Mental Disorders of the New Millennium

MENTAL DISORDERS OF THE NEW MILLENNIUM

Volume 2
Public and Social Problems

Edited by Thomas G. Plante

Praeger Perspectives

Abnormal Psychology

Westport, Connecticut
London

Library of Congress Cataloging-in-Publication Data

Mental disorders of the new millennium/edited by Thomas G. Plante.
    p.; cm.—(Praeger perspectives. Abnormal psychology, ISSN 1554–2238)
    Includes bibliographical references and index.
    ISBN 0–275–98781–7 (set) — ISBN 0–275–98782–5 (v. 1) —
    ISBN 0–275–98783–3 (v. 2) — ISBN 0–275–98784–1 (v. 3)   1. Psychiatry.
2. Mental illness.   I. Plante, Thomas G.   II. Series.
    [DNLM: 1. Mental Disorders. WM 140 M548326 2006]
    RC454.M462   2006
    616.89—dc22   2006015096

British Library Cataloguing in Publication Data is available.

Library of Congress Catalog Card Number: 2006015096
ISBN: 0–275–98781–7 (set)
        0–275–98782–5 (vol. 1)
        0–275–98783–3 (vol. 2)
        0–275–98784–1 (vol. 3)
ISSN: 1554–2238

First published in 2006

Praeger Publishers, 88 Post Road West, Westport, CT 06881
An imprint of Greenwood Publishing Group, Inc.
www.praeger.com

Printed in the United States of America

The paper used in this book complies with the
Permanent Paper Standard issued by the National
Information Standards Organization (Z39.48–1984).

10 9 8 7 6 5 4 3 2 1

Dedicated to my family patriarchs—
Bernard Plante, the late Henry McCormick, and
Eli Goldfarb—who have taught me much
about the human condition.

Contents

Preface

Tragically, the daily news is filled with stories about significant and remarkable problems in human behavior. Each morning we are greeted with news reports about murder, suicide, terrorist acts, drunken driving accidents, child molestation and abduction, drug abuse, gambling troubles, gang violence, various criminal behavior, and so forth. Other frequent stories reported in the press involve the betrayal of trust among highly respected and regarded members of society. These stories include the legal, sexual, financial, and general ethical lapses of politicians, leading sports celebrities, and movies stars. Some reports include the sexual abuse perpetrated on children and teens by school teachers, coaches, and members of the clergy. Other stories focus on the stress-related troubles soldiers experience following their duty in war. Still others focus on more and more reports of what appear to be mental problems such as autism, dementia, attention deficit disorders, panic, eating disorders, and depression, among both children and adults.

These troubles are reflected in recent cover stories in magazine news weeklies such as *Time*, *Newsweek*, and *US News and World Report*. Problems such as attention deficit hyperactivity disorder, autism, Alzheimer's disease, depression, panic disorder, murder-suicide, eating disorders, and child sexual abuse, among others, have been featured many times over as cover stories in these and other popular media outlets. The fact that these topics appear frequently on the covers of these news weeklies means they must impact significant numbers of people.

Perhaps just about everyone in the United States is affected by mental illness and abnormal behavior to some extent. Many people either suffer from one or more of the various mental disorders or live with those who do. It is likely that almost everyone in our contemporary society knows someone in his or her immediate family or circle of close friends and relatives who suffers from a significant abnormal behavior, psychiatric condition, or behavioral pattern that causes the person and his or her loved ones a great deal of stress.

Consider just a few of these statistics from our chapter contributors:

1. About 1 million people will die by suicide every year. The worldwide mortality rate of suicide is 16 per 100,000, or one suicide every 40 seconds. Fifty-five percent of suicides occur before age 44. Suicide is the third leading cause of death for both sexes.
2. About 1 million older Americans (1 in 35) is a victim of elder abuse each year, and between 3 and 5 percent of older adults over the age of 65 are or will be victims of abuse and/or neglect.
3. Epidemiological studies suggest the prevalence rate of child and adolescent depressive disorders ranges from 2 to 9 percent.
4. Over 18 million Americans suffer from some type of depression each year, and about 20 percent of the U.S. population will experience a significant depressive episode in their lifetime.
5. The number of probable adult pathological gamblers varies from just under 1 percent in the United Kingdom to between 1 and 2 percent in the United States and about 2.5 percent in Australia.
6. About 20 percent of all American women and 15 percent of all American men report being sexually abused by an adult while they were still a child.
7. About 4 percent of Catholic priests and 5 percent of school teachers have had a sexual encounter with a minor child in their care.

Clearly, mental illness and abnormal behavior touch the lives of just about all of us!

What's going on? How can it be that so many highly problematic psychiatric disorders, abnormal behaviors, and problems in living impact so many people? It wouldn't be an exaggeration to state that the vast troubles of the world stem from abnormal behavior. From ignoring global warming to terrorism, from murder to suicide, from divorce to gambling, from autism to dementia, it seems that abnormal behavior is at the root of so many challenges of our day.

Sadly, most of the books available in the field of abnormal psychology are not especially useful for the average educated lay reader. Much of the literature currently available tends to fall into two categories. The first includes academic books written by academics for an academic or scholarly audience. These books are often written in a very dry, jargon-filled, data-driven manner that is challenging for the general reader to get through. In fact, these books are often challenging for professionals in psychology and related fields to understand as well. The second category includes trade books that tend to be very simplistic and often tell the story of someone suffering from a particular problem. These books are often located in the self-help or inspirational section in a bookstore. Books of this type are written by those who experience the particular disorder, mental health professionals who treat the problem, or journalists who tell a remarkable story about a particular case that made news. Very few books are written for the educated lay reader that balance academic, scholarly, and clinical information with a readable, engaging, and user-friendly style.

The purpose of this series on mental disorders is to help bridge this gap between academic and self-help /inspirational books written on abnormal psychology topics that impact society—those topics that potential readers see on the covers of weekly news magazines or in daily newspapers. The series focuses on contemporary abnormal behavior topics and is compiled from contributions by experts for an educated lay audience. Leading experts who study, treat, evaluate, and reflect upon these troubles and issues have been asked to write chapters for you to help you better understand these contemporary problems. The chapters are based on the most up-to-date research and practice evidence and go well beyond the information provided in popular media outlets. Hopefully, you will find that the books are highly informative, contemporary, and readable.

If we better understand the factors that contribute to these contemporary abnormal behaviors and patterns, then perhaps we can find better ways to prevent some of these problems from emerging and better evaluate and treat those who suffer from these experiences. In an effort to create a better world for ourselves and our children we must do all that we can to prevent abnormal behavior and help those who are troubled by abnormal behavior in themselves, their loved ones, and their communities. In doing so, we will be better able to create an improved world.

Acknowledgments

Many people other than the author or editor assist in the completion of a book project. Some contribute in a direct way while others help in a more supportive manner. I would like to acknowledge the assistance of the people who worked to make this book idea a reality and who have helped me in both direct and indirect ways.

First and foremost, I would like to thank the contributors to this volume. Leading experts who represent the very best that the professional community has to offer graciously agreed to contribute quality chapters to this book project. Second, I would like to thank my associate editors, Drs. DeLeon, Kaslow, and Plante, for agreeing to serve as associate editors for this book and all the books in the abnormal psychology book series. Third, it is important to recognize the wonderful people at Greenwood who published this book. Most especially, many thanks go to Debbie Carvalko, our editor at Greenwood. Fourth, I would like to thank Santa Clara University, which has supported me and allowed me many opportunities to pursue my scholarly academic activities and interests.

Fifth, I would like to acknowledge the anonymous persons who are referred to in this book, who have allowed their life experiences and traumas to become instruments of learning for others. Sixth, I would like to thank my family patriarchs (Bernard Plante, the late Henry McCormick, and Eli Goldfarb) and matriarchs (Marcia Plante, the late Anna McCormick, the late Margaret Condon, and Marilyn Goldfarb) and my sisters (Mary Beauchemin and Leeann Sperduti), all of whom have taught me much about the human condition. Finally, I would like to thank my wife, Lori, and son, Zachary, for their love and support while I worked on yet another compelling book project.

Chapter 1

Post-Traumatic Stress Disorder among U.S. Combat Veterans

Stanley Krippner and Daryl S. Paulson

The greatest weapon against stress is our ability to choose one thought over another.

William James

Traumas are assaults on the human mind or body that disrupt the typical functioning of such subsystems as the biological, psychoneurological, social-emotional, or spiritual-existential subsystems. Psychological trauma often leads to a constellation of psychiatric disorders that do not seem to mend, such as persistent anxiety and depression. Such a constellation, labeled *post-traumatic stress disorder* (PTSD), is described by the American Psychiatric Association's *Diagnostic and Statistical Manual of Mental Disorders* (fourth edition, text revision) as a condition following the experiencing or witnessing of life-threatening events that exceed one's psychological coping capacity, emotional resources, and/or existential worldview.[1]

PTSD AS A SOCIAL CONSTRUCT

The term *post-traumatic stress disorder* is a socially constructed label that Western mental health workers have affixed to noticeable changes in someone's behavior, attitudes, and/or values following accidents, natural disasters, armed combat, rape, torture, or abuse. The putative causal incident can last a few seconds (as in the case of two automobiles colliding or a person shot by an unseen sniper) or several years (as in cases of spousal abuse or protracted armed insurgency).[2] When the person who suffers the trauma fails to recover, regain equilibrium, or "get on with life," psychotherapists typically diagnose patients with PTSD as a way of describing this type of dysfunction following an assault on one's mind/body system (hence the term *post-traumatic*).

Definitions of the condition include the word *stress* as a reference to the irreparable or terminal impact of the catastrophic stressor, or event responsible for the symptoms. In other words, PTSD victims have never returned to a socially functional condition from their dysfunctional state.

In 1980, the American Psychiatric Association added PTSD to the classification scheme in its *DSM–III–R*. This was an important historical event in that it implied that the logical agent (the *traumatic stressor*) was outside the individual rather than an inherent, internal condition (as in *traumatic neurosis*) or a transient reaction to a stressful situation (as with *adjustment disorder*). PTSD is unique among other *DSM* diagnoses because it is the only psychiatric diagnosis with an identifiable cause. The traumatic stressor is given paramount importance; indeed, a mental health practitioner cannot make a PTSD diagnosis unless the patient has actually met the stressor criterion. Implicit in the diagnosis is the assumption that the patient has been exposed to an event considered so traumatic that it lies outside the range of "usual human experience," a 1980 description later modified because rape, severe accidents, and armed struggle are no longer considered "unusual."

For the diagnosis of PTSD to be made, a person's response to the event must involve intense fear, helplessness, or horror; in children the response must involve disorganized or agitated behavior. The characteristic symptoms resulting from extreme trauma, as specified in the *DSM–IV–TR* include:

> Persistent re-experiencing of the traumatic event, persistent avoidance of stimuli associated with the trauma and a cognitive-emotional numbing of general responsiveness, and persistent symptoms of increased arousal. The full symptom picture must be present for more than a month and the disturbance must cause clinically significant distress or impairment in social, occupational, or other important of areas of functioning. (p. 424)

Virtually all survivors of the Nazi Holocaust and the atomic bombings at Hiroshima and Nagasaki would be considered at risk for developing PTSD and its symptoms. The experiences responsible for PTSD retain the power to evoke panic, terror, dread, grief, or despair as manifested in daytime fantasies, traumatic nightmares, and flashbacks for years, decades, or lifetimes.

Although the term *PTSD* is a socially constructed label for a qualitatively distinctive internal experience, it involves phenomena that can be qualitatively measured.[3] Sometimes, it can be better understood as the result of histori-cally situated intersubjective transformations of value and meaning among people, the nature of which differ from time to time and place to place. Each person's innate psychological capacity to handle stress varies; a situation may leave one individual with a PTSD diagnosis while others emerge from stress unscathed.[4] Some cultures reportedly have endured (and even thrived) amid strings of plagues, massacres, and calamities, while similar events devastate cultures that fail to develop the technological or psychological resilience needed for long-term survival.

Experiencing combat or other trauma does not always lead to psychopathology. Interestingly, suffering is a necessary, but not sufficient causative factor in PTSD. Some individuals and groups respond to distress with an understanding that their response is appropriate for the climate (be it war or natural disasters). For them, post-traumatic stress would be a pseudocondition. For example, the Buddhists Nargarjuna and Chandrakirti, in developing the Mādhyamaka system (the Middle Way) of Buddhism, argue that attachment and clinging to static conditions, concepts, and ways of life are the fundamental causes of suffering. The First Noble Truth of the Buddha was that all life is suffering, trying to make permanent that which is transitory.

Arthur Kleinman[5] has pointed out how serious illnesses "embody" a dialectic between shared intersubjective cultural meaning and values that always provides a particular meaning of illness for suffering patients, their families and friends, and their professional caregivers, and that this meaning affects their lived experiences. That is, shared cultural values, goals, beliefs, and meaning interact with the lived experience of individuals and their perceptions of wellness or sickness.

Kleinman,[5] an anthropologist, and Thomas Greening,[6] a psychologist, both have argued that the most challenging aspect of a traumatic emotional disturbance involves the loss of a familiar world; a loss that cannot be "cured" or mended by drugs, catharsis, deconditioning, or social support. If these interventions do produce long-term changes, it is largely because they have imbued the patient's life with fresh meaning and new perspectives that enhance or vitalize meaning. Conceptualizing PTSD as a social construct enables therapists and patients alike to work with it as a fluid condition. As a result, there are no universal truths in an event, or in the treatment of PTSD. Trauma, like pain, is not an external phenomenon that can be completely objectified. Like pain, the traumatic experience is filtered through cognitive and emotional processes before it can be appraised as an extreme threat. Nevertheless, the term can be used descriptively to refer to people who are suffering, and prescriptively to identify therapeutic responses that help relieve that suffering.

Several psychological and psychobiological mechanisms are at work when a person achieves relief from PTSD. For example, PTSD, characterized by high physiological arousal, resembles state-dependent learning in which brain states affect the retention of knowledge. Cognitive and emotional relief, therefore, occur when this arousal is dulled, or when traumatic experiences are reformulated, reframed, or integrated into one's ordinary behavioral and experiential repertoire. Greening speaks of moving "beyond trauma" to higher levels of personality integration and development.[6]

History of the Diagnosis and Treatment of PTSD

Exposure to potentially traumatic stressors is inseparable from the human condition. People were healing one another long before there were accepted definitions for *illness, sickness, disease, syndromes,* and *disorders.* Before the term *PTSD* was constructed by the mental health care community, many recognized, as documented in mythological, literary, and historical sources, the toxic emotional effects of early childhood traumas. For example, after Isaac was bound and nearly sacrificed by his father, Abraham, there is little mention of him in biblical accounts. Those that do appear include an arranged marriage at the age of 40, a dispute over the ownership of local wells, and a deception by his son, Jacob, who stole his brother's birthright. These incidents indicate that Isaac's behavior was passive and marked by social altercations, two hallmarks of what today is called PTSD.[7]

Additionally, psychopathologies of trauma have been described by individuals living in prescientific eras. For example, Samuel Pepys's description of the 1666 Great Fire of London indicates that he suffered from insomnia, nightmares, anxiety, and outbursts of anger—all symptoms of unresolved exposure to trauma. Shakespeare, well known today not only for his plays, but also for his profound psychological insights, illustrates the lasting effects of trauma in *Henry IV,* when Lady Percy describes her husband, Hotspur, as melancholy, socially withdrawn, and talking in his sleep following a bloody battle in which he lost a kinsman.

A few physicians on both sides of the Atlantic posited cause-and-effect relations between traumatic experiences and psychiatric disabilities in the 19th century. American physicians described cardiac and respiratory problems coupled with anxiety among several Civil War veterans, while French physicians noted that natural disasters and accidents were often followed by emotional numbing. During the First World War, similar conditions were referred to as *shell shock,* and during the Second World War as *battle fatigue.* This development coincided with a revival of interest in hypnosis, which became a frequently utilized treatment for symptoms now associated with PTSD. Some followers of Sigmund Freud used the term *war neurosis,* but denied an organic basis to the condition, hypothesizing that it was the consequence of adult trauma and recommending psychoanalytic treatment. Abraham Kardiner, a psychoanalyst, conducted a study of psychiatrically disabled World War I combat veterans, terming the condition *physioneurosis*. S.L.A. Marshall,[8] a World War II military analyst, was the first to systematically collect data during and immediately following battle.

The first two editions of the *DSM* gave brief mention to *combat stress reactions*, but Robert J. Lifton and other psychiatrists, after working with Korean War and Vietnam War veterans, helped ensure the disorder a separate category in future *DSM* editions. The nature of traumatic stressors was described in some detail by the authors of the *International Classification of Disease* (Volume 10), who claimed that stressors could be mental or physical, and rarely included common life trials like illness, divorce, job dismissal, romantic rejection, financial reverses, and the like. Because of the slow recognition of PTSD as a singular disorder, Katz[7] has proposed that "it represents the least studied major psychiatric disorder and our ignorance is as significant as our understanding" (p. 555). To meet this need, various screening instruments have been developed in an attempt to facilitate treatment and expand the data base.[3]

Because PTSD is a social construct, it is important to note that it is generally diagnosed and treated by clinicians from Western industrialized nations who work with patients from the same background. However, the psychological impact of traumatic exposure may be a major difference between Western and non-Western societies. For example, Mādhyamaka Buddhists of Southeast Asia cite clinging to particular desires as a prime cause of suffering. According to several researchers, acceptance of one's suffering may promote resilience against psychic trauma. Katz's lament about the lack of clinical research is urgent when one considers the absence of comparative cross-cultural data and culturally appropriate models for treatment in developing countries.[2]

INCIDENCE AND TYPES OF PTSD AMONG COMBAT VETERANS

Both prospective and retrospective epidemiological studies indicate that most people in the United States will experience a major traumatic stressor during their lifetime.[8] In addition, about 10 percent of them will develop PTSD at some point. These statistics are also more nuanced than they appear. For example, PTSD is twice as common among U.S. women as among U.S. men; however, this difference may be due to women's tendency to seek professional help more often than men.

A study of PTSD among U.S. Vietnam veterans found similar patterns for female veterans (mostly nurses) as for males relative to their level of exposure to war-zone stressors (like dead or wounded soldiers). Yet, for women exposed to high war-zone stress, up to 20 percent were diagnosed with PTSD. Overall,

53 percent of male Vietnam veterans and 48 percent of female veterans have experienced clinically significant stress reaction symptoms, not all of them warranting a PTSD diagnosis. In addition, several scholars have compared PTSD in combat veterans with similar symptoms in female victims of rape or incest. In both cases there is a conflict between the will to deny horrible events and the will to proclaim them aloud. This internal conflict has often been described as the result of a "shattered self" where basic trust has been obliterated. Therefore, PTSD not only is a traumatic stress disorder, but also is one that results from a combatant's isolation from home and community, combined with the uncertainty of the near future.

PTSD can be conceptualized as a three-stage process. First, there is the presence of highly diverse predisposing biological, psychoneurological, socioemotional, and spiritual-existential factors. When a person is subjected to a traumatic stressor, his or her initial reaction activates the sympathetic component of the autonomic nervous system. This becomes evident through both physical symptoms (e.g., tachycardia, hyperventilation, increased muscle tension, sweating, hyperactivity) and subjective reactions (e.g., anxiety, hypervigilance). Not surprisingly, prolonged stress weakens immune system function. A cohort study of 1,400 U.S. Vietnam veterans followed over two decades demonstrated that those with PTSD (nearly a quarter of the total) were twice as likely to have chronic conditions such as cardiovascular disease. Additionally, those with PTSD have a smaller hippocampus, which is associated with memory and learning.[9]

Regarding socioemotional factors, one's developmental stage in life and one's place in the community can play predisposing roles in PTSD. One's level of maturational development, defensive coping style, worldview, and social standing are part of a complex socioemotional system that can buffer individuals against the effects of trauma or increase their vulnerability. Apparently, the more flexible a person's self-concept, the more resilient that person can be.

At the heart of PTSD's social sequelae is isolation, or a feeling of disconnection from family and friends. In situations of terror, people spontaneously seek their first experienced source of comfort and protection; wounded soldiers and raped women often cry for their mother or for God. When their cry is not answered, basic trust in the world is destroyed. Traumatized individuals feel utterly abandoned and alone, cast out of the divine system that sustains life. From that moment on, a sense of alienation and disconnection pervades each relationship. In addition, predisposing social attitudes can encourage one's family and friends to exhibit compassion or to withdraw support. The media's presentation of events can enhance support or undermine resilience.

Much of the anguish suffered by returning Vietnam veterans was the result of their rejection by society. Many felt shunned, as did Daryl Paulson, who faced combat in the Vietnam War.[10]

> When our 707 landed at El Toro Marine Air Station, I was secretly preparing for a hero's welcome. I think all of us reasoned that we would get a double strong welcome, because we had fought, in spite of the absence of any explicit government plan to win the war.... We landed and walked out of the plane to our homecoming reception. I saw three people waiting for us. That was it! They were Marine wives who had volunteered to serve cookies and Kool-Aid to us. Where was everyone else? ...
>
> Once in the air terminal, we were escorted to waiting military buses and driven to Camp Pendleton Marine Base for discharge or reassignment. During the drive, some college-age people screamed obscenities at us and flipped us the bird. I can still remember them yelling something about being "war mongers." At Camp Pendleton, we were swiftly processed and bussed to Los Angeles International Airport to schedule flights home. At the airport, I went to a bar to have a couple of drinks while waiting for my flight. This was an especially big event for me. It was my first legal drink in the United States, for I was of age—21. I felt like being friendly, so I tried to start a conversation with two women sitting next to me, but they ignored me. Then I tried to talk to a couple of guys, but they, too, ignored me. It began to dawn on me that no one cared that I had served in the Vietnam War. I felt like a misfit.

In parts of the former Yugoslavia, victims of the tragic mass rapes were seen as "poisoned containers," even by family members. However, victims of those wars were also dehumanized by some of the United Nations peacekeepers sent to protect them. One Finnish solider admittedly created a psychological distance to preserve his own equilibrium. He simply asked a refugee for a name, then stamped a document, admitting in retrospect that "a life was nothing" (p. 560).[11]

One's external membership in organized religion and/or one's internal spiritual-existential belief system can also be powerful predisposing factors in how a traumatic event is handled. Paulson[10] illustrates the problem of existential guilt:

> Plagued with guilt, I tried to find a place where I could go for forgiveness, to get away from this hell [guilt, anxiety, and despair]. I felt too guilty to go to God and church, for I had killed, I had injured, and I had tortured my fellow human beings with intense delight. No, I could not go to God or church, for I had too much blood on my hands. I reasoned that no one wanted me now, not even God, for I had killed His children.

Social and personal myths are narratives that address life meanings and, therefore, an individual's day-by-day decisions. A child who has been sexually abused by a priest might be devastated (if his/her personal myth holds that "Priests are God's representatives on earth"), or might assimilate the experience (if his/her personal myth summons the response, "My mother told me not to trust older men, not even priests"). Evolutionary psychology takes the position that human behavior is not completely reducible to biological factors or genetic determination. Humans have evolved to interact with the environment over thousands of generations. Anxiety is valuable to the species, as individuals can determine quickly whether to flee or fight when threatened. While the adaptation is valuable, there is a substantial lag period between when the tools are needed and when they actually evolve. In some ways, humans meet postmodern challenges with primordial reactions. According to Lifton,[13] the intrusion of death imagery (i.e., being killed) during a traumatic incident is what threatens the core belief in one's safety. As a result, PTSD often arises from a general violation of deeply held beliefs and expectations about the world and one's place in it.

At the beginning of 2005 some two dozen countries were engaged in, or were recovering from, a civil conflict. Researchers studied four of these countries, Afghanistan, Democratic Republic of the Congo, Somalia, and Sudan, finding that factors such as malnutrition, lack of sanitation, nadequate water supplies, and poor public health services predisposed civilians to PSTD, as well as to illness or death.

Given that each person faces a traumatic stressor with a different set of predispositions, a traumatic event and its context serve as the activating factor. Whether the stressor (or, in some cases, the series of stressors) will trigger PTSD depends on its severity and its interaction with one's predisposing factors. About one out of four individuals exposed to traumatic stressors threatening their life or physical integrity (e.g., war combat, rape) develops PTSD, a much higher figure than the overall 10 percent estimated for all types of potential trauma. In 2005, the U.S. National Center for PTSD reported that up to 30 percent of combat veterans suffer from the condition at some point in their lives, a phenomenon that has been described as the psychological consequence of killing. Earlier, a 1990 study of 1,582 Vietnam War veterans found precombat personality factors were less important in eliciting PTSD than war-zone stress itself.

Finally, incidents later in one's life that provoke traumatic memories often serve to reinforce, or even aggravate PTSD. Again individuals differ. Generally, a war veteran working in a fireworks factory will be at greater risk for memory recall than one filling orders for organic food supplies. Yet, some individuals feel that stress is imminent even in times when stress is low. This has been described by one study as "waiting for the other shoe to fall." Individuals become aroused and anxiety-ridden, looking for a threat or danger to activate their free-floating nxiety. For example, Paulson[10] writes:

> I tried to go on relaxing picnics with my friends, but I became too uneasy, even with tranquilizers, to enjoy the picnic. I kept feeling that someone—the enemy—was hidden in the trees, stalking me, just as I had felt in Vietnam. At times, I became so tense and anxious on these picnics that I would have to drink a couple belts of whiskey just to get through the ordeal. No fear impacted me as the fear I felt during thunder storms. Even though I knew thunder was caused by lightening, the sound of thunder would send me right back to Vietnam. I would drop to the ground to protect myself.... Other veterans I have talked to reported similar experiences. They reported panic attacks when a fire alarm was set off, when a helicopter flew over them, and when hearing loud noises.

Military PTSD victims are rarely sent back into combat, even in a different war, despite a professed desire to take up arms again. The similarity of a new battleground with the original traumatic stressor typically makes these soldiers a potential threat to themselves and to others.

PTSD among Vietnam, Gulf, Afghanistan, and Iraq War Veterans

Greening[6] has provided a case history highlighting three important aspects of PTSD: (1) character structure, (2) family background, and (3) social background. Greening observed that his patient's character structure (one with a strong manipulative streak), family background (replete with alcoholic and depressed relatives), and societal background (a business career involving unethical practices) provided a predisposition to PTSD that was activated while fighting in Vietnam. Although the patient performed well in combat, he experienced an atrocity that disturbed him to his core. As time went on, he became involved with illegal drugs and became cynical about the way the U.S. government was conducting the war. He returned home with an unmanifested PTSD that quickly emerged with an array of symptoms, including flashbacks. He was hounded by a particularly disturbing flashback in which he remembered a soldier's corpse that looked like him, and he had a hard time differentiating between himself and others. He filled his social life with "fast" women, one of whom he impregnated, and whose unannounced abortion made him feel guilty. His acute PTSD symptomatically manifested with generalized depression and distrust of others, leading him into a period of psychotherapy. During this time, he was able to greatly reduce PTSD symptomatology and found a worthwhile job as a hospital fund-raiser.

Others were not so fortunate. In a study conducted by Paulson,[10] the plight of two Vietnam veterans was described. "Joey" went back to college and his fraternity when he returned from Vietnam. He found, however, that he was no longer wanted. His fraternity brothers no longer wished to associate with him. He was "flawed." He was a Vietnam veteran. He could not deal with that, so he shot himself in the head.

The second combatant used a different mechanism to escape his pain:

> Art, a Marine Corps veteran, came back to the states and went to college. He suppressed his entire Vietnam experience and never spoke a word about it to his non-military friends. By this action, he found that he was harboring tremendous amounts of guilt. To compensate for this, he tried to be all things to all people. He tried his best to be the most caring friend to the women he knew, he tried to be the best, most caring friend to the men he knew. In the process, however, he denied his own needs. On the outside, he put on a good show, but his inner conflict was betrayed by his ever present need for a drink, an R&R on the rocks. Art ultimately withdrew from college, moved to Mexico, lapsing into alcoholism.

The media has publicized the number of U.S. combatants killed in the Afghanistan and Iraq wars but less attention has been given to those who have been so seriously injured that they had to be evacuated. Based on interviews with Department of Defense officials, National Public Radio in October 2004 estimated the number to be 20,245. An additional 800 people were evacuated for treatment of PTSD and depression, and 600 for skin diseases resulting from insects and parasites.

Combat is a huge potential traumatic stressor because it exposes combatants to situations that involve killing others, as well as being killed. It is not theoretical, nor can it be deferred into the future. It is a long, persistent, seemingly endless now.[9] One must remember that military action itself does not occur in a vacuum; Vietnam veterans' flashbacks might represent unsuccessful attempts to make sense of an experience that many of the veterans' fellow Americans considered to be pointless or wrong.

Paulson[10] has described his dilemma of trying to have a relationship with women. Before going to Vietnam, he fantasized about finding a warm and caring woman to marry. However:

> When I did return, things were different. I found I did not really like to be with women; they made me nervous. To be held by a woman made me feel very vulnerable. Instead of feeling good, I would feel terribly sad and afraid in her arms. It was almost like being a little boy again, in need of a mother to hug away my pain.

He continues, describing why he felt vulnerable:

> We had to distance ourselves from any meaningful encounters with women, because we felt that we could not share with them what we had experienced. How could you tell your girlfriend what it was like for you to shoot another human being? How could you tell her how vulnerable and scared you had felt, never knowing if you would live another hour the whole time you were in Vietnam? How could you tell her what it was like to kick dead [enemy] soldiers because you were so angry at them for killing your friends? I was afraid to tell any woman what it was like. How could I tell her about the horror I felt watching a dump truck taking the corpses of seventeen of my friends to be embalmed? How could I tell her what I felt when I watched their blood drip and flow from the tailgate onto the ground? How could I tell her how deeply I hurt, of the agony I was in, and how gnawing my suffering was? How could I tell her that the pain and guilt followed me like a beast tracking its prey? How could I tell her that the pain hounded me day and night, even while making love? What would she think of me if I told her? I feared that if any woman knew this about me, she would freak out, go into convulsions, vomit, and totally reject me for being such a disgusting human being. What was I to do? I did what seemed best: I drank and drank and drank.

Besides flashbacks, common symptoms of PTSD among veterans include hypervigilance, dejection, panic attacks, substance abuse, inappropriate acting out, unaccountable episodes of rage, depression, and cycles of anxiety and guilt (guilt often fuels anxiety, and this anxiety later fuels additional guilt). Moralizing noncombatants sometimes reinforce these symptoms by attacking soldiers for their role in the conflict. Some veterans may feel they have lost everything of value and are thrown into utter alienation from friends, lovers, family, and themselves.

The *DSM–IV–TR*[1] lists some 17 symptoms or symptom clusters and stipulates that at least 6 must be present (and long lasting) for the diagnosis of PTSD to be made. The *DSM–IV–TR* groups the symptoms into reexperiencing the stressor (e.g., intrusive thoughts and images, nightmares, flashbacks);[2] avoidance and emotional numbing (avoiding stimuli associated with the trauma, inability to experience a full range of emotions);[3] hyperarousal (e.g., exaggerated startle response; vigilant sleep disruption). Anxiety is often generalized to areas that were not associated with the actual trauma. The stressor finds many ways to intrude into the patient's stream of consciousness; whether the stressor is reexperienced or avoided, it brings about some type of arousal. Paulson[10] describes this situation:

> I felt completely alone and totally isolated. I lived in an alien world with which I could not communicate. I did not fit in with the other college students, since I was a Vietnam veteran, but I did not fit in with the military, either. I spent a little

of my time studying, but most of my time, I spent drinking to assuage the pain of life's all-too-obvious meaninglessness. The recurring visions and dreams of the killing I had seen and the killing I had done began to intensify. I just could not stop visualizing—and reliving—the emotional scenes of my comrades' deaths. Even the alcohol was not taking the edge off. I could not sleep, and I could not bear the pain of being awake. I could only suffer and hurt and despair over the meaninglessness and aloneness I endured, but even these were not as painful as the guilt.

In each of these ways, the stressor comes to dominate the veteran's awareness, particularly his/her worldview, usually unexpectedly and often in ways that are maladaptive and dysfunctional. Veterans often try to avoid reexperiencing the stressor in a number of ways. They attempt to forget anniversaries of the traumatic event, attempt to stay away from activities or feelings that arouse recollections of the event, and engage in "emotional numbing," not sharing feelings about the event with anyone. This numbing is often carried to extremes, leading to the avoidance of marriage, children, long-term employment, and close friendships. It may lead to emotional detachment from others, if the involvement becomes anxiety-producing. Veterans may even forget key elements of the traumatic event, engaging in defensive repression, suppression, or denial.[9]

The veteran may experience persistent anxiety due to increased arousal that was not present before the traumatic experience. For example, sleep disorders (especially difficulty falling asleep and staying asleep) are common, as are outbursts of anger, irritability, paranoid-like hypervigilance, and exaggerated startle responses. Friends learn not to take the veteran by surprise, even for benign purposes, for fear of being verbally admonished or physically attacked. If a scene from a movie, theatrical event, or television show is reminiscent of the traumatic stressor, it is not uncommon for the veteran to leave the room to avoid "losing it" or acting inappropriately.

From an evolutionary psychological perspective, this behavior is founded in what anthropologists call "survival benefit." In a combat situation, it is normal to be hypervigilant, to drop to the ground upon hearing explosions, and to have sleep problems. What makes the behaviors maladaptive is the change from a war zone to a non-war zone. And because the combatants cannot instantly drop their combat theatre behavior, many, upon their return from combat, cognitively judge their behaviors negatively, reinforcing inner conflict between "what is" and "what should be."[9]

TREATMENT PROCEDURES FOR VETERANS WITH PTSD

Most treatment procedures for PTSD are aimed at reducing symptomatology to help the client to acknowledge that his/her reaction to the initial threat is normal, and to help take ownership of his/her existential situation.

Following these steps, adequate coping methods (e.g., self-regulation, self-management) need to be introduced to permit awareness of the traumatic experience, but without allowing the memory to interfere with daily activities. PTSD is not easy to treat therapeutically, but is often more treatable than anxiety disorders encountered in normal maturation because combat trauma is experientially removed from day-to-day civilian life.

Anxiety resulting from intrapsychic conflict (e.g., feelings of inferiority or inadequacy) dominates a veteran's life. He or she may feel like a victim, expressing anger and pain that continue to backslide without resolution. Various defense mechanisms assist veterans with otherwise unbearable trauma, but also present barriers to psychological therapy.

For example, when Paulson[10] first started to reveal his experiences in Vietnam to his therapist, he thought that the therapist would also abandon him. He recalled, "I could visualize him clutching his throat and gasping in horror as he fell from his chair over the disgusting, disgraceful things I had done in Vietnam. When I did tell him, fearing he would kick me out of his office, he merely said, 'Thank God that is out in the open now.' He did not reject me."

Many therapists stress the importance of having a support system. A support system offers the veteran positive reinforcement in the confrontation with his/her anguish, and a buttress for a more functional and healthier self-concept. This gives the veteran a firm platform on which to build a more auspicious understanding of the traumatic events without fear of rejection. For example, Juan, an Army infantry officer, described his experience to us:

> When I came back from war, everything was different. I did not know who I was, what I was, or where I should be going in my life. I was off balance. But since I was perceived as tough combat veteran, I felt that if I told anyone how off balance I felt, I would somehow be thought a very weak person. So, at first, I played the role of a tough infantry officer. But I became more and more cynical, unhappy, and more confused. I wanted to drop the whole stage performance and tell everyone, including myself, how scared and miserable I was. But where could I go? There was no psychological support system that I knew of at the time. So I found another answer, that of drinking. I began to live my life with a little on-going "buzz." It blunted the sharp sting of life's cruel horror. But soon, I found myself drinking more and more, and within two years, I was a drunk. I was hospitalized in an alcohol treatment program and, during that time, something marvelous occurred. Several representatives from Alcoholics Anonymous (AA) visited me. I decided to join AA and, to my surprise, I found a very supportive group of people who had "been there." They had hit the bottom in their lives and now were working their way back. They gave me the strength to deal with Vietnam just by being accepting. I could question my motives, my life, anything, and they did not judge me. After I had

this support base, I used it to launch my life. I quit drinking. I learned a lot about the benefits of a support group from that experience.

Often, people who have not endured significant emotional trauma wonder why it is so difficult to mollify suffering. This underscores the divergent reality that the pain generates for victims of PTSD. They cannot relate to notions of self-fulfillment or self-actualization, or to people who can, because their world is one of constant danger, and most of their day is consumed with maneuvers to guard themselves from those dangers and potential destruction.[9] Because this constructed reality is one in which the world is a perilous place, they must constantly be vigilant and removed. Hence, part of the reason for their severed bond with collective reality is a fundamental distrust of the world and its inhabitants. After all, the origin of their distress is easily traced to the mercurial world outside of themselves.

A comprehensive clinical assessment of PTSD needs to include carefully structured interviews, administration of self-report psychometrics, and a thorough evaluation of past traumatic experiences. A "cookbook" approach is contraindicated because each case of PTSD is quite different. Several instruments have been designed specifically for the identification of PTSD (e.g., the PTSD Checklist, the PTSD Diagnostic Scale) while others are based on existing inventories (e.g., the Minnesota Multiphasic Personality Inventory).

Several therapists have suggested an integrative approach to treating PTSD.[15] In this approach, the therapeutic procedure is relative to the needs of the patients and to their unique existential situation. Second, insight therapies (e.g., psycho-dynamic and humanistic-existential therapies) are important for understanding and integrating traumatic experiences into daily life. However, applied therapies (e.g., cognitive behavior and behavioral therapies) are important for confronting anxiety brought on by exposure to unavoidable events (e.g., thunderstorms, loud noises).[14]

At present, no one therapeutic approach for PTSD has demonstrated its superiority to the others, though mainstream psychologists favor cognitive-behavioral therapy. Significant results have been found for all psychological therapies on which data exist, especially behavioral therapies.[15] In the field of medicine, the development of psychotropic medications has led to other innovations, either as the primary mode of treatment or as an adjunct to psychological therapy.

Treatment methodologies can be classified as either[1] exposure-based approaches (e.g., systematic desensitization, implosion, flooding, prolonged exposure, imaginal therapy),[2] cognitive restructuring therapies (e.g., cognitive-behavioral therapy, modeling, rational-emotive behavior therapy),[3] or anxiety management (e.g., relaxation training, biofeedback training, meditation, pharmacology). These categories, of course, are arbitrary; some writers combine implosion and flooding, some place biofeedback under behavioral approaches, and others make pharmacological treatment a separate category.

In addition, Greening[6] would add humanistic-existential psychotherapy to this categorization. This approach often helps clients deconstruct their story of trauma, and reconstruct a story of survival. However, clients are encouraged not to remain content with their status as survivors but to marshal such psychological and spiritual resources as optimism, resilience, and hardiness. Clients may be asked to create narratives to deal with trauma, loss, and death, using not only verbal dialogue but expressive art and dance therapy as well.

The Therapeutic Spiral Model is based on the assumption that traumatic memories are stored in the combat veteran's brain. This short-term approach uses adaptations of psychodrama and role-playing to focus on those brain centers involved in nightmares, flashbacks, and other emotional sequelae, areas that purportedly are bypassed by talk therapy. Others advocate a variety of approaches that are body based in an attempt to break the veteran's behavioral pattern of defense and avoidance.

Whichever approach is used, the severity of PTSD may be reduced by the judicious and timely use of trauma counseling.[7] For example, critical incident stress debriefing (CISD) was attempted with adult survivors of the September 11, 2001, attacks in New York City, but follow-up studies failed to demonstrate its effectiveness. As an alternative to CISD, some therapists have recommended brief cognitive-behavioral therapy two to four weeks after the trauma, when they claim it is most efficacious for treating high-risk PTSD populations.[16]

Positive outcomes of cognitive-behavioral therapy are reported in literature on the subject, and one of the best known is Albert Ellis's rational-emotive behavior therapy (REBT). Veterans are taught how to alter their own irrational belief systems; because these systems drive behavior, it is assumed that their transformation will lead to changes in veterans' daily lives. REBT, although highly cognitive, emphasizes feelings—both those that add to one's life and those that sabotage it. REBT is often used in combination with other therapies.

Hypnotically facilitated psychotherapy is frequently used to alleviate the suffering associated with PTSD. One study found that when combined with cognitive-behavioral therapy, there was a greater reduction of symptoms (at six-month follow-up) than when the latter was used alone.[17] One of several procedures is to ask the client to "relive" the experience several times while hypnotized; suggestions are given to desensitize the client until the images of the trauma no longer evoke distress.[12] Ernest Rossi has proposed that both hypnosis and traumatic dissociation are rhythmical, occurring at predictable intervals, usually between 90 and 120 minutes, during the day. Peter Brown[17] has noted that a therapist's knowledge of these rhythmic patterns can enhance the deconditioning process, especially if she or he has attempted to trace the physiological pathways responsible for these patterns and has described how they can be mobilized for therapeutic "tuning."

Behavioral therapies cover a wide range of approaches ranging from systematic desensitization and implosion or flooding, to relaxation training. The improvement attributed to behavioral therapies has been more noticeable in lessening symptoms related to depression, anxiety, fear, and intrusive thoughts and images, but less effective in treating emotional numbing and avoidance behavior. Some studies have found implosion to be especially effective in the treatment of anxiety, but it also has a high rate of complication, including escalated depression and panic episodes as well as the relapse of alcohol abuse. Systematic desensitization and similar approaches appear to facilitate a decrease in such target symptoms as intrusive phenomena, avoidance, and flashbacks, but psychodynamic and cognitive therapies seem to be better suited to address such issues as low self-esteem and hopelessness.

Many practitioners of so-called energy psychology claim to have treated PTSD successfully. Using an approach based on Chinese medicine's meridian theory, the energy psychologist typically combines mental imagery and/or verbal affirmations with the stimulation of acupuncture points to effect attitudinal and behavioral changes. David Feinstein and his associates[18] relate the story of "Rich," a hospitalized Vietnam War veteran disabled by insomnia, haunting war memories, and height phobia (due to several parachute jumps made during combat operations). During treatment, he was asked to imagine a situation involving heights; his fear level increased immediately. While holding the image of these stressful events, Rich was asked to stimulate a number of points on his skin by tapping them with his fingertips. Within 15 minutes, Rich reported no fear reaction; the therapist tested this report by having Rich walk onto the fire escape on the third floor with no resulting anxiety.

The therapist then asked Rich to retrieve several of his most intensive combat memories, using the same tapping procedures. These memories were "neutralized" within an hour; Rich still recalled the experiences but they had lost their emotional charge. The therapist taught Rich several apping procedures as homework assignments. Within a short period of time, his insomnia ceased, war memories left his immediate consciousness, he discontinued his medication, and he checked himself out of the hospital. A two-month follow-up indicated that Rich was symptom-free. Several war veterans in the same hospital were treated with similar methods, reportedly achieving similar results. It is clear that the claims of energy psychology need to be investigated by outside observers. If this modality proves to be an empirically validated approach, it could rehabilitate many combat victims in a cost-effective manner through short-term treatment.

Traumatic incident reduction (TIR) is another novel short-term treatment procedure for PTSD and related disorders.[19] TIR operates on the principle that a permanent resolution of a case requires the recovery of repressed memories rather than mere catharsis or coping. It purports to take a "person-centered" perspective, finding out what made the triggering (or "root") incident traumatic from the client's viewpoint. The client is encouraged to express and experience the traumatic incident fully, enabling the incident to be "discharged," at which point it becomes a past, rather than an ongoing, incident. The client tells and retells the TIR practitioner everything he or she remembers about the root incident, each time "peeling off" layers of thoughts, considerations, emotions, decision, and opinions. The incident, or incidents, undergoes reframing and cognitive restructuring, often accompanied by imaginal flooding, sometimes facilitated by hypnosis, gestalt work, and systematic desensitization.

TIR therapists claim to arrive at lasting results in as little as two or three hours; in one research study yielding favorable results, the average length of time per session was 71 minutes.[19] In this study, TIR was compared with two varieties of energy psychology treatments (i.e., thought field therapy, eye movement desensitization and reprocessing), both of which require very little verbalization and claim to "interrupt" the post-traumatic reaction on a physiological level. The contention of TIR practitioners, in contrast, is not that it interrupts the reaction, but "extinguishes" it. One of the treatment modalities, thought field therapy, was credited by the chief medical officer of Kosovo for rehabilitating 105 victims of violence.[19]

Practitioners of eye movement desensitization and reprocessing (EMDR) ask the client to focus on several aspects of a distressing experience. At the same time, the client's attention is grounded on some form of bilateral stimulation such as eye movements, tapping, or sound stimulation. This combination of dual focus and bilateral stimulation is said to generate a reduction in the emotional charge associated with the distressing experience, desensitizing the client. As this desensitization occurs, the client is guided through a process of cognitive restructuring in which the personal meanings associated with the disturbing experience are transformed (e.g., "I am in danger" becomes "I am safe now").

Proponents of EMDR point to research data supporting the long-term effectiveness of this technique (see www.EMDR.com), claiming that talk therapies attempt to train the left frontal cortex (the verbal/conscious part of the brain) to override an already aroused right limbic system (i.e., the emotional/arousal part of the brain), the area directly accessed by EMDR.

Elizabeth Earle-Warfel, in her 2005 doctoral dissertation written for Saybrook Graduate School, proposed a model of PTSD based on chaos theory. For her, EMDR and energy psychology may be effective because, according to chaos theory, only slight perturbations of a few crucial neurons may be needed to alter the stability of whole neuronal systems.

Group therapy is commonly used as an adjunct to other treatments, especially in the Veterans Benefits Administration system. Its benefits include providing a structure of social support and stability for PTSD clients, as well as enhancing socialization and decreasing the intensity of avoidance behavior. Readjustment for Vietnam veterans appears to be enhanced if the other veterans led discussion groups, family counseling, and workshops in coping skills.

The use of various psychotropic medications has become prevalent PTSD, especially since they often entail pronounced positive effects. With the advent of specific serotonin reuptake inhibitors (e.g., Prozac, Paxil, Effexor), few negative side effects are noted, with the benefit of noticeable reduction in anxiety and depression.[20] There is considerable benefit in employing these pharmaceuticals, but their use generally requires contiguous psychotherapy and/or counseling to accomplish more than symptom reduction. Pharmacology can be used in combination with psychotherapy or by itself. In some studies, however, psychological therapies have been more effective than psychotropic medication, although both treatments led to greater symptom reduction than comparison groups of clients who received no treatment.[21]

Acute anxiety is typically treated by the minor tranquilizers. Tricyclic drugs, including amitriptyline, have been employed with some success,[7] especially to treat avoidance syndromes. Other tricyclic antidepressants have been used with greater success to treat intrusive symptoms. Fluoxetine appears to reduce reexperiencing, while sertaline and parexetine are among the most commonly prescribed medications for other PTSD symptoms.

Relapse following medication has been attributed to its failure to address veterans' existential issues and to move them beyond trauma.[6] For example, Iraq war veterans have described the problems and uncertainty accompanying their participation in that conflict; initially they viewed the war as protecting their homeland and liberating Iraq from a despot. Later, combat zones were no longer demarcated, and threats appeared from suicide bombers, snipers, rocket-propelled grenade launchers, and roadside detonation devices. It should come as no surprise that an estimated one out of every six U.S. military men and women returning from Iraq appears to be in need psychotherapeutic care.[22]

Once the most effective approaches have been identified through evidence-based practices,[23] it would be commendable if selected procedures could be taught to health care workers who lack extensive training in psychotherapy, yet possess the personal skills and sensitivity needed to treat raumatized veterans. These men and women are survivors of a protean type of warfare. Terrorists, especially in Iraq and Afghanistan, often take combatants by surprise, use civilians as human shields, and justify their techniques to capitalize on errors in judgment and practice committed by Americans and their allies.

The nature of such warfare takes a toll on caretakers and practitioners as well as combatants. *Compassion fatigue* is a condition that affects many practitioners who work with people suffering from trauma. It can be described as a preoccupation with the trauma of their clients and subsequent weariness in their attachment. Compassion fatigue is associated with sleep disturbances, irritability, tension, and anxiety; if not detected and treated, it can lead to practitioner burnout. As one counselor remarked, "I lost my ability to feel. I . . . could not feel sad, angry, scared, or happy" (p. 24).[24]

Interaction of PTSD and Other Combat-Related Disorders

When a therapist contemplates which treatment strategy to use for PTSD, he or she needs to consider possible associated conditions, since they will have a direct impact on the client's response to treatment. A concomitant episode of major depression is an especially important related disorder to keep in mind, given the high rate of suicide attempts, successful and unsuccessful, among combat veterans. Other taxing conditions include anxiety disorders, phobic disorders, depression, substance abuse, and organic mental disorders.[25]

Chronic exposure to trauma has been known to lead to dissociative identity disorder (DID). Given the socially constructed nature of self-identity, it should be no surprise that a condition such as PTSD, which often devastates a veteran's prewar identity, could lead to the emergence of alternative identities. Maldonado and Spiegel[26] have remarked that it is rare to see a DID patient who has not been exposed to intense trauma, usually in the form of repeated physical or sexual abuse.

There is one other diagnostic issue that must be carefully considered. Therapists must consider that after a PTSD diagnosis a patient may receive immense secondary gain in the form of financial reimbursement and legal benefits, not to mention increased attention from powerful people in the mental health hierarchy. When a differential diagnosis is made, the possibility of factitious disorder or malingering is present and must be considered, because the presence of either can have a major impact on the patient's treatment.[26] Misdiagnosis may occur for any of the *DSM* categories but the accurate diagnosis of PTSD is especially crucial.

Treatment Procedures for Family Members of PTSD Veterans

Families of combat veterans with PTSD face challenges as well.[27] The mother of a guilt-ridden Vietnam veteran with PTSD told the investigative reporter Seymour Hersh, "I gave them a good boy and they sent me back a murderer." Many of these veterans cannot sustain their marriages; others commit acts of violence against family members, including murder. In these cases, incarceration becomes a "treatment" to limit the harm that can be done to others.

A PTSD diagnosis is not needed for family problems to exist. Williams and Williams[28] reported that one out of three combat veterans experienced readjustment difficulties without evidence of concurrent psychological trauma. Nonetheless, may therapists object to labeling returning combat veterans "psychiatric time bombs," claiming that Vietnam veterans were no worse off for their experiences than survivors of previous wars and were about as likely to lead successful lives as nonveterans.

Historically, psychology has focused primarily on addressing individual psychological consequences of war and designing appropriate interventions in turn. The psychological literature on the impact of war stress on families is scarce, and there is a lack of theoretical models, assessment tools, and psychologically based modes of intervention on a large scale to aid civilian victims of war, and families of PTSD victims. Consequently, psychologists and other aid workers who attempt to address the needs of these populations locally, either directly or in a consultancy role, are faced with a lack of resources. This need has generated efforts from various areas of psychology, in collaboration with other disciplines, to provide research and experimentation with different models of intervention with civilian victims of war.[29]

Current information regarding assistance for veterans with PTSD is posted on several Web sites: www.deepthought.org, www.menstuff.org, www.crisisinfo.org, and www.ncptsd.org, the latter under the supervision of the U.S. Department of Veterans Affairs.

PTSD as a Consequence of Modern Warfare

Terror and trauma seem to be dialectally related, yet little clinical research has appeared for either of them. Based on 72 interviews with survivors of five decades of terrorist attacks, genocides, concentration camps, and military bombings of civilian centers, Charles Webel[30] has referred to political terror as the external terrorizer and trauma as the internal terrifier. Both present threats to self-identity at its very core, and nonviolent ways are available to confront these twin horrors.

PTSD is one of several war traumas. All of them reflect the effects of war as an extreme stressor that threatens human existence.

In early 1990, the celebrated author Barbara Ehrenreich[31] gave a resentation on war and warrior elites to a group of sociologists. They were supportive and interested but reminded her that war had run its course. The cold war had ended, and they informed Ehrenreich that war was only subject for historical interest. Later that same year, the United States was at war in Kuwait and Iraq, and a little more than a decade later, in Afghanistan and Iraq. The conviction that war is obsolete has a venerable history of its own; the introduction of the gun and, later, artillery seemed to promise levels of destruction so immense that no state would want to risk them. After the bloodletting of the Napoleonic Wars, Auguste Comte and John Stuart Mill predicted that war would phase out as nations turned to industrial production. World War I was "the war to end all wars"; World War II introduced atomic weapons and a similar sobriquet. Since then, there have been nearly 200 wars of various shapes and sizes, taking more than 200 million combatant and civilian lives.[31]

At the same time, however, organized human resistance to war has been on the rise. While the practice and passions of war have been the province of a warrior elite, popular opposition to war largely has taken the form of opposition to the elite. Ehrenreich[31] comments, "It is a giant step from hating the warriors to hating the war, and an even greater step to deciding that the 'enemy' is the abstract institution of war" (p. 240).

In 2005, the Public Broadcasting Service aired a film titled *A Soldier's Heart*. One segment of it included an interview with a Marine sergeant who opened fire on an Iraqi civilian just as she was reaching into her handbag for a white flag as she approached the sergeant's checkpoint. When he realized his mistake, he broke into tears, crying over her dead body. Thereafter, he was unable to carry out his duties. Such are the consequences of modern warfare. And such is the nature of the enemy against which the defenders of peace will mobilize if war trauma, at last, is to take its place with the plagues of the past rather than remain a malady of the present.

ACKNOWLEDGMENTS

The authors express their gratitude for The Chair for the Study of Consciousness, Saybrook Graduate School, San Francisco, for its support in the preparation of this chapter, and to Jeffrey Kirkwood, Carlos Adrian Hernandez Tavares, and Steve Hart for their editorial assistance.

REFERENCES

1. American Psychiatric Association (2000). *Diagnostic and statistical manual of mental disorders* (4th ed., text revision). Washington, DC: Author.
2. De Jong, J. (2002). *Trauma, war, and violence*. New York: Plenum.

3. Brown, C. R., Rose, S., & Andrews, B. (2002). A brief screening instrument for post-traumatic stress disorder. *British Journal of Psychiatry, 181*, 158–162.

4. Marra, T. (2005). *Dialectic behavior therapy*. Oakland, CA: New Harbinger.

5. Kleinman, A. (1986, February 26). When you're the one with AIDS, it's a different fight. *Los Angeles Times Book Review*, p. 8

6. Greening, T. (1997). Posttraumatic stress disorder: An existential-humanistic perspective. In S. Krippner & S. Powers (Eds.), *Broken images, broken selves: Dissociative narratives in clinical practice* (pp. 125–135). Washington, DC: Brunner/Mazel.

7. Katz, R. (1994). Post-Traumatic stress disorder. In V. S. Ramachandran (Ed.), *Encyclopedia of human behavior* (Vol. 3, pp. 555–562). San Diego: Academic Press.

8. Marshall, S.L.A. (1947). *Men under fire: The problem of battle command in future wars*. New York: William Morrow.

9. Boscarino, J. (2001). Disease among men 20 years after exposure to severe stress: Implications for clinical research and medical care. *Psychosomatic Medicine, 59*, 605–614.

10. Paulson, D. S. (2005). *Walking the point: Male initiation and the Vietnam experience* (Rev. ed.). New York: Paraview.

11. Foreman, W. C. (2005). *The subjective experience of UN peacekeeping duty: The concerns of Finnish police officers on war zone duty in the former Yugoslavia*. Unpublished doctoral dissertation, Saybrook Graduate School, San Francisco.

12. Brown, P. (1994). Toward a psychobiological model of dissociation and posttraumatic stress disorder. In S. J. Lynn & J. Rhue (Eds.), *Dissociation: Clinical and theoretical perspectives* (pp. 94–122). New York: Guilford.

13. Lifton, R. J. (1979). *The broken connection*. New York: Simon and Schuster.

14. Wilson, J. P. (1989). *Trauma transformations and healing: An integrative approach to theory, research, and post-trauma therapy*. New York: Brunner/Mazel.

15. Kulka, R. A., Schlenger, W. E., Fairbank, J. A., Hough, R. L., Jordan, B. K., Marman, C. R., & Weiss, D. S. (1990). *Trauma and the Vietnam War generation: Report of findings from the National Vietnam Veterans Readjustment Study*. New York: Brunner/Mazel.

16. Gist, R., & Devilly, G. J. (2002). Post-trauma debriefing: The road too frequently traveled. *Lancet, 360*, 741–742.

17. Bryant, R. A., Moulds, M. L., Guthrie, R. M., & Nixon, R. D. (2005). The additive benefit of hypnosis and cognitive-behavioral therapy in treating acute stress disorder. *Journal of Consulting and Clinical Psychology, 73*, 334–340.

18. Feinstein, D., Craig, G., & Eden, D. (2005). *The promise of energy psychology*. New York: Jeremy P. Tarcher/Penguin.

19. Volkman, V. R. (Ed.). (2005). *Beyond trauma: Conversations on Traumatic Incident Reduction* (2nd ed.). Ann Arbor, MI: Loving Healing.

20. Catell, P. (2004). *Drugs & clients: What every psychotherapist needs to know*. Petaluma, CA: Solarium.

21. Van Etten, M. L., & Taylor, S. (1998). Comparative efficacy of treatment for post-traumatic stress disorder: A meta-analysis. *Clinical Psychology and Psychotherapy*, 5, 126–144.

22. Hamod, S. (2005, March). *33 things you should know about the Middle East and America.* Retrieved March 6, 2005 from http://smirkingchimp.com/article. php?sid = 20176

23. Roberts, A. R., & Yeager, K. R. (Eds.). (2004). *Evidence-based practice manual: Research and outcome measures in health and human services.* New York: Oxford University Press.

24. Kennedy, A. (2004, November). ACA Foundation releasing revised edition of trauma guidebook. *Counseling Today*, pp. 1, 24, 26, 42.

25. De Jong, J. T. V. M., Komproe, I. H., & Van Ommeren, M. (2003). Common mental disorders in postconflict settings. *Lancet, 361*, 2126–2130.

26. Maldonado, J. R., & Spiegel, D. (1994). The treatment of post-traumatic stress disorder. In S. J. Lynn & J. Rhue (Eds.), *Dissociation: Clinical and theoretical perspectives* (pp. 215–241). New York: Guilford.

27. Carr, C. (2002). *The lessons of terror: A history of warfare against civilians, why it has always failed and why it will fail again.* New York: Random House.

28. Williams, C., & Williams, T. (1987). Family therapy for Vietnam veterans. In T. Williams (Ed.), *Post-traumatic stress disorder: A handbook for civilians* (pp. 75–92). Cincinnati, OH: Disabled Veterans of America.

29. Krippner, S., & McIntyre, T. M. (Eds.). (2003). Overview: In the wake of war. In S. Krippner & T. M. McIntyre (Eds.), *The psychological impact of war trauma on civilians: An international perspective* (pp. 1–14). Westport, CT: Praeger.

30. Webel, C. P. (2005). *Terror, terrorism, and the human condition.* New York: Palgrave/ Macmillan.

31. Ehrenreich, B. (1997). *Blood rites: Origins and history of the passions of war.* New York: Henry Holt.

Chapter 2

Family Violence and Its Degrees of Deviance: Understanding the Truth or Paying the Consequences

Christina M. Dalpiaz

REDEFINING "DOMESTIC VIOLENCE" AS "FAMILY VIOLENCE"

The purpose of this chapter is to redefine violence between intimate partners as "family violence" rather than "domestic violence" and demonstrate how this type of violence affects society as a whole. This new definition thus expands the implications of family violence to all its victims. Unwittingly, society has tended to lessen the atrocity of battered victims and their children by minimizing their experiences as tiffs between two partners, excluding the impact on children, extended family, and society. These violent episodes are much broader, far-reaching, and complex than previously imagined. In 2000, 1,247 women and 440 men were killed by their intimate partners.[1] In many of these cases, the couples had children who were left without one or both parents.

The best available data regarding violence against women suggests that about 1.3 to 5 million women are abused annually. On the lower end of the scale, according to one study, 76 percent of these women were abused by current or former husbands, cohabiting partners, or dates. Interestingly, 835,000 men also reported being abused by their intimate partners.[2] These numbers suggest that society should take a closer look at the dynamics of family violence and understand that the entire family unit is being impacted and that no one, regardless of gender or position in the family, should be overlooked. The troubling aspect of all of this is that the children who are exposed to violence against a parent, grand-parent, other relative, significant adult, or themselves are also being harmed. This exposure is robbing them of their childhood innocence and producing a new generation of violence, one that appears to be increasingly more violent than the last. In another study, between 50 and 75 percent of children living in homes where there is domestic violence were themselves abused.[3] As a result, one troubling statistic estimated that 63 percent of boys 11–20 years old who commit homicide kill a man who is abusing their mother.[4] And according to the Columbus Coalition against Family Violence, 80 percent of incarcerated juvenile offenders and adult prisoners reported coming from violent homes.[5] Consequently, society is building more facilities to house these children and young adults. These numbers are staggering. Imagine the monetary savings in the judicial system alone, if our country's response to family violence was more immediate, effective, and proactive. The system has become reactive and cannot financially manage these numbers adequately. Then the overpopulated prisons are forced to reduce sentences and the abusers are set free and often reoffend.

Throughout history, family violence has often been ignored. A desensitized society has resigned itself to the notion that two people in conflict are simply mismanaging their emotions and outsiders should mind their own business. The reality, however, is much graver and more insidious. Most victims and their children are essentially imprisoned and held hostage under inhumane conditions. Victimized families are forced to endure high levels of stress through emotional terrorism. The tactics batterers use to achieve fear are quite remarkable. For example, they may destroy precious items, threaten other family members with bodily harm, or kill family pets to gain compliance. The resulting fear generates conditioned responses that often permanently impact behavior and cognitive processing, enabling batterers to "groom" their victims into submission, making the victims psychologically incapable of leaving their abusers. The devastating impact this psychological conditioning has on families victimized by violence is therefore referred to as the *grooming process*.[6] As a result of this conditioning, victims often assume the blame or responsibility for their own abuse. They have been taught that they caused and deserved their mistreatment. Victims are constantly reminded that they are inadequate and that somehow they were responsible for their abusers' violent behavior.

In order to understand these families better, it is imperative to understand the family violence psychological process more fully. Batterers usually will not physically strike until they know that the victims cannot psychologically leave the relationship. The basis for this reasoning is that many batterers fear abandonment and cannot afford to lose their partners by miscalculating their victims' emotional state or possible response. They learn their partners' vulnerabilities very well and then exploit them. Their keen ability to recognize how to groom their victims eventually makes physical violence possible. This adeptness guides them to carefully choose their victims. They know how to target their victims' strengths and weaknesses to manipulate the environment in order to meet their need for control. Once conditions are favorable for abuse, the physical violence can commence. A gradual breakdown occurs where victims' identities are stripped from them and their perpetrators' influence is all that they comprehend.

Being able to support members in family violence involves assessing and recognizing how this psychological terrorism and emotional deprivation become precursors to physical assault and contribute to victimization. Therefore, it is imperative to dispel the myth that a fight between two adults is only a private issue. This concept only perpetuates the cycle of violence, which plays a significant role in revictimizing battered families who are genuinely interested in fleeing the abusive relationship.

With our increasingly changing culture, definitions of family have also changed. Family and child advocates as well as criminal justice and other system personnel must be sensitive and respectful of these changes without judgment in order to include anyone experiencing personal violence within a broadly defined family environment. There are intimate relationships that do not fit the traditional nuclear family stereotype yet still qualify as families suffering with violence. Their plight is as significant as the traditional family and should not be minimized. These abused families may include:

- Men who are assaulted by women
- The "sandwich generation," where both grandparents and children are abused
- Same-sex relationships as well as heterosexual ones
- Step-, kinship, or foster families

Each family constellation presents a different dynamic of family violence that must be addressed individually. There is no place in these victims' lives for advocates and other system personnel who do not understand the seriousness of their situation.

Mind-set of the Abuser and the Victim

The degree of deviance in the dynamics of family violence becomes more insidious and methodical as the batterers repeatedly succeed in their psychological assaults. To prevent violence, the perpetrators' viewpoint and mind-set must first be recognized. The abusers' perspective can be outrageous, unrealistic, and incomprehensible to the average person. Their thought process generates cognitive distortion that influences their victims' perceptions, rendering victims incapable of making informed choices. Abusers can rationalize their distorted thought process so well that the victims believe them. Consequently, batterers can manipulate and lie much more eloquently than their victims can tell the truth. As a result, many outsiders view abusees as hysterical, irrational, and unstable. Victims constantly exposed to this mindset may come to share this same viewpoint and often admit that they feel as though they are going crazy. Over time, the exposure to their batterers' frame of mind gradually breaks down the victims' self-worth and -esteem, which alters their ability to comprehend their circumstances, ultimately limiting their effective coping options. These preliminary behaviors become causal factors that allow physical abuse to eventually occur. In order to more accurately predict the progression that escalates into physical violence, we must assess the relationship between precursors and subsequent behaviors.

Some methods used to groom victims include the following:

+ Isolation
+ Manipulation
+ Humiliation
+ Guilt
+ Name-calling
+ Emotional deprivation
+ Fear
+ Sexual assault
+ Terror or the potential threat of bodily harm

Forecasting these tactics can prospectively lead both victims and perpetrators toward a healthier interpersonal relationship and away from the cycle of violence. First, however, the inappropriate behaviors must be taken seriously. What much of society minimizes or overlooks is how emotional violence imparts fear and contributes to the perception of a threat. The following case illustrates this point.

Case 1: One batterer would tap a watch to indicate that it was time for a beating. In court, the abuser began tapping and the victim quickly became hysterical. The court found that the gesture was insignificant and that the victim overreacted.

The key element to consider when working with families is that emotional terror alone can control victims, even in the absence of physical violence. Most often physical assault is used as a last resort. The potential threat generates conditioning and distorts the victims' perception of reality.

Society tends to believe that couples can work out their conflicts by negotiating with each other. But in an abusive, controlling, and unilateral relationship this means that victims must comply with their perpetrators' demands. Negotiation is never an option and compromise doesn't happen. The batterers' behavior can often be interpreted or justified as a mood or impulse that implies a temporary attitude or situation. Unfortunately, this is rarely the case. Their abusive and controlling mind-set has patterns that are perpetual and long-lasting. Stephen Hart, a Canadian expert, describes this as *ladder behavior*, which means deviant behavior ascends. He eloquently articulates this psychological process by stating, "It's the thought that counts." It is not the actual physical violation that is so important but rather the intent and the perception of the violation. Consequently, to combat the misconceptions about family violence, we must recognize its psychological and emotional implications.

Most victims, whether they are male or female, stay in abusive situations for a variety of reasons. First and foremost is the issue of children. A male victim feels the need to protect the kids and will not want to leave them alone with an abusive mother. He also fears that the legal system will rule that the children belong with their mother and therefore he would lose access to his children. A female victim fears that the abuser will follow through on his threat to prove that she is a bad mother and that she will lose custody of her children. Both fathers and mothers often worry about financially caring for their children, and they may perceive a two-parent home as more emotionally stable.

Other reasons victims stay may be attributed to their beliefs and cognitions. They have been groomed to think that they are too inept to survive in the "real" world and that no one else would ever desire them. They come to believe that they are lucky to have their relationship and should feel grateful for it. They are conditioned to either excuse or ignore the abusive behavior and accept what the abusers say as true. Some victims become overly reliant on their abusers and desperately fear independence. The abused man or woman may be mentally, emotionally, or financially dependent on the batterer. The thought of leaving the relationship generates significant feelings of loss, anxiety, or depression. These painful emotions can be so intense that they are often confused with love. Over time, the victim becomes psychologically connected to the abusing partner, making it difficult to separate. Progressive mastery of grooming techniques provides control for the batterers and keeps their victims trapped.

Family dynamics determine how individuals behave or feel as a result of the abuse. These behaviors ultimately impact the entire family and contribute to how members interact with one another. To help move them in a more healthy direction, it is important to understand how victims and abusers react to their partners. The following list reviews some of the results that occur when abusive behavior is persistent.

Characteristics typically present in victims include:

+ Depression—experiences feelings of helplessness and/or hopelessness
+ Anxiety/hypervigilant reactions—mimics hyperactivity or learning difficulties
+ Poor self-image—behaves the way they feel, unwilling to excel or be self-reliant
+ Incompetence—experiences feelings of inadequacy as a result of constant berating or browbeating
+ Fear of failure—learns that making mistakes has grave consequences so they either avoid trying or strive for perfection, believing they can manage the violence
+ Poor social skills—develops inadequate relationship or interpersonal skills
+ Poor eye contact—generates detachment issues and potential pathologies
+ Overreactive startle response—fears severe repercussions due to relentless abuse; body is held in a high state of arousal
+ Inadequate protective factors—accepts that they cannot protect their children or themselves or minimize danger
+ Poor impulse control—attempts to meet internal needs through external sources that can never be satiated
+ Meltdowns—reacts inappropriately due to inability to cope with stress
+ Regressive behavior—reverts to age-inappropriate behaviors such as bed-wetting or thumb sucking
+ Passive or passive/aggressive behavior—expresses extreme or improper behavior due to low self-esteem and worth; believes they do not deserve to have needs met appropriately

Characteristics typically present in batterers include:

+ Pessimistic attitude—expresses dissatisfaction; rarely happy, demands perfection from others through constant criticism and coercion
+ Inadequacy—projects negative self-image onto victims
+ Jealousy or abandonment issues—desperately fears the loss of the relationship and uses guilt and accusations to maintain relationships
+ Aggressive or passive/aggressive behavior—rationalizes that this is the only successful way to get needs met
+ Controlling and excessive behavior—believe they must control environment to maintain status quo
+ Unrealistic or demanding expectations—requires victims to achieve the unachievable
+ External locus of control—allows external environment to control internal thoughts and behaviors; ironically this reaction gives away the very control they are so desperately trying to maintain
+ Depression—generates irritability and general malaise
+ Fearful—promotes anxiety and terror

- Cognitive distortion—thinks in a twisted or crooked manner and can rationalize or justify their behavior
- Trust issues—suspects others' motives and cannot trust environment to meet needs

As a result of these conditions, the toxicity of the relationship and the desperate need for the batterers and victims to bond with each other ultimately generate chaos and dissension. The link they share is referred to as *trauma bonding*. Regardless of the physical violence, the emotional connection between them is insurmountably strong. This dysfunctional interaction poisons every aspect of their lives, prohibiting a healthy and violence-free relationship. Tensions are high and generally unpredictable, so the attacks can erupt at any given moment and under any circumstance. These explosive personalities create an unsafe environment for the entire family.

Abusees may not know how to cope with the violence and may displace their feelings onto other family members. For example, children deeply struggle with their emotions, in part because they do not understand their feelings. On one hand, they might feel comfortable enough to emote or unleash their pent-up frustration onto the nonabusing parent in an effort to relieve the pressure. On the other hand, they will desperately attempt to please the abusive parent to gain validation. Essentially, victims' attempts to resolve issues never come to fruition because they hardly ever defend themselves and batterers are rarely satisfied with their family's performance. In cases where both parents are abusive, the children are faced with double jeopardy: unable to get their emotional needs met by anyone regardless of their attempts, they feel inadequate and unworthy, and view themselves as constant failures. These imprinted messages are rehearsed and embedded into their self-image. Eventually, they emotionally beat themselves up and no longer require external input. That is why it is so important to understand that a child can be taken out of a violent environment, but it may take years to take the violent environment out of the child.

Evaluating the impact that violence has on child development can generate a more accurate account of children's behaviors. When we can see their reactions as a cry for help rather than defiance, we are one step closer to the healing process. Children are our most precious investment in our future, and we are obligated to create an environment that meets their emotional needs and interrupts the cycle of violence for the next generation.

Family Violence Once Victims Flee

The social question posed to most victims is, Why did you stay? The answer is clear. Fleeing the abusive relationship guarantees the escalation of physical violence. Batterers do not recognize boundaries. They do not understand that no means no, stop means stop, and don't means don't. Abuse is based on control, and when that control is lost (i.e., the victims flee), the batterers are placed on the offensive. Their mission, now, is to regain their position. Their objectives are often achieved through stalking their victims or creating havoc. The generated fear forces victims to return in order to secure perceived safety.

Victims and their extended families report the following list of behaviors that significantly increase when victims attempt to terminate the relationship:

- Kidnapping children
- Breaking into the home
- Killing or stealing pets
- Stealing or damaging property
- Physically restraining victims
- Stalking
- Relentless harassing telephone calls
- Threatening suicide or homicide
- Disturbing workplace, with resulting job loss for the victim
- Holding victims hostage
- Murdering victims and their children

In the face of such conditions, survival instincts may dictate victims' choices. They understand that leaving increases their risk of physical injury or even death. Statistics verify their fears. Seventy-five percent of the victims killed by intimate partners had fled the relationship.

WHY SHOULD OUTSIDERS CARE?

The community's response to family violence can, to a large extent, determine the outcome for victims—negative or positive. This section has three primary objectives. The first is to alert outsiders to many of the current procedures that unwittingly contribute to the plight of victims. The second is to demonstrate how their cases consequently fall between the cracks in the system. The third objective illustrates how the community can help save lives when it responds appropriately.

Obviously, our culture does not consciously set out to harm these families. People too often simply do not understand them. Abusers have aberrant behaviors that are difficult to grasp, and this can generate expectations for victims that are unrealistic and naive. The general population still places the onus on victims to terminate the abusive relationship. People do not fully comprehend or acknowledge the dynamics that force victims to stay. Reports by battered women and men state that they fear leaving the relationship due, in part, to the system's lack of appropriate and immediate response to their predicament. Victims believe this indifference allows perpetrators to abuse them again and again, emotionally, sexually, and physically, with little or no ramifications. Victims realize that they are facing a double-edged sword: "Damned if you do leave, dead if you don't." Most victims truly believe that they cannot fight against their batterers and win.

An increasing number of abusers, both male and female, know how to manipulate the legal and social service system to further the assault on their runaway families. The community then generates barriers and obstacles that prevent victims from fleeing by prejudging them. Victims may hear statements such as "You made your bed, now lie in it," or "It takes two to tango." Compassion is often missing because society generally believes that the victims shouldn't have gotten themselves into this mess in the first place. Some feel if that if victims were stupid enough to tolerate the abuse then they need to figure things out on their own. Additionally, the cultural perspective often still maintains that children need both parents, whether they are abusive or not. Pressures are applied to comply with court orders; yet, we chastise victims for not protecting their children. Instead, the legal and social service systems need to recognize the impending danger and mandate treatments that work.

Contrary to what many might believe, some of the most dangerous abusers can be very much in control of their emotions. They often appear more credible in court than their victims and can usually win custody of their children based on their ability to present themselves well and to use tactics that manipulate the legal system. For example, *continuance* is a term that every victim comes to know and understand. Continuances are granted to individuals who need to extend their cases to adequately prepare for the judicial outcome. This right gives batterers the ability to prolong the legal proceedings. The perpetrators' skills along with their lawyer's creative tactics make the possibilities for continuances endless.

Case 2: One victim shared that her husband's lawyer had exhausted every possible continuance imaginable, so he suggested that the only recourse his client had was to fire him because the courts respect the right to representation. So the abuser heeded his attorney's advice, causing yet another delay. Next, he employed another lawyer who would be just as skilled. This attorney delayed filing the divorce papers so that her client could file for bankruptcy and ruin the victim's credit. Although the victim was paying her mortgage and his credit card debt, the batterer placed those items on his bankruptcy statement causing financial havoc. With time and a few thousand dollars in legal fees, she should be able to rectify this problem, but why should she have to?

The system often impedes victims' efforts to leave an abusive situation by generating case plans that are impossible to complete. Yet, they judge victims with condemnation or disgust when they stay in the relationship. Professionals working in the realm of family violence need to read between the lines and react more appropriately. One way to respond differently is to look beyond the surface. For example, victims often admit or assume responsibility for their part in the violent interaction, whereas, the batterers normally will not. Without the proper assessment skills, the easiest and least expensive means of resolving the legal conflict is to accept the victims' acknowledgement of responsibility, which relieves the perpetrators of any liability and obligates the victims to meet legal requirements. Take for instance the following case.

Case 3: A young woman fled her abusive partner with her son. The estranged husband subsequently broke into her apartment while she slept and began choking her. She dug her nails into his arm to break the chokehold, which left deep marks. The police responded and saw the injury to her ex-partner's arm. She then admitted that she scratched him. Although she had bruises on her neck, the claw marks on him seemed more serious. Rather than assessing who the real primary aggressor was, the police made a dual arrest and charged them both with domestic violence. This batterer had prior convictions, but the woman was noted as primary aggressor due to the severity of his injuries. The violence did not stop here. The batterer then threatened to get even with the victim and worked with another woman to set her up. He keyed an old girlfriend's car and got the new girlfriend to say she witnessed his wife commit the crime. The police called the victim and insisted that she turn herself in because there was a witness. While she was in jail, the victim was served with custody papers. It would appear that the perpetrator had mastered the system. And the victim's only crime was doing what society wanted her to do—leave the abusive relationship. The escalation of his behavior suggests that he recognized the potential assaultive maneuvers available to him and used them impeccably against his victim.

Researchers, therapists, and law enforcement personnel are often missing the mark. Rather than recognizing the batterers' escalating behavior as higher levels of abuse, they see these perpetrators as different types of batterers. This compartmentalization according to different types of violence fragments and dilutes the assessment, because treatment plans are not generated to measure the abuse as a sum of all parts. To adequately respond to violence, professionals need to recognize and accept that abusive behaviors accelerate to higher levels and that they do not belong to different personality types. With this assumption, we can predict with greater accuracy what victims can expect. Most batterers start out the same way, using emotional violence; then, as they perfect their skills, they graduate to the next level. Compare the behavior with college students who are selecting their majors. Students essentially start out at the same point, taking basic core classes. When they have passed the prerequisite courses, they are permitted to take the upper level classes. Abuse is analogous. The course is Violence 101. When abusers can manipulate their victims through guilt and accomplish their objective, then they can move to the next level, which might be shame or isolation. But when society condemns their behavior and says, "This is unacceptable," the abuse is momentarily thwarted. Consequently, they either fail the course and stop abusing, or they do extra credit to continue the bad behavior. If you look more closely at the abusers' lives, most are not violent with anyone other than their partners or family, which suggests that they understand that there are no societal sanctions for their actions. The following example illustrates what happens to behavior when family members either accept or denounce the intervention.

Case 4: A couple, both with abusive tendencies, was in conflict. The wife initiated a fight then went to bed to "punish" her husband. Brooding over the "unfinished" business, he waited for his wife to fall asleep then threw a glass of water in her face. The conflict escalated and the police were called. Both were ordered into family violence treatment. The results were that the husband eventually recognized that his behavior was abusive and altered his actions. The wife, however, could not acknowledge her part in the abuse and continued using her current behavior to deal with conflict. Although both were treated, one's behavior graduated to the next level whereas the others did not.

Deviant behaviors can have distinct and predictable patterns that could be examined and profiled. Over a lifetime, batterers can have multiple victims, which suggests that they possess serial behavior that warrants study. We have developed useful profiling techniques to assess serial murderers, pedophiles, and rapists based on their behaviors. Would it not make sense, then, to evaluate serial batterers? We could predict future behavior with relative accuracy if we recognized the escalating emotional behavior as progressive. Not all cases of emotional violence erupt into physical violence, but, according to victims' reports, all physical violence started with emotional abuse.

For victims, fleeing an abusive relationship often means leaving with only the clothes on their back. Proving the abuse becomes difficult when, in the past, victims feared the possible consequences and thus rarely or never reported the assaults. Now that danger is eminent and fleeing is their only chance of survival, the onus is placed on the victims to prove to the court that their mates are abusive. Some researchers go so far as to suggest that victims make up the abuse to harm the other parent. The term used to describe this behavior is *parent alienation syndrome* (PAS). PAS theorizes that "alleged" victims want to hurt their spouses by severing the relationship between the other parent and the children. However, although situations arise where parents pit children against their estranged partners, it is more likely the batterers and not the victims who are capable of this type of manipulation. Victims have been beaten down so badly emotionally and physically that this any attempt to deliberately alienate children from a spouse would be too frightening. It makes more sense to conclude that the batterers are the ones who use this tactic because they need to regain control. Most professionals denounce PAS and believe it to have no merit. Unfortunately, some attorneys and psychologists have been able to introduce this theory in court and victims have thus lost custody of their children. The following is an example of how a perpetrator can utilize the legal system to further the abuse.

Case 5: A vice president of a prominent bank tried to report to the doctors, police and social services that her ex-husband was sexually assaulting their six-year-old daughter. When no one would assist her, she made a desperate decision. She went into hiding in a foreign country to save her daughter from the horrific abuse. She gave up a prestigious job and salary to live in secret. Her ex-husband then hired a private detective to find the young girl. At this point, the child was recovered and the mother was arrested and put in prison for two years for denying parental visitation. Subsequently, the woman has never been able to see her daughter again and her ex-husband is free to do whatever he pleases to his daughter. The answer to the question, "Why didn't the victim leave?" is clear—leaving can mean total devastation and loss.

Yet, victims who stay jeopardize losing their children as well. A relatively new trend, which is gaining momentum and should be cause for great concern, is how child protective services (CPS) responds to children exposed to family violence. Many victims now lose their children to CPS under the guise of "failure to protect." Sometimes the assessment is so off target that CPS gives custody to the very person who inflicted the abuse. While all measures should be taken to protect children from being exposed to family violence, the system needs to ensure that social services are not generating more traumas for these families. Some caseworkers will go so far as to force interaction between parents, knowing there is a restraining order. The victims understand the eminent danger but the system often does not. Take for example the following cases.

Case 6: One social worker told a male victim, "Your ex-wife hasn't hit you for years so stop presuming she'll hurt you now." The fact may be that she hasn't hit him but she stalked him on a regular basis and was arrested several times for violation of a restraining order. Those behaviors need to be strongly considered as part of the abusive cycle when dealing with families of violence. Victims who are forced to stay in the traumatized state cannot think clearly or make informed decisions.

Case 7: A Special Advocate, or what was previously known as a Guardian Ad Litem (GAL), is a representative, usually a lawyer, who is assigned by the courts to protect children involved in custody cases. In this particular case, the GAL forced a victim into mediation, which ended with deadly results. Although the GAL reported, "That guy was the scariest person I have ever met," he still insisted that the victim negotiate and compromise with her abuser. His minimization of the danger cost the victim her life. The abuser brought a gun into the mediation process. He shot and killed his wife leaving behind two children. The GAL's response was, "The system failed this man. If we would have only let him see his children maybe he wouldn't have done this." This response completely absolves the perpetrator of his behavior and caused the victim's death. The paradigm needs to shift to see that the persons whom the system failed, in this case, were the victim and her children. The system's failure to recognize the dynamics of abuse is evident in this next case as well.

Case 8: An abusive boyfriend warned his victim, while riding home from a Christmas party, "Wait until we get home, you're in for a real beating." She frantically tried to stop the vehicle, but he punched her in the face and broke her nose. She jumped out of the car and started running down a residential street, banging on doors and pleading for help. The police arrived, and the perpetrator told them that she was drunk and tried to drive home. He said that his elbow accidentally hit her in the struggle for the keys. They arrested her for domestic violence and for disturbing the peace because she knocked on the neighbors' doors. The police did not verify her story and they never tested the man for intoxication. The woman was initially taken in handcuffs to the hospital, where the doctor looked at her and sneered, "Wow, he got you good," then he walked out of the room and left her there alone for three hours. Because she was considered the perpetrator, she did not qualify for a victims' advocate. She was forced to spend three nights in jail for a crime her abuser had committed.

Case 9: One social worker clearly discounted an accusation that a child was sexually assaulted when she declared, "I was abused by my father and I hated him. This girl loves her dad and doesn't act like a victim." What this social worker does not understand is that each victim has to access the skills she or he has learned and use them at all costs to survive. There is no place in this system for emotional projection. A standardized list of requirements should be made to eliminate or minimize subjective assessments. With a regulated protocol, there is less opportunity for providers to be prejudiced by personal experiences. It is also imperative that providers be emotionally healthy before they attempt to assist others with victimization. Victims' reactions vary and considerations should be made for those differences. Each victim develops different degrees of coping skills, physiological defenses, and psychological perspectives. Each mind-set must be respected and all efforts should be made not to minimize victims' trauma, regardless of the professionals' experience.

Case 10: A father openly admitted to a caseworker that he had been sexually abused as a child and was sexually abusive as an adolescent. He walked in on his daughters touching each other and flew into hysteria. He thought he had protected his children from his abusive family members. Now, the cycle of violence was continuing with his daughters despite his efforts. With his worst fear realized, he overreacted and inappropriately spanked them leaving bruises. He compared his reaction to spanking a child who darts out into the street—he panicked. As a result of the physical marks, the family was referred to human services where the children were immediately removed. Both parents complied with the case plan, but when they met the goal, the social worker wasn't satisfied. She decided that the mother, who was a nonoffending participant, must be mentally ill for staying in the relationship and forced her to take a psychological exam. This was clearly a misuse of power. For whatever reason, the social worker was convinced that this father was a child molester, and she had no intention of returning the children no matter how compliant the family was. The irony is that the social worker placed the children with the people this man feared most—his abusive family members.

Parents often have no recourse because child protective agencies are sheltered under the guise of confidentiality. The agencies are essentially permitted to do whatever they want without being monitored or challenged. Unless the families can afford adequate representation, the chances are great that the children will be removed permanently.

These examples are provided to alert the community (as well as advocates and service providers) that current practices should be reevaluated. Also, these professionals might want to determine whether they are genuinely being objective in their evaluations. Although it is obvious that these cases can stimulate various emotional responses, it is important to underscore the responsibility and need for an objective perspective when it comes to family violence. Depending on the worker's position and point of view, there may be an inappropriate level of sympathy or apathy toward family members. Instead, professional objectivity must rule the day.

Case 11: A district attorney (DA) insisted on incarcerating a family member even though support services were being offered and the family complied willingly. The DA became irate when the advocate said that progress was being made. The DA insulted the advocate, accusing her of being a "psycho babbler" with no interest in protecting the children. Luckily, the judge was familiar with the advocate's work and reprimanded the attorney. This DA obviously had some emotional baggage that altered his ability to adequately perform his duties.

Although these examples may make the judicial system seem inept, there are many judges, advocates, therapists, and social workers who are making outstanding strides and contributions in the area of family violence. The following case is an excellent example.

Case 12: A father physically struck his daughter, leaving a bruise across her face. Social services ordered the father to be removed from the home and treatment began. Initially, the abuser minimized and rationalized his behavior. However, with counseling and classes on domestic and parenting, he was able to recognize the gravity of his behavior and change it. This man made significant progress with his wife and children, and the family was able to remain intact.

So, when treatment and intervention programs are done effectively, positive changes can occur. As we learn how to manage the dynamics involved in family violence, our success rate can improve.

Cost to the Victims and to the Community

Family violence extends past the immediate family and impacts everyone to some degree. The cost psychologically, sexually, physically, and financially affects not only families but also the community as a whole.

This section begins with perhaps the most vulnerable—the children. The information provided here explains the influence family violence has on their development and the significant damage they experience when caught in the crossfire. Because most behavior is taught, the violence alters the outcomes of their lives. Children love their parents innately and desire harmony. Unfortunately, however, children who witness abuse rarely experience peace. They are deeply traumatized when one parent or both assaults the other. According to one study, 85 percent of one group of children who witnessed family violence displayed moderate to severe symptoms of post-traumatic stress disorder (PTSD).[7] The study also reported that exposure to domestic violence appeared to be a stronger risk factor for PTSD than being a direct victim of physical abuse. The reason this may be true is that children's symbiotic bond with their parents is so strong that when they see the blow that created the black eye, fat lip, or broken bone, they can empathize with their parent's pain. They experience an overpowering sense of helplessness, which in turn generates guilt for not being able to control the situation. This exposure is teaching children how to treat or be treated by members of the opposite sex. Their relationship skills are being developed in a maladaptive manner, and the effects of these observed behaviors can last a lifetime.

Parents from abusive homes (whether perpetrator or victim) participate in behaviors that emotionally damage the welfare of their children. Over time, parents run the potential risk of losing their ability to recognize the protective factors necessary to keep their children emotionally and physically safe.

Case 13: One child disclosed that her abusive father would push her head under the water until she couldn't hold her breath any longer. When the mother was asked why she didn't rescue her daughter, she claimed, "Oh, her father was just playing." Regardless of what the batterer thought he was doing, the young girl was terrorized. It matters not what the inflicter feels but rather how the receiver processes or interprets the event. These families need assistance with understanding how their behavior impacts future outcomes. The system falls short when it does not adequately identify, evaluate, or respond appropriately to the severity of the abuse. Take this next court case as an example.

Case 14: A victim and two children were diagnosed with PTSD and the abuser was not. He instead was given the diagnosis of narcissistic personality. No one bothered to theorize that perhaps the reason the abuser did not suffer from PTSD or appear emotionally debilitated might be because he created the terror. Rather than look at that possibility, human services concluded that since the other parent was traumatized and emotionally incapable of caring for the children, then the nontraumatized parent was more suitable for custody.

The more deviant batterers may learn how to manipulate the system and threaten to take away the victims' children. In many cases, batterers either win custody or financially devastate their victims by taking them to court. When victims cannot take care of their children's basic needs, they feel forced to return to the abusive relationship. In an increasing number of cases where abusive men fight for custody, they win. The important role of fatherhood for a long time was grossly underestimated and prejudices worked against men, and because the court system wants to rebalance the scales of justice, they now often award custody to fathers. Unfortunately, in many of the custody cases today, it isn't the "good" guys who are fighting for their children, but rather the abusers in an attempt to control and punish their victims for running away. Abusive women are also using the same twisted manipulation to punish their partners. The batterers' mind-set is that victims must pay for their transgressions. As a consequence, victims spend whopping sums of $20,000–$40,000 to obtain or legally maintain custody of the children, and these costs can rise as high as $150,000. In many situations, while in the relationship victims were not permitted to work or money was controlled so tightly that now financial resources are not available to fight for custody. Meanwhile, legal maneuvers by batterers, such as seeking continuances, currently cost victims at least $2,000 per hearing. The more often the abusers can drag their victims to court, the greater their chances are of financially devastating them. When victims cannot afford the attorney's fees, they are forced to give up. Someone once said, "America has the best justice money can buy." Unfortunately, children often are the ones who pay the price. More precise evaluations are needed to measure what society's next step should be in the fight against family violence. We must research and find methods to change these outcomes.

Although statistical research is undoubtedly invaluable and generates much-needed baselines for understanding the frequency and significance of victimization, one must be cautious regarding how they are interpreted. Studies can be difficult to assess. Because many are designed with a specific objective, they can represent subjective goals. Therefore, some can be misleading while others seem to make sense. Statistics in this chapter have been provided simply to underscore the large numbers of families affected by violence. Without them, the system cannot see the value in prevention and intervention treatment strategies.

In order to justify spending public funds, society appears to need facts and figures to quantify the problem of family violence. Unfortunately, it is estimated that from 50 percent to 70 percent of incidences of abuse go unreported. One study concludes that only one in seven incidences of domestic assault come to the attention of police.[8] Because of underreporting, we genuinely have no idea how many victims are suffering in silence: as I once heard it expressed, "If victims were beaten in the woods and no one was there to hear their screams, were they really abused?" The plight of battered families thus needs to be evaluated and responded to by looking past the numbers. There are still two significant elements missing from relevant quality research: the planning and executing of prevention strategies. Although we need to continue tracking the casualties, it would serve society better to preemptively respond rather than react to violence, to prevent the devastation where we can.

The single underlying misapprehension that most impedes progress is when our culture conceives the family violence problem as a gender issue. Both sides feel compelled to protect their gender as a whole rather than look for resolution. Each side's need to protect or preserve its position makes both willing to completely disregard the other's point. There is absolutely no compromise, and when confronted with different values or agendas, the groups are like cornered dogs that bite. Blinded by their respective positions, each group becomes more strongly convinced and more irate each time the other side tries to state or inflict its perspective. The issue is increasingly polarized, and nothing is accomplished. We need to strategize, not personalize, the work ahead. This is not specifically a gender issue.

A solution begins when each participant in violence, whether victim, perpetrator, or witness, is educated on the impact the violence has on their family. The judicial system, advocates, and community leaders tend to resist acknowledging this need and taking action for two reasons. First is the widely accepted view that imposing mandatory classes further victimizes family members who are not abusive. My own experience has shown that adults court-ordered to parenting or family violence classes admitted that they would never have taken these courses voluntarily. Yet, they remarked that they enjoyed the classes because they learned skills to be better parents and partners. Most individuals don't consciously want to be violent; but sometimes, owing to generational learning, it is all they know. Once they develop better communication tools and have access to healthy alternatives, they gain personal control that makes them feel confident and competent. The old adage, "Knowledge is power," pertains here. Therefore, education should be regarded as a tool and not a punishment. Second is the presumption of innocence and our need to ensure that no one is wrongly accused and loses the right to participate in family life. If we implemented educational programs more swiftly, we could potentially prevent this occurrence. This point is made in the following example.

Case 15: In one county, a psychologist performed evaluations and therapy while families were taught parenting strategies. This type of response keeps the family intact and potentially avoids traumatizing children further. In many of these cases, removal of children generates abandonment and trust issues that negatively affect the outcome of their lives.

When families are committed to changing their behavior, the results are extremely positive and effective. So the concept isn't to change who they are but rather what they do. I personally believe that a class on family violence should be required before marriage and/or upon the birth of children. Some couples might choose not to unite if they learn that they are in a violent relationship, or they could get into couples counseling before the violence escalated into physical assault. Additionally, education could thwart the leading cause of injury in pregnant women—partner assault. The following example is a happy testimony to the positive effects of education.

Case 16: A father was court ordered to parenting class as a part of his plan to avoid prison time. He had been convicted for running a methamphetamine lab. After his sentencing hearing he returned to class even though he could no longer use the class as leverage in court. When queried as to why he returned to class, he stated, "Well, I am still going to be a dad when I get out and I am learning a lot and my kids need me."

Drug and alcohol abuse are present in most cases where children are removed from their homes. However, this does not mean that substance abuse causes physical abuse. Permitting people to excuse their behavior because they are intoxicated takes away their responsibility for their actions. It gives them an excuse that allows them to continue hurting others. A better explanation for why substances are present in family violence is that being physically assaulted precipitates substance abuse. Generally speaking, substances serve to self-medicate and mask trauma. The numbing effects allow parents to mistreat children or to not be consciously available to meet their emotional or physical safety needs, as intoxication becomes the priority. Self-medication in the form of substance abuse contributes to the poor choices people make regarding many areas of their lives. So if we want to see substance abuse lessen, we have to stop family violence. Currently, 50 percent of male batterers and 20 percent of female victims abuse alcohol.[9] Experts agree that regardless of age, children living with family violence tend to have higher risks of alcohol/drug abuse and juvenile delinquency. Adolescents living in such troubled environments are likely to be experiencing difficulties in a number of areas, including family relationships, physical abuse/sexual victimization, educational performance, and emotional/psychological functioning. Many of these difficulties can be traced to an early age and, if not addressed, place these youths at high risk of future drug use and delinquency/crime.

The effects trickle down into other facets of society as well. Take for example the labor force. American corporations lose from $3 billion to $5 billion annually as a result of managers who were abused as children and now abuse their own employees, creating health problems, limited concentration, and poor peer relations.[10] Compound this with employees who are battered at home then attempt to work. The results are lower productivity; increased absenteeism, and high turnover rates that substantially raise corporate costs.

Assertiveness Training

To generate healthier boundaries and limitations that are respectable for all those affected by family violence, new tools must be provided. Teaching individuals how to effectively get their needs met is a great place to start. The underlying behavior displayed by abusers is aggression. They have learned through trial and error what works. An effective compromise then would be to provide assertiveness training to help families through this process. Currently, the system uses reactive and punitive approaches to dealing with violence. Batterers' intervention programs force abusers into containing their behavior and rarely teach assertiveness skills to compensate for the lost behavior. Fearing further retribution from the court system, many batterers revert to extremely passive behavior, thereby swinging the pendulum in the complete opposite direction. Unfortunately, this is as damaging as the aggressive behavior because it gives children, especially adolescents, the upper hand over their recovering batterers. The new attitude or perspective becomes, "It's payback time." The abuse and its dynamics are now transferred from one family member to the next and no resolution is made. One father called and passionately pleaded, "I need a tool to deal with this kid right now because I want to deck him. Please give me another choice."

With coaching, perpetrators and victims alike can be more effective parents. Without assistance however, the results seem black or white, right or wrong. Members of dysfunctional families use aggressive or passive/aggressive behavior because they feel that is the only way to get their needs met—not necessarily to hurt their families. The key point to make here is that most people are not bad, but their behaviors can be. When given options that allow them to have control over their lives in a purposeful way, individuals are able to replace those abusive tendencies with healthier tools and options, thus reducing the level of deviance.

Assertiveness training benefits not only the batterers, but the victims as well. When people can assert boundaries and limitations, they can protect themselves and their children against abuse. Perpetrators only hurt the people that they know they can. Establishing boundaries early in the relationship allows for healthier interactive skills. Otherwise, a breakdown occurs, and the batterers' insidious manipulation style lends itself to later emotional abuse and eventual physical attacks. To help abusers and their victims, options must be provided that make everyone feel confident and competent. These families, however, need outside assistance to make this happen. Therefore, a coordinated community response that requires communication and conflict-management skills will ensure better results.

CONCLUSION

The plight of abused families has improved dramatically over the past two decades, but there is still a great deal of work to be done. Emergency shelters, advocates, and other resources are now available to assist with the safety of many victims, but services are still lacking in important areas. For instance, very few shelters exist for male victims or for children over the age of 12. To assist all victims, we should consider their dilemma as well. Additionally, personnel working in the area of family violence need more adequate training to serve the best interest of these families. Programs must be implemented to educate parents on how their behavior influences their families.

The bottom line, however, is that in order to combat and eradicate family violence, we have to see that it exists and recognize how devastating its impact is on the world as a whole. There is a saying, "If you are not outraged you are not paying attention." We must stop the cycle of violence and alter its outcome for children, their parents, and ultimately our society. We have been successful with making driving while drunk socially unacceptable; we have made smoking in public buildings socially unacceptable. Now, it is time to make family violence socially unacceptable as well.

NOTES

1. C.M. Rennison, *Intimate Partner Violence* (NCJ 197838), (Washington, DC: U.S. Department of Justice, Office of Justice Programs, Bureau of Justice Statistics, Crime Data Brief, 2003).

2. J.E. Samuels and S.B. Thacker, *Findings from the National Violence against Women Survey* (NCJ 183781), (Washington, DC: National Institute of Justice and the Centers for Disease Control and Prevention, 2000), p. 6.

3. U.S. Department of Justice, *Bureau of Justice Statistics* (Washington, DC: U.S. Department of Justice, 1997).

4. Federal Bureau of Investigation, *Uniform Crime Report* (Washington, DC: Federal Bureau of Investigation, 1994).

5. Columbus Coalition against Family Violence, *Family Violence Statistics* (Columbus, OH: Columbus Coalition against Family Violence, 2002), http://thecolumbuscoalition.org/news/family/php.

6. C.M. Dalpiaz, *Breaking Free, Starting Over* (Westport, CT: Praeger, 2004).

7. National Council of Juvenile and Family Court Judges (NCJFCJ), "The Role of the Juvenile and Family Court Judges in Context" (Reno, NV: NCJFCJ, 2000).

8. Florida Governor's Task Force on Domestic and Sexual Violence, *Family Violence Statistics* (Tallahassee, FL: Florida Mortality Review Project, 1997).

9. American Psychological Association, *Facts about Family Violence*, APA press release (Washington, DC: American Psychological Association, 1996).

10. Bureau of National Affairs, *Violence and Stress: The Work and Family Connection* (Washington, DC: Bureau of National Affairs, 1990).

Chapter 3

Abuse and Neglect of Older Adults: What Do We Know about It and How Can We Identify It?

Daphne Nahmiash

This chapter addresses the phenomenon of violence against vulnerable, dependent older adults, most of whom are women, who live in the community and are being cared for by or are caring for a family member, friend, or neighbor. Others are living in nursing homes or senior residences and are being abused by a paid caregiver. It is hard for us to even imagine that such violence exists and in fact has always existed. A recent study[1] from Greece notes that "ancient Greek history recorded clear cases of selfish carelessness or coarse insolence toward the old and offers instances of children taking over their parents' property . . . without proof of incapacity in the elders."

Case study: Elinor is a 64-year-old woman abused verbally and physically by her 35-year-old son, who is addicted to drugs.

"Let's talk about your relationship with your son [who] is living with you."

"Verbal abuse from all my children: my older son . . . who's a drug addict. He started on his drugs when he was 15 . . . with his friends. They started on the drugs and it never stopped. Then it went into stealing to get his drugs. I put him in jail once, which everybody thought was the worst thing in the world . . . he's been in jail three times [for] stealing. Then, he went right on and stole from me. You see my wedding rings?"

"There are no wedding rings. He stole them. All for drug deals. Now it's worse because he's on the coke . . . when he's on the drugs, it's okay. It's the withdrawal

I can't take . . . when he doesn't have any money for his . . . drugs. He's abusive . . . I have three cats, right. But when he's on withdrawal, the least little thing, there's a cup upside down or, the cats . . . he tore the place apart . . . the other day, the cat threw up in his room. He wrecked my kitchen, he wrecked it and smashed everything. He says, 'I don't have my rent.' He went from babysitter to babysitter, he did not have chances when he was young. I blame myself for his problems today and that's the guilt feeling that you get. My outlet is to have a drink when I want. I'm an alcoholic."

Elinor tells about a friend of her son's whom she had treated like a son and at one point was on drugs and was asked to leave the house. One day, he received a phone call that the friend was dead.

"He had been drinking and on the drugs. He laid on his back and choked on his vomit and suffocated and died. Now you know why he lives with me. Everybody says, 'Kick him out.' And I says, 'yeah and look at what happened to S when you kicked him out. He's dead, isn't he?' I said, 'that'll never happen to my son . . . put me through . . . hell, but I'm never going to have it on my damn back that my son died because I put his ass out. It'll never happen.'"

This case study illustrates not only the horror of elder abuse but also the complexity of family problems and relationships and why all participants have a difficult time getting out of the situations because of their beliefs and codependent relationships.

The subject of violent and neglectful behavior is increasingly becoming a topic of conversation in the media, our schools, and our social gatherings. This is not because violence did not formerly exist in private relationships in our society, but rather because we were not aware of its existence and it was a taboo subjects until the 1960s, when we first began to discuss the phenomenon of child abuse. In the 1970s conjugal violence was brought into the open, and in the past three decades people have become increasingly aware of other types of violence, such as dating violence between adolescents in schools and young adults and diverse forms of harassment in the workplace. Thus the context of elder abuse and neglect is part of a broadening awareness of domestic and societal violence. However, elder abuse has its own specific characteristics.

After establishing the extent of the problem, in this chapter I will discuss definitions of abuse and neglect and the difficulties in arriving at a common definition and terminology. I will briefly explore some possible causes and explanations. I will describe the different forms that abuse and neglect can take and present a brief outline of signs and symptoms that can help identify the presence of some types of abuse. Risk factors for abusers and victims are presented, and screening tools discussed. Finally, I will discuss some possible ways of preventing elder abuse and helping both abusers and victims.

PREVALENCE AND INCIDENCE OF ELDER ABUSE AND NEGLECT

There have not been many studies measuring the prevalence of abuse and neglect of older adults in our society. In one nationwide study[2] in Canada, 1 in 25 older adults (over the age of 60) stated that they were victims of some form of abuse or neglect, most often perpetrated by a family member. Similar estimates have been made for the United States; one study[3] reported that over one million older Americans (1 in 35) is a victim of abuse every year. We can estimate that between 3 percent and 5 percent of adults over 65 are victims of abuse and/or neglect.

In the past few years, more and more countries have been identifying the problem and finding ways to bring it to public attention. A British study[4] observed that work on abuse of older adults has been reported in 22 European countries, although much of the work is still in the formative stages. However, one study[5] compiled research from 10 countries in different parts of the world from international and cross-cultural perspectives and concluded that the problem will probably augment as a major world social problem as the overall population ages and the number and proportion of older adults increase.

All authors in all countries conclude that the topic of violence against older adults is taboo even among seniors themselves and is rarely reported. We can thus conclude that studies underestimate the number of cases of elder abuse. One study[6] has also demonstrated that there is a greater incidence of abuse and neglect of older adults (7–10%) as they become more vulnerable and in greater need of health and social services. Thus, abuse of older adults is a serious social problem that practitioners and others must recognize in order to identify, treat, and prevent it. It must also be noted that many forms of abuse and neglect of older adults criminal offenses, and when they are unreported, the perpetrators are not held accountable.

DEFINING ABUSE AND NEGLECT

Definitions of abuse and neglect are problematic. There are still no agreed-upon definitions or standardized conceptualizations, despite attempts in this direction by several authors.[7] Definitions are important because they give a clear understanding of the problem in question and differentiate the phenomenon from others. At present, terms may be interpreted differently by different authors and their meaning may depend upon the purpose of a given study. Some people use the term *mistreatment* to cover violence against older adults, others use the terms *abuse and neglect*. Stones[8] offers the following general broad definition of abuse: "a misdemeanor against acknowledged standards by someone a senior has reason to trust." This chapter uses this definition because it acknowledges the importance of social norms in defining these behaviors. Stones has also developed EAST, a comprehensive tool that contains 71 items grouped into the following nine categories: physical assault, excessive restraint, putting health at risk, failure to give care by someone acting as a paid or unpaid caregiver, abuse in an institution, material exploitation, and verbal humiliation. In my own research I found high agreement between seniors and professionals on items that indicate greater or lesser abuse, and the items rated as most abusive were mainly examples of physical abuse. However, most researchers have chosen the following definitions to operationalize and observe the types of abuse and neglect encountered.

- *Physical abuse* includes any form of physical aggression, rough handling, burning, pushing, assault, kicking, and so forth.
- *Sexual abuse* includes any form of assault of the person in a sexual way or forcing her or him to perform or engage in any sexual activity against her or his wishes. Sexual abuse is often part of physical or psychological abuse, but it is kept as a separate category because it is often not identified by health and social practitioners or older adults themselves.
- *Psychological abuse* is when the older adult is subject to repeated or chronic verbal assault that insults, threatens, humiliates, or excludes. Lack of affection, betrayal, social isolation, or denying the chance to make or participate in decisions that pertain to the individual's own interests are included.
- *Material/financial abuse* (sometimes called *exploitation*) involves misuse of the senior's money, possessions, or property. It includes fraud or using the senior's funds for purposes contrary to her or his needs and interests. This type of elder abuse has been noted as the most common, possibly because seniors themselves find it relatively easy to identify.
- *Passive or active neglect* involves the withholding of items or care necessary for daily living. This type of abuse can be intentional (active or physical) or nonintentional (passive), and it is most common among seniors living in institutional milieus.
- *Self-neglect,* or an individual's failure to provide adequate care for herself or himself, has also been identified as a form of elder abuse and is the most common type of mistreatment identified by Adult Protection workers. Although there is no outside perpetrator of this type of abuse, relatives or others may be aware of the problem and fail to help.
- *Violation of a person's rights* has also been recognized as a form of abuse. This consists of preventing an individual from making personal decisions or forcing the individual to do something against her or his wishes, such as going go to a nursing home. Other authors include this in the psychological abuse category.

+ *Social, systemic, or collective abuse* has been identified as a societal form of abuse. It includes ageism and other ways of treating elderly persons that affect their personal dignity and identity. This type of abuse was highlighted in a British study[4] that pointed out that abuse and neglect are socially structured through a range of policies and professional ideology relating to dependency in old age. Some authors include this type of abuse and neglect in the category of psychosocial abuse.

+ *Care abuse* is abuse which is perpetrated by the care receiver toward the caregiver. It is usually reported among caregivers responsible for an older adult who is suffering from dementia or mental illness; according to one study,[4] care abuse represents about 3 percent of the overall abuse.

Few studies have taken into account how multicultural or aboriginal groups define abuse and neglect. Most studies ignore cultural nuances and seem to assume that all seniors are similar in their attitudes and perceptions. Thus future studies should pay attention to particular subgroups, because each society and group has different standards and norms as to what constitutes abusive and neglectful behavior. Some standards and norms are laid down in the criminal code or the charter of rights; others are laid down by organizations and in professional codes of ethics, but those presenting the most difficulty are usually defined by common consensus within a society or group.

Psychological abuse and some types of neglect or self-neglect tend to fall into this consensus-based category. For this reason it is a good idea to try to arrive at common meanings for the definitions used. It is also important to note that often several types of abuse or neglect are present and there is sometimes more than one abuser. Occasionally abuse is mutually perpetrated by both the older adult and the caregiver, especially in cases in which there is mental illness or dementia.

IDENTIFYING VICTIMS OF ABUSE OR NEGLECT

My collaborator Susan Kurrle and I, in a book chapter on geriatric medicine,[9] identified some common indicators of the main types of elder abuse and neglect. We are presenting these along with some additional signs and indicators in Table 3.1.

PERPETRATORS AND VICTIMS OF ELDER ABUSE

Authors have noted in all studies and articles that abuse and neglect of seniors is a taboo subject. Seniors themselves rarely report being the victim of abuse and neglect, either in the community or in an institutional setting. Further, in different cultural milieus abuse and neglect may be accepted or unrecognized. For example, in some families screaming insults and obscenities

Table 3.1
How to Recognize Abuse and Neglect

Type of abuse or neglect	Signs to look for
Physical	
Evidence of punching, kicking, biting, burning, pushing, dragging, shaking, or arm twisting; , physical restraints such as being tied to a bed or chair or being locked in a room.	Presence of bruises, abrasions on face, forearms, or lower legs (history of unexplained accidents or falls). Bald patches on head or bruising on scalp (possible hair pulling). Black eyes or bleeding in white part of eye. Swelling in lips or nose, lacerations, and missing teeth. Fractures of skull, nose, and facial bones. Bruises on arms due to belt buckles, walking sticks, hair brushes, or ropes. Pinch marks or grip marks on upper arms. Bite marks or scratches. Burns from cigarettes, chemicals, ropes, hot or boiling water. Fractured ribs related to being pushed against an object or furniture.
Sexual	
Evidence of sexual assault or unwanted affection or touching.	Bruising, bleeding, or pain in genital areas. Torn, stained, or blood-stained underwear. Evidence of sexually transmitted diseases. Difficulty walking or sitting.
Psychological	
Evidence of mental or emotional anguish; repeated shouting at the person, threats, or humiliation. Emotional isolation; i.e., left alone in a room all day, withdrawal of affection. Emotional blackmail or infantilization of the person.	Huddled body position, nervous around the family or caregiver. Insomnia or sleep deprivation. Loss of interest in self or environment. Fearfulness, helplessness, hopelessness, passivity, resignation, or withdrawal. Paranoid behavior or confusion not due to dementia. Anger, anxiety, frustration, or agitation. Ambivalence toward the caregiver; reluctance to talk when caregiver is present, avoiding eye contact.
Material / financial	
Evidence of improper use of the person's property, money, or assets.	Loss of money, bank books, checks, or credit cards; cashing large checks or sudden, unexplained withdrawals of money from bank. Sudden inability to pay bills or buy food. Receiving incorrect change from the person purchasing the food or goods. Loss of jewelry, silverware, paintings, furniture, or sculptures. An unprecedented transfer of money or property to another person (often a child or nephew/niece). A new will is drawn up. Power of attorney or mandate improperly obtained from someone mentally competent.

Table 3.1
(continued)

Type of abuse or neglect	Signs to look for

Active or passive neglect

| Evidence of deprivation of the basic necessities such as food, medication, drink, clothing, care, etc. | Malnourishment due to lack of food and drinks, weight loss, wasting and dehydration (without an illness-related cause). Constipation or fecal impaction, inadequate or inappropriate use of medication (over- or underseda-tion). Decaying teeth, lost or nonreplaced eyeglasses, hearing aids, walkers, or other necessary prostheses. Poor hygiene or inadequate skin care (dirty and smells strongly of urine or infested with lice). Urine rash with excoriation and chafing. Clothing is dirty and in poor repair or inappropriate for the weather or gender. Pressure areas over the sacrum, hips, heels, or elbows. Withholding of medical or nursing care and attention. |

Self-neglect

| Evidence of an older adults who lives alone in housing and living conditions that are unsanitary and unsafe for the person or others. | Presence of poor hygiene, inadequate skin care, strong odor related to the person or living area, dirty clothing in poor repair, clothing inappropriate for weather or gender. Sometimes may have no clothing, decaying teeth, overgrown nails, malnourishment, weight loss, wasting, and dehydration. Constipation or fecal impaction. Inappropriate use of alcohol, medications, or other substances. Bizarre behavior that includes disturbing others. The adults often have a long history of mental illness. |

Violation of a person's rights

| Evidence of forcing a person to do something against their wishes or intentionally depriving them of their rights. | Being forced to live in inadequate housing against the person's will, for example a nursing home or in a son's or daughter's home (often to save money). A landlord who is not doing appropriate repairs to the person's property or who is raising the rent too high. A child who is refusing to allow a grandparent to see his grandchildren. |

Social or systemic abuse

| Evidence of discrimination against an older person on account of his or her age. Institutional or systemic abuse of an older adult through practices that deny the person's dignity or identity. | Societal images or depicting seniors as marginal, frail, vulnerable, and dependent (through media, policies, and laws). Discriminatory social policies for older adults, such as inadequate pensions, etc. Conditions in societal systems and institutions for older adults that impair quality of life. Institutions that do not uphold rules or that provide substandard care; for example, seniors suffering from dementia may be mistreated because caregivers are ignorant of how to treat these patients. |

(Continued)

53

Table 3.1
(continued)

Type of abuse or neglect	Signs to look for
Career abuse	
Evidence that an older adult is abusive physically, psychologically, or financially toward the caregiver.	Usually a situation in which an older adult suffers from mental or emotional illness or from dementia and mistreats the person providing their care. Sometimes codependent relationships in which the senior is abused and abuses the abusive caregiver in turn.

may have been a way of life for decades, and many different interpretations of what constitutes appropriate and inappropriate behavior still exist.[9] Until recently it was difficult to penetrate these groups to provoke some discussion and awareness. Nevertheless, it can be stated that elder abuse is experienced by both men and women, and victims may live in their own homes, share their homes with others, or live in nursing homes, residences for the aged, or long-term care facilities. It is also known that such inappropriate behaviors are for the most part perpetrated by unpaid caregivers, mainly family members, but also by paid caregivers, mainly in institutions, and that all these abusers are held by the older adults to be in a position of trust.

Beyond these general conditions, several studies have identified more than 40 indicators that predict whether older adults are likely to be abused and neglected and whether caregivers, paid or unpaid, are likely to perpetrate such abuse. These indicators have been summarized in several book chapters.[5,9–13] The main characteristics of abused and neglected older adults are summarized in the following 12 indicators:

Characteristics of the Abused

1. Gender: mostly women, although a few studies have found more men
2. Marital status: mostly widows or spouses
3. Generally in poor physical or mental health
4. Advanced age
5. Substance abuse
6. Living arrangements: usually with or in close proximity to the abuser
7. Psychological factors: depression, stress or resignation
8. Presence of problem behavior, often related to dementia or mental illness
9. Dependence in terms of activities of daily life
10. Social isolation
11. Reports history of relationships problems
12. Reports current marital or family conflicts

Characteristics of the Abuser

Eleven characteristics of the caregivers have also been reported in the same studies. These are:

1. Substance abuse (mainly alcohol) or gambling
2. Emotional illness (depression often associated with caregivers who care for persons with dementia or mental health problems).
3. Mental health or behavioral problems; personality disorder.
4. Reports poor or lacking social supports
5. Lack of caregiving experience
6. Reports reluctance to be a caregiver
7. History of abuse
8. Dependency (often financial) on the care recipient
9. Confusion and dementia (an older caregiver's spouse)
10. Reports feeling burdened and stressed in the caregiving experience
11. Personality traits related to control, depression, and blame; being overly critical and unsympathetic

---

Case study: Mary is a 73-year-old divorced and separated woman who is the mother of 13 children and is abused physically, financially, and psychologically by two of her sons.

"It's been a long time that I'm fighting violence. I accepted it. It happened ... I've had three phases of abuses ... I've had my husband. I divorced because he was too violent. He was a boxer ... I had seven children and he became really violent, especially related to drinking ... he gave me bad treatment, hit me, hit two of the children. I started a second page of my life. I wasn't a victim of violence. I was in the work market. I was doing fine ... the children started growing up and my husband was coming back ... Every week he started to be violent towards me ... it started to get rough. But let's say since the Golden Age, it's important to note that I was victim of violence."

She explains that this was after the separation and death of her third common-law partner when her sons became violent.

"He didn't directly hit me ... it's the alcohol ... when he arrives home, there is arguments ... they all have problems. One it's drugs, hard drugs. Another it's a separation, it's difficult he's not working. He didn't hit me, he hit his brother and I put myself in between and, of course, I got a little hit there because I got pushed against the wall ... it goes back about four or five years ... the police arrived. I called the police. I had to arbitrate, separate ... he held my arm a little tight, but not really that tight for me not to be able to work so I was trying to stay in between both and the fight continued. He still succeeded in hitting ... it's been three times that it happens like this. It's the police who brought the charges. This morning I cut his sentence by one year ... because he's too sick. He's discouraged ... he's a guy who's lost everything. He takes drugs . . . he is always depressed, sick and a little desperate. Sometimes . . . he take me by the ropes of the heart [pulls at my heart strings]. I try to help him get along as much as I can.

"If he's drunk . . . he wants money. He's going to steal a radio . . . a sound system. I'm well aware that lots of people, 60, 65 that are victims of violence by their children. It happens. I don't know why."

"You have only your pension?"

"Yes, but even then it's not much. It's poverty level, in the bottom of poverty. I can't manage so it creates difficulties. It's been two years . . . violence with words and threats . . . I went to court this morning. I have about half of an apartment and to be robbed by (my son).

"Maybe, the abuse happens because I support them . . . help them . . . open the door . . . tolerate them. If I didn't have a sensitive heart . . . I think these are my sons. Eventually they'll understand . . . If I'd been more authoritarian, maybe the father would have been avenged instead of me. I am still convinced they can get out of it and I am hopeful. I'd have to completely kick them out . . . but I give them one more shot."

This case study shows how the learned gender role of a female caregiver and mother who sacrifices herself for the family contributes to the continuation of the pattern of abuse. It shows how alcohol and drug abuse, if untreated, contributes to violence and abuse, long part of this family's history. Another issue raised is how helpful the criminal justice system is in solving crimes of this type. This elderly mother was severely physically abused three times by her sons, and each time the judge allowed the middle-aged boys to come back and live with their mother, so that the abuse started all over again.

Besides the personal characteristics relating to the abused and the abuser, researchers have identified some characteristics in the social, cultural, and economic environment that may indicate abuse and neglect. These are as follows:

The Social Context of the Care Situation

Six indicators have been related to the social context of the care situation:

1. Financial problems (from unemployment or welfare)
2. Family violence, especially related to physical and psychological abuse
3. Lack of social support
4. Family disharmony
5. Living arrangements (lack of privacy, overcrowding, and substandard housing conditions)
6. Intergenerational transmission of violence (violence that has existed for a long time within the family relationships and is passed on from generation to generation)

The Cultural Context of Care

Attitudes, beliefs, and values can determine whether individuals engage in or deter from engaging in the abuse and neglect of older adults. Six such indicators have been identified:

1. Ageist attitudes, beliefs, and policies (discrimination against an older adult or group on account of their age)
2. Sexist attitudes, beliefs, and policies (discrimination against an older adult or group on account of their sex)
3. Cultural beliefs and attitudes about violent behavior (e.g., abuse is perceived as a "family affair")
4. Reactions to abuse (personal beliefs due to religious convictions, family, or cultural backgrounds may influence help-seeking behaviors and patterns)
5. Negative attitudes toward the disabled and sick
6. Imperatives for family caregiving (expectations and perceived obligations)

The Economic Context of Care

Four indicators are observed that influence abusive situations:

1. Poverty
2. Limited finances
3. Lack of informal resources to help (other family members who could help provide care)
4. Lack of formal resources, or services that are too costly

Six Key Risk Factors Associated with Abusive and Neglectful Care Situations

Although many risk indicators have been identified in the studies and combinations of these indicators have been found in all types of abuse and neglect cases, it is still difficult to clearly state which particular indicators will appear in which scenarios. However, six indicators have been found to exist in all studies and in most abuse cases, and will be discussed in more detail in this section. These are:

+ Codependent relationships
+ Social isolation; lack of social support; keeping abuse and neglect a family secret
+ Substance abuse by perpetrators
+ Living arrangements
+ Gender issues
+ Depression and loss of identity

Codependent Relationships

The existing literature and my own research[9,11–13] show that abuse and neglect situations usually, though not always, also involve codependent relationships between the perpetrator of the abuse and neglect and the abused individual. Furthermore, these codependent relationships prevent the abused persons from moving out of or reporting their abusive situations. For example, I have observed many older women who did not tolerate the abusive behavior of a spouse and divorced him, but nonetheless tolerate physical, psychological, and financial abuse from their middle-aged sons who have a drinking or drug problem. The mothers explain that if they separated from these sons, the child would fall ill or become suicidal and the mothers would feel responsible. The sons depend on their mothers for food, money, and housing. Some mothers say they are afraid to live alone, and living with their son provides companionship and security for them. Others depend on their sons for their activities of daily living, such as grocery shopping. The mothers feel they have to sacrifice themselves for the well-being of their children.

I also observed that both the abused adult and the abuser in the codependent relationships are in a cycle of powerlessness that results in a loss of identity for both the abused and the abuser. They are unable to act or move out of this cycle of powerlessness. One study[14] compared groups of older battered women and found that the wives were more likely to be dependent on their husbands for some instrumental activities of daily living, and the husbands depended upon them for emotional support. Adult children were usually dependent on their mothers for housing and financial support, whereas the mothers depended on them for activities of daily living. The husbands of the battered women were more likely to use physical aggression against their wives than adult children against their mothers, but the verbal aggression shown by adult children was perceived to be more serious than similar acts by husbands toward their wives.

Social Isolation, Lack of Family Support, and Family Secrets

Social isolation and lack of social support are important risk factors associated with abuse and neglect situations.[15]

The isolation contributes to the persons continuing to stay in the abusive situation because the victim has no one to whom to complain. The abuser encourages and forces the person to stay in an isolated situation so that the abuse will continue to be tolerated and will go unreported. This type of situation is frequent in cases of older spousal abuse, usually by the male spouse. The male threatens the spouse that if she confides in friends or reports the abuse to another family member, the violence will augment. These are unequal power relationships and result in controlling the wife and keeping her in an isolated situation. Ménages à trois, or situations involving three individuals living in the same household, have also been observed to demonstrate the same dynamics. In some of these situations, the wife remained in the abusive situation, playing the role of perfect wife to save her marriage, in spite of the fact that the husband's lover was in the situation for many years. Similar situations have been observed in same-sex relationships.[16]

Substance Abuse

Abuse of drugs and alcohol is frequently associated with caregivers who are abusive. For example, under the influence of alcohol a son physically and psychologically abuses his sick mother, who cannot defend herself because she suffered herself at the hands of an alcoholic father who physically and psychologically abused his children. Another son, addicted to cocaine, abuses his mother physically and psychologically in order to extort money from her to pay for his drugs. The relationships between the mothers and sons, daughters or spouses are usually codependent relationships. For example, a battered wife was buying the beer for her husband who abused alcohol. She was emotionally dependent upon her husband and could not leave the situation. Caregiver sons who have gambling addictions were also associated with abusive behavior and codependent relationships with family members.

Living Arrangements

Living in the same house, nursing home, or residence as the abuser has also been found to be a factor frequently associated with abusive behavior toward older adults, especially in cases of neglect, which is most common in nursing homes and residences and in cases of conjugal violence. Sometimes the abused and the abuser do not live in the same house but live in close proximity to one another. It is evident that it is easier for an individual to mistreat another person if they live in close contact. For example, one case of abuse started between a mother and her daughter when they copurchased a duplex and moved in together. An older man, after the death of his wife, was persuaded to move in with his son's family and was severely neglected by them. Another man who developed Alzheimer's disease was abused physically when his wife could no longer take care of him and a social worker moved him into a private residence for older adults. The move happened so quickly that the man's wife did not have a chance to check out the quality of care provided by the residence in advance, a step that might have prevented the abuse incident.

Gender

Most studies have shown that older women run more risk of being abused than older men.[14] However, it has also been observed that as many men as women are exploited financially and physically.[17] Nevertheless, in cases of physical abuse the consequences of the abuse have been found to be more serious in women than in men. As will be discussed in greater detail below, learned gender roles have also been observed to be associated with abusive situations.

Depression and Loss of Identity

In several reports,[18] it has been observed that abusive caregivers often show symptoms of depression, and sometimes they, as well as their victims, have even attempted suicide or have ideas of taking their own lives, when they both feel powerless to remove themselves from the situations they are in. They describe their situation as "like living in a black hole" or having no meaning in their lives. Some females feel that they have always cared for others and never had a life of their own, and thus have lost a sense of their self or their own identity; for other, their only sense of identity is that of their abusive husband or child. Even after an abusive husband dies or is placed, an abused female may still believe she needs his permission to act.[9,12,14]

POSSIBLE UNDERLYING CAUSES AND EXPLANATIONS FOR ABUSE AND NEGLECT OF OLDER ADULTS

Many explanations have been put forward about why seniors experience abuse and neglect. This chapter will not discuss these theories at length, but will merely point the way for readers to find out more about some of the explanations.[19]

The four principal theories explaining abuse and neglect of older adults are as follows: the situational model, the social exchange theory, the symbolic interaction model, and the empowerment model.

1. *The situational model* suggests that acts of abuse are an irrational response to environmental conditions and a situational crisis. The situational variables are (1) those associated with a caregiver, (2) those associated with an older adult, and (3) additional sociostructural factors, and the three elements interact with one another to produce an abusive situation. However, this theory has not yet been proven, and two studies actually contradict one another.

2. *The social exchange theory* assumes that older adults have less access to power and resources and are progressively more vulnerable and less able to perform their activities of daily living than young adults. However, other

studies have demonstrated that the abusers are also vulnerable and dependent upon the abused adults.

3. *The symbolic interaction model* posits that abuse and/or neglect is a process involving at least two persons. It is produced over time and is composed of several repetitive steps, which are interrelated and which involve constant negotiations and renegotiations. This model is based on the social learning, family violence, and feminist theories, in which abuse and neglect is seen as a recurrent cyclic phenomenon in the family associated with past violent relationships. However, this model does not apply to all types of abuse, in that not all are rooted in family violence.

4. *The empowerment model*, which I use, sees both perpetrators and victims as being in a process of powerlessness from which they cannot extract themselves due to a number of varied explanations, including those mentioned in all the above theories. Being able to extract oneself from a position of powerlessness involves a struggle, the use of resources and strategies, the development of a personal identity and awareness of one's situation, and a critical knowledge and understanding of the forces that reshape one's social and political environment. Furthermore, individuals need to develop a greater knowledge and reaction competence to attain their personal and collective goals.

Using the empowerment model, the dicussion will next turn to how abuse and neglect can cause an inability to act and feelings of powerlessness to change or move out of the situation.

WHY VICTIMS AND PERPETRATORS OF ABUSE AND NEGLECT FEEL POWERLESS TO CHANGE THEIR SITUATIONS

Below are some examples[14] of abused older adults who feel powerless to move out of their situations, followed by examples of some caregivers who feel powerless to change their situations. Assessment of their family histories, gender roles, cultural contexts and their environmental situations can help explain their feelings of powerlessness.

Powerlessness in the History of the Family

A caregiver of a sick husband was being sexually abused by her 40-year-old son, who had left the house but was constantly bargaining with his mother to let him back in. She feels responsible for his welfare as a mother and a caregiver because she is a survivor of the Holocaust and feels she survived in order to be able to take care of her family. There is a direct relationship between the oppression experienced by the mother in the concentration camp and her abusive situation with her son. She claims, "I can do nothing . . . I cannot leave . . . I have to be here . . . I was condemned to death and I survived. Now I condemn myself to life." The sexual abuse began shortly after the son's wife divorced him, leaving him unable to control his life, dependent on his mother, and powerless.

Gender Issues

Learned gender roles of female abusers and abused older adults have been associated with abusive situations and the victims' inability to extract themselves from the abuse and neglect.

Bertha is a 69-year-old woman who has been forced into the role of care-giver and protector of her family ever since she was a child growing up with a physically abusive alcoholic father. Even though she seems to be a relatively strong and autonomous woman in general, she is unable to defend herself when her son and daughter-in-law attack her physically and psychologically. She says, "I just went helpless. I was in shock . . . Oh probably if it wasn't one of the family I could defend myself . . . because you have been nurturing your brothers and sister, you still have that sense that you have to protect somebody."

Cultural Context

Different cultural values, religious beliefs, and class positions can also contribute toward maintaining the abuser and the abused in a powerless situation.

An 83-year-old Indian man was neglected and abused by his common-law North American spouse and three stepchildren. He describes a complex clash of learned cultural values and beliefs from two different societies which especially manifest themselves in relation to ideas about punishment for the children and stem from the victim's own experience of punishment at school. He explains how when he found the children had stolen from him. "My punishment for them was to write lines . . . So that's the way I was brought up when I was punished in school . . . I was like, from the old school." His spouse resented him punishing her children, and this led to an incident of severe physical abuse of the older man. The stepchildren were stealing money from man because they thought he was old and could not defend himself: "'Look, you're going cuckoo, you're losing it. You're going senile.' Sort of like telling me, you're not thinking properly." These are also ageist attitudes internalized by the children and contributing to the man's feeling of powerlessness. Economic and class issues were also involved in this abuse case, because the common-law spouse and the children were attracted to moving in with the man because of their own poor economic circumstances and feelings of powerlessness.

Environmental Context

Social and environmental factors also contribute to how an abusive situation can develop and keep abusers and abused persons in a powerless situation. Living arrangements most often illustrate these situations, whether they occur because an older adult is moved into a nursing home or residence for seniors or moves into a living arrangement with adult children and grandchildren who benefit from the move for financial reasons.

In one case,[21] an abusive situation developed when a young couple moved next door to an older couple and felt they could exploit the seniors by taking over part of their property. The younger couple perceived the seniors to be too old to defend their rights. As the older spouse stated, "He [the neighbor] would do crazy things so we couldn't get out. It was like that for three years. We were stuck . . . They hosed us, hosed us in our yard, spit on our yard, waited for us at 10:00 at night . . . I couldn't handle it anymore. I could only see black . . . I was loving weight and I was sick. I was admitted four times at the hospital by ambulance . . . If it would have been somebody young, that would have thrown them . . . but they knew they were dealing with an old woman crazy and an old man so they took advantage of it." The older woman's vulnerability and powerlessness are directly related to her living arrangements and the behavior of her new neighbors toward her and her disabled husband. She describes her feelings of powerlessness as "not capable," "giving up," "can't handle the situation," "hitting a wall," and "can't fight," all of which led to an inability to act. The situation was eventually resolved, not because justice was done but because the neighbor lost his job, becoming also powerless, and had to move away.

WHAT CAN WE DO TO HELP? SIX EMPOWERMENT STRATEGIES

Many strategies have been described which involve using screening, evaluation and clinical tools to intervene in and prevent such cases of abuse and neglect of older adults.[21-25] It is important to note that effective preventive strategies involve addressing the problems of the caregiver abusers as well as the abused or vulnerable seniors. In many cases there are several abusers and also many types of abuse present, and all must be addressed. In addition, sometimes when one type of abuse, such as physical abuse, is stopped, another type, such as psychological abuse, may become more severe. Most of the documented intervention models fall into the categories of family violence, family therapy, social action, adult protection services, or multidisciplinary-based interventions. Space constraints in this short chapter make it impractical to describe the many existing models or the tools used, but and readers may refer to the books and articles noted in the reference at the end of this chapter. However, seven strategies that help abused persons and their abusers move out of their powerless and abusive situations to empowerment are presented: use of a facilitator, telling the story, transformation of energy, action, documentation and resolution of the problems, offering resources and referral, and self-control.

The Need for a Facilitator

Since situations of abuse and neglect force older adult victims into a process of powerlessness and an inability to act, the abused may be unable to move out of their situations without the help of another person, referred to as a *facilitator*. Abusive caregivers are also in a powerless position in their lives through their inability to move out of their dependencies on drugs, alcohol, or other problems, and they, too, need an independent facilitator to help them move out of their situations.

Telling the Story

The process of recognizing that a person has a problem and identifying the problem is the first step to solving it. Thus, the facilitator helps individuals describe through their family history, cultural history, and context, assessing their gender roles and responsibilities and environmental situations to determine how they and their abuser got into the abusive situation. As individuals tell their story, they are able to reflect on the circumstances that created their situation and develop insight and awareness into the forces that shape their present reality. The role of the facilitator is mainly to listen carefully and guide each individual in exploring the issues.

Transformation of Energy

By describing the situation in great detail and developing a critical awareness about the reasons why the individual is in the current situation the negative elements blocking the individual's energy are released and replaced by positive energy flows which enable the individual to be able to act to develop strategies to move out of his or her abusive situation.

Action

Many strategies and actions are used by the abused individuals to help them move out of their situations. These include confrontation of the abuser, breaking their silence and the isolation that has maintained them in an abusive situation, participation in a self-help group with people experiencing the same or similar problems, returning to school to educate themselves or finding employ-ment, participation in community activities, participation in caregiver support groups, obtaining information about rights or how to use the criminal justice system to protect themselves from the abuse and neglect situations.

Sometimes, especially in the case of more vulnerable older adults, someone is needed to accompany the person through the process. Victims' rights and advocacy organizations often have such resources available.

Documentation and Resolution of the Problems

It is extremely important to document carefully in writing or by tape record-ing the sequence of events leading up to and involved in the abuse situation and the steps and strategies taken or to be taken to help the person out of the situ-ation, especially in cases in which specific crimes are committed. Photographs and videos are effective means of producing hard evidence of such crimes. This documentation should be done as soon as possible while the events are still fresh in the minds of the persons involved.

Other strategies to solve problems could involve changing the locks of the house to ensure the abusive caregiver may not return. Arrangements can be made for pension checks to be deposited directly into a bank account to pre-vent an abusive nephew from stealing them. A court order may be needed to remove an abusive relative from the home.

Offering Resources and Referrals to Other Services

A variety of public and private services may be needed to assist abused seniors or their abusers during this time. For example, home care services or respite services and post-traumatic stress counseling can be helpful for abused seniors. Caregivers with substance abuse or gambling problems should be referred to appropriate treatment programs. Adult protection services are avail-able in many states and provinces in North America. A range of strategies and interventions are also used in nursing home and long-term care hospitals, such as reporting systems, quality assurance programs, and so forth. Police services, notaries, day care centers, and activities can help prevent seniors from experi-encing social isolation.

Self-Control

In the final step, the formerly abused senior or abusive caregiver has solved the problem and is once again in control of life. This step may entail finding time for a break from caregiving, such as having lunch once or twice a week with friends, or planting a small garden. Older adults and caregiver should be encouraged to think of and satisfy their own needs and not only the needs of others by finding pleasurable activities.

CONCLUDING REMARKS

This chapter's focus has been the prevalence of abuse and neglect of older adults by people in a position of trust, defined as paid or unpaid caregivers. The present estimates of abuse and neglect may only represent the tip of the iceberg: we are living in an aging society, and abuse and neglect of older adults is higher among those who are frail and cannot defend themselves.

The chapter presents the ways in which abuse and neglect manifest themselves and the characteristics of those who are abused and those who abuse. In particular, the six key risk factors associated with abuse and neglect situations are noted.

Finally, the problem of why older victims of abuse and their abusive caregivers feel powerless to change their situations is addressed. The discussion touches on some ways which can be used to help, in particular, six strategies that can move the abused or the abuser to a process of empowerment and out of the abuse situations.

There is a need for far greater awareness of the problem of abuse and neglect toward older adults. More resources and services need to be coordinated and made available by governments and organizations, so that seniors can live out their lives in comfort and security.

REFERENCES

1. Council of Europe. (1992). *Violence against elderly people.* Brussels, Belgium: Author.
2. Podnieks, E., Pillemer, K. A., Nicholson, J. P., Shillington, T., & Frizzell, A. F. (1990). *National survey on abuse of the elderly in Canada.* Toronto, Ontario, Canada: Office of Research and Innovation, Ryerson Polytechnic Institute.
3. Select Committee on Aging. (1981). *Elder abuse: An examination of a hidden problem* (pp. 99–277). Washington, DC: U.S. Government Printing Office.
4. Biggs, S., Phillipson, C., & Kingston, P. (1995). *Elder abuse in perspective.* Rethinking Ageing Series. Buckingham, UK: Open University Press.
5. Kosberg, J. I., & Garcia, J. L. (Eds.). (1995). *Elder abuse: International and cross-cultural perspectives.* New York: Haworth.
6. Reis, M., & Nahmiash, D. (1995). When seniors are abused: An intervention model. *The Gerontologist, 35,* 666–671.
7. Hudson, M., & Johnson, T. F. (1986). Elder abuse and neglect: A review of the literature. *Annual Review of Gerontology and Geriatrics, 6,* 55–83.
8. Stones, M. (1991). *A lexicon for elder mistreatment.* St. John, Newfoundland, Canada: St. John's Provincial Work Committee.

9. Nahmiash, D., in collaboration with S. Kurrle (2002). Abuse and neglect: Identification, screening and intervention. In R. N. Ratnaike (Ed.), *Practical guide to geriatric medicine* (pp. 851–866). Sydney, Australia: McGraw-Hill.

10. Ansells, E. F. (1996). Causes and theories. In L. A. Baumhover & S. C. Beall (Eds.), *Abuse, neglect and exploitation of older persons: Strategies for assessment and intervention* (pp. 9–29). Baltimore: Health Professions.

11. Kosberg, J. I., & Nahmiash, D. (1996). Characteristics of victims and perpetrators and milieus of abuse and neglect. In L. A. Baumhover & S. C. Beall (Eds.), *Abuse, neglect and exploitation of older persons: Strategies for assessment and intervention* (pp. 31–50). Baltimore: Health Professions.

12. Nahmiash D. (2000). Les mauvais traitements et la négligence à l'égard des personnes âgées. In P. Cappeliez, P. Landreville, & J. Vézina (Eds). *Psychologie clinique de la personne âgée* (pp. 197–216). Ottawa, Ontario, Canada: Presses de l'Université d'Ottawa.

13. Reis, M. & Nahmiash, D. (1997). Abuse of seniors: Personality, stress and other indicators. *Journal of Mental Health and Aging, 3,* 337–356. New York: Springer.

14. Nahmiash, D. (2002). Powerlessness and abuse and neglect of older adults. *Journal of elder abuse and neglect, 14,* 21–47.

15. Wolf, R. S., & Pillemer, K. A. (1997). The older battered woman: Wives and mothers compared. *Journal of Mental Health and Aging, 3,* 325–336.

16. Pillemer, K. A. (1984). Social isolation and elder abuse. *Response, 8,* 2–4.

17. Pillemer, K. A., and Finkelhor, D. (1988). The prevalence of elder abuse: A random sample survey. *The Gerontologist, 28,* 51–57.

18. Pittaway, E., Gallagher, E., Stones, M., Nahmiash, D., Kosberg, J. I., Podnieks, E., Strain, L., & Bond, J. (1995). *Services for abused older Canadians.* Ottawa, Ontario, Canada: Health Canada, Department of Family Violence.

19. Paveza, G. J., Cohen, D., Eindorfer, C., Freels, S., Semla, T., Ashford, W., Gorelick, P., Hirschman, R., Luchins, D., & Levy, P. (1992). Severe family violence and Alzheimer's disease: Prevalence and risk factors. *The Gerontologist, 32,* 493–497.

20. Phillips, L. R. (1986). Theoretical explanations of elder abuse: Competing hypotheses and unresolved issues. In K. A. Pillemer & R. S. Wolf (Eds.), *Elder abuse: Conflict in the family* (pp. 197–217). Dover, MA: Auburn House.

21. Reis, M., & Nahmiash, D. (1995). *When seniors are abused: A guide to intervention.* North York, Ontario, Canada: Captus.

22. Nahmiash, D., & Reis, M. (2000). Most successful intervention strategies for abused older adults. *Journal of elder abuse and neglect, 12,* 53–70.

23. Wolf, R. S. (1986). Major findings from three model projects on elderly abuse. In K. A. Pillemer & R. S. Wolf (Eds.), *Elder abuse: Conflict in the family* (pp. 219–238). Dover, MA: Auburn House.

24. Pritchard, J. (Ed.) (1999). *Elder abuse work: Best practice in Britain and Canada.* London and Philadelphia: Jessica Kingsley.

25. Baumhover, L. A., & Beall, S. C. (Eds.) (1990). *Abuse, neglect and exploitation of older persons: Strategies for assessment and intervention.* Baltimore: Health Professions.

Chapter 4

Homicide-Suicide: An Overview

Julie E. Malphurs and Maria D. Llorente

Las Vegas, Nevada, March 2005: A man shot and killed his wife in the middle of a busy intersection last night then turned the gun on himself. The woman jumped out of a car in the intersection and ran toward the median, the man following her. He fired, she fell to the ground, and then he stood over her and shot her in the head at close range. The man then shot himself in the head. Detectives said that it appeared that the victim was the estranged wife of the killer and that the couple had a history of domestic violence.

Boston, July 2005: The deaths of a mother and her nine-month-old daughter, who fell from a downtown high-rise apartment, have been ruled a murder-suicide. Detectives said that two suicide notes were found, one on the woman's body.

Garner Valley, California, May 2005: A 44-year-old man shot and killed his 14-year-old son, 10- and 8-year-old daughters, his 75-year-old mother, and his wife before dialing 911 and shooting himself with a 9-mm semiautomatic handgun. Neighbors and friends told reporters that there was nothing about his behavior prior to this incident that would have indicated he was capable of such action.

Killeen, Texas, July 2005: Police have indicated that the deaths of two soldiers this week have been ruled a murder-suicide. Officials found the female victim on the front porch of her home, shot in the head. Her estranged husband was found a short time later in the parking lot of an apartment complex across the street with a self-inflicted gunshot wound to the head. The couple had a violent domestic history, and a two-year protection order had been issued last week ordering the husband to stay away from his wife.

Chesterfield, Virginia, July 2005: A murder-suicide has left a mother and her two daughters dead of gunshot wounds. Investigators believe that the 36-year-old mother fatally shot her daughters and then killed herself.

Columbus, Ohio, May 2005: An 18-year-old shot his grandparents, his mother, his sister, and two of his friends while they were sleeping. The young man, who was to graduate from high school the next morning, then shot himself in the head.

The events described above are just a sampling of homicide-suicide events that occurred within a five-month period in 2005. *Homicide-suicide*, or *murder-suicide*, refers to violent events in which a perpetrator takes his or her own life either immediately or within a very short time after killing one or more victims. Homicide-suicide is a psychosocial and public health problem. Homicide-suicides are rare relative to suicides and homicides, but these lethal events are an emerging public health concern. Homicide-suicides are nearly always committed by a man, typically involve family members, and nearly always involve a firearm.

Homicide-suicides have a mortality count similar to meningitis, pulmonary tuberculosis, influenza, and viral hepatitis,[1] and the rate may be increasing in the United States, especially among older persons.[2-5] Homicide-suicides have a traumatic and lasting impact on the health and well-being of family covictims and disrupt the communities in which they occur, especially when they involve mass killings.

Several prominent homicide-suicides have received national attention. In May 1998, a 23-year-old corporal in the Pope's Swiss Guard killed the newly appointed commander of the Guard, age 42, and his wife before turning the gun on himself in the Vatican. Also in May 1998, the comedian and actor Phil Hartman, age 49, was shot and killed by his wife Brynn, age 41, before she committed suicide in Los Angeles. The tragic mass killings of 13 people by Eric Harris and Dylan Klebold at Columbine High School in Littleton, Colorado, that occurred in April 1999 were a homicide-suicide event. Atlanta day trader Mark Barton killed his wife and children at their home and then went to brokerage offices and killed nine more people before killing himself in the summer of 1999.

EPIDEMIOLOGY OF HOMICIDE-SUICIDE

The rate of homicide-suicide in the United States is relatively stable, averaging .20–.30/100,000, and ranging from .19 to .55 per 100,000 persons.[6] From 1.5 percent to 4 percent of all suicides and 5 percent of all homicides in the United States occur in the context of homicide-suicide.[7-10] Homicide-suicides, reported in terms of percentage of total suicides, vary regionally in the United States, but average between 2 percent and 4 percent. Suicide pacts are not classified as homicide-suicides because there is mutual agreement of death between two persons; suicide pacts are thus excluded from all reported rates of homicide-suicide events.

Although there is no national surveillance system for homicide-suicides in the United States, they are estimated to account for 1,000–1,500 deaths a year. Marzuk and associates[1] derived this mortality count from the results of a *Time* magazine national survey of all deaths by guns in a one-week period, where 11 gun-related homicide-suicides with 22 deaths occurred.[11] If these seven days were representative of an average week, 572 suicides and at least 572 related homicides would be expected over a year. Most homicide-suicides are the spousal/consortial type, but there are multiple victims in 10 percent to 15 percent of cases.[6,12]

Homicide-suicide rates have been consistently reported to range from 0.2–0.3/100,000 persons in most studies,[1,6,13] although a few investigators have reported higher rates of 0.4–0.5 per 100,000.[12,14] All of these epidemiological studies have been based on retrospective analyses of information from medical examiner's and coroner's reports where cause of death was classified using the *International Classification of Diseases (ICD)* external cause of injury codes, or E-codes.[15] Homicide-suicides can only be ascertained by comparing homicide and suicide lists using available information, including date, name, location, and method of death.

Although empirical descriptive epidemiological studies of homicide-suicide are not available for the country, print media surveillance has been used to estimate the number of intentional injuries, including homicide-suicide.[1,16–20] Newspaper accounts are often sources of supplemental information to accompany medical examiner's and coroner's reports, but used alone they vary in the accuracy and type of information provided and underreport intentional injuries.[16,18]

Despite the rarity of these events, recent research has indicated that homicide-suicides, especially among older persons, may be increasing.[2] The lack of a national surveillance system or standardized definition for homicide-suicide may be affecting the low reported rates of this phenomenon. Accurate accounting of homicide-suicides can only be accomplished through the use of a specific ICD E-code classification similar to those used for homicide and suicide by the Centers for Disease Control and Prevention (CDC). Recently, the CDC pilot-tested a National Violent Death Reporting System (NVDRS), in which detailed information regarding violent deaths is collected from multiple sources in order to increase surveillance of homicide and suicide in individual states.[19] This surveillance system is being implemented in six states and, if successful, may also serve to link specific intentional injuries to each other, thus creating surveillance of homicide-suicide events. The implementation of a national surveillance system of homicide-suicides using standardized classification and reporting methods would be a valuable mechanism to identify and prevent this increasingly violent public and mental health problem.

TYPES OF HOMICIDE-SUICIDE

Homicide-suicides often occur suddenly and all parties directly involved are dead. There is little, if any, prior clinical documentation, and often the possibilities for psychiatric intervention are limited.[10] Of the articles published in this area, most are descriptive reports or epidemiological studies that do not empirically document the biopsychosocial complexities of these acts. Most homicide-suicides are perpetrated by men, and most of their victims are female. Cultural differences do exist; for example, most of the homicide-suicides in the United States are perpetrated by men who kill their spouse or lover, while in Japan most homicide-suicide perpetrators are mothers who kill their children and then themselves.[10] Further, in the United States, nearly all (~90%) of all homicide-suicides are committed by non-Latino white perpetrators.

The number of victims associated with homicide-suicide events varies, and depending on the type of homicide-suicide can range from one victim, which is commonly seen in intimate partner homicide-suicides, to two or more victims, frequently seen in familicides or mass murders.

Spousal/Consortial (Intimate Partner) Homicide-Suicide

Homicide-suicide between spouses or lovers represents one-half to three-fourths of all homicide-suicides in the United States,[10] and are typically interpreted as dyadic deaths, double suicides, or homicide-suicides with altruistic motives. Frequently, the spousal homicide-suicide is the culmination of a chaotic, abusive relationship marked by amorous jealousy.[1,10,22–27] Intimate partner homicide-suicides are also frequently associated with a real or threatened dissolution in the partnership, that is, an impending separation or divorce. There is sometimes a history of domestic violence in the couple prior to the homicide-suicide, but not always. The victims are nearly always female and are typically killed at home with a firearm.

Homicide-suicides occurring in older couples or spouses (see Special Topic below) have been typically considered, and often described in the media, as suicide pacts or mercy killings. Recently, it has been determined that homicide-suicides among older adults share similar characteristics with homicide-suicides in younger couples, although the precipitating stressor in older couples is more likely chronic illness or caregiving rather than impending separation.[5]

Familial Homicide-Suicide

Homicide-suicide events can take several forms other than spousal/consortial, including fillicide and infanticide, which occur when a parent kills his or her child or children and then commits suicide; and familicide, which occurs when a parent kills the entire family and then commits suicide.

Homicide-suicides involving children are most frequently committed by the mother and are discussed in depth in another chapter. In these cases, the mother will almost never kill her spouse along with her children. Conversely, fathers who kill their children and then themselves are more likely to also kill an intimate partner at the time of the event.

An estimated 30 percent of all homicides involving children in the United States each year are committed by a parent.[28] Children are killed by a parent who then subsequently commits suicide for varied reasons: the infant or child may be caught in the middle of an argument between the parents; the child may be killed for revenge against one parent related to divorce or separation; mothers with severe post-partum depression may develop psychotic features and kill their children to "save" them; children may be killed by parents for altruistic reasons. Nearly all cases of homicide-suicide can be related to either an acute or chronic stressor as a predisposing factor to the homicide-suicide event.

Other Homicide-Suicide

Extrafamilial homicide-suicide occurs when an individual kills one or more strangers, usually a group of people, and then commits suicide. Mass murders, including workplace killings, in which the perpetrator kills several persons and then commits suicide are also homicide-suicides.

Special Topic: Homicide-Suicide in Older Adults

Mr. M., age 91, shot his wife, Mrs. M., age 88, while she was sleeping in their bedroom. Mr. M. then dialed 911, stated that there was a homicide-suicide, and hung up. When police arrived, they found Mr. M. lying next to his wife in bed with a gunshot wound to the head. Mr. and Mrs. M. had been married for 71 years. Investigators found several notes, including detailed instructions for their daughters, around the house. Mr. M. had been caring for his increasingly frail wife for many years. Mr. M. had been on more than 10 medications, including antianxiety and antidepressant drugs, at the time of his death.

Mr. B., age 85, shot his wife, Mrs. B., age 83, in their apartment at an assisted living facility. Mr. B. then shot himself. The couple had recently been told that Mrs. B. was going to have to be transferred to a nursing home due to her declining health.

Mr. P., age 67, shot his 65-year-old wife and then shot himself. The couple had a history of marital problems, and the homicide-suicide occurred after a lengthy and heated argument. Mrs. P. had recently sought the advice of a divorce attorney due to the discovery of her husband's illegitimate child.

Mr. S., age 87, shot his wife, age 84, in the parking lot of the nursing home in which Mrs. S. had lived for over a year. Mr. S. wheeled his wife out to the parking lot during his regular daily visit to his wife, who had Alzheimer's disease. Mr. S. had recently been diagnosed with liver cancer. After Mr. S. shot his wife, he then shot himself in the head. Three suicide notes were found, one on his wife's wheelchair.

In the United States, persons age 65 and older have always had a higher suicide rate than other age groups, and the rate has been increasing since 1980.[29–31] Older men have substantially higher rates than older women, committing 70 percent to 80 percent of all suicides.[29,30,32] Suicide rates increase with advancing age, and white men age 85 and above have rates of 60.4 per 100,000, almost six times that of the general population.[31]

Although death rates for suicide in older persons are substantially lower than the rates for heart disease, cancer, and infectious diseases, the number of older persons who die by suicide and homicide-suicide is substantial. The Surgeon General's recent report, *Call to Action to Prevent Suicide*, declared suicide a serious public health problem and specifically targeted the older population for prevention efforts.[33] Suicide took the lives of 8,700 people age 55 and older in the United States in 1997, or 167 individuals each week.[29] Since most homicide-suicides in older people involve couples, at least eight people died of this cause each week of 1997.

Although many papers have been published about homicide-suicide since the first reports by Ferri[34] and Provent,[35] it was not until the late 1990s that the rates and clinical patterns of homicide-suicide were reported in older persons.[2,4–5,20] In the few earlier studies where older perpetrators and victims were even identified, only the number of events was reported or the deaths were attributed to mercy killing.[36–38] These lethal events were erroneously believed to be more common in the young and to be suicide pacts or altruistic homicide-suicides where both spouses were old and sick.[29]

Research findings to date indicate that homicide-suicides in older persons are not suicide pacts and most homicide-suicides are spousal/consortial,[2,5] a finding consistent with other studies[23,38–39] Motivations behind these homicide-suicides are complex, with psychopathology, marital and family dynamics, caregiving burden, and other life stressors, as well as other individual, family, and community factors implicated. Homicide-suicides involving older persons are perpetrated by men who are older than their victims, have been to a physician within a few weeks of the event, and use guns as the method of death.[2] These are all factors similar to the observed pattern for suicide in the older population.[29-30]

Chronic physical illness, the single most distinguishing feature of old and young homicide-suicides, impacts mood and destructive behavior. The differential effect of illness and other chronic stressors prevalent in late life on the risk for intentional lethal injury toward self and others remains to be clarified.

PSYCHOPATHOLOGY AND HOMICIDE-SUICIDE

Psychopathology, especially depression, has been consistently linked to the killing of family members as well as other forms of intentional violence, including homicides and suicides.[40-41]

Almost all homicide-suicides occur in a family context, and most involve only one homicide victim, usually a wife or intimate. Homicide-suicides are rare events, but the traumatic stress can have significant and long-lasting effects, including depression and post-traumatic stress syndrome, in family survivors who are covictims of these sudden lethal events.[1, 10, 42]

Palmer and Humphrey[43] first suggested that homicide-suicide is a suicidal process and that perpetrators have characteristics similar to individuals who only commit suicide, but there have been no empirical studies. It has long been known that between 75 percent and 95 percent of individuals who kill themselves have a treatable psychiatric illness,[29,30,32,44] and that psychopathology is also prominent in individuals who commit homicide-suicides.[2,8,10]

The important role of undetected and untreated depression as well as other psychiatric problems in homicide-suicide cannot be overemphasized. Rosenbaum,[8] in a psychological autopsy series of cases, reported that 75 percent of perpetrators of homicide-suicide suffered from depression and 33 percent had an Axis II personality disorder. Personality factors such as low openness to experience on the NEO five-factor inventory[45] have been linked to completed suicide in persons age 50 and older, and other traitlike factors such as aggression, impulsivity, and inflexibility have been related to completed suicide.[46-47] Autopsy reports of homicide-suicide victims reveal that a very low number of perpetrators test positive for antidepressants, and that perpetrators have a low prevalence of previous psychiatric treatment.[4-5]

Alcohol misuse has been associated with both suicide and homicide-suicide.[4,39,48-51] The use of alcohol and other drugs, including benzodiazepines, among homicide-suicide perpetrators may serve to decrease inhibitions to commit these violent acts.[52-54]

Marital difficulties resulting from caregiving burden, marital conflict, and other circumstances, have been implicated in both homicide-suicide and suicide.[2,29] Marital conflict involving an impending or previous divorce occurs in about a third of couples who die in a homicide-suicide.[1,4,12] Jealousy and conflict are the most common motivations reported for younger couples.[2,22-23,25-26,39] The extent to which prior marital conflict may have been characterized by domestic violence is documented in only a fraction of homicide-suicide cases.

A number of homicide-suicide events can also be characterized by situations where the male perpetrator was a caregiver, including familial cases where adult children caregivers kill their parents. Older men who are caregivers appear to be at risk for homicide-suicide.[2,4-5] Caregiving is a stressful burden, and persons providing care are known to be at risk for depression, a factor known to be related to homicide-suicide, especially in older men.[2,4-5,8,55-57] Physical illness in the perpetrator and victim has also been noted to increase the risk for homicide-suicide.[2,8,58-61]

Special Topic: Diathesis-Stress and Homicide-Suicide

Homicide-suicidal and suicidal behaviors are complex acts determined by many factors that interact over time to lower the threshold for action. Although there are a number of theoretical approaches to suicide,[29] only a few have been proposed for homicide-suicide.[10] A diathesis-stress model has been proposed to explain risk for homicide-suicide.[62]

Homicide-suicides can be described as the result of additive or multiplicative effects of diatheses, that is, vulnerabilities and multiple biopsychosocial and environmental stressors, as well as protective factors. The diathesis-stress model, originally developed to predict schizophrenia[63] has been a useful model for the explanation of depression and hopelessness.[64-67] Diathesis-stress models have also previously been used as theoretical frameworks for the study of lethal behavior.[68,69]

Diatheses for lethal violent injury may include psychopathology, physical health problems, pain and suffering, personality characteristics, attitudes and beliefs, or cognitive attributions. Stressors may include a real or perceived change in health, inability to master the challenges of being a caregiver, pending institutionalization, social isolation, and marital and family conflict. The mechanism through which interpersonal and life stressors influence the vulnerability of older perpetrators to commit homicide-suicide or suicide remains to be clearly specified.[68-69]

Protective factors may include biological, psychological, social, cultural, or environmental influences that serve as buffers or increase the resilience of vulnerable individuals.[70] Social support, help from health care professionals and family and friends, support to seek domestic violence protection, or assistance with conflict management and resolution may also be protective for homicidal and suicidal behavior.

SUMMARY

Restricted access to guns may be one of the most potent ways to prevent homicide-suicide and other lethal intentional violence. Almost all homicide-suicides involve guns, and homicide-suicides are rare in countries with strict gun control laws.[6] The risk of a homicide occurring in a home with a gun present is almost twice as high as a non-gun-owning household, while the risk of suicide increases nearly tenfold in homes with guns.[71]

Risk factors, protective factors, and their interactions are the basis of an empirical prevention model for homicide-suicide and suicide.[10,33,47,70] Early intervention to prevent these tragic deaths based on the potential for a homicide-suicide or suicide could save lives. The available data make it clear that substantial efforts are needed to increase the knowledge of primary care physicians, other professionals, and families about the detection and appropriate treatment of depression and marital stress in vulnerable population groups.

REFERENCES

1. Marzuk, P., Tardiff, K., & Hirsch C. (1992). The epidemiology of murder-suicide. *Journal of the American Medical Association, 267,* 3179–3183.
2. Cohen, D., Llorente, M., & Eisdorfer, C. (1998). Homicide-suicide in older persons. *American Journal of Psychiatry, 155,* 390–396.
3. Cohen, D., & Eisdorfer, C. (1999, August). Clinical patterns of spousal/consortial homicide-suicide in the aged. Paper presented at the ninth congress of the International Psychogeriatric Association, Vancouver, British Columbia, Canada.
4. Malphurs, J. E., Eisdorfer, C., & Cohen, D. (2001). A comparison of antecedents of homicide-suicide and suicide in older married men. *American Journal of Geriatric Psychiatry, 9,* 49–57.
5. Malphurs, J. E., & Cohen, D. (2005). A statewide case-control study of spousal homicide-suicide in older persons. *American Journal of Geriatric Psychiatry, 13,* 211–217.
6. Milroy, C. M. (1995). The epidemiology of homicide-suicide (dyadic death). *Forensic Science International, 71,* 117–122.
7. Wolfgang, M. E. (1958). An analysis of homicide-suicide. *Journal of Clinical and Experimental Psychopathology, 19,* 208–216.

8. Rosenbaum, M. (1990). The role of depression in couples involved in murder-suicide. *American Journal of Psychiatry, 147,*1036–1039.

9. Clark, D. C., & Fawcett, J. A. (1992). Review of empirical risk factors for evaluation of the suicidal patient. In B. Bongar(Ed.), *Suicide: Guidelines for assessment, management, and treatment* (pp. 16–48). New York: Oxford University Press.

10. Nock, M. K., & Marzuk, P. M. (1999). Murder-suicide: phenomenology and clinical implications. In D. G. Jacobs (Ed.), *The Harvard Medical School guide to suicide assessment and intervention* (pp. 188–209). San Francisco: Jossey-Bass.

11. Leviton, J., & Riley, M. (1989, July 17). 7 deadly days. *Time,* 31–52, 57–61.

12. Hanzlick, R., & Koponen, M. (1994). Murder-suicide in Fulton County Georgia 1988–1991: Comparison with a recent report and proposed typology. *American Journal of Forensic Medicine and Pathology, 15,* 168–173.

13. Coid, J. (1983). The epidemiology of abnormal homicide and murder followed by suicide. *Psychological Medicine, 13,* 855–860.

14. Hannah, S. G., Turf, E. E., & Fierro, M. F. (1998). Murder-suicide in central Virginia: a descriptive epidemiologic study and empiric validation of the Hanzlick-Koponen typology. *American Journal of Forensic Medicine and Pathology, 19,* 275–283.

15. U.S. Department of Health and Human Services, Centers for Disease Control and Prevention (1997, August 29). Recommended framework for presenting injury mortality data. *Morbidity and Mortality Weekly Report, 46,* No.RR14;1. http://www.cdc.gov/mmwr/preview/mnwrhtml/mm4953a1.htm.

16. Aderibigbe, Y. A. (1997). Violence in America: A survey of suicide linked to homicides. *Journal of Forensic Sciences, 42,* 662–665.

17. Danson, L., & Soothill, K. (1997). Murder followed by suicide: A study of the reporting of murder followed by suicide in the *Times* 1887–1990. *Journal of Forensic Psychiatry, 7,* 310–322.

18. Fine, P. R., Jones, C. S., Wrigley, M., Richards, J. S., & Rousculp, M. D. (1998). Are newspapers a viable source for intentional injury surveillance data? *Southern Medical Journal, 91,* 234–242.

19. Rainey, D.Y., & Runyan, C. W. (1992). Newspapers: A source for injury surveillance? *American Journal of Public Health, 82,* 745–746.

20. Malphurs, J. E., & Cohen, D. (2002). A newspaper surveillance study of homicide-suicide in the United States. *American Journal of Forensic Medicine and Pathology, 23,* 142–148

21. U.S. Department of Health and Human Services, Centers for Disease Control and Prevention (2005, April 22). Homicide and suicide rates—national violent death reporting system, six states, 2003. *Morbidity and Mortality Weekly Report, 54,* No.MM15;377. http://www.cdc.gov/mmwr/PDF/wk/mm5415.pdf.

22. Morton, E., Runyan, C. W., Moracco, K. E., & Butts, J. (1998). Partner homicide-suicide involving female homicide victims: A population-based study in North Carolina, 1988–1992. *Violence and Victims, 13,* 91–106.

23. Palermo, G. B., Smith, M. B., Jenzten, J. M., Henry, T. E., Konicek, P. J., Peterson, G. F., Singh, R. P., & Witeck, M. J. (1997). Murder-suicide of the jealous paranoia

type: A multicenter statistical pilot study. *American Journal of Forensic Medicine and Pathology, 18*(4),374–383.

24. Felthous, A.R., Hempel, A. G., Heredia, A., Freeman, E., Goodness, K., Holtzer, G., Bennett, T. J., & Korndorffer, W. E. (2001). Combined homicide-suicide in Galveston County. *Journal of Forensic Science, 46*, 586–592.

25. Bourget, D., Gagne, P., & Moamai, J. (2000). Spousal homicide and suicide in Quebec. *Journal of the American Academy of Psychiatry and Law, 28*, 179–182.

26. Lindqvist, P., & Gustafsson, L. (1995). Homicide followed by the offender's suicide in northern Sweden. *Nordic Journal of Psychiatry, 49*, 17–24.

27. Walsh, S., & Hemenway, D. (2005). Intimate partner violence: homicides followed by suicides in Kentucky. *Journal of the Kentucky Medical Association, 103*, 10–13.

28. Byard, R. W., Knight, D., James, R. A., & Gilbert, J. (1999). Murder-suicides involving children: A 29-year study. *American Journal of Forensic Medicine and Pathology, 20*, 323–327.

29. McIntosh, J. L., Santos, J. F., & Hubbard, R. W. (1992). *Elder suicide: Research, theory, and treatment.* Washington, DC: American Psychological Association.

30. Pearson, J. L., & Conwell, Y. (1995). Suicide in late life: Challenges and opportunities for research. *International Psychogeriatrics, 7*, 131–136.

31. U.S. Department of Health and Human Services, Centers for Disease Control and Prevention (2000, May 2). *United States injury mortality statistics.* www.cdc. gov/ nchs/products/pubs/pubd/hus/2010/2010.htm.

32. Gallagher-Thompson, D., & Osgood, N. J. (1997). Suicide in later life. *Behavior Therapy, 28*, 23–41.

33. U.S. Public Health Service. (1999). *The Surgeon General's call to action to prevent suicide.* Washington, DC.

34. Ferri, E. (1934). *Homicidio-suicidio.* Madrid, Spain: Editorial Reus.

35. Provent, P. (1928). Le suicide "post-agressionnel." *Annales de Medicine Légale, 8*, 232–239.

36. West, D. J. (1965). *Murder followed by suicide.* Cambridge, MA: Harvard University Press.

37. Brown, M., & Barraclough. B. (1999). Partners in life and death: The suicide pact in England and Wales 1988–1992. *Psychological Medicine, 29*, 1299–1306.

38. Berman, A. L. (1996). Dyadic death: A typology. *Suicide and Life-Threatening Behavior, 26*, 342–250.

39. Felthous, A. R., & Hempel, A. (1995). Combined homicide-suicides: a review. *Journal of Forensic Sciences, 40*, 846–857.

40. Reid, W. H. (2004). Killing family members: Mental illness, victim risk, and culpability. *Journal of psychiatric practice, 10*, 68–71.

41. Daniels, K. (2005). Intimate partner violence and depression: A deadly comorbidity. *Journal of Psychosocial Nursing and Mental Health Services, 43*, 44–51.

42. Herman, J. (2000). *Trauma and recovery.* New York: Pfizer.

43. Palmer, S., & Humphrey, J. A. (1980). Offender-victim relationships in criminal homicide followed by offender's suicide, North Carolina, 1972–1977. *Suicide and Life Threatening Behavior, 10*, 106–118.

44. Conwell, Y., Duberstein, P. R., Cox, C., Herrmann, J. H., Forbes, N. T., & Caine, E. D. (1996). Relationships of age and Axis I diagnoses in victims of completed suicide: A psychological autopsy study. *American Journal of Psychiatry, 153,* 1001–1008.

45. Duberstein, P. R. (1995). Openness to experience and completed suicide across the second half of life. *International Psychogeriatrics,7,*183–198.

46. Mann, J. J., Waternaux, C., & Haas, G. L. (1999). Toward a clinical model of suicidal behavior in psychiatric inpatients. *American Journal of Psychiatry, 156,* 181–189.

47. Conwell, Y. (1997). Management of suicidal behavior in the elderly. *Psychiatric Clinics of North America, 20,* 667–683.

48. Stillion, J. M., & Macdonnell, E. E. (1996). Suicide among the elderly. In *Suicide across the lifespan: Premature exits* (pp. 169–196). Bristol, PA: Taylor and Francis.

49. Duberstein, P. R., Conwell, Y., & Caine, E. D. (1993). Interpersonal stressors, substance abuse, and suicide. *Journal of Nervous and Mental Disease,181,* 80–85.

50. Conwell, Y., Rotenberg, M., & Caine, E. D. (1990). Completed suicide at age 50 and over. *Journal of the American Geriatrics Society, 38,* 640–644.

51. Purcell, D., Thrush, C. R., & Blanchette, P. L. (1999). Suicide among the elderly in Honolulu County: A multiethnic comparative study, 1987–1992. *International Psychogeriatrics, 11,* 57–66.

52. Moscicki, M. (1997). Identification of suicide risk factors using epidemiologic studies. *Psychiatric Clinics of North America, 20,* 499–517.

53. Neutel, C. I., & Patten, S. B. (1997). Risk of suicide attempts after benzodiazepine and/or antidepressant use. *Annals of Epidemiology, 7,* 568–574.

54. Hirshfeld, R. M., Keller, M. B., & Panico, S. (1994). The national depressive and manic-depressive association consensus statement on the undertreatment of depression. *Journal of the American Medical Association,277,* 333–340.

55. Lesco, P. A. (1989). Murder-suicide in Alzheimer's disease. *Journal of the American Geriatrics Society, 37,* 167–168.

56. Cohen, D., & Eisdorfer, C. (1988). Depression in family members caring for a relative with Alzheimer's Disease. *Journal of the American Geriatrics Society, 36,* 885–889.

57. Cina, S. J., Smith, M. T., Collins, K. A., & Conradi, S. E. (1995). Dyadic deaths involving Huntington's disease: A case report. *American Journal of Forensic Medicine and Pathology, 17*(1), 49–52.

58. Cohen, D. (2000). Homicide-suicide in older persons. *Psychiatric Times, 17,* 49–52.

59. Cohen, D., & Malphurs, J. E. (2000). Antecedents of homicide-suicide and suicide in older married men. *SIEC Current Awareness Bulletin, 26*(3), 16–18.

60. Allen, N. H. (1983). Homicide followed by suicide: Los Angeles, 1970–1979. *Suicide and Life Threatening Behavior, 13,* 155–165.

61. Sakuta, T. (1995). A study of murder followed by suicide. *Medicine and Law, 14,* 141–153.

62. Malphurs, J. E., Cohen, D., & Eisdorfer, C. (1997, August). A diathesis-stress model of homicide-suicide. Paper presented at the 103rd annual meeting of the American Psychological Association, Chicago, IL.

63. Zubin, J., & Spring, B. (1977). Vulnerability: A new view of schizophrenia. *Journal of Abnormal Psychology, 86,* 103–126.

64. Metalsky, G. I., & Joiner, T. E. (1992). Vulnerability to depressive symptomotology: a prospective test of the diathesis-stress and causal mediation components of the hopelessness theory of depression. *Journal of Personality and Social Psychology, 63,* 667–675.

65. Spangler, D. L., Simons, A. D., & Monroe, S M. (1993). Evaluating the hopelessness model of depression: diathesis-stress and symptom components. *Journal of Abnormal Psychology, 102,* 592–600.

66. Linehan, M. M., & Shearin, E. N. (1988). Lethal stress: A social-behavioral model of suicidal behavior. In S. Fisher & J. Reason (Eds.), *Handbook of life stress, cognition and health* (pp. 265–285). New York: Wiley.

67. Rubenstein, D. H. (1986). A stress-diathesis theory of suicide. *Suicide and Life Threatening Behavior, 16,* 100–115.

68. Plutchik, R., Bostis, A. J., & Weiner, M. B. (1996). Clinical measurement of suicidality and coping in late life. In G. J. Kennedy (Ed.), *Suicide and depression in late life: Clinical issues in treatment, research, and public policy* (pp. 83–102). New York: Wiley.

69. Leenaars, A. A. (1996). Suicide: A multidimensional malaise. *Suicide and Life Threatening Behavior,26,* 221–236.

70. Steffens, D. C., & Blazer, D. G. (1999). Suicide in the elderly. In D. G. Jacobs (Ed.), *The Harvard Medical School guide to suicide assessment and intervention* (pp. 443-462). San Francisco: Jossey-Bass.

71. Wiebe, D. J. (2003). Homicide and suicide risks associated with firearms in the home: a national case-control study. *Annals of Emergency Medicine, 41,* 771–782.

Chapter 5

Mothers Who Kill Their Children: Considering Patterns, Prevention, and Intervention

Cheryl L. Meyer and Michelle Oberman

Filicide, or the crime of killing one's children, is as old as human society. Even a brief consideration of written history confirms this. It appears in the Old Testament. It is written into Roman law. Filicide is not new, and yet, because it undermines some of our most cherished myths—that mothers are unfailingly altruistic and that nuclear families are safe, happy, and loving havens—society tends to react to stories of filicide with shock and horror.

The most certain way to prevent filicide is to understand its genesis. When considering contemporary cases of maternal filicide, in particular, a surprisingly clear set of patterns emerges. These patterns reflect specific cultural norms and imperatives, both unwritten and written, that govern practices such as motherhood, family, mental health, and violence in contemporary life.[1] In the discussion that follows, we will explore these norms, illustrating the manner in which they shape contemporary maternal filicide cases, as well as the broader spectrum of child abuse and neglect.

It is impossible to determine the *exact* frequency of modern American infanticide for a number of reasons. For example, the perpetrator may be a juvenile and the records are sealed, or an infant is found dead but the cause of death or the perpetrators are never identified. In 1997, the Federal Bureau of Investigation estimated that nearly five infants under the age of one are killed each week (based on 1995 data), although the agency's report did not specify who committed the crimes.[2] However, children under age one are at a great risk of homicide and their killers are more likely to be their own mothers than anyone else.[3] Meyer and Oberman's data suggests that a mother murders her child approximately every three days in the United States.[1] This number is derived from the fact that we found over 1,000 reports of maternal filicide in the United States from January 1, 1990, to December 31, 1999, or more than 100 per year, which averages to one murder every three to four days. It is *very* likely that this number is also an underestimate.

We were able to find extensive information on 219 of those 1,000 cases. From them, we created a typology of mothers who kill their children. After publishing that typology, we interviewed 40 women who had been convicted of killing their children and were incarcerated for their actions. Their responses added a qualitative dimension to our original research, and we include some of their stories in the discussion below.

This chapter begins with an overview of our two research methodologies. It proceeds with a comprehensive review of our typology of filicide cases, which incorporates both our qualitative and quantitative research findings for each of the five types of filicide we identify. Following the discussion of the typology, we turn to a consideration of prevention and intervention strategies. In closing, we discuss some interventions and advocacy issues as they relate to the social construction of motherhood.

METHODOLOGIES

Oberman's research provided the impetus for our typology.[3] Using NEXIS, a news database that provides full text articles and publications from news-magazines, regional, and national newspapers, newsletters, trade magazines, and abstracts, Oberman identified 96 reported cases of filicide. Using these cases, the primary researchers for the project and a team of additional researchers read all 96 cases and formulated a draft typology. This draft typology was refined by testing it in classifying new cases, culled from the 10-year span between 1990 and 2000. Although more than 1,000 cases were found, cases that could not be followed up extensively through further searching were deleted from the sample. More details regarding case selection and exclusion are included in Meyer and Oberman.[1]

In order to determine patterns, the researchers tracked available information for each case regarding the following factors: age of the mother, age and gender of child, method of death, marital status, number of children in the family and in the home, geographical location, date of crime, charge/conviction, mother's behavioral response after death, history of domestic violence, mental health history, substance abuse history, socioeconomic status, the need for public assistance, children's protective service involvement, frequency of weapon use, any motive mentioned, birth order of child. Following publication of the typology and our findings, a second research team was provided with an opportunity to interview mothers incarcerated for killing their children. The women's reformatory with which we worked housed 69 women (out of approximately 1,800 inmates) who were incarcerated for killing their children. Forty of these women participated in a two-hour interview. Of the remaining 29, 13 were unable to be interviewed because they were in prerelease (9), the residential treatment unit (2), lock-up (1), or on judicial release (1). One woman killed her adult son and was not invited to participate. Two women had scheduling difficulties. Only 13 women out of 69 refused to participate. Each interview lasted approximately two hours. The interviews took place in offices within the prison medical facility. Some of the case studies that follow are drawn from this research. Where names and details are part of the public record, we have used them without alteration. When a case study only includes the woman's first name, the name and details of the crime have been changed to protect confidentiality. The quotes are paraphrases from the interviews.

UNDERSTANDING PATTERNS RELATED TO MOTHERS KILLING THEIR CHILDREN: A TYPOLOGY

Our typology was not the first typology related to filicidal parents.[1] However, it is the only typology based exclusively on cases from the United States. Additionally, the cases were all recent, occurring during the 1990s. In creating the typology, we believed that because infanticide has reflected cultural norms and imperatives throughout history, the unique interaction of social, environmental, cultural, and individual variables needed to be addressed *within each category* of filicidal mothers. In that way, we could arrive at as complete a picture as possible of the factors that come together to result in filicide in each case. Patterns and characteristics associated with each of the five types are described below, beginning with a representative case study. The types of filicide are described in descending order, from the most to the least common.

Filicide Due to Neglect

Linda was the victim of physical and sexual abuse at the hands of her uncle from age 2 to age 11. At the age of 13, she was raped by another man. As an adolescent, she received some counseling because she was acting out in school, but Linda doesn't feel this was very helpful for her. At the age of 18, she became pregnant as a result of a relationship with a man she eventually married. They had another child together. However, Linda describes the relationship as troubled. They eventually divorced and Linda moved into her own apartment in the same neighborhood. Her ex-husband began stalking her and making threatening phone calls to her. She was forced to move to a different town in order to get away from him. The apartment into which she moved was where the incident occurred in which both of her children were killed.

Linda had been living at the new apartment for over a year and had begun dating a young man who lived in a nearby house. On the evening of the incident, Linda put her two children down to bed and decided to go visit her new boyfriend, ostensibly for just a short time. She left her apartment, leaving a space heater on in the master bedroom where her children were asleep. While she was gone, the space heater somehow caught the bedding on fire and both children died. Linda was charged with two counts of involuntary manslaughter and received a prison term of 10 years.

Linda talks about her circumstances in the following excerpt:

A lot of people here call me "baby-killer" and it bothers me. People say I'm a violent killer. It's not that I purposefully did anything to them ... I am not a violent person. When they call me baby-killer, it is really painful. I don't think I killed my children ... it's hard to deal with being in here ... and it's hard to understand how my family can stick by me ... because I have a lot of guilt and I started hating myself and I am thinking, "how can they not hate me?"

This category of cases is marked by several strikingly consistent patterns. The mothers in these cases generally had more than one child, and the events that led to the death of one of her children are most readily viewed as accidental. Rather than intending to kill their child, these women emerge as mothers who were attempting to care for their children under conditions that were suboptimal, at best. These mothers overwhelmingly received little or no support from the fathers of their children. They had limited financial means. Their living conditions tended to be tenuous, and their support systems were fragile and seldom extended to child care. All of these factors limited the mother's ability to find work to support herself and her children, as well as to find ways to provide herself with the sort of respite care that all mothers, and particularly single mothers, need.

In our original study, we had a total of 76 cases of neglect. The majority of these women became mothers between the ages of 17 and 20 years. In addition, the overwhelming majority (85%) of mothers in this category were single parents, which likely further compounded their economic situation and available resources. Moreover, among the cases reviewed, 41 percent of the families had three or more children. Not surprisingly, 90 percent of the cases in this category involved mothers living in poverty. Finally, in at least 41 percent of the cases there were mental health issues, including mood disorders, such as depression, or chemical dependency.

We subdivided cases in this category into neglect-omission and neglect-commission cases, respectively. Neglect-omission cases included instances where the mother did not attend to health, nutrition or safety needs of the child, often by not providing adequate supervision. There were six predominant ways children died: fire, automobile suffocation, bathtub drowning, layover suffocation, poor nutrition, or inattention to safety needs. In neglect-commission cases, an irresponsible action of the mother caused the death, such as shaking the baby too hard or placing something over the child's head to stop the child from crying. In all cases, the mother did not purposely kill the child.

Neglect-related filicide is not only the most common form of maternal filicide in contemporary society, it is also one of the most entrenched. The challenge when articulating ways in which one might intervene or prevent neglect-related filicide is that one immediately comes up against seemingly immovable forces: poverty, social isolation, and limited access to resources such as child care, job training, and support systems. In a sense, one might view these cases as situational in nature, rather than involving individual psychopathology. Prevention therefore would involve forging connections—whether through neighborhood communities, work, or perhaps places of worship—that would serve to support both the mother and her children.

Filicide Related to an Ignored Pregnancy

Rebecca Hopfer played flute in the high school marching band and spent a lot of time at home. When she was 17, a boy convinced her to have sexual intercourse and then promptly broke off the relationship. In January 1994, Rebecca Hopfer realized she was pregnant, but she concealed the pregnancy. She later told her mother she concealed the pregnancy from her because she loved her too much to tell her. In August, after she had worked all day at an ice cream social, she went into labor at home and gave birth over a toilet. Hopfer maintains the baby was born dead with the umbilical cord wrapped tightly around her neck. The baby weighed four pounds and was 21 inches long. Hopfer wrapped the child's body in plastic bags and put it in the trash. Although she was 17, Hopfer was bound over to adult court and found guilty of murder and abuse of a corpse. She was sentenced to 15 years to life. She failed in two bids for clemency but eventually, in 2004, her sentence was commuted by the governor of Ohio and she was paroled after serving approximately eight years in prison.

Rebecca Hopfer's story helps to highlight perhaps the most strikingly patterned set of cases that we identified in our research: neonaticide. *Neonaticide* was a term first coined by Resnick,[4] to refer to the killing of a newborn within 24 hours of birth. Thirty-seven women in our sample of 219 (approximately 17%) had committed neonaticide. They ranged in age from 15 to 39, but the average age was 19.3. Thirty-six out of 37 of the women in our sample were single. Several of the intimate relationships that produced the pregnancy ended when the future father found out about the pregnancy. More than a third of the women gave birth in their bathrooms at home. In 70 percent of the cases, the child died from being smothered.

These cases were marked by an extreme degree of emotional isolation and fear. The women who committed neonaticide were relatively young and often socially immature. Their pregnancies were, for the most part, accidental, and yet, most of the women were ambivalent about the thought of ending their pregnancies. On the one hand, some feared that the birth of their child would bring about the demise of their life as they knew it. On the other hand, some hoped that the child might be a source of love and affection in their otherwise emotionally isolated existences.

The fears triggered by the pregnancy tended to be both practical and emotional. Most of these women felt their families would not be supportive during their pregnancies, let alone in their lives as mothers. In particular, they expressed fears that they might be ostracized or even physically punished. In general, they were overwhelmed by feelings of shame, guilt, and/or fear. Because they were relatively young, many of these women feared they would be kicked out of their homes, and they worried about how they would support themselves and their baby. Due to these fears, some of these girls and women, like Rebecca, actively concealed their pregnancy. One woman we interviewed, who had concealed her pregnancy and then committed neonaticide, described her experiences as follows:

> I hid the pregnancy from everyone . . . that was the hardest part—ignoring my pregnancy. It was so hard to deny and hide knowing that there is a life inside you. I had no medical care . . . I didn't even see a doctor. I kept thinking, 'it can't be true . . . this isn't happening to you'. Several times I wanted to talk with my family but I was too scared . . . several times I wanted to sit down and tell them but I thought 'they'll think less of you or that it was your fault'. It was not that way at all. Now they tell me: you should have come to us and we would have helped you any way we could . . . It's hard being in here [prison] knowing that I am convicted of killing my child—the hardest thing is knowing that I am convicted of killing my child. People turn up their nose up at you and treat you differently. Some don't care and treat you human but a lot don't. I don't even talk to people about my case. I just want to be treated like a human. We are all here and we all made mistakes.

Other women denied the pregnancy, even to themselves. Some were able to deny the pregnancy because they continued to menstruate and gained minimal weight. When they began to experience the abdominal cramps and indigestion that often comes with labor, many thought they needed to defecate. Given their lack of prenatal education, this confusion is not surprising.

For all of their fears, however, at least some of these women reported wanting a baby, viewing it as a potential source of unconditional love and attention. It is important to note that these women were, in many cases, still girls, living at home with their parents. Although their families of origin might appear to have been loving ones, it must be noted that these girls felt unable to confide in *any* of the adults in their lives. Moreover, the adults either did not notice the girl's advancing pregnancy, her emotional state, or the broad hints that the girls dropped in their effort to get an adult to intervene and take care of them, or they chose to deny them, just as the girl was denying her pregnancy. As a result, the girls were left alone with their desperate secrets. In such circumstances, it is not surprising that an adolescent might have some positive fantasies about the sort of love, affection and attention that a baby would bring to her life.

In hindsight, one might identify multiple opportunities for prevention in these cases. A surprising number of these girls were seen by doctors or nurses during the course of their pregnancies—some for school-related care, and some even for routine gynecological exams. Unfortunately, the health care providers typically failed to ask direct questions relating to the girl's health, or to probe a bit when met with the girl's silence. In some cases, they allowed the girl's mother to remain in the examination room, which chilled the girl's willingness to confide in her health care provider.

An additional opportunity for prevention might have involved any of the numerous unrelated adults who were present in these girls' lives, and who might have had reason to recognize her pregnancy. In almost all cases, there were teachers, coaches, youth group leaders, religious leaders, friends, and friends' parents who either missed the signs of pregnancy, or perhaps suspected it but hesitated to intervene. Adolescents in our society often are remarkably isolated from adults, who view them with some degree of fear or alienation. This isolation leaves them vulnerable when attempting to exercise responsible decision-making in "adult" situations. These girls, and their babies, might well have been rescued had even one of the adults in these girls' lives shown concern, rather than disinterest or fear.

Recently states have been enacting "safe haven" laws in an attempt to prevent neonaticide and newborn abandonment. Although well intentioned, "safe havens" have had little, if any, impact on the number of neonaticides to date. This may be due to the fact that there is some element of planning involved in dropping a child off at a "safe haven," and that the girls and women who commit neonaticide are so emotionally paralyzed that they are perhaps uniquely unlikely to engage in such advance planning. Nonetheless, if fully implemented, these laws may raise awareness about unwanted, concealed pregnancy. Indeed, were a teacher to be assigned to educate young people about these laws, this might have the secondary benefit of revealing a safe adult in whom a girl might confide.

Purposeful Filicide and the Mother Acted Alone

Beth was an extremely withdrawn and shy child who grew into a quiet and rebellious adolescent. At 15, she met a very charismatic 29-year-old man named Bob. Within a year she was pregnant, and she had given birth to four children by the time she was 20. Bob had a job in sales and traveled extensively, taking his family with him. This forced Beth to drop out of high school. Beth felt isolated and alone most of the time. Bob had numerous affairs and was an alcoholic who could be extremely violent when he was drinking. When she was 21, Beth left Bob and returned home. She brought her four children with her, all of whom were under the age of six. They lived in her parents' partially finished attic. The conditions were less than ideal: there were no windows and the temperature would average 88 degrees during the day and 74 degrees in the evening. Still, Beth held a part-time job to support her family and completed her high school degree.

One evening at a party, Beth went for a walk with an acquaintance and was brutally raped. In response to this crisis, on top of her chronic exhaustion and depression, Beth determined that she no long could bear living. However, she did not want to leave her children behind. She stated, Beth started with the youngest child and one by one smothered each child. She then ingested 40 over-the-counter sleeping pills. Beth survived and was sentenced to life in prison without parole. As she looks back on her crime she states:

> I don't consider it over. As long as I live I don't consider it over . . . I will live with the pain of killing my children the rest of my life . . . Before I committed the crime, I didn't like any of me anymore. I didn't feel I could be a good person for many years. I didn't accept I could have a life after killing my children . . . Once I reached the point where I felt responsible, I stopped having nightmares about my kids. I had good dreams, of us doing things together.

At many levels, the purposeful filicide cases, in which a mother deliberately takes the life of her child or children, are the most difficult to comprehend. Perhaps because of this, in some sense, they seem to be the most intriguing. Mental health problems are woven through the overwhelming majority of the cases in this category, and yet, there is a remarkably broad spectrum of diagnoses relevant to these cases. At one end of the spectrum are cases like Beth's, in which there was no history of treatment for mental illness, and yet, clearly the rape was a trauma that likely awakened and exacerbated anxiety Beth had experienced through domestic violence. In addition, long before the rape that precipitated her homicidal acts, she was clearly exhibiting signs of depression.

At the other end of the spectrum are cases such as that of Andrea Yates, the Texas mother who drowned her five children in a widely reported case in 2001. Yates had a long history of struggles with mental illness, including numerous hospitalizations for postpartum mental illness. At the time of her crimes, she was in the throes of postpartum psychosis.

Other cases in this category are somewhere between these two extremes. Consider the equally notorious case of Susan Smith, a South Carolina mother who killed her two small children by leaving them in the car and rolling the car into a lake. Although she had a long history of struggles with mental illness, suicide attempts, and ongoing sexual abuse by her stepfather, Smith was not under medical supervision at the time of her crime.

Conventional wisdom suggests women in this category are either "mad or bad." Women portrayed as "mad" have been characterized as "good mothers" who have conformed to traditional gender roles and whose crimes seem to be the result of mental illness. In contrast, women characterized as "bad" do not seem to suffer from mental illness and are labeled as cold, callous, evil mothers who have often been neglectful of their children or their domestic responsibilities. This dichotomy can be seen in portrayals of Andrea Yates. The prosecutor suggested Yates was "bad," in that she purposely and selfishly killed her children. Yates's defense claimed the opposite—that she was "mad" and the deaths were the result of mental illness. This simplistic dichotomy cannot begin to address the complexities underlying these cases.

Despite the diversity these cases presented in terms of maternal mental illness, striking and clear patterns emerged among the 79 cases we reviewed. These commonalities include the killing of multiple children, the experience of a recent failed relationship, the extent to which these mothers felt desperate and suicidal, and finally, issues of cultural and religious ideology.

Unlike mothers in other categories, nearly 39 percent of mothers within this category killed more than one child; when considering only cases of murder-suicide, the number jumped to 68 percent. In addition, the majority of the mothers in this category (57%) attempted to kill not only their children, but also themselves. Almost 42 percent of the mothers in this category experienced a recent failed relationship, separation, or divorce prior to the murders. This number increases if the experiences are expanded to include the death of a loved one. For example, Andrea Yates lost her father shortly before killing her five children.

Of these fact patterns, the suicide attempt by the mother is perhaps the most salient. The criminal justice system often diminishes or ignores these attempts, yet those seeking to understand and prevent these crimes must pay attention to the fact that it is the mother's determination that she can no longer go on living that typically leads her to take the lives of her children. A surprising number of these mothers sought to arrange alternative care for their children, asking parents, siblings, or friends whether they would be willing to take responsibility for them in the event that something happened to her. Only after such attempts failed did they decide to "take their children with them." Often, this decision was rendered more acceptable to the mothers because of deeply held religious convictions regarding guilt, forgiveness, and an afterlife.

Another distinctive feature of these women's stories was their devotion toward their children. For instance, Beth describes herself as having been a loving mother and devoted to her children:

> They always came first. They were more of an appendage. I loved them very much. Killing them was not out of hate. It was a suicide. I could never envision them without me. I could not accept that my ex-husband could raise them better than me. I wanted to die and I wanted the kids with me in death. Everything I valued was my kids and if I had them with me in death then there was nothing holding me back and the thought that I could kill them—I was totally worthless and once I started thinking that and felt that way about myself I couldn't stop myself.

The overwhelming majority of these mothers had no history of abuse or neglect toward their children, and most people who knew them agreed they exhibited undying love for their children.

Finally, issues of culture and ethnicity seem to play a significant role within this category, particularly as they relate to immigrant women. A large number of immigrant women were represented, in comparison to the other categories of filicide. Many of these women were reported to have had difficulty assimilating to life in the United States.

Although postpartum mental illness receives a considerable amount of attention in the popular and professional literature, a relatively small percentage of mothers within this category suffered from postpartum disorders (8%). Overall, when all 219 cases are included, the postpartum cases accounted for less than 3 percent of the sample. Certainly, it is possible that some of the women may have suffered from postpartum depression or psychosis without being diagnosed or even identifying it themselves. However, in applying this standard to the sample of 40 incarcerated women whom we interviewed, 10 women killed their child in the postpartum period (defined as one year postpartum) and only 6 of the cases might arguably have involved postpartum disorders. Of those six, only one woman attempted to raise a postpartum illness-related defense at trial.

Nonetheless, a significant number of women in this category recognized their need for mental health treatment and sought care. Unfortunately, those who did seek help, or were referred for treatment, often were not candid with their health care providers about their distress, and in particular about their fears or plans. For example, they usually did not discuss their fears of being a bad mother or their thoughts of committing filicide. In part, this may stem from embarrassment or shame about not being a good mother. Such reticence may also be due to real fears of losing custody of their children were the mothers to reveal their darkest thoughts. Thus, their health care providers failed to recognize the immediate threat that these women posed to their children and to themselves. Those who wish to work toward the prevention of filicide should anticipate these fears and concerns when treating mothers for mental health problems, and must create an environment that feels safe enough for the mothers to disclose the true nature of their distress.

Abuse-Related Filicide

Felicia was incarcerated in her early 20s for involuntary manslaughter and child endangerment. She was sentenced to up to 25 years for fatally beating her four-year-old child. Felicia readily admitted that she had a history of abusing her daughter and that Felicia herself was the victim of extensive and severe physical and psychological abuse and neglect by her stepfather. She also observed incessant violence against her mother by her stepfather, which, she noted, led to her mother abusing drugs heavily. In addition to abuse she experienced and witnessed at home, Felicia was later assaulted by her baby's father, who beat and raped her. This rape resulted in the conception of her daughter.

Felicia has spent much of her time in prison thinking about why she hurt her daughter and has finally concluded that she learned her behaviors from her parents' modeling. She states:

> My mother and stepfather are both recovering addicts. The abuse came at the hand of my stepfather. I recall my stepfather hitting me . . . and he also hit my mother. He threatened me with a knife several times if I didn't do exactly what he said. I tried to commit suicide three times when I was a kid. I was tired of being hit on—you know what I mean?

In most respects, Felicia is representative of mothers who killed their children through abuse. Mothers who abuse their children or who kill their children through abuse have not received much research attention. In part, this may be due to definitional issues. Abuse and neglect are not clearly distinguished, and there are ethnic and cultural variations in what constitutes acceptable discipline practices and what is abusive.

In our original research we had only 15 cases in this category, and there was very little information available on 3 of those cases. The children killed ranged in age from six weeks to six years. However, only two were under a year old. The women had an average of four children, but 10 of the women had four or more children. All of the children but one, who drowned, died as a result of beatings. Almost half of the fatal assaults involved a blow to the head. Although the mothers seemed to abuse all their children, several cases mentioned that the victim seemed to be a target of violence more often than the other children. We found similar patterns in our interviews with women who killed their children through abuse.

One of the most troubling aspects of this particular form of filicide was that, in the vast majority of cases, state child welfare authorities were aware of the trouble in these families long before the child was killed. In our original sample, child protective services had previously intervened with at least 12, and possibly even 14 of the 15 cases. In two-thirds of the cases, the mother had previously lost custody and killed the child after reunification. Although it was unclear how long the mother and child had been reunited, in at least five cases it had been less than six months. Of the five cases that were not reunifications, three of the mothers had previously been reported to child welfare.

In addition, child protective service workers were involved with most of our interviewees who killed through abuse. However, the fear of seeking help because children's services might remove children from the home was a theme in all our interviews. One woman stated, "I think maybe when people come to ask for help instead of penalizing them—that's probably what my husband was afraid of—they should provide resources. If a person goes and tells them, 'I'm on the edge,' they take the chance of having their kids taken away from them." As a result, the involvement of children's protective services did not seem to prevent abuse-related deaths.

Although none of the mothers in the abuse-related category of our original research was an adolescent at the time of the crime, many were adolescents when they first bore a child. The average age was 27 with a range of 21–39 years old. Substance use was clearly a factor in eight of the cases and at least a third of the victims had been born addicted to substances. At least two of the women were pregnant at the time of the killings.

When we were able to interview the women who had killed their children through abuse, we determined that most of these women reported being abused as a child. The *intergenerational transmission hypothesis*[5] suggests that being abused as a child, or observing abuse as a child, is related to prepetrating abuse as a parent. Some of the women we interviewed had come to understand their predisposition. For example, Felicia stated:

> When I finally saw a counselor, she told me about the cycle of abuse and the "generational curse." She really helped me to understand myself. In my

case, my daughter was just doing something she knew she wasn't supposed to do . . . I never had any patience and I slapped her real hard in the face. She fell, hitting the corner of the wall and she died two days later in the hospital.

Most of the women we interviewed did not understand the cycle of violence in which they had unwittingly participated. The women often said something to the effect of, "I had an Ozzie and Harriet childhood. I was sexually abused for a few years but beyond that we were a typical family." Their descriptions reflected a sense that the abuse they had experienced was a relatively unremarkable part of growing up, and they were simply noting it for the record.

The perception that abuse is typical is all the more troubling in light of the fact that it is a common theme in at least three of our filicide categories: abuse-related, assisted/coerced, and neglect. Perhaps the best hope of preventing filicide cases that grow out of chronic abuse and/or neglect is to heighten awareness regarding the patterned nature of child abuse and the support that is needed to assist those who survive abusive childhoods when they themselves undertake parenting. For instance, Felicia long had been involved with children's services and had undergone court-ordered counseling, yet until she was incarcerated, no one had ever explained the intergenerational transmission hypothesis to her, nor described the way in which her own abuse as a child might have shaped her responses to parenting. Felicia told us, "I feel like the system failed me until I saw the psychologist who told me about the cycle of abuse . . . My whole thing is to get to the core of it and try to prevent it. I feel like in my situation had that been done, I wouldn't be here."

Assisted/Coerced Filicide

Lisa never knew her father and her mother worked as an erotic dancer. When Lisa was 18 she became pregnant, and the father of the child left Lisa with her new daughter, Angie. Lisa admits she did not know how to raise a family and was struggling to make ends meet. Several times, state child welfare agents came to her home to investigate reports of child neglect. When she met Matt, everyone encouraged her to get married to him because he would be her "knight in shining armor." What Lisa did not know was that Matt was on medication to control his manic-depression and he would stop taking his medication periodically and attempt self-medication. Matt began to discipline Angie in relatively innocuous ways. However, by the time Angie was five, Matt began beating her and administering harsh punishments. One day, Matt beat Angie severely, but Lisa did not think that Angie required medical attention. The child died of internal injuries that night. Matt and Lisa were both convicted of involuntary manslaughter.

In assisted/coerced filicide cases, mothers kill their children while acting in conjunction with a partner—generally a romantic partner—who contributes in some manner to the death. We subdivided our original 12 cases in this category into two subcategories: active and passive. In the active subcategory, the women were directly involved in their children's death. In the passive subcategory, women like Lisa were charged with their child's death due to their failure to protect the child.

The characteristics of women in this category are unlike those of women in other filicide categories. Most notably, unlike most of the other types of filicide, during the time period in which they kill their children, these women are involved with a partner, one who usually is not the biological parent of the child who is killed. The relationship with her partner typically is quite violent in nature. In most cases, state child protection agencies have been involved with the family. As Lisa indicated,

> Domestic violence was not new to me but it doesn't start with someone dying. There's a gradual escalation of violence. I knew that and I was going to stop the relationship with Matt, but I was afraid that since they [the state child protective services workers] saw him as such a hero, they would take my kid away again if I left him.

All of the children in this category who were in our original sample had been physically abused. For the most part, the deaths of these children resulted from discipline-related abuse that escalated into fatal beatings. These incidents occurred during times that are typically stressful for parents, such as bedtime.

When thinking about prevention, it is vital to recognize that state child welfare agencies were aware of the risks facing the families in these cases long before the children were killed. The prevention problem therefore is less one of detection, than it is one of discernment. How is the state to distinguish households in which the children are safe from those in which the children are so vulnerable that they should not be permitted to remain with their mothers? Surely, it is important to note the range of social stressors in these mothers' lives, including poverty and the presence of multiple children in the home. In addition, there is the presence of domestic violence, which brings with it the possibility that the mother might perceive her own exit options as limited. Finally, there is the fact that the men in these cases seldom are the biological fathers of the victims. In and of itself, this is not a warning sign, as few stepparents kill their stepchildren. However, when considered in conjunction with other factors, this may be part of a risk pattern.

FILICIDE AND THE SOCIAL CONSTRUCTION OF MOTHERHOOD

In this chapter we have provided an overview of five different types of mothers who kill their children. Within each category, we have provided some suggestions for ways in which these particular forms of filicide might be prevented. In addition to these case- and category-specific observations, there is one overarching theme, present to some degree in all forms of filicide, that we believe is vital to understanding the persistence of filicide in contemporary society. Specifically, filicide cases result in part from the manner in which society has defined and constructed the role of mother.

The social construction of motherhood has two central and interrelated components. First of all, mothers are held accountable to their children, and are defined by their role as mother, in a manner that is far more comprehensive than is true for fathers. Second, and particularly in the United States, mothers today parent in relative isolation, far removed from the social supports that are present for mothers in other cultures, and throughout history.

With regard to the accountability of mothers, it goes almost without saying that societal expectations for mothers are different than expectations for fathers. A small example: our research failed to identify a single "failure to protect" case in which a father faced homicide charges for his failure to stop his wife or girlfriend from harming their child. Indeed, in the many, many cases we found discussing filicide, there is not a single mention of the fact that the fathers failed to protect their children from the mothers. And yet, the law is replete with such cases brought against mothers. We take for granted the assumption that it is a mother's job to protect her children, and that a mother who is remiss in this duty is, by definition, a bad mother.

The social construction of mother as one who is all-seeing, altruistic, and endlessly loving contributes to filicide in a variety of ways. It makes it risky to share fears and self-doubt with others, for instance. Not surprisingly, a mother's feelings of fear and self-doubt often are aggravated by the social expectation that she should be feeling unadulterated joy about being a mother. Instead of reaching out for help, a mother who is struggling frequently will withdraw from friends and family, hoping to hide the "fact" that she is a "bad mom" from others.

In fact, our research revealed that isolation was a warning sign across all categories, from the teens who conceal their pregnancies and later commit neonaticide to the mothers who experience postpartum mental illness. Although isolation may be self-imposed in some women's circumstances, such as in the case of neonaticide, or imposed by others in different circumstances, such as in the case of domestic violence, the end result was the same—the mothers felt unable to confide in others about their increasingly desperate struggle.

One of the most frequent comments we heard in our interviews of mothers was that the one thing they had learned in prison was to reach out for help when they needed it, despite the fear and shame that kept them from doing so before. While saying this, they also recognized the very real danger in reaching out. For a mother to admit that she needs help, or that she feels unsure about how to raise her child, creates the very real risk she may thereby invite the scrutiny of state child protective services workers into her life, and ultimately, that she may lose custody of her children. This creates a catch-22: a mother can reach out and put herself at risk, or remain isolated and therefore at risk. Once again, the social construction of motherhood helps to shape this risk. Fathers who reach out for help may not suffer the same scrutiny. Consider the response when a father is widowed versus when a mother is widowed. When a father is left to raise children alone there is an outpouring of parenting support we rarely see for mothers in the same circumstances.

Isolation, the second component of the social construction of motherhood, plays an equally central role in contributing to contemporary cases of filicide. The demise of the extended family, and indeed, of the nuclear family, means that mothers today experience a profound degree of isolation from support systems. In the past, and in other cultures around the world today, a new mother receives substantial support from her own mother, from her siblings, her extended family, and indeed, her entire community. With others who will shop, clean, cook, and care for her and her family, the mother of a young child is free to devote her attention to her baby or babies. In contemporary U.S. society, even a relatively wealthy mother is likely to spend long hours alone with her child, apart from her spouse, isolated from her neighbors, and away from her family.

Isolation is particularly menacing when one considers the needs of mothers who are struggling with mental illness, dire poverty, substance abuse, and/or domestic violence. The mere fact of becoming a mother does not automatically endow one with the coping skills needed to respond patiently and gently to the demands of a young child. Together, the isolation of mothers and the shame that mothers feel if they are less than "perfect" create an environment in which harm to a child becomes predictable, if not inevitable.

CONCLUSION: THOUGHTS ON INTERVENTION AND PREVENTION OF FILICIDE

The researchers involved in both of these projects approached the topic with varying levels of sympathy and horror. By the end of these projects what was striking to us was how our sympathy toward the women had grown and the horror had become redirected. It started as horror toward the women for their heinous acts. By the end it was a different horror, borne of our recognition that these women were not monsters. In fact, there were many similarities between them and us. It made us aware of our privilege and thankful for our resources. While none of us in any way wanted to absolve these women of their responsibility for their crimes, we wondered whether, given the right circumstances, almost any mother would be capable of such acts.

The disturbing observation that, *on the whole*, we could empathize with many of these mothers derived from our recognition of the challenges inherent in the circumstances under which they were attempting to parent. Isolation, poverty, violence, and mental illness are a terrible foundation upon which to raise a family. In the last paragraph of our 2001 book, we stated, "If there is one central point to this book, it is this: to the extent that we conceive of the crime of infanticide as a rare and exceptional act committed by a deranged or evil woman, we are dangerously wrong" (p. 177).[1] This sentiment was reiterated in numerous interviews. One mother stated:

> People have to stop thinking we are cruel and hard, we just went through an emotional battle. I've had girls tell me that they went through what I went through but they had their husbands and mothers to help them through it. The family has to get involved. People are so closed they don't want to see anything. They see everything in black and white but they really need to see color.

Nothing in this chapter is meant to excuse these mothers or to justify their acts. It is a crime to kill a child, and those who do so should be held responsible for their actions. What is particularly challenging about these cases is the attempt to discern the extent to which these mothers are culpable or blameworthy. By asking questions about their blameworthiness, we increase our understanding of these mothers and the circumstances that surrounded them at the time that they took their children's lives. From this inquiry, we learn that filicide is not incomprehensible. Instead, filicide occurs at the intersection of isolation and despair. It is only in this understanding that we can find the road to preventing what all of us hope will one day be truly incomprehensible: the death of a child at her mother's hands.

ACKNOWLEDGMENTS

Parts of this chapter previously appeared in the following publications: C. Meyer, "Enhancing Understanding and Awareness of Patterns Associated with Maternal Filicide," in *Innovations in Clinical Practice: Treatment and Prevention of Violence*, ed. L. VandeCreek and T. L. Jackson (Sarasota, FL: Professional Resource Press, 2004); C. L. Meyer and C. Weisbart, "Listening to Women's Voices: Considering Why Mothers Kill Their Children," in *It's a Crime: Women and Justice* (3rd ed.), ed. R. Muraskin (Englewood Cliffs, NJ: Prentice Hall, 2003).

REFERENCES

1. Meyer, C. L., & Oberman, M. (with White, K., Rone, M., Batra, P., & Proano, T., 2001). *Mothers who kill their children: Understanding the acts of moms from Susan Smith to the "Prom Mom."* New York: New York University Press.
2. Nearly 5 babies killed weekly, FBI data show. (1997, June 27). *CNN Interactive.* Retrieved July 5, 2001, from http://www.cnn.com/US/9706/27/killed.babies/index.html.
3. Oberman, M. (1996). Mothers who kill: Coming to terms with modern American Infanticide. *American Criminal Law Review, 34,* 1–110.
4. Resnick, P. J. (1970). Murder of the newborn: A psychiatric review of neonaticide, *American Journal of Psychiatry , 126,* 1414–1420.
5. Milner, J. S., Robertson, K. R., & Rogers, D. L. (1990). Childhood history of abuse and adult child abuse potential. *Journal of Family Violence, 5,* 15–34.

Chapter 6

When the Peer Group Becomes the Parent: Social and Developmental Issues Associated with Youth Gangs

Michael Axelman and Sara Bonnell

While youth gangs have been part of the urban landscape for over a century, the number of cities and counties experiencing youth gang problems increased substantially between the mid-1980s and mid-1990s. While the overall level of gang activity appears to have stabilized over the past decade, gang members, according to studies based on large urban samples, are responsible for a large proportion of violent offenses.

Along with impacting society, gang involvement exerts an extremely heavy toll on youth's psychosocial development. Early risk factors associated with gang involvement include: lack of paternal involvement, problematic parent-child relations, low school attachment and achievement, association with peers who engage in delinquency, and disorganized neighborhoods characterized by high unemployment, a factor always correlated with large numbers of youth in trouble. The possible developmental consequences of youth gang involvement can be quite profound and include: reduced access to prosocial goals, school dropout, early parenthood, and unstable employment.

This chapter situates what has been referred to as the youth gang problem within historical, sociocultural and developmental contexts. The fist section presents youth gangs from a historical perspective. This is followed by a discussion of the way in which gangs impact society, and how social and cultural forces influence youth who are at risk for gang involvement. In order to understand the thoughts and the behavior of youth who have been socialized by youth gangs—behavior which is often misrepresented and poorly understood by the popular media—we must first understand how these youth construct and make meaning of the world in which they live. The lives of these youth are embedded, to a large extant, in a different social system and a unique set of constraints that are significantly different, especially with respect to safety and opportunity, from mainstream American culture. Although the psychological, the social, and the cultural are often discussed independently in this paper, these domains should be understood as interdependent. Gang violence and intimidation are understood as both a response to, and a re-creation of, the economic and social disorganization that characterizes many inner cities and impoverished rural communities in America.

The chapter concludes with an examination of current efforts to address youth gang issues. This includes a review of the several of the more effective community-wide interventions that have been used to address the youth gang problem. Strategies that employ local resources, provide opportunities for education and job training, and engage in collaborative problem solving have been found to be particularly effective.

HISTORY OF GANGS IN AMERICA

From the often romanticized days of Al Capone to contemporary street gangs, urban America has a long history of youth gangs. Youth gangs first emerged in large northeastern cities in the United States among ethnic European immigrants during the industrial era. Outside of the large cities, gangs developed rural pockets in the Southwest following the Mexican Revolution. It is generally agreed that gang growth and activity developed at four distinct periods in the United States: the late 1800s, the 1920s, the 1960s, and the 1990s.[1]

Street gangs first emerged in the United States in the 1800s. As the Industrial Revolution gained momentum, immigrant minorities such as the Jewish and Irish formed gangs in urban centers like New York and Philadelphia.[2] Gangs formed as a response to social conditions such as prejudice and poverty.[3] Mexicans residing in the southwestern United States simultaneously emerged from similar conditions, possibly as a result of the Mexican Revolution of 1813.[4]

During the 1920s and 1930s, youth gangs had a notable presence in lower-income neighborhoods in cities such as New York and Chicago.[5] In Los Angeles, African American gangs began to form in the 1940s, as protective mechanisms against white clubs. However, it was not until the 1960s that the Los Angeles Police Department began identifying these groups as gangs. Some of these very same gangs participated in the Watts Rebellion of 1965. Some street gangs evolved into political or radical movements, while others continued as street gangs.[6] In the 1930s and 1940s, Mexican American gangs gained momentum, again as a response to social and economic conditions. A distinctive clothing style often marked gangs of this era. For example, the Pacheco fashion and the zoot suit differentiated Latino gang members from other groups. Street gangs continued to evolve throughout the 20th century, as harassment of and poor economic conditions continued for minority populations.[7]

The historical shift to today's multiracial gang membership reflects the changing face of the inner city. Gangs, as we know them today, transformed during the crack cocaine epidemic of the 1980s. This mobilization of gang culture was centered in poor, minority inner-city communities. The failure of the civil rights movement outside of southern cities resulted in little progress advancing economic opportunity for minority communities in northern and western cities. The loss of large numbers of blue-collar jobs in large cities in the North and Midwest throughout the 1980s contributed significantly to the disenfranchisement of young adult males in the inner city.[8] The infamous public housing projects of the 1960s and 1970s, proposed as the solution to housing America's poor, further concentrated poverty in the inner city.

YOUTH GANGS—AN INTRODUCTION

Considerable disagreement exists regarding the nature and definition of youth gangs. A gang is broadly defined by the National Youth Violence Prevention Resource Center as a group of teens and young adults that hang out together and are involved in joint delinquent activity. This definition can potentially encompass small groups hanging out in the local shopping mall as well as adult criminal organizations. Our society tends to see gang members as "super predators" when in fact, the majority of these youths carry on a lifestyle similar to that of their peers—sleeping, going to school, and hanging out with friends.[9] The group will have a name and a common name or symbol, and they often choose to wear a certain type of clothing or to display some other identifying item. While gang members range from age 12 to 24, roughly half of members are 18 or older.[10]

Traditionally, women have been a branch of male gangs or as part of a sexually mixed gang. Currently, there is a rise in autonomous female gangs.[11] In a 1992 nationwide survey, only 3.7 percent of gang members were female.[12] It is important to note, however, that a large portion of those surveyed do not identify any females as gang members. Female gangs appear to be less likely to engage in violent behavior than their male counterparts.[13] As Puerto Rican gangs such as the Latin Kings were evolving in the latter half of the twentieth century, a female counterpart, the Latin Queens, became the social counterpart of male-dominated gang life. As a large number of gang-associated Latinos were sent to prison, females visiting these incarcerated members received new status as the link between prison and street gang members.[14]

Gangs range across ethnicity and gender and exist in both rural and urban areas. In 2002, the National Youth Gang Survey found that 731,500 members were active in 2,300 American cities.[15] The contemporary ethnic makeup of gangs is primarily Latino and African American. In the 1998 survey, gang members were 46 percent Latino, 34 percent African American, 12 percent Caucasian, and 6 percent Asian.[16]

Latin gangs have increased steadily in recent years. In the 1950s, many violent, often gang-affiliated Latino males from southern California were incarcerated. For protection against the non-Latino inmates and prison staff, the gang La Eme, or Mexican Mafia, was formed. As the number of Latino gang members from northern California grew, the gang Nuestra Familia was formed for the protection of incarcerated gang members. These prison-affiliated gangs manifested as street gangs known as the Surenos (Southerners) and Nortenos (Northerners). La Eme and Sureno gang members identified with the number 13 (the order of M in the alphabet) and the color blue. The gangs Nuestra Familia and Nortenos identified with the number 14 (letter N in the alphabet) and the color red. These gangs were, and continue to be, strongly connected to illegal drug trafficking. In addition to violent street and prison gangs such as the Nortenos and Surenos, there were less violent street groups known as Tagger Crews, named for their acts of vandalism. Initially engaged in nonviolent delinquent behavior, Tagger Crews became incorporated into traditional gang life in Latino California as a way of marking territory.[17]

YOUTH GANGS: IMPACT ON SOCIETY

Currently, gang activity remains an unchecked, unmeasured "hidden war" in our society.[18] Gangs that have traditionally operated in Los Angeles and Chicago have spread throughout America's urban environment. Additionally, deportation of undocumented gang members to countries such as El Salvador has resulted in an internationalizing of gangs to urban cities in other countries. Current gang culture varies from relatively structured criminal organizations to small, local hate groups. While some youth gangs are involved in drug trafficking, other street gangs are involved in other types of delinquent behavior. Modern drug gangs have become organized around economic, hierarchical structures, from foot soldiers on the bottom, up to imprisoned gang members serving mandatory sentences, sending out directives from prisons throughout the country. Gang problems extend to juvenile detention and correctional facilities as well.[19]

There is a strong correlation between youth gangs, violence, and drugs. In Denver, for example, only 14 percent of teens were gang members, but they were responsible for committing 89 percent of the serious violent crimes.[20] The ability to obtain firearms easily has increased the violent nature of gang warfare. Most gang violence is related to conflicts with other gangs. These turf disputes[21] generally occur in specific neighborhoods between gangs. However, gangs engage in criminal activity at several levels. Their violence spills over and impacts neighborhood residents or shop owners who are not involved in gangs. Gang activity also enables the black-market drug trade to pervade society. In a 1998 survey, drug sales accounted for 27 percent of gang-related crime, while theft and illegal entry constituted 17 percent and 13 percent, respectively.[22]

In addition to these social costs, the gang members themselves are victims in gang activity. Members face injury, death, and incarceration due to their delinquent behavior. The 1999 National Report on Juvenile Offenders and Victims found that 2.8 million juveniles were arrested in 1997. The violent death rate for drug-selling gang members is 7 percent per year.[23] The 1999 survey also reports that arrested juveniles accounted for 19 percent of all arrests, 14 percent of all murder arrests, and 17 percent of all violent crime arrests.[24] While there is much we can say about the causes of gang violence and involvement, we can only estimate the actual involvement of gang membership and gang warfare's toll on society. Current studies estimate that 25,000 individuals, mostly minority gang members, have been killed through gang-related violence.[25]

RISK FACTORS CONTRIBUTING TO GANG INVOLVEMENT

Individual

There are several personal attributes of at-risk youth that make them more susceptible to becoming gang members. Prior delinquency, drinking, and aggressiveness have been associated with early gang membership. One appeal of membership is that gangs can provide a way of solving social adjustment problems and the difficulties associated with adolescence. These inner-city youths attend the worst schools in the poorest neighborhoods with the highest dropout rate. Typically, they perform well below average. At-risk youth characteristically get into trouble at school and are labeled as "losers" by teachers and administrators. These youths are less committed to their academic performance and have limited educational expectations. Gang members may exhibit deviant attitudes, a fatalistic view of the world, and in extreme cases, socio-pathic characteristics.

When the Environment is Socially Toxic

The surrounding neighborhood for at-risk youths is characterized by the presence of gangs, drugs, and violence. In these neighborhoods, joining a gang can be a form of protection for youth. The community tends to be socially disorganized, featuring high mobility, poverty, welfare-dependency, and single-parent households.[26]

At-risk youth tend to come from dysfunctional families. Single-parent households contribute to a socially disorganized environment. Lack of parental role models, parental drug abuse, and a criminal model in the home negatively influence children. Gang members are often victims of abuse and neglect; abused and neglected girls are twice as likely to be arrested as juveniles.[27]

Children and adolescents growing up in situations of chronic danger from community violence, domestic violence, and interpersonal conflict face developmental challenges and increased health and educational risk.[28] Trends in urban violence and victimization suggest that youth are especially vulnerable. Though violent crime rates have been dropping over the past 10 years, the 1990s were devastating years for youth residing in the inner cities of America. In 1992, for example, 1 in 13 juveniles was a victim of a violent crime, a rate twice that found in the general population.[29] Although children are clearly at risk for being victims of violent encounters, as they transition into adolescence their risk steadily increases, with the victimization rate peaking between the ages of 16 and 19.[30] Youth are the most vulnerable age group with respect to violence, and African Americans experience an extremely disproportionate rate of victimization. Although African Americans constituted less than 15 percent of the U.S. population in 1992, half (50%) of all homicide victims in the United States were African American.[31] Homicide is the leading cause of death for black males between the ages of 14 and 44, with the majority of adolescent homicide victims killed by guns.[32] The trends are similar for nonfatal assaults. In 1992, African Americans were victims of robbery and aggravated assault at two to three times the rate of whites.[33] Inner-city African American adolescents may be the most vulnerable of all. Carl Bell, in a study of high school–aged youth residing in an impoverished Chicago neighborhood, reported that nearly one-quarter of teenagers in his sample had witnessed a shooting.[34] Another survey found that 45 percent of inner-city high school students had been threatened with a gun or had been shot at, and that one-third have been beaten up traveling to and from school.[35] Evidence suggests that exposure to severe violence in childhood and adolescence is correlated with drinking, drug use, fighting, carrying a weapon, and trouble in school.[36] A Harris poll from 1996 found that one in eight youths carries a weapon for protection.[37]

There is reason to be cautiously optimistic, as the adolescent homicide statistics have declined steadily in recent years. From 1995 to 2002, the firearm homicide rates for black and Hispanic males declined substantially, from 101 to 48 per 100,000 for black males, and from 47 to 22 per 100,000 for Hispanic males.[38]

Peer Group and Protection

Along with neighborhood and family influences, the peer group is a significant factor influencing at-risk youth. Sustained interaction with antisocial youth is a key indicator for future gang affiliation. Socialized on the street, youth develop a tough, street-smart attitude. A strong affiliation to delinquent peers who use or distribute drugs is typical of urban at-risk youth. However, these peers are not necessarily reliable and dependable friends. In fact, it is not unusual to hear urban youth reporting a pervasive sense of distrust of their peers. This lack of trust is expressed in the marked distinction urban youth make between friends and associates. The less intimate term, *associates*, has arisen in some youth circles to describe the members of one's social network. Weak emotional attachments coincide with a perception of the world as unstable and unpredictable. "I don't have friends, only associates," is a phrase commonly used by both boys and girls to describe peers in their social network.

In an effort to feel safer by having a dependable group of youth to back them up when threatened, some youth turn to relatives for support, while others turn to gangs for protection. Eddie,[39] a small, rather unassuming youth, discusses his thoughts about joining a gang for protection:

Michael
Axelman (MA):   Do you worry about gangs?
Eddie (E):   Not in my neighborhood, like around the corner in another neighborhood, yeah.
MA: Do you think you'll ever join a gang?
E: I doubt it.
MA: Have you been approached, have you thought about joining?
E: Kind of, I hang with them a lot, but I ain't, in none of the gangs. I hang with a lot of different gangs. Like my cousin's in a different gang.
MA: What gang is he in?
E: One of my cousins is a Gangster Disciple, and my brother is a Stone [Black P Stone].

MA: Does your brother want you to join the Stones?

E: Not really. My other cousin's a Stone.

MA: What are some of the advantages and disadvantages of joining the gangs?

E: Like, say you get into it with somebody and they go get a lot of people they know. But you ask somebody to help and they like, "We ain't got nothing to do with that." But if you're in a gang, you know you could ask for their help, and you know they'll help. You know when you're in a gang or something, you're more than good friends, y'all like brothers or something.

MA: Is that appealing to you, to get that kind of help?

E: Yeah sometimes.

MA: How about the disadvantages? What do you think the problems are?

E: Like, the police mess with you all the time. It's like you hang around, the police come around and start just searching people for no reason. You'll probably get shot at, chased. You can't go in other neighborhoods.

MA: Well, now that you're not in any gang, do you feel like you can go into any neighborhood?

E: Not really. 'Cause they'll probably think you're in a gang. 'Cause it's if you walk in their neighborhood, and you're not in their gang, you know, they'll think you're, in the opposing gang, the opposite gang to them. And they'll try to jump on you. To me, let me tell you, I don't know. I might go in a gang, 'cause what's the sense? You can't go nowhere without somebody thinking you're in a gang. You're gonna get chased, jumped on, regardless, so you [might as well] have somebody in your corner. You know, you go in somebody else's neighborhood and you ain't nothing. They're still gonna jump on you.

MA: So you think maybe this summer you might join one, huh?

E: Uh huh.

MA: Which one do you think you're gonna join?

E: Um, probably the Stones like my brother.

Eddie is not alone. Protection is frequently cited by youth as the reason they joined a gang. Eddie resisted the temptation to join gangs until the 10th grade, but his reasons for staying out of the gangs appear now to be outweighed by the perceived benefits of joining. After enduring nearly two years of intimidation and aggression from peers who are in gangs, along with encounters with the police who assume that he is a gang member, Eddie seems to have had enough. Even though he is not in a gang, his movement through South Side Chicago[40] neighborhoods is compromised because when he enters certain neighborhoods, the youth who control the block will "probably think [he] is in a gang." As Eddie notes at the end of the excerpt, "You're gonna get chased, jumped on regardless, so you [might as well] have somebody in your corner." The youths' perspective on joining gangs is at odds with school staff and law enforcement, who view gang symbols and gang membership unequivocally as a form of intimidation.[41]

Economics

In addition to the sociological factors, potential gang members are also motivated by economic factors. Young inner-city residents are limited by both poor education and limited skills training near to home. Entry-level jobs are often located outside economically distressed inner-city neighborhoods, and these jobs offer little more than minimum wage. Participation in a drug gang's economy is enticing. At the lowest level of involvement, foot soldiers can earn up to and above minimum wage by selling drugs. More so than this immediate opportunity, is the chance to progress up the hierarchical ladder. At the higher levels of gang involvement, members earn far more than any comparable job.[42] Along with the glamour attached to gang life, the possibility of higher profits motivates lower-level members to participate in the drug economy despite risks of incarceration, injury, and death.

THE SOCIOCULTURAL LANDSCAPE OF THE INNER CITY

The Social Context

The inner city has been identified as a difficult context for development.[43] The disappearance of employment opportunities and the traditional family headed by a married couple has become a characteristic feature of the inner-city ghetto.[44] Social and psychological problems abound in families, neighborhoods, and schools struggling with limited resources and depleted spirit.

William Julius Wilson, in his widely cited book, *When Work Disappears*,[45] discussed the decline of social organization as one explanation for the rise in social problems in the inner-city ghettos. Social organization is associated with the ability of residents to maintain effective social control and realize common values:

[N]eighborhood social organization depends on the extent of local friendship ties, the degree of social cohesion, the level of resident participation in formal and informal voluntary associations, the density and stability of formal organizations, and the nature of informal social controls.[46]

Wilson posits a relationship between high rates of unemployment and the organization of family and community life. His research suggests that neighborhoods plagued with high levels of joblessness and poverty are more likely to experience problems with social organization, family stability, and marital commitment. Work anchors and organizes life with a system of concrete expectations and goals. Along with providing a way to make a living and to support one's family, work also constitutes the framework for daily behavior and patterns of interaction because of the discipline and regularities it imposes on a life. Youth reared in families and neighborhoods plagued by persistent unemployment frequently lack role models living structured lives. Without a sense of cohesion and stability in everyday life, the ability to plan one's future and set realistic goals is significantly diminished. In sum, the high rates of joblessness and endemic poverty that plague ghetto neighborhoods significantly affect the social context of the inner city.

Elijah Anderson, an urban sociologist who has conducted extensive ethnographic research in Chicago[47] and Philadelphia,[48] has examined the values and codes of families and individuals living in the inner city. He reports that the inner city is composed of two distinct family orientations—the "decent," and the "street." Anderson characterizes the vast majority of families living in the inner city as sharing mainstream values. These values include hard work, education, and the maintenance of a positive mental attitude and a spirit of cooperation. Most residents endorse the mainstream values associated with child rearing, honesty, and hard work. However, despair, poverty, and joblessness have spawned an "oppositional" culture—"the street"—whose norms and values are often at odds with those of mainstream society. "Street-oriented" parents tend to resolve disputes through verbal and physical aggression, and even young children from these homes perceive the world to be unpredictable, uncaring, and violent.[49] These children frequently experience a disorienting discrepancy between the expectations of home and street life, and the more mainstream values that characterize the school environment. This is especially true of aggressive behavior that is seen as necessary for survival, or at least for the preservation of manhood and respect.[50]

The violent and unpredictable life circumstances that many inner-city teens face on a daily basis shape the perception of both youth and adults concerning the nature of successful developmental outcomes. The commonality and unpredictability of violence can lead to preoccupying vigilance accompanied by blunted emotional reactivity,[51] as well as a host of stress-related disorders.[52]

The Code of the Streets

The "street" is the primary mode of socialization for youth residing in the inner-city ghetto who lack a stable, structured family life organized by mainstream values. A particular aspect of this local cultural milieu has been referred to by Anderson as, "the code of the street."[53] The code revolves around the presentation of self. Inner-city peer culture in adolescence to a large extent is organized around suspicion of others. Support from peers is not expected, and blood and fictive kin, and at times fellow gang members, are seen as the only reliable sources of peer support. Folk beliefs about "making it" in school and on the streets highlight independence and self-reliance.[54]

An important requirement is the display of a certain predisposition to violence. In public, one must send a convincing message to the next person that one is capable of taking care of oneself and will engage in violence when necessary. When possible, one must avoid appearing weak, ineffectual, or cowardly.

Gang affiliation or lack of affiliation in many ways defines who you are as a person on the streets. In Chicago for example, it is not uncommon to hear gang-affiliated youth referring to one another with phrases like "he GD," or "no man, he Folk." Gangs in Chicago traditionally belong to one of two alliances, Brothers or Folks. Both alliances were established in the 1980s in the penitentiary system by incarcerated gang members, seeking protection by forming coalitions. There are many symbols the gangs use to distinguish themselves as Brothers and Folks, but the two most common are the star symbol and the way in which members wear their baseball caps or hats. The five-pointed star is used by the Brothers and the six-pointed star represents the Folks. The symbols are displayed on gold rings, necklaces, and earrings as well on tattoos on the upper arms and calves. Brothers cock their hats to the left, while the Folks wear their hats to the right.

Males who are not affiliated with street gangs are called Neutrons. "Neutron" implies group affiliation through nonmembership, and street-oriented males who are not in gangs use the term frequently when asked about their status. Neutrons by definition are not involved with the selling of drugs and consequently lack the money to buy name brand clothes and fancy jewelry. They have only one defining characteristic: they do not cock their hats in either direction. When I asked Larry, who is a Neutron, about whether he was concerned about wearing a baseball cap he said emphatically, "not really, I just keep it straight. I make sure that it's straight!"

Culture of Respect

The norms and values that frame the world for these youth are embedded, to a large extent, in the code of the street. At the heart of this code is the issue of respect.[55] Respect involves being treated right and being granted the deference one deserves.[56] Respect and associated behaviors are inseparable from the way in which adolescents attribute meaning to the world, and it underpins face-to-face encounters, on all levels of interaction.

A standard way of augmenting one's respect is to challenge other's status and "win." In the following excerpt, an 18-year-old former gang member discusses the importance of "proving yourself," and maintaining your respect on the streets:

MA: How about proving yourself? You told me you had to prove your-
             self. Now is that part of being on the streets?

Nick (N):   Yea, see prove yourself, you know you gotta. Somebody gonna
             try you. You know somebody gonna say you a punk mark and
             all this and they gonna want to kick your butt. And you gotta
             prove yourself, you know that you ain't no punk and stand your
             ground.

MA: . . . So everybody, whether you are in gangs, whether you are not
             in gangs, you have to give people the message [interruption].

N: You ain't no hole, you ain't no punk, and you're gonna stand for
             what's yours and you ain't gonna let nobody take that down.

Although this type of posturing is especially important in relations between gangs and within gangs, it is also central to interactions that are not directly affiliated with gang life. On the streets, to engage in violence is respected, and having respect is essential for, and interconnected with, the expression of power. The following excerpt with the same former gang member makes clear how violence for reputation is connected with violence as an expression of brute force, power.

MA: But you said you participated in some drive-bys. What was the reason
             for those?

N: Just to build my name up. I ain't gonna lie. That's so people say, "Yeah,
             he went out and shot some somebody man, that nigga's cold. Don't
             mess with him."

MA: So it wasn't like you were shooting somebody over drugs or turf?

N: Just to go out and do it?

MA: It was a random person?

N: Yeah. Just to, you know, just to get the feeling, put a gun in your hand
             and shoot it.

MA: How did it feel when you did it?

N: I was amazed by it. I ain't gonna lie. The first time I shot a gun . . . , you
             might get a little trigger happy. You might want to go and shoot some
             more people, you know what I am saying. And once you get the feel
             for it, it's amazing, like you never felt nothing that powerful in your
             hand in your whole life. And when you shoot it you get this tense jerk

back, and you know you like, I got the power in my hand. Just like, if you seen the movie *Juice.*

It is important to emphasize that this youth, who was 16 years old at the time of this particular shooting, engaged in random drive-by shootings both as a means of conveying his sense of power and as a relational strategy in the service of self-preservation. His intent was to send the message—back off—to others whom he felt were encroaching on his turf. He wanted others to know that he was capable of these types of acts.

In this narrative excerpt, we see the way in which particular behaviors, especially violent behaviors, are both a response to and a re-creation of the social disorganization of the neighborhood and the unpredictability that characterizes street culture. Violence in the service of self-preservation has a destabilizing effect on the community, and it often results in the re-creation of violence and unpredictability.

The Psychology of Dissin'

The word "diss" is used frequently by street-oriented youth. It is derived from the word *disrespect* and it often used as a verb. For instance, one may say: "don't diss me," or "don't be dissin' me." To diss is to violate or insult one's status or personhood, and these violations are perceived to have a zero-sum quality.[57] That is, if someone gains in respect, others are diminished. Dissing ranges from an outright threat of physical violence to more subtle, but no less threatening, forms of eye work such as staring someone down.

What follows is an excerpt from a 15-year-old gang member, who was thrown out of high school for fighting and eventually enrolled in an alternative school. The discussion begins with him talking about the problems he has had avoiding fights at school:

MA:	What do you think is going to happen in your new school?
Jack (J):	I could see myself in that school, probably having a fight, which I don't want to do.
MA:	What if you decide not to fight, what happens?
J:	You're beat up.
MA:	You'll get beat up. So you have to defend [yourself]?
J:	Right. Like the same situation I got kicked out of South Side High. Having to defend myself.
MA:	So it's really is the school's fault because you don't have a safe environment to get an education in, that's what you're telling me.
J:	Right. It shouldn't be like that.

MA: You have to watch your back.

J: It shouldn't be like that.

MA: Every day?

J: Yeah, shouldn't be like that.

MA: But I . . . who's at fault? Letting the school get like that?

J: I can't really blame it on the school. The people who's supposed to be doing things, but they got they minds somewhere else, so.

MA: Why would somebody want to beat you up at school?

J: Probably jealousy.

MA: Jealous about what?

J: Yeah, um, I'm not sure.

MA: So if somebody wants to beat you up, a lot of times you don't even know why?

J: Ain't gotta be doing nothing, you ain't gotta say nothing, just "Why" you know, like, "Why you looking at me so hard?" Then that's that right there.

MA: And if somebody said that to you what would you say to them?

J: Hey, you got a right to look where you want to, really. As long as I ain't disrespecting you, you shouldn't have a problem with it.

MA: Can you disrespect somebody just by looking at 'em?

J: Yeah. I say you can.

MA: And how would you do that?

J: I don't really know, it's you know how a person look at you. Like, look you up and down like. You know. And shaking their head and then that would be disrespecting.

To be "dissed" is an extremely humiliating experience for urban youth. These encounters involving the "theft" of one's pride are emotionally painful, and youth attempt to avoid these encounters at all cost. The notion of respect and associated behaviors are inseparable from the way in which adolescents attribute meaning to the world and underpin face-to-face encounters on all levels of interaction.

A diss encounter may involve taking something of material value from another (i.e., gym shoes, jewelry, jackets), but also involves an immaterial theft of someone's pride. Pride is often the primary motivation for dissing another person. Diss encounters are anchored on the shame-pride axis and involve stealing one's pride through shaming. These aggressive interpersonal encounters are extremely humiliating and are avoided by inner-city youth at all costs.

Research on emotions from clinical psychology indicates that when one is publicly shamed, he or she is thrust into an extremely unpleasant emotional state.[58] One's history of prior experiences with shame, and the meaning one attaches to these painful moments, determine the intensity and duration of one's embarrassment.[59] Four defensive scripts that represent strategies for dealing with shame have been identified: withdrawal from the situation, avoidance of affect, attacks directed towards the self, and attacks directed towards the other.[60] Although each of these scripts affects interpersonal relations in important ways, attacks directed towards the other, which involve the transformation of shame into rage, are particularly damaging to community relations because these externalizing responses perpetuate the shaming process. An individual who employs this strategy purges unwanted, negative affects by transforming shame into rage and then "infecting" another person. The shame-rage cycle toxifies community relations, with one shaming encounter leading to another.

IMPLICATIONS FOR ADOLESCENT DEVELOPMENT

Peer Group as Parent

Erik Erikson's theory of psychosocial development[61] has provided an important framework for understanding the role of adolescence within the life course. Adolescence, the developmental period between childhood and adulthood, is marked by significant physical and psychological changes. During adolescence, along with coming to terms with the hormonal and physical changes associated with puberty, youth are confronted with identity formation as the central developmental task. While engaged in this psychosocial process, youth become increasingly focused on questions related to self-definition. Identity formation is a complex developmental process composed of multiple psychological, sociocultural, and intrapsychic components. Experimenting with one's persona, and determining whether it brings affirmation or denigration from others, is a typical emotional experience for the adolescent preoccupied with the challenge of identity formation.[62] Adult role models are among the most important social components for adolescents.[63]

The quest for self-definition does not take place in a social vacuum. The search for the answer to the question, "who am I?" involves experimenting with a variety of identities. This search is embedded in particular sociocultural contexts.[64] The creation of one's identity happens locally, and is significantly influenced by three social institutions: the family, the secondary school, and the peer group.[65] The family is the chief socializing influence on adolescents, and parental expectations and evaluations play and important role in shaping the adolescent's search for self-definition. Adolescents who are further along in identity formation are more likely to have parents who encourage self-assertion and freedom to disagree, while at the same time encouraging connectedness to the family.[66] Frequent interaction with a parental role model seems to positively affect the intellectual and social maturation of adolescents.[67] However, although the family plays a critical role in the development of adolescents, typi-cal teens spend a significant portion of their time, almost three and half hours a day, at home without parents or other adults present.[68]

Evidence suggests that inner-city adolescents may be even more estranged from their parents than suburban teenagers. When questioned, inner-city youth had difficulty identifying significant role models in their lives.[69] Though the youth in Darling and colleagues' study expressed strong affection for family members, nearly half of his sample reported no significant role model iden-tifications. In addition, inner-city youth have less positive identification with parents, especially fathers. Fewer than a third of inner-city African American adolescents mentioned their father as a positive source of influence on their lives, and an almost equal number characterized their father's influence as largely negative or indifferent.[70] Considering the lack of positive identifications with fathers in inner-city families, adult males outside of the family play a par-ticularly important role.

Increasing attention has been placed on school and community influences on adolescent development, and on the potentially ameliorative properties of adolescents' relations outside of the family.[71] Schools serve an important social function by bringing adolescents into daily and sustained contact with adults outside of the family. Studies on resiliency suggest that relationships with teachers have the potential to buffer youth from stress, as well as provide them with essential role models.[72] However, research suggests that social support and role models available to urban youth may be limited. Shortages of minor-ity teachers may detrimentally affect minority youth's attempts to forge stable identities.[73]

The peer group also has a major impact on the adolescent socialization pro-cess. Peers serve as a reference point for adolescents to compare their emerg-ing sense of competence in a variety of psychosocial, intellectual, and physical areas. Within the peer group, the adolescents test their developing identities and their evolving sense of independence and autonomy.[74] The important role of the peer group for low-income youth has been noted by a number of researchers.[75] The increased value of peer relationships in urban settings has been linked to the breakdown of the traditional family and the subsequent loss of parental authority,[76] and to the collapse of mentor/protégé relationships in the inner city.[77]

Elijah Anderson, in his urban ethnography, *Streetwise*, discusses the collapse of nonparental adult-adolescent relationships in African American communi-ties in the inner city.[78] He reports the disappearance of particular adult male role models, old heads, who provided guidance and advice to urban black youth. He describes the "old head" as a man who was employed in a stable job and was strongly committed to family life. His role in the community was to socialize young men to meet their community and family responsibilities.

> The old head was a kind of guidance counselor and moral cheerleader who preached anti-crime and anti-trouble messages to his charges. Encouraging boys to work and make something of themselves, he would try to set a good example by living, as best he could, a stable, decent, worry-free life.[79]

The reasons for the collapse of this mentor/protégé relationship are complex and involve many sociological and economic factors. However, one thing is certain: the breakdown of this relationship has had a devastating impact on urban black families, especially on inner-city youth.

For African American youth, successfully completing the tasks associated with adolescent development has often been problematic due to a complex set of sociocultural and historical forces that often inhibit success.[80] Due to the stress and poverty associated with inner-city life, it is not uncommon for inner-city youth to reach adolescence with a basic mistrust for their environment; mistrust that contributes significantly to role confusion and doubts about their ability to make it in the world.[81] Self-doubt and lack of trust in others make the process of identity consolidation problematic. This is compounded for many inner-city boys who must engage in the process of identity formation with minimal or no positive adult male role models.[82]

Psychological Sense of Belonging

Through gang involvement, youths are able to believe in something greater than themselves and to achieve a sense of belonging. Each gang community has its own name—the Latin Kings, Aryan Nation, Conservative Vice Lords, and Gangster Disciples, to name a few. Language and dress distinctively mark each gang, and members may be identified by gangs colors, such as blue or red. A person becomes a member through being "jumped in" by fellow gang members. Youths are personally invested in the gang's activities, and the gang as a whole has influence over its members and determines behavior and activities such as drug sale or turf warfare. As a member progresses up the chain of command, the more that member influences the gang's activity. Thus, members' behavior is also determined by the desire to move up in the gang and gain power.

However, the sense of community in a society offered by a gang fails to provide for the basic needs of disenfranchised urban youth. According to researcher Samuel Sarason, "a sense of community is one of the major bases for self-definition."[83] A sense of community is defined by four elements: membership in the group, influence in the group, fulfillment of need, and shared connection.[84]

Gangs provide a sense of community through the fulfillment of needs not met in the inner city. As a member of a gang, an individual is able to carve out an identity—each person is identified by a different name and establishes respect through their tough behavior. Gang members are rewarded for their actions within the gang community. Honor and humiliation are taken seriously: an attack on a member results in retaliation by the gang. Individuals are rewarded for being tough, and in return are provided a community that offers support and protection—two key elements in the rough environment of the street.

Gang membership is subject to a natural "aging out" process. While 6 percent of youths will continue criminal activity throughout their lifetime, the large majority of juveniles desist in their behavior.[85] As gang members transition into adulthood they have little or no useful life skills. In the past, youths engaged in antisocial behavior would transition to jobs. However, there are notably fewer jobs for delinquent youth to age into as we have shifted into a postindustrial economy with more focus than ever before on cognitive and interpersonal skills.

SOLUTIONS

Providing educational and job training opportunities to disenfranchised neighborhoods has been identified as a key ingredient of successful community programs that aim to reduce gang violence. Gang members frequently lack the skills and educational background to obtain jobs, and with fewer and fewer jobs available, youth are more motivated to join gangs. Thus, the provision of better schools, job and skills training, and a significant increase in job opportunities to urban youth are considered necessary public policy interventions to resolve gang activity.

In *Street Wars*, Thomas Hayden argues that participation in the drug trade and working "McJobs" should not be the standard for urban youth's economic options.[86] Public policy interventions are required to eliminate the delinquent activity of inner-city gangs. Again, focused prevention as opposed to late intervention or suppression has been unanimously approved as the best practice solution.[87] Prevention efforts should begin early, target youth exposed to multiple risk factors, and address all facets of youths' lives.[88] Public policy efforts can be informed through research and evaluation of existent programs. Programs often have short life spans because changes either did not provide a quick solution or because of changing administrative positions and priorities.

Harsh police responses have been found to negatively impact and perpetuate gang violence. Beyond the legal process of incarceration itself, the state of prison life is deplorable. Instead of rehabilitation for inmates and detained youth, guards are known for violent acts towards inmates and fostering intergang rivalry.[89]

The consensus that police suppression is not effective comes from analysis of several programs implemented by law enforcement agencies around the country, such as Operation Hammer by the Los Angeles Police Department and the Flying Squad program by the Chicago Police Department. During a typical weekend under Operation Hammer, 1,000 police officers descend on a small section of south-central Los Angeles. In one weekend, 1,453 arrests were made, half of whom were not gang members. Ultimately, charges were filed against only 32 of those arrested.[90] These types of police practices humiliate and traumatize adolescents and young adults, and further erode the fragile sense of trust that urban youth have in law enforcement.

Another type of program has been implemented by the Bureau of Alcohol, Tobacco and Firearms called Gang Resistance Education and Training (GREAT). This school-based gang prevention curriculum consists of a nine-week course discouraging kids from delinquent and gang behavior. Similar to the Drug Abuse Resistance Education, or DARE program, GREAT uses a cognitive approach to teach alternative methods of solving problems in order to avoid delinquent and violent behavior. This program has now spread throughout schools in 50 states and several other countries.[91]

Policy interventions have also been undertaken by the Bush administration: Project Safe Neighborhoods (PSN) is a federally funded one billion dollar initiative to reduce the use of guns in violent crime.[92] The Boston Reentry Initiative of PSN has had some initial success in assisting violent criminals and former gang members in their transition out of prison.[93]

In addition to public policy efforts, the efficacy of community-based organizations is of notable importance in reducing gang activity and violence. Community building can provide a sense of belonging and respect to youths who have no other option but street culture and can prove effective in reducing gang activity and violence. The program Barrios Unidos is one of the most successful organizations targeted at reducing gang violence. The program has four main principles: to learn constructive self-discipline, to create positive self-image, to develop skills, and to implement skills learned.[94] Community-based economic initiatives such as Westside, a clothing store in Los Angeles, are outgrowths of the Barrios Unidos efforts.

Irving Spergel of the University of Chicago, who has conducted extensive community-based research on the youth gang problem, has concluded that the lack of social opportunities available to teens and young adults in a particular neighborhood and the degree of social disorganization present in a community largely account for its youth gang problem. Spergel has developed the five-part "Comprehensive Gang Model to address these very issues: 1) to mobilize community leaders; 2) reach out to gang-involved youth; 3) provide economic, social, and educational resources; 4) include law enforcement suppression; and

5) facilitate cooperation by community agencies to provide holistic services to youths."[95] Results from the evaluation of the Little Village Gang Violence Reduction Project in Chicago show that the model is effective in lowering crime rates among youth gang members.[96]

Another example is the Boys and Girls Club of America. This organization developed the Gang Prevention Through Targeted Outreach program. It targets youth at risk for gang involvement and seeks to alter their attitudes and perceptions. The approach consists of structured recreational, educational, and life skills programming.[97] It illustrates a key feature of Spergel's recommended approach to gang prevention and intervention: the mobilization of community efforts by community-based agency staff.[98] The consensus of most research and program evaluation is that prevention efforts geared toward at-risk youth is the best-practice solution to dealing with gangs in our society.

Successful measures in community-based solutions to gang violence often include local clergy. Some successful programs were initially started by clergy committed to at-risk youth. In contrast to the Los Angeles Police Department's Anti-gang unit, Operation Hammer, Jesuit priest Gregory Boyle started Jobs for a Future (JFF) in the housing project neighborhoods of Pico Gardens and Aliso Village. There are several organizations within JFF that employ former gang members, such as a bakery. Through this organization, former gang members can have their tattoos removed and receive clothing and training for job interviews.

CONCLUSION

Adolescents coming of age in the impoverished inner cities and rural towns throughout America are at risk to becoming involved in youth gangs. Gang life seemingly offers a ready-made solution to teens living in situations of chronic poverty and danger and struggling with the developmental tasks associated with adolescence. Youth gang membership provides an identity and an intense sense of belonging to a group built upon loyalty and obedience. Though gang membership solves many of the short-term issues faced by disenfranchised teens, these youth frequently lack the basic educational and job skills to succeed in mainstream society. The youth gang problem cannot be solved by scapegoating urban teens. Youth gang violence is a social problem that must be addressed through social solutions.

In order to facilitate the education and development of youth who are at risk for becoming gang members, we need to learn how to best create and maintain positive, trustworthy intergenerational relationships for these youth at home and in school. We also need to find ways to make the social and educational institutions of the inner city more conducive to the forming of these essential relationships. It is only through interactions with caring, healthy, society-minded adults that adolescents can move into adulthood. The developmental and social consequences are grave indeed when the peer group becomes the parent.

NOTES

1. G.D. Curry and S.H. Decker, *Confronting Gangs: Crime and Community* (Los Angeles: Roxbury Publishing Company, 1998).

2. Lou Savelli, "National Gang History," East Coast Gang Investigators Association, 2001, available at http://www.gripe4rkids.org/his.html.

3. Al Valdez, "A History of California's Hispanic Gangs," National Alliance of Gang Investigators Associations, http://www.nagia.org/Hispanic_Gangs.htm.

4. A. Alonso, "Los Angeles Gangs: A Brief History," streetgangs.com, 1999, available at http://www.streetgangs.com/history/history/html.

5. Savelli, "National Gang History."

6. Alonso, "Los Angeles Gangs."

7. Valdez, "California's Hispanic Gangs."

8. W. J. Wilson, *When Work Disappears: The World of the New Urban Poor* (New York: Knopf, 1996).

9. Finn-Aage Esbensen, *Preventing Adolescent Gang Involvement* (Washington, DC: U.S. Department of Justice, Office of Juvenile Justice and Delinquency Prevention, 2000).

10. National Youth Violence Prevention Resource Center, *Youth Gangs* (Washington, DC: National Youth Violence Prevention Resource Center 2002).

11. Larry J. Siegel, Brandon C. Welsh, Joseph J. Senna, and Thomas Wadsworth, *Juvenile Delinquency: Theory, Practice and Law* (Belmont, CA: Wadsworth Publishing, 2003).

12. I. A. Spergel, *The Youth Gang Problem: A Community Approach* (New York: Oxford University Press, 1995).

13. G. David Curry, "Female Gang Involvement," *Journal of Research in Crime and Delinquency* 35 (1998): 100–119.

14. A. Hamid, "Resurgence of drugs/gangs/violence in New York City," unpublished manuscript, New York: John Jay College, 1996.

15. *National Youth Gang Survey, 2002* (Washington, DC: U.S. Department of Justice, Office of Juvenile Justice and Delinquency Prevention, 2002).

16. *National Youth Gang Survey, 1998* (Washington, DC: U.S. Department of Justice, Office of Juvenile Justice and Delinquency Prevention, 1998).

17. Al Valdez. *A History of California's Hispanic Gangs* (National Alliance of Gang Investigators Association, 1998), available at www.gangstyle.com/reality/hisp.php.

18. T. Hayden, *Gangs and the Future of Violence* (New York: New Press, 2004).

19. James C. Howell and Scott H. Decker, *The Youth Gangs, Drugs, and Violence Connection* (Washington, DC: U.S. Department of Justice, Office of Juvenile Justice and Delinquency Prevention, 1999).

20. D. Huinziga, "The Volume of Crime by Gang and Nongang Members," Paper presented at the annual meeting of the American Society of Criminology, November 1997, San Diego, CA, cited in Howell, *Youth Gangs: An Overview*.

21. Howell and Decker, *The Youth Gangs, Drugs, and Violence Connection*.

22. Cited in *National Youth Gang Survey, 1998*.

23. Steven D. Levitt and Sudhir Alladi Venkatesh, "An Economic Analysis of a Drug-Selling Gang's Finances," *Quarterly Journal of Economics* 115, no. 3 (2000): 755–789.

24. U.S. Department of Justice, Office of Juvenile Justice and Delinquency Prevention, *Juvenile Offenders and Victims: 1999 National Report* (Washington, DC: U.S. Department of Justice, Office of Juvenile Justice and Delinquency Prevention, 1999).

25. Thomas Hayden, *Street Wars: Gangs and the Future of Violence* (New York: New Press, 2004), p. 6.

26. W. J. Wilson, *When Work Disappears*.

27. Beth R. Richie, Kay Tsenin, and Cathy Spatz Widom, *Research on Women and Girls in the Justice System* (Washington, DC: U.S. Department of Justice, 2000).

28. J. Garbarino, K. Kostelny, and N. Dubrow, "What Children Can Tell Us about Living in Danger," *American Psychologist* 46 (1991): 376–383; D. Prothrow-Stith and M. Weissman, *Deadly Consequences: How Violence Is Destroying Our Teenage Population and a Plan to Begin Solving the Problem* (New York: HarperCollins, 1991).

29. M. R. Rand, *Guns and Crime* (Washington, DC: U.S. Department of Justice, 1994).

30. A. J. Reiss and J. A. Roth, *Understanding and Preventing Violence* (Washington, DC: National Academy Press, 1993).

31. Federal Bureau of Investigation, *Uniform Crime Rates, 1991* (Washington, DC: Government Printing Office, 1992).

32. D. A. Hamburg, *Today's Children: Creating a Future for a Generation in Crisis* (New York: Times Books, 1994).

33. L. D. Batian, *Criminal Victimization 1992* (Washington, DC: U.S. Department of Justice, 1993).

34. C. Bell, "Preventing Black Homicide," in *The State of Black America 1990*, ed. J. Dewart (New York: National Urban League, 1990) pp. 143–155.

35. J. F. Sheley and J. D. Wright, *Gun Acquisition and Possession in Selected Juvenile Samples* (Washington, DC: U.S. Department of Justice, 1993).

36. E. J. Jenkins and C. C. Bell, "Violence Exposure, Psychological Distress and High Risk Behaviors among Inner-City High School Students," in *Anxiety Disorders in African-Americans*, ed. S. Friedman, (New York: Springer, 1994) pp. 76–88.

37. P. Applebome, "Crime Fear Is Seen Causing Changes in Youth Behavior, *New York Times*, January 12, 1996, p. A12.

38. Centers for Disease Control and Prevention, "FastStats A to Z: Assault/Homicide," (November 14, 2005) available from www.cdc.gov/nchs/faststats/homicide.htm.

39. Pseudonyms have been used to protect the identities of informants. Observations and interviews were conducted by senior author in Chicago between 1993 and 1998.

40. Institutional names have been changed to ensure anonymity.

41. M. Axelman, "The Relational Experiences of African-American Adolescents and the Role of Signicant Adults: An Examination of Teenage Lives during the Transition to High School," Ph.D. dissertation, University of Chicago, 1999; abstract in *Dissertation Abstracts International*, publ. nr. (9951758).

42. Levitt and Venkatesh, "Drug-Selling Gang's Finances."

43. J. Garbarino, *Raising Children in a Socially Toxic Environment* (San Francisco: Jossey-Bass, 1995); M. W. McLaughlin, M. A. Irby, and J. Langman, *Urban Sanctuaries: Neighborhood Organizations in the Lives and Futures of Inner-City Youth* (San Francisco: Jossey-Bass, 1994).

44. Wilson, *When Work Disappears.*

45. Wilson, *When Work Disappears.*

46. Wilson, *When Work Disappears,* p. 3.

47. E. Anderson, *A Place on the Corner* (Chicago: University of Chicago Press, 1978).

48. E. Anderson, *Streetwise: Race, Class, and Change in an Urban Community* (Chicago: University of Chicago Press, 1990).

49. E. Anderson, *The Code of the Street: Decency, Violence, and the Moral Life of the Inner-City* (New York: Norton, 1999).

50. Anderson, *The Code of the Street*; Prothrow-Stith and Weissman, *Deadly Consequences.*

51. Garbarino, Kostelny, and Dubrow, "What Children Can Tell Us."

52. C. Bell, "Stress-Related Disorders in African-American Children," *Journal of the National Medical Association* 89, no. 5 (1997): 335–340.

53. Anderson, *The Code of the Street*; Prothrow-Stith and Weissman, "What Children Can Tell Us."

54. E. Anderson, "The Code of the Streets," *Atlantic Monthly* 273 (1994): 80–94;. P. Bourgois, *In Search of Respect: Selling Crack in El Barrio* (Cambridge: Cambridge University Press, 1995).

55. Anderson, "The Code of the Streets."

56. Anderson, "The Code of the Streets."

57. Axelman, "Relational Experiences of African-American Adolescents."

58. H. B. Lewis, *Shame and Guilt in Neurosis* (New York: International University Press, 1971).

59. D. L. Nathanson, "The Shame-Pride Axis," in *The Role of Shame in Symptom Formation*, ed. H. B. Lewis (Hillsdale, NJ: Erlbaum, 1987) pp. 183–205; Nathanson, *Shame and Pride.*

60. Nathanson, *Shame and Pride.*

61. E. H. Erikson, *Identity and the Life Cycle* (New York: Norton, 1959); E. H. Erikson, *Identity: Youth and Crisis* (New York: Norton, 1968).

62. S. Harter, "Developmental Differences in the Nature of Self Understanding," *Cognitive Therapy and Research* 14 (1990): 113–142.

63. Erikson, *Identity: Youth and Crisis*.

64. D. P. Swanson and M. B. Spencer, "Developmental and Cultural Context Considerations for Research on African-American Adolescents," in *Children of Color: Research, Health, and Policy Issues*, ed. H. E. Fitzgerald, B. M. Lester, and B. S. Zuckerman, (New York: Garland, 1999) pp. 53–72.

65. C. C. Lee, "Adolescent Development," in *Nurturing Young Black Males*, ed. R. B. Mincy, (Washington, DC: Urban Institute Press, 1994) pp. 33–41.

66. C. R. Cooper, H. D. Grotevant, and S. M. Condon, "Individuality and Connectedness in the Family as a Context for Adolescent Identity Formation and Role-Taking Skill," in *Adolescent Development in the Family*, ed. H. D. Grotevant and C. R. Cooper (San Francisco: Jossey-Bass, 1983) pp. 43–60.

67. M. Csikszentmihalyi, K. Rathunde, and S. Whalen, *Talented Teenagers: The Roots of Success and Failure* (New York: Cambridge University Press, 1993).

68. M. Csikszentmihlyi and J. Schmidt, "Stress and Resilience in Adolescence: An Evolutionary Perspective," in *The Adolescent Years: Social Influences and Educational Challenges*, ed. K. Borman and B. Schneider, (Chicago: University of Chicago Press, 1998) Part 1, pp. 1–17.

69. R. L. Taylor, "Black Youth, Role Models, and the Social Construction of Identity," in *Black Adolescents*, ed. R. L. Jones, (Berkeley, CA: Cobb and Henry, 1989) pp. 155–171.

70. Taylor, "Black Youth."

71. N. Darling, S. F. Hamilton, and S. Niego, "Adolescents' Relations with Adults outside the Family," in *Personal Relationships during Adolescence*, ed. R. Montemayor, G. R. Adams, and T. P. Gullotta (Thousand Oaks, CA: Sage, 1994) pp. 216–235.

72. E. Werner, "Resilience in Development," *Current Directions in Psychological Science, American Psychological Society* 4, no. 5 (1995): 81–85.

73. D. P. Swanson, M. B. Spencer, and A. Petersen, "Identity Formation in Adolescence," in *The Adolescent Years: Social Influences and Educational Challenges*, ed. K. Borman and B. Schneider, (Chicago: University of Chicago Press, 1998) Part 1, pp. 18–41.

74. Erikson, *Identity: Youth and Crisis*.

75. U. Bronfenbrenner, *Two Worlds of Childhood* (New York: Russell Sage Foundation, 1970); Taylor, "Black Youth."

76. Taylor, "Black Youth."

77. Anderson, *Streetwise*.

78. Anderson, *Streetwise*.

79. Anderson, *Streetwise*, p. 69.

80. J. T. Gibbs, "Black Adolescents and Youth: An Update on an Endangered Species," in *Black Adolescents*, ed. R. L. Jones, (Berkeley, CA: Cobb and Henry, 1989) pp. 3–28.

81. Lee, "Adolescent Development."

82. Lee, "Adolescent Development"; Taylor, "Black Youth."

83. S. B. Sarason, *The Psychological Sense of Community: Prospects for a Community Psychology* (San Francisco: Jossey-Bass, 1974).

84. D. W. McMillan and D. M. Chavis, "Sense of Community: A Definition and Theory," *American Journal of Community Psychology*, 14, no. 1 (1986): 6–23.

85. Siegel, Welsh, and Senna, *Juvenile Delinquency*, p. 45.

86. Hayden, *Street Wars*, p. 72.

87. Howell and Decker, *The Youth Gangs, Drugs, and Violence Connection*.

88. K. G. Hill, C. Lui, and J. D. Hawkins, *Early Precursors of Gang Membership: A Study of Seattle Youth* (Washington, DC: U.S. Department of Justice, Office of Juvenile Justice and Delinquency Prevention, 2001).

89. Hayden, *Street Wars*, p. 42.

90. M. W. Klein, *The American Street Gang* (New York: Oxford University Press, 1995); Esbensen, *Preventing Adolescent Gang Involvement*.

91. (http://www.great-online.org/).

92. http://www.projectsafeneighborhoods.gov/.

93. Department of Corrections Advisory Council, "Mentors Help Reduce Recidivism," (Boston: Department of Corrections Advisory Council, 2005).

94. Hayden, *Street Wars*, p. 72.

95. Spergel, *The Youth Gang Problem*.

96. I. A. Spergel, S. F. Grossman, K. M. Wa, S. Choi, and A. Jacob, *Evaluation of the Little Village Gang Violence Reduction Project: The First Three Years, Executive Summary* (Chicago: Illinois Criminal Justice Information Authority, 1999).

97. Esbensen, *Preventing Adolescent Gang Involvement*.

98. I. A. Spergel, R. Chance, K. Ehrensaft, T. Regulus, C. Kane, R. Laseter, A. Alexander, and S. Oh, *Gang Suppression and Intervention: Community Models* (Washington, DC: U.S. Department of Justice, Office of Juvenile Justice and Delinquency Prevention, 1994); Howell, *Youth Gangs: An Overview*.

Chapter 7

Substance Abuse among Adolescents

Steve Sussman, Silvana Skara, and Susan L. Ames

Substance abuse and dependence are among the most prevalent causes of adolescent morbidity and mortality in the United States.[1] Adolescent substance abusers experience numerous social, academic, physical, and legal consequences[2] (e.g., problems at school, truncated development). Substance-dependent adolescents endure additional problems such as drug tolerance effects, withdrawal symptoms, and preoccupation with drug use to the exclusion of other activities. At present there is a paucity of systematic research on adolescent substance abuse and dependence.[3,4] This chapter provides a review that synthesizes major aspects of the recent scientific literature on adolescent substance abuse and dependence. This chapter is divided into four sections. The first section begins by discussing distinctions between substance use, abuse, and dependence. This section then includes a brief review of differences between adolescent and adult substance abuse. Next, data are presented regarding the current trends in substance abuse among adolescents, including the prevalence of the different types of drugs. Then, the many consequences of drug use are briefly discussed, followed by a summary of the correlates or predictors of adolescent substance abuse and dependence disorders, as well as treatment outcomes. The second section of the chapter presents various assessment methods available to diagnose adolescent substance abuse and dependence. This section discusses separately the assessments of alcohol abuse and abuse of other drugs.

The third section of the chapter briefly discusses prevention and then provides a more in-depth presentation of treatment approaches. Specifically, it provides a brief discussion of the key elements of effective adolescent substance abuse and dependence treatment programs, addresses the important issue of the individuals' motivation to enter or remain in a treatment program, provides descriptions of the primary treatment modalities currently being implemented among adolescents, and provides a summary of studies that have contrasted or evaluated the various treatments. This section also presents information on other potentially useful treatment options for adolescents and provides information on recovery and relapse prevention. Finally, the fourth section of the chapter examines future potential directions and needs for more effective programming in the treatment of substance abuse and dependence among adolescents.

SUBSTANCE USE, ABUSE, AND DEPENDENCE

Substances of Abuse

The term *substance*, when defined in the context of substance abuse and dependence, refers to substances that are taken into the body, have a direct or indirect effect on the central nervous system, are not used as prescribed by a professional, and may lead to various negative consequences for the drug user. The American Psychiatric Association's *Diagnostic and Statistical Manual of Mental Disorders* (fourth edition, text revision)[5] currently ascribes substance abuse to the following 10 classes of substances: (1) alcohol; (2) amphetamines (including "crystal meth," amphetamine-like substances found in appetite suppressants, and medications used in the treatment of attention deficit and hyperactivity disorder [ADHD]); (3) cannabis (including marijuana and hashish); (4) cocaine (including "crack"); (5) hallucinogens (including LSD, mescaline, and MDMA ["ecstasy"]); (6) inhalants (including compounds found in gasoline, glue, and paint thinners); (8) opioids (including morphine, heroin, codeine, methadone, oxycodone [OxyContin (TM)]); (9) phencyclidine (including PCP, "angel dust," ketamine); (9) sedative, hypnotic, and anxiolytic (antianxiety) substances (including benzodiazepines such as valium, barbiturates, prescription sleeping medications, and most prescription antianxiety medications); and (10) other substances (this category permits recording new or other substances). Nicotine and polysubstance use are referred to when substance dependence is diagnosed. Caffeine has also been identified as a substance in this context; however, currently there is insufficient evidence to establish whether caffeine-related symptoms constitute substance abuse and dependence. As indicated, substances of abuse may be widely available substances such as alcohol or glue, over-the-counter drugs, or prescription medications. In many cases, the substance of abuse may have been legal and even medically prescribed for the user; however, abuse occurs when the pattern of use diverges from use as intended or prescribed.

Definition of Substance Use, Abuse, and Dependence

Substances are widely used by adolescents as a means of enjoyment, independence, rebellion, instant gratification, escape, or self-medication, or as an effort to belong to a peer group or achieve a desired adult-like identity.[6] Substance use by adolescents may follow certain progressive patterns, for example, as delineated by the gateway drug theory.[7] Generally, alcohol and tobacco, followed by marijuana, are the first drugs of abuse that young people experiment with or use. If use of the gateway drugs continues, cocaine, hallucinogens, inhalants, and black-market prescription medications are likely to be used next. Research on substance-use onset trajectories has also indicated some interesting findings regarding use of multiple gateway drugs, including data that suggest that use of both alcohol and tobacco is more likely to lead to other substance use, as opposed to use of alcohol only, and experimental use of tobacco but not alcohol (in the seventh grade) may accelerate the initiation and progression of other substance use, as measured one year later.[8] Further, research conducted by Collins and colleagues[9] has shown that caffeine may also be an early step (i.e., gateway) drug because heavy caffeine use has also been shown to be related to a progressive pattern of type of drugs used.

The initiation and progression of substance use may be characterized on a substance use, abuse, and dependence continuum. This continuum begins with initial drug use and may progress to harmful use and addiction, with various problems present along the spectrum. Substance use may be defined as low to moderate use with no social, role-based, environmental, psychological, health, economic, legal, or familial consequences. However, use may be complicated by potential legal consequences (and attempts at concealment) if illicit drugs are involved.

Substance abuse, as defined by the *DSM–IV–TR*,[5] is a maladaptive pattern of substance use leading to clinically significant impairment or distress as manifested in a 12-month period by at least one of the following: (1) recurrent substance use resulting in failure to fulfill major role obligations at work, school, or home (e.g., poor performance at school or work, neglect of children or younger siblings); (2) recurrent substance use in hazardous situations (e.g., driving while intoxicated); (3) recurrent substance-related legal problems (e.g., DUIs); and (4) continued substance use despite having recurrent social or interpersonal problems related to substance use (e.g., arguments with family members about consequences of intoxication).

Substance dependence has been defined by the *DSM–IV–TR* as a maladaptive pattern of substance use leading to clinically significant impairment or distress as manifested in a 12-month period by three or more of the following: (1) tolerance (with repeated use, a person will no longer achieve the same degree of pleasurable effect experienced in the past and must use increasing amounts of the substance to get the same pleasurable effect); (2) withdrawal (when physically dependent on a substance, individuals will develop withdrawal symptoms that cause distress or impairment when use stops or the amount is cut down; the person will continue to use the substance to avoid the withdrawal symptoms); (3) the substance is taken in larger amounts or over a longer period of time than intended; (4) the person experiences a persistent desire or unsuccessful efforts to cut down or control substance use; (5) a great deal of time is spent in activities necessary to obtain the substance, use it, or recover from its effects; (6) important social, occupational, or recreational activities are given up or reduced because of substance use; and (7) the substance use is continued despite knowledge of having a persistent physical or psychological problem that is likely to have been caused or exacerbated by the substance.

Differences between Adolescent and Adult Substance Abuse

The ways in which adolescents differ from adults in the development and expression of substance abuse raises important questions as to whether different criteria should apply to youth than those currently applied to adults. Adolescent substance abuse may differ from adult substance abuse in at least six ways. First, regular use may or may not be considered abuse in adults, whereas it might be considered abuse in youth because of the potential of such use to interfere with brain developmental growth and adjustment tasks.[3,10,11] Conversely, some researchers and practitioners have argued that some substance use represents normal development among teens as they begin to explore different life roles.[12] Second, adolescents may tend to exhibit less physical dependence and fewer physical problems related to use (alcohol, in particular) and consume less overall. Rather, teens may exhibit more binging-type behavior—for example, drinking as much as adults when they do drink, but drinking on fewer occasions and presumably being less prone to blackouts.[3,13–15] On the other hand, adolescents who do begin to drink (or use other drugs) more heavily will tend to become dependent on alcohol (or other drugs) much more quickly than will adults[15] (e.g., less than a year versus over several years).

Third, high-risk situations may differ between adolescents and adults. In particular, adolescents may be more likely to use drugs in situations in which they are not responsible for taking care of others. Fourth, teens may have relatively higher rates of dual diagnosis, that is, comorbidity of substance-use disorders and other mental health disorders.[1] More than half of the youth in treatment for substance-use disorders have other psychopathology in addition to substance-use problems[16,17] (e.g., depressive and anxiety disorders, social phobia, PTSD, conduct disorders, or oppositional defiant disorder). Fifth, teens may be less likely to seek treatment and relapse more quickly than adults do after treatment.[18,19] Finally, adolescents may have a higher likelihood of suffering social consequences specific to adolescence[2,20] (e.g., problems at school, statutory difficulties, truncated development). More systematic research is needed to increase our understanding of the specifics of adolescent substance abuse.

The *DSM–IV–TR* criteria may be less applicable when diagnosing adolescent substance-use disorders than adult substance-use disorders in one other notable way.[12,20,21] The stochastic process of substance abuse to dependence is not clear cut among teens (this may be true of adults too, but to a less extent). For example, an early consequence of teen substance use is the development of tolerance to a drug, a substance-dependence criterion. Another early consequence is excess time spent on getting the drug, using it, and recovering from its effects. Eventually, the young drug user develops social and role consequences, shows unsuccessful efforts to control use, legal consequences, and use in dangerous situations. Even later in the temporal order of consequences, the user exhibits withdrawal symptoms, uses larger amounts over a longer period, important activities are given up, and the user demonstrates continued use despite drug-related problems (e.g., paranoid reactions, leading to hospitalization). This order of symptoms has led some researchers to suggest the "withdrawal gating hypothesis," that is, that a greater weighting on substance abuse dependence given to withdrawal symptoms would preserve the stochastic perspective of abuse to dependence disorders.[22,23]

Currently, only 10 percent of the estimated 1.4 million teens with an illicit drug problem are receiving treatment, compared to 20 percent of adults.[24] In fact, the first systematic investigation of highly regarded treatment programs for teens in the United States has only very recently been conducted.[1] The results of this evaluation indicate that much improvement is needed in existing programs. Given potential differences in the nature of teen versus adult substance abuse disorder, it is also possible that teen-specific substance abuse is currently underestimated in prevalence.

Prevalence of Substance Use and Abuse among Adolescents

Despite recent national data indicating some small and sporadic declines in adolescent use of various substances since the beginning of the last decade (and somewhat larger declines relative to 1980), substances of all types are still being widely used or abused by both younger and older teens in the United States.[25] In 2004, the proportions of 8th, 10th, and 12th graders who reported that they had used an illicit drug in the prior 12 months were 15 percent,

31 percent, and 39 percent, respectively. The proportions that had reported ever trying an illicit drug in their lifetime were 22 percent, 40 percent, and 51 percent, respectively. Marijuana, by far the most widely used illicit drug, showed lifetime rates of 16 percent, 35 percent, and 46 percent, respectively. At the same time, use of stimulants remained widespread, with respective lifetime prevalence rates of 8 percent, 12 percent, and 15 percent for amphetamine use; 3 percent, 5 percent, and 6 percent for methamphetamine use; and 3 percent, 4 percent, and 8 percent for ecstasy use. Prevalence data on opiate use, such as heroin, for example, indicate lifetime rates among 8th, 10th, and 12th graders of 1.6 percent, 1.5 percent, and 1.5 percent, respectively. Rates of use of legal drugs also were rather high among teens. For example, respective lifetime prevalence rates of tobacco use were 28 percent, 41 percent, and 53 percent, while rates of lifetime alcohol use were 44 percent, 64 percent, and 77 percent, and of ever being drunk were 20 percent, 42 percent, and 60 percent, respectively.

According to Tarter,[11] approximately 5 percent of adolescents in the United States qualify for a diagnosis of substance abuse disorder. Among older teens, some studies are finding alarmingly high substance abuse and dependence rates. As examples, within a sample of New Jersey regular high school students ($n = 1044$), 13.4 percent and 3.9 percent of the sample were found to suffer from substance abuse and dependence disorders, respectively,[26] and within a sample of southern California alternative high school students ($n = 1936$), 36.7 percent and 19.1 percent were found to suffer from these disorders.[27]

Consequences of Use

Substance abuse and dependence disorders cross all ages, gender, ethnicities, and educational and socioeconomic status, leaving virtually no group unaffected. Substance use may result in a variety of negative physical, psychological, and social health effects to an individual, and its effects can be acute[6] (resulting from a single dose or a series of doses) or chronic (resulting from long-term use). The toll of drug use can be especially great during adolescence or in young adulthood.[27,28] A multitude of negative consequences may befall substance abusers. First, for example, adverse immediate consequences occur[29] (e.g., overdoses and accidents; the incidence of older adolescent and young adult drinking and driving is double that of the general population). Second, those teenagers who are heavy drug users also tend toward early involvement in family creation, and divorce or unhappiness in these relationships. Third, crimes such as stealing, vandalism, and violence are associated with heavy drug use in adolescence. Fourth, drug-abusing youth are less likely to graduate from high school, or take longer to graduate. Fifth, while these youth tend to earn more money than nonusing same-age peers, they also tend to seek less skilled employment sooner than their peers and job stability is lower. Sixth, drug-using youth are more likely to develop disorganized thinking and unusual beliefs that may interfere with problem-solving abilities and emotional functioning. Seventh, adaptive coping and achievement behavior are lessened. Eight, heavy hard drug use predicts greater social isolation and depression. Finally, drugs of abuse also may lead to health consequences, including cardiovascular complications, lung problems, and digestive or excretory problems.[6]

Substance abuse and dependence may also be viewed as a public health problem with far-ranging health, economic, and adverse social implications. Substance use-related disorders are associated with societal problems such as teen pregnancy and the transmission of sexually transmitted diseases, as well as failure in school, unemployment, homelessness, and crimes such as rape and sexual assault, aggravated assault, burglary, robbery, and homicide. The estimated cost of alcohol-related disorders alone (including health care expenditures, lost productivity, and premature death) in the United States was over $160 billion in 1995.[30]

Correlates or Predictors of Adolescent Substance Abuse and Dependence Disorders

Substance abuse is a multifactorial biopsychosocial process.[6] Consequently, there are multiple factors and causal pathways that influence substance abuse and dependence. Many suspected influences contributing to substance abuse are not easily modified (e.g., genetics, although the future of genetic engineering is promising), whereas other influences are more amenable to change (e.g., peer influence). Several concurrently or prospectively measured influences have been found to be associated with substance abuse and dependence disorders among adolescents. These variables or influences can be categorized as extrapersonal or intrapersonal predictors. Extrapersonal predictors include environmental, cultural, and social influences. These influences are exogenous to the individual (i.e., external to or outside the individual) and include interactions with others in various contexts and locations, as well as the learning of social behaviors from significant others. Some key extrapersonal determinants found to be predictive of substance use among adolescents include environmental variables such as distance from a drug distribution route or neighborhood disorganization,[6,31,32] social variables such as peer substance use,[2,33,34] parental substance abuse,[33,35-38] and family history of psychopathology and conflict.[35,36,39,40]

Intrapersonal predictors or processes contributing to individual differences in substance abuse etiology include physiological susceptibility, as measured in research on genetics[40,41] (e.g., twin studies and investigation of phenotypes), and the affective traits and personality correlates of neurobiological processes; explicit cognitions, including beliefs or expectancies as a motivation to engage in alcohol or other drug use behavior;[42-47] and implicit cognitions, including attentional and behavioral biases influenced by associative learning and memory processes.[48-50]

Intrapersonal influences also include comorbidity variables such as suicidal ideation and depression,[33,51,52] trauma exposure and post-traumatic stress disorder,[38,53] attention-deficit hyperactivity disorder, and conduct disorder. Other trait correlates of neurobiological processes that have been shown to influence substance use initiation and problem consequences from use include impulsivity, sensation seeking, anxiety sensitivity, and aggression.[27,33,40,51,54-57] Additionally, neuropsychological differences (e.g., in attention, executive cognitive function, behavioral self-regulation, and emotional regulation) have been found between teen drug abusers and nonabusers; however, the order of causation is not clear.[40,58] Intrapersonal influences that affect substance abuse likely play a more active role than external influences in explaining why some individuals who use do not go on to abuse or become dependent while others do. Integrative theories of substance abuse and dependence incorporate a variety of influences in an attempt to explain substance use trajectories.

For example, one theoretically based prospective study of the prediction of substance abuse and dependence was conducted by Sussman, Dent, and Leu.[34] These researchers examined one-year prospective predictors of self-reported substance abuse and dependence among a sample of 702 youth at high risk for drug abuse from 21 southern California continuation (alternative) high schools. Triadic influence theory was used as a theoretical guide, from which predictors were selected for assessment.[32] Triadic influence theory attempts to classify experimental drug use into three substantive domains (interpersonal, attitudinal/cultural, and intrapersonal), with differing distances from performance of drug use behavior (ultimate, distal, and proximal). Within the interpersonal domain, ultimate variables include home stress, distal variables include drug use role models, and proximal variables include social-related drug beliefs (e.g., perceived social approval for drug use, estimates of prevalence of drug use). Within the attitudinal/cultural domain, ultimate variables include community disorganization (community stress), distal variables include development of hedonic values or alienation, and proximal variables include expectancies regarding drug use benefits minus costs. Finally, within the intrapersonal domain, ultimate variables include biological temperament (biological stress), distal variables include low self-esteem and poor coping, and proximal variables include refusal self-efficacy and intentions to use drugs.

The Sussman, Dent, and Leu study[34] measured distal and proximal variables of triadic influence theory. Among 13 predictors, a drug use and intention index, and concern that one is or will become an addict or alcoholic, were consistently predictive of self-reported substance abuse or substance dependence one year later, controlling for baseline abuse or dependence status. In addition, baseline substance abuse, white ethnicity, and relatively poor prosocial coping predicted later substance dependence. Apparently, adolescents can predict their future use, and abuse or dependence status. This research also suggests that instruction in prosocial coping (e.g., seeking social support) may help inhibit the transition from substance abuse to substance dependence.

In addition, various other problem behaviors have been found to correlate with and predict substance abuse, including teen gambling[59] (of 97 substance abusers in an outpatient program in Connecticut, 57 percent were classified as social, nonpathological gamblers, and 9 percent were transitioning into pathological gambling), eating disorders,[40] school drop-out,[60] and criminal behavior.[54,60] Also, it has been documented that up to 75 percent of teen substance abusers are also daily cigarette smokers.[61]

Correlates or Predictors of Adolescent Substance Abuse Treatment Outcomes

Treatment outcomes among teens (e.g., 6 months to 12 months posttreatment), which generally have consisted of use of measures of drug use and abuse, and sometimes also quality of family relations, school behavior, or well-being, are affected by pretreatment factors. These pretreatment factors include pretreatment levels of parental substance use (in some studies but not all,[62]) sibling substance use, deviant attitudes, deviant behavior, impulsivity,[63–65] low self-esteem,[66] young age of first use, and multiple drug use,[62,66] but not pretreatment severity of drug abuse. Treatment outcomes are also predicted by comorbidity of substance use disorders and other mental health disorders. Studies on adolescents with both substance use disorders and other mental health disorders have found greater severity of post-treatment drug involvement as well as higher relapse rates.[17,67]

Conversely, having abstinent friends, being socially and academically connected, and being goal-oriented are protective.[64,65] These are very similar to the protective factors that might inhibit the development of substance abuse or dependence, which include relatively high intelligence, problem-solving ability, social skills, high self-esteem, good family relationships, positive role models, and good affect regulation.[40]

Treatment outcomes also are predicted by some treatment factors. These include length of stay (a longer stay predicts better outcomes), degree of parental involvement (more involvement predicts better outcomes), aftercare participation[63] (attendance predicts better outcomes), having a realistic attitude and being able to achieve social support,[68] and ease of post-treatment contact with professionals.[69] Relapse rates appear similar to those of adults.[70]

ASSESSMENTS USED TO DIAGNOSE SUBSTANCE ABUSE AND DEPENDENCE

Several types of assessment methods are available to aid in the diagnosis of substance abuse among adolescents, including examinations of the individual's behavioral and family characteristics, physical findings and complaints, and laboratory tests. Clinically, assessments to determine diagnosis and treatment planning typically rely on an in-depth drug use history and psychiatric and physical examinations. This section reviews the various assessments commonly used, starting with examples of unstructured examinations and interviews, followed by examples from the large inventory of structured assessments. It should be noted that due to the paucity of treatment research among adolescents, many of the structured assessments available for use with this population are adaptations of adult interviews and questionnaires.

Reasons for and Goals of Assessment

There are several circumstances in which adolescents might be assessed for potential drug misuse.[6] These include situations that involve employment in which public safety is paramount (e.g., lifeguards, delivery personnel, driving vehicles, babysitters), obtaining a driver's license, student athletics, sharply worsened school performance, avoidance of social situations and sudden changes in mood, parental suspicion of social problems related to drug use, and individuals with a history of use.

The initial goals in assessment are to determine the nature of an individual's involvement with drugs of abuse and to assess psychological and medical status, psychosocial functioning, social supports, attitudes toward drug use, and motivation for initial abstinence. Detailed information is obtained regarding the individual's drug use history and related consequences, and comorbidity. Questions that might be asked include: Have you taken or tried any drugs? What do you use? How much (quantity)? Do your peers use any drugs? Does your best friend use drugs? Do your parents use drugs? What are your beliefs about drug use and abuse? How did you get into using drugs? How old were you when you first used? Have you experienced any legal or social problems from drug use? What do the drugs do for you? How do they make you feel? Have you ever gone to a psychiatrist or other professional for mental health concerns? Any suicidal or homicidal ideation, or sexual or physical abuse? (Any disclosure of intended physical harm to self or others would need to be reported by the interviewer to the appropriate agency.) How much control do you think you have over your drug use? How long do your using episodes last? What happens? Do you seem to lose control over any other areas of your life? How about gambling? Sex? Spending? Eating? Exercising a lot? Studying or working long hours?[6]

Due to response demand problems, it is helpful to use corroborative methods of assessment, including family members' reports or biochemical methods. Of course, some differences in judgment as to whether or not an individual is a drug abuser should be based on variables such as age. For example, any use of an illicit drug, or a drug such as inhalants, by a child or young teen indicates potential immediate danger.

Mental Status Examination

A mental status examination generally is conducted as a systematic means of gathering psychological and behavioral data. The purpose is to provide an initial screening of an individual's mental health status, and to help suggest other means of assessment to determine whether or not a diagnosis of a formal psychiatric disease should be made. The mental status examination includes the assessment of appearance, attitude and behavior, speech, affect, thought and language, and perceptions and cognitive functioning such as insight and judgment.[71]

When performing a mental status examination, questions such as the following help provide a guideline to determine whether or not an adolescent is suspected of drug abuse or other psychopathology. Does the individual appear to be withdrawn, socially isolated, undernourished, agitated or depressed, tired, unable to concentrate, or uninterested in pleasurable activities, or unkempt in physical appearance? Is the individual hostile or uncooperative, evasive or defensive, and are there any discrepancies in reports of autobiographical events (i.e., lies, missing information)? Are any delusions or visual or auditory hallucinations reported? If so, what were the circumstances? Was the individual under the influence of mood-altering drugs at the time? After answering these questions, the individual might be assessed through a more specific interview assessment.

Drug Treatment History

The use of interviews or self-reports that elicit information regarding an individual's prior involvement in drug treatment programs, psychiatric facilities, self-help support groups (e.g., 12-step programs), or public sanctions (e.g., court, juvenile hall, camps, or community schools) can be quite useful. Such data can assist in understanding the level of drug dependence (where individuals fall on the drug abuse continuum), occurrence of other compulsive behaviors and psychiatric difficulties, and motivation to stop using. It is also useful to assess the longest period of abstinence endured, both with and without the help of a structured environment. Many individuals will disclose that while in juvenile hall or prison ("locked up"), or while in treatment, they can remain abstinent, but when in the community, without some structure, they are unable to remain abstinent.

Frequency, Quantity, and Method of Drug Use, and Family Drug Use

Although questioning individuals about the frequency and quantity of drug use may not be essential in making a diagnosis of substance abuse, it is nonetheless associated with drug abuse–related dysfunction.[72,73] Of course, some individuals experience severe consequences while using relatively low levels of drugs (e.g., experiences of some Asian groups with alcohol), while other appear to experience few consequences on relatively high levels of regular use. However, high quantities of intake are highly correlated with occupational, social, and medical impairment. Frequency of use indicates how often individuals are using a drug. Frequency of drug use can be measured through self-reports of estimated lifetime use, yearly use, monthly use, and/or daily use. Unfortunately, this type of assessment lacks precision because of memory biases, social desirability, denial, and other response demands.

Recency of use does not indicate the duration or extent of the addiction, but it helps disclose the most current and reliable autobiographical events. Quantity of use is more predictive of problems or disruptive drug use than frequency[74,75] (e.g., binge drinking vs. small amounts of daily use). According to the National Household Survey on Drug Abuse, binge drinking is defined as consuming five or more drinks on one occasion at least 1 day in the past 30 days. Alternatively, heavy drinking is defined as drinking five or more drinks on the same occasion on 5 or more of the past 30 days.

The assessment of the method of drug intake may also help one to understand the level of addiction for those drugs that vary in means of use (e.g., cocaine and heroin). For instance, many individuals with crack cocaine addiction may have originally started by snorting powdered cocaine. Eventually, they switch to a different form of the drug—smoking crack—which is cheaper, readily available in small quantities, and which immediately potentiates dopamine transmission in the brain (e.g., nucleus accumbens).

Assessment of family history of drug use may further help to assess the level of addiction, perceived problems and consequences, attitudes toward drug use, and probability of relapse. Current use among significant others, and perceptions that drug use is simply a part of normal behavior, would lead one to expect future struggles with drug use.

The Structured Clinical Interview

The *DSM–IV–TR* is widely used in establishing whether or not an individual has a drug abuse disorder.[5] This manual also contains specific criteria sets for substance abuse, dependence, intoxication, and withdrawal applicable across different classes of drugs. The *DSM–IV–TR*'s Structured Clinical Interview (SCID-IV) is a broad-spectrum instrument that adheres to the standardized decision trees for psychiatric diagnosis and encourages multiple paths of exploration, clarification, and clinical decision making. It can be tailored to a variety of populations.[76] This interview is a primary measure of substance abuse disorder and substance dependence, with clarification particularly regarding efforts to decrease or control use, continued use despite problems, specific withdrawal symptoms of a drug, and assessment of comorbidity.

Structured Assessments of Alcoholism That Could Be Used with Adolescents

The *CAGE questionnaire*[77] is a self-report screening instrument that uses the mnemonic CAGE to assess problems with alcohol. It is a relatively sensitive four-item instrument that assesses attempts to Cut down on drinking; Annoyance with criticisms of drinking; Guilt feelings about drinking; and use of alcohol as a morning Eye opener. When one answers yes to two or more questions, that individual is suspected of having alcohol problems. These questions could be adapted for other drug use, as well, by replacing the word *drinking* with *drug use*, and *a morning eye opener* with *the drug to get you started in the morning*.

The *RAFFT Test* (Relax, Alone, Friends, Family, Trouble) was developed similarly to the CAGE, but as a brief screen specifically for teens; it consists of five items[78] (e.g., "Do you drink to relax, to feel better about yourself, or to fit in?"). Recently, Knight and colleagues[79] adapted RAFFT along with several other measures to create a brief screening of alcohol and other drug abuse. A six-item *CRAFFT Test* measure resulted (Car, Relax, Alone, Forget, Family or friends complain, Trouble). Items addressed riding in a car driven by someone under the influence, drinking or using to relax, drinking or using alone, forgetting things while drinking or using, family or friends telling the person to cut down, and getting into trouble while under the influence. The CRAFFT shows good convergent validity and internal consistency.

The *Adolescent Alcohol Involvement Scale (AAIS)* consists of 14 items and examines type and frequency of drinking, last drinking episode, reasons for drinking, drinking situations, effects of drinking, and perceptions about drinking.[80] The measure shows a moderate internal consistency and convergent validity with a substance use disorder diagnosis.

The *Adolescent Alcohol Expectancy Questionnaire (A-AEQ)*[81] was developed to evaluate anticipated effects of alcohol consumption among adolescents. This 100-item inventory addresses expected effects in several domains, including global positive changes, changes in social behavior, improved cognitive and motor abilities, sexual enhancement, cognitive and motor impairment, increased arousal and relaxation, and tension reduction.

The *Comprehensive Effects of Alcohol (CEOA)* questionnaire[82,83] was developed to assess positive and negative alcohol effects and the subjective evaluation of those effects. This 76-item measure consists of several expected positive effects, including factors that address sociability, tension reduction, liquid courage, and sexuality, and several negative effects, including factors addressing cognitive and behavioral impairment, risk and aggression, and self-perception. The CEOA was developed among college students but has been found to be comparable to the A-AEQ.[84]

The *Alcohol Abstinence Self-Efficacy Scale (AASE)*[85] consists of temptation and self-efficacy items that are self-rated to assess an individual's confidence to resist use in several drinking situations. This instrument contains 20 efficacy and 20 temptation items (with four subscales). Key outcome variables include cues related to negative affect, social, physical, and other concerns, and withdrawal and urges.

Structured Assessments of Other Drugs of Abuse That Could Be Used with Adolescents

The *Substance Dependence Severity Scale (SDSS)*[86] is a clinician-administered structured interview (comprising 13 items) that was developed to assess severity and frequency of dependence across a range of drugs, based on the *DSM–IV–TR*. The test-retest, joint rating, and internal consistency reliabilities across alcohol, cocaine, heroin, marijuana, and sedative users is good.

The *Chemical Dependency Assessment Profile (CDAP)* is a 235-item multiple-choice and true/false self-report instrument used to assess substance use, dependency problems, and treatment needs among adolescents and adults. Domains addressed include quantity/frequency of use, physiological symptoms, situational stressors, antisocial behaviors, interpersonal problems, affective dysfunction, treatment attitudes, impact of use on life functioning, and expectancies.[87]

The *Problem-Oriented Screening Instrument for Teenagers (POSIT)* is a 139-item self-administered yes/no questionnaire that was developed by the National Institute on Drug Abuse as part of their Adolescent Assessment/ Referral System.[88] POSIT contains 10 scales: substance use/abuse, physical health status, mental health status, peer relations, family relations, educational status, vocational status, social skills, leisure and recreation, and aggressive behavior/delinquency. This measure has good convergent validity, internal consistency, and test-retest reliability; it takes 20 minutes to complete.

The *Drug and Alcohol Problem (DAP) Quickscreen* consists of 30 yes/no items, and discriminates well between high-risk and low-risk users.[89] It was developed to be used in primary care offices, and includes the prototypical item: "Has anyone (friend, parent, teacher, or counselor) ever told you that they believe that you may have a drinking or drug problem?"

The *Rutgers Alcohol Problem Index (RAPI)*[90] consists of 23 items that address consequences of alcohol and other drug use related to psychological functioning, delinquency, social relations, family, physical problems and neuropsychological functioning. This measure has been found to correlate highly with *DSM–III–R* criteria for substance use disorders[91] (.75–.95).

The *Inventory of Drinking Situations (IDS)*[92] or the *Inventory of Drug Use Situations*[92] assesses the contextual aspects of alcohol or other drug use and provides information about relapse situations. This inventory consists of either 42 or 100 items (with eight subscales) to evaluate drinking/drug use situations, including unpleasant emotions, physical discomfort, pleasant emotions, testing personal control, urges and temptations, conflict with others, social pressures, and pleasant times with others.

The *Adolescent Diagnostic Interview (ADI)*[93] is a 15-minute evaluation used to assess the need for treatment of drug use among adolescents. This interview includes the evaluation of various cognitive, interpersonal, and school functioning factors that may contribute to alcohol or drug use. The instrument consists of 24 items. The *Personal Experience Inventory (PEI)*[94] is a comprehensive questionnaire used for detection of problem consequences and potential risk factors believed to predispose youth to use or maintain drug use. This 276-item questionnaire helps to quantify level of involvement with a variety of drugs and the severity of problems in personal, family, and psychosocial domains.

The *Adolescent Drug Abuse Diagnosis (ADAD)* is a comprehensive structured interview consisting of 150 items used to assess substance abuse and other problem areas. The format is adapted from the well-known adult tool, the Addiction Severity Index (ASI).[95] This interview addresses nine life areas including medical, school, work, social relations, family relationships, legal, psychological, and alcohol and drug use.[96]

The *Comprehensive Addiction Severity Index for Adolescents (CASI-A)* is an instrument designed to provide an in-depth, comprehensive assessment of the severity of adolescents' addiction and problem consequences. This structured interview is also adapted from the Addiction Severity Index (ASI).[95] Ten domains are assessed, including psychological functioning, peer relationships, family history and relationships such as sexual and physical abuse, significant life changes, use of free time, substance use effects and treatment experiences, leisure activities, educational experiences and plans, legal history, and psychiatric status, including prior treatment experiences.[97]

The *Substance Abuse Subtle Screening Inventory (SASSI-A)* consists of 81 items and 10 scales (face-valid alcohol, face-valid other drugs, family-friends risk, attitudes, symptoms, obvious attributes, subtle attitudes, defensiveness, supplemental addiction measures, and correctional experiences). This measure takes about 15 minutes to complete. However, it is not clear that the different scales are measuring empirically separable phenomena, and the face-valid content measures show the best convergence with interview-based measures on substance use impairment.[98,99]

Other promising measures of alcohol or other drug abuse among teens includes the Global Appraisal of Individual Needs (GAIN),[100] Form 90 Timeline Followback (TLFB),[100] Perceived Benefits of Drinking and Reasons for Drug Use Scale,[101,102] Adolescent Drug Involvement Scale (adapted from the AAIS),[103] Adolescent Problem Severity Index (APSI),[104] the Juvenile Automated Substance Abuse Evaluation (JASAE),[105] and the Minnesota Multiphasic Personality Inventory-Adolescent.[40] For more information on adolescent substance use screening inventories, see http://www.testsymptomsathome.com/DSO01_screening_assessment_instruments.asp

Biochemical Assessment of Drug Use among Teens

Urine toxicology screening can play an important role in assessment and treatment of adolescents with substance use disorders. These tests provide validation of the accuracy of self-reported substance use when properly conducted and when the results are properly interpreted to minimize errors (e.g., false-positive or false-negative test results). Other reasons why biochemical assessment of drug use might be ordered among adolescents include early initiation of treatment, to rule out other possible illness or potential health problems, when individuals are brought into the emergency room, fair play in sports and scholarship, and for proof of innocence in legal cases.[6] Positive test results for any substance are generally confirmed by a second test on the same urine sample using a different analytic method. Alternative, but more expensive, drug screening methods are hair, saliva, and blood analyses.

For initial drug use screening, the most commonly used tests are immunoassays (e.g., radioimmunoassay, enzyme immunoassay, and flourescence polarization immunoassay). Immunoassays involve the measurement of labeled and unlabeled antigen (drug or metabolite) and antibody interactions.[106] In drug testing, the antigen is a drug or metabolite; its corresponding labeled analog and the antibody is a protein grown in an animal and directed towards a specific drug, metabolite, or group of similar compounds. More selective screening assays used for confirmation include gas chromatography/mass spectrometry (GC/MS), gas chromatography (GC), and high-performance liquid chromatography (HPLC). Chromatography consists of a variety of techniques used to separate mixtures of drugs, their metabolites, and other chemicals into individual components based on differences in relative affinity for a mobile phase and a stationary phase.

PREVENTION AND TREATMENT OF ADOLESCENT SUBSTANCE ABUSE AND DEPENDENCE DISORDERS

Both prevention and cessation approaches encourage adoption of new, healthy behavior. However, the central focus of cessation work is on stopping a current behavior to arrest ongoing consequences and permit recovery of health, whereas the central focus of prevention work is on antecedents of the behavior, to anticipate and prevent future negative consequences from occurring. Cessation often deals with coping with psychological dependence on a drug and with physiological withdrawal. Prevention generally does not assist drug users through such hurdles. The choice between using a cessation or prevention approach is not always clear. There are high relapse rates in adult cessation programs; perhaps prevention might halt the addiction process that makes cessation so difficult. Alternatively, youth at highest risk may not benefit from prevention measures. They may only benefit when they perceive some costs occurring to them, making them appropriate candidates for early cessation efforts. This section will briefly discuss prevention efforts for youth and then more completely discuss what is known about youth cessation.

Prevention

An increasing number of prevention programs are developing specific strategies for altering risk factors (or enhancing protective conditions) empirically demonstrated to be related to decreased drug use. Universal interventions, that is, prevention programming delivered to an entire population regardless of risk status, have been utilized most often. Targeted interventions, which are designed to tailor programming to those groups at higher psychosocial-based risk (selective) or individuals who have demonstrated to be at greatest risk of continued drug use behavior (indicated), have also been implemented, but relatively few such programs exist.[107]

Prevention modalities that have provided some evidence of effectiveness include school-based educational programs, family-based informational programs, community-based activities, and mass media campaigns. However, the most widespread prevention approaches are those implemented through the school system and designed to counteract the psychosocial influences that promote drug use initiation.[108] The two major psychosocial approaches used in schools are the social-influences approach[109] and more comprehensive personal- and social-skills-enhancement approaches (e.g., Life Skills Training,[110] Project Towards No Tobacco Use[111]). Social-influences programs are designed to increase the awareness of social factors that promote drug use, alter norms regarding the prevalence and acceptability of drug use, and build drug resistance skills. Skills-enhancement programs incorporate the social-influence approach and also include general self-management and social-competence skills.

Research on substance use prevention programs have indicated short-term (under 24 months) reductions in the rate of initiation of substance use generally ranging from 10 percent to 15 percent or more in students exposed to social-influences programs compared to control students.[108] A few targeted programs implemented with older high-risk teens have found 25 prevalence reductions in, for example, methamphetamine use lasting up to two years post-program.[107,112,113] These programs utilize a skill-enhancement approach and also incorporate motivation-enhancement material to effect changes in personal attitudes that may impede skill development and behavior change. Although much more research is necessary, a comprehensive substantive approach that utilizes multiple intervention modalities (school setting, community, mass media, etc.) may be most effective in controlling and preventing substance use initiation and escalation.

Treatment of Adolescent Substance Abuse and Dependence Disorders

Many adolescents may not receive or be helped by available prevention programming. Some may need formal treatment. Given the heterogeneous nature of substance use and the relative lack of adolescent treatment research to date, it is not possible to recommend one specific treatment modality that is likely to be effective for all adolescent patients.[114] Instead, researchers and clinicians generally recommend the inclusion of specific treatment elements and a continuum of care in all treatment modalities (e.g., the *Quick Guide for Clinicians*[115]). Currently, several treatment modalities are available and have been utilized in the treatment of adolescent substance abuse and dependence. Most of these are based on adult treatment models; however, they typically include modifications to address the special needs of adolescents. This section provides a brief review of adolescent treatment issues (current status of treatment and youths' motivation for treatment), types of treatment, evaluation of treatment programs, potential further treatment options that may be effective when implemented among adolescents, and recovery and relapse prevention.

Effective Elements of Treatment for Adolescents

Beginning in the 1980s there was a dramatic increase in substance abuse treatment programs for youth. However, relatively few treatment effectiveness studies have been completed.[116] Of note, Brannigan and colleagues,[1] with assistance of a 22-member advisory panel, created a checklist of nine key elements of effective substance abuse treatment for adolescents. First, the panel agreed that programs should conduct comprehensive assessments that cover psychological and medical problems, learning disabilities, family functioning, and other aspects of youths' lives. Second, program services should address all aspects of the youths' lives (e.g., school, home, public activities). Third, parents should be involved in the youths' drug treatment. Fourth, the programming should reflect developmental differences between teens and adults. Fifth, treatment programs should build a climate of trust to maximally engage and retain teens in treatment. Sixth, staff should be well trained in adolescent development, comorbidity issues, and substance abuse. Seventh, programs should address the distinct needs of youth as a function of their gender and ethnicity. Eighth, programs should include information on continuing care (e.g., relapse prevention, aftercare plans, and follow-up). Finally, programs should include rigorous evaluations to measure success and improve treatment services.

Next, the researchers conducted in-depth telephone surveys of 144 broadly distributed (throughout the United States), highly regarded adolescent substance abuse treatment programs to determine the extent to which available programs met the criteria. Results indicated that the best programs were not more likely to be accredited, but were more likely to be 20 years old or older and to involve family therapy and a therapeutic community approach. Only approximately 19 percent of the treatment programs provided adequate comprehensive assessment, 33 percent provided adequate comprehensive treatment, 34 percent emphasized adequate family involvement, 44 percent adequately considered developmental appropriateness, 25 percent adequately established means that could encourage good retention, 54 percent reported adequately qualified staff, 10 percent adequately considered gender and cultural sensitivity, 39 percent adequately considered continuing care, and 6 percent adequately addressed process and outcomes evaluation.[1] One might infer that most treatment provided to adolescents nowadays is far from ideal.

Youths' Motivation to Receive Treatment

Not only are many treatment programs far from ideal; youth may not be motivated to enter or remain in treatment regardless of the type of treatment facility.[19] For example, among 600 teens entering outpatient treatment primarily for marijuana abuse and dependence at facilities located in four urban U.S. locations, only 20 percent stated that they needed help for their problems associated with alcohol or drug abuse.[117] Thus, motivating youth to obtain assistance and stay in treatment is a difficult task, because most of them may not feel they need any formalized treatment.

Likewise, Weiner et al.[118] utilized both open-ended and multiple-choice surveys, as well as health educator–led focus groups, to assess issues relating to marijuana use and cessation among a population of high-risk youth. A total of 806 students participated, assessed as two separate samples from 21 continuation (alternative) high schools in southern California. Approximately 70 percent of the students were current marijuana users. Over half of the marijuana users surveyed had tried to quit and failed. Still, social images associated with marijuana smokers were predominantly positive, and subjects expressed a lack of confidence in the efficacy of marijuana cessation clinic programs. "Quit in private, on your own, without any policies" received the highest mean rating for effectiveness out of a list of ten different cessation strategies. Other highly rated methods of marijuana cessation were either restrictive or punitive. "Inpatient stay" received the second-highest mean effectiveness rating and "jail time" the third-highest effectiveness rating. "Fines" and "driver's license suspension" received the fourth- and fifth-highest effectiveness ratings, respectively. Thus, subjects believed that self-help and restrictive or punitive methods are the most effective types of marijuana cessation activities. Minors can consent to their own treatment in most states without parental notification, and perhaps providing awareness of and emphasizing confidentiality of treatment could help motivate more youth to seek help.[119] Based on available research reported below, it does appear to be the case that treatment (of some kind) for substance abuse is superior to no treatment, and that aftercare services are important.[20]

Current Treatment Modalities for Adolescents

There have been four primary treatment models used with adolescents: (1) the Minnesota Model, which is based on the 12 steps of Alcoholics Anonymous (AA);[120] (2) the therapeutic community (TC) model; (3) family therapy; and (4) cognitive-behavioral therapy.[20] The Minnesota Model emphasizes the following: inpatient or residential care for a few weeks or months; a focus on psychoactive substance use disorder with little attention directed to associated psychiatric conditions or individual psychosocial factors; use of AA concepts, resources, and precepts, including the 12 steps central to recovery; referral to self-help groups such as AA upon discharge from residential or inpatient care, with limited or no ongoing professional treatment; provision of limited family therapy, although the family may be oriented to AA principles and Al-Anon; and nonacceptance of psychotherapy and pharmacology for either substance abuse or psychiatric disorder. Traditionally, counselors have been recovering alcoholics or addicts, though now professional staff have been added to the related treatment facilities, and attention to dual diagnosis and other issues is increasing.[20]

In the therapeutic community (TC) group model, the community serves as the primary therapist. While the client may have a primary counselor, all members of the community have the responsibility to act as therapists and teachers. Nearly all activities are part of the therapeutic process. Peer-group meetings are often led by a peer. Clients are provided with increased responsibilities and privileges as they pass through structured phases of treatment within the TC. One-on-one counseling, remedial education, and occupational training also are provided.[20] Modification of the TC model for teens includes use of shorter stays, participation by families, limited use of peer pressure, and less reliance on use of life experiences to foster self-understanding.[120]

Family therapy tends to view alcohol and drug abuse as a family (systems) problem. Family relationships are viewed as problematic and family boundaries are viewed as distorted. Family therapy with professional staff is the main treatment modality,[20] although therapies that involve specific training for parents and the teen substance abuser also have been developed.[107] Some prevalent family-based treatments in the teen substance abuse disorder treatment literature include Structural Strategic Family Therapy (SSFT), Multidimensional Family Therapy (MDFT), and Multisystemic Family Therapy (MST). In general, these treatments attempt to involve all family members, improve parent-child communication, and provide skills training for parents (child management practices: limit setting, appropriate parent behavior) and youths (appropriate role as a teen[40,121]).

Behavioral and cognitive-behavioral approaches seek at least three goals. First, they aim to decrease the frequency of behaviors compatible with drug use and increase the frequency of behaviors incompatible with drug use. Second, they aim to shape new adaptive behaviors (e.g., social skills development). Finally, they aim to appropriately modify cognition (i.e., decrease the frequency of cognition compatible with drug use and increase the frequency of cognition incompatible with drug use). Training new behaviors can be accomplished through use of shaping, modeling or observational learning, role playing, and assertiveness training. Further, modifying one's thinking or inner speech can be accomplished through using strategies such as self-instructional training and cognitive restructuring.[122] Other thought-modification strategies include self-verbalizations, positive affirmations, thought stopping, rehearsal and imaging.[122] Cognitive-behavioral approaches such as social-control contracting, emotional-regulation training and anger management, social and environmental support seeking, problem solving, coping skills training, environmental resource–acquisition skills, and relapse prevention also ideally would be taught.[40]

A few other modalities have also begun to be used with teens. These include emphasis on group therapy and pharmacotherapy. Group therapy provides a means for youth to provide corrective feedback to each other and is less expensive than individual therapy. On the other hand, the potential for peer deviancy modeling could result by group participation.[19] Group therapy, with other clients and/or the family, provides peer support, feedback, and confrontation, guided by a trained leader. In-depth attention on psychological issues that might occur in group therapy is relatively unlikely to occur in self-help groups. In early recovery, the therapist serves as a coach and a monitor. As recovery progresses, the therapist helps group members resolve issues of trauma and learn intimacy with others, as well as learn how to express feelings appropriately.

Kaminer[123] discusses the option of using pharmacotherapy with teens, just as it has been used with adults. Possibly, medication might help ease potential withdrawal symptoms, and might help in mood stabilization after quitting alcohol or other drugs. There has been very little research on the safety of using pharmacotherapy among teens.[124] Studies on use of pharmacologic adjuncts to assist with tobacco use cessation have not been promising thus far as applied to teens.[112] Desipramine (a tricylclic antidepressant) has been used to treat cocaine dependence in a few case studies with mixed results.[123] Additionally, little evidence exists for the efficacy of drug-related medications for teens such as use of methadone and naltrexone during detoxification.[40] However, while there is some debate, use of selective serotonin reuptake inhibitors (SSRIs) or selective norepinephrine reuptake inhibitors (SNRIs) is recommended for those young patients who are highly depressed or anxious. Medications for Attention Deficit and Hyperactivity Disorder (ADHD), including Ritalin, could be abused but generally are not by prescribed users (some do provide these medications to their friends). Medications for ADHD with less potential for abuse are being developed. The future of the use of medications with teens is not clear, and ethical concerns exist with this special population, including consideration of parental rights and child rights, potential interference of the rapidly developing brain of the young person, and limited life experience that might preclude giving fully informed consent regarding use of a medication, that limit experimentation in this arena.[123]

Treatment Program Evaluations and Contrasts

There are several types of treatments for teens that have been tested for therapeutic change and/or contrasted recently. Kaminer, Burleson, and Goldberger[125] compared the efficacy of group cognitive-behavioral therapy versus group psychoeducational therapy for 88 adolescents who were randomized into two 8-week outpatient conditions. Subjects in the cognitive-behavioral therapy condition reported significantly lower relapse rates compared to those subjects in the psychoeducational therapy condition at three-months follow-up. However, cognitive-behavioral therapy subjects failed to report significant improvements in relapse rates compared to the psychoeducational therapy at nine months post-treatment. This loss of differential short-term gains of cognitive-behavioral therapy compared with psychoeducational therapy is similar to findings reported in another study.[126]

Battjes et al.[127] found that 194 youth who attended a structured, outpatient, group-based treatment program reported a decreased level of marijuana use but not alcohol use up to 12 months post-entry into treatment. Liddle et al.[128] contrasted outpatient peer group therapy with family-based treatment (MDFT) among 80 low-income, urban youth and found the family therapy to be superior over the course of treatment.

In several recent studies, family-based teen substance abuse treatment has been found to lead to greater recruitment and retention than other modalities.[129] It is less clear if family-based treatment is superior in behavioral outcomes to other treatments. An outpatient combined cognitive-behavioral group therapy and family therapy program (Family and Coping Skills, or FACS; 3-month duration) for treatment of substance abuse and depression was found to be feasible and was associated with improvement in mood and substance abuse–related behavior (for marijuana, not alcohol) the week following treatment among a sample of 13 teens.[130] A similar pattern of results was found in a randomized clinical trial involving 114 teens.[129] At four months follow-up, a significant reduction in marijuana use was found in the combined treatment and functional family therapy condition. At seven months follow-up, the combined treatment and psychoeducational group therapy were relatively effective. Thus, a combined/comprehensive approach in treatment appears to work better than family or group approaches. The latter two approaches show equivocal relative effects on behavior.

Weekly or twice-a-week individual outpatient treatment, which includes psychoeducation and instruction in use of decision making, has been found to be associated with improvement of depression and anxiety-related symptoms eight weeks later among 129 teen substance abusers.[55] Dasinger, Shane, and Martinovich[131] evaluated a variety of treatment models and found that programs that involved placing teens in long-term residential care showed the greatest magnitude in drug use reduction but with the highest relapse rates. Regarding types of patients, one study of 187 teens revealed that those teens with a history of victimization show better outcomes in residential care than as outpatients.[132]

Cultural Sensitivity and Treatment

Ethnic, gender, and drug use history differences have been found between involvement in residential (inpatient) and outpatient modalities of treatment. As reported by Rounds-Bryant, Kristiansen, and Hubbard[133] in a survey conducted from 1993 through 1995 of 3,382 subjects from six nationally dispersed urban areas, residential patients tended to be male, African-American or Hispanic, and had often been referred by the juvenile or criminal justice system. Outpatients reported the least criminally involved lifestyles, lowest levels of drug use, and least drug treatment experience. Very little quantitative empirical work on cultural sensitivity has been completed in the teen substance abuse treatment arena. However, research has shown that cultural factors should be considered in, for example, treatment placement decisions. A study conducted by Dinges and colleagues[134] found that Native American adolescents showed intense emotional strain, which can be counterproductive to treatment, when removed from their family for inpatient setting treatment. Thus, for some youth, it may be advantageous to ensure that family bonds are not disrupted by out-of-home placement.. Instead, such youth may be better served through a more intensive outpatient setting; if inpatient treatment is deemed more appropriate, it should be accompanied by frequent family contact and support.

Summary of Contrast Studies of Different Treatment Programs

Generally, improvements were found for those who remained in treatment, regardless of type of treatment, although numerous methodological flaws in the study designs were present. Some noted methodological flaws included small sample sizes, lack of placebo-type control groups, lack of random assignment to conditions, insufficient descriptions of treatments or facilitators, inadequate follow-up of dropouts, and lack of biochemical validation.[121,125,135]

The first randomized trial to provide follow-up data beyond 12 months was completed by Henggeller and colleagues[136] in their evaluation of Multisystemic Therapy (MST) at a four-year follow-up among juvenile offenders (80 of 118 youth that had been randomly assigned to MST or usual community services). Effects were maintained for aggressive criminal activity but not for property crimes, and an effect was apparent for marijuana abstinence.

Consideration of Other Treatment Options

Reach of Programming

Reaching young substance abusers in multiple settings has been suggested as being potentially very important to strengthen treatment for youth. There are many examples of means of providing treatment for youth in community settings. Two examples are student assistance programs in schools and physician assistance. Student assistance generally is available first through a contact with someone at the school, perhaps a teacher, the security guard, other students, or the school nurse. Typically, there may be around five hours of in-service training for staff and peer counselors regarding addiction, how to recognize drug problems, and referral skills. Peer counselors may lead education groups that teach coping skills and values development. Peer support groups may also be available for youths who are struggling to get and stay sober. Usually these groups also provide referral information and take a 12-step, group-support model approach. Finally, sometimes a resource library and peer advising are available.[137]

Primary care physicians can learn to screen for problems and refer youth to drug and mental health counseling.[138] In addition, they can be trained as agents of outpatient treatment,[139] particularly if minimal programming can be used. There is very little research completed on using the physician as a point of contact or as a treatment agent for teen drug abuse; however such work has begun.

When dealing with extreme populations such as runaway youth, screening for drug abuse is more difficult because these youth are relatively unlikely to have contact with traditional systems of care. Public health care facilities often screen for drug abuse among teens as part of all standard care. In addition, stabilization of living situations for homeless youth is very important (e.g., easy access to housing shelters and outreach) to be able to draw these youth into treatment.[140]

Aftercare Self-Help Programming

Twelve-step programs that include groups for young people provide another promising modality to help teens maintain sobriety (e.g., an Internet search conducted June 7, 2005, yielded 250 links for young people in Alcoholics Anonymous). Twelve-step programs such as Alcoholics Anonymous (AA) and Narcotics Anonymous (NA) are abstinence-oriented, multidimensional, nonprofit, humanistic, voluntary, supportive, self-help fellowships for individuals for whom drug use is problematic. All of the 12-step, sobriety-based programs are based on a disease model of addiction and require complete abstinence from all drugs except cigarettes (nicotine) and coffee (caffeine).

The essential principle of these 12-step programs is that a recovering alcoholic or drug abuser can altruistically and effectively help a fellow addict to gain or maintain sobriety. Members openly talk about their struggles and successes and develop problem-solving skills, as well as friendships with others, comforted in the knowledge that they are not alone in their plight. An important adjunct to the program is self-selecting a sponsor who provides support and helps to guide the individual in the program.[6]

At present, approximately 9 percent of the members of AA are 21 to 30 years old and only 2 percent are under 21 years old.[141] Admitting to a sense of powerlessness, a key principle of 12-step programs, may conflict with teens' search for autonomy as can perceiving themselves as having to remain abstinent (perceiving themselves as having "hit bottom[55]"); both are thus potential barriers to participating in a 12-step program. Treatment for teens needs to grapple with the tendency to engage in a great deal of limit-testing.[142] However, attendance at 12-step meetings specifically for teens has been found to predict better outcomes. These outcomes are mediated by motivation but not coping.[143]

Many drug abusers (alcoholics and addicts) may best regain control of their lives through a program that does not require moral betterment or belief in a higher power to gain sobriety. Some individuals do not want to feel powerless or dependent upon others, or to attend meetings for the rest of their lives. Other self-help treatment alternatives to AA include Rational Recovery, SMART Recovery, and Secular Organizations for Sobriety.[6] Use of these programs with teens is not yet prevalent.

Motivational Interviewing

Motivational Interviewing has been considered for use with teens, particularly because of its potential to be delivered as a brief intervention.[144]

Motivational Interviewing[145] is based on principles of cognitive therapy, Carl Rogers's client-centered approach, and the Transtheoretical Model. It involves a series of procedures for therapists to help clients clarify goals and follow through with their efforts to change behavior. Motivation is conceptualized as the probability that a person will enter into, continue, and adhere to a specific change strategy.[146] Motivation for change fluctuates over time, and *addressing this ambivalence* is considered a key for facilitating behavioral change. Motivational Interviewing involves eight strategies to motivate behavior change. One is *giving advice*, which entails identification of the problem, clarification of the need for change, and encouraging the specific change. A second is *removing impediments to change* through problem identification, effective problem solving and cognitive restructuring. A third is *providing choices*. A fourth is *decreasing desirability (of not changing)* by promoting benefits of behavior change. A fifth is providing *empathy*, which is marked by warmth and understanding. A sixth is *providing accurate feedback* of one's behavior and outcomes to aid in altering or modifying risky behaviors. A seventh is *clarifying goals by* confronting the individual about discrepancies between future goals and the present situation. Finally, an eighth is *supporting the development of self-efficacy (active helping)*. Motivational Interviewing may prove a valuable brief treatment option for teens, although current data suggest its advantage over no treatment or other modalities in only approximately 30 percent of the studies in which it has been examined.[144]

Relapse and Recovery

Recovery from substance abuse is widely known to be extremely difficult, even with exceptional treatment resources. For example, although relapse rates are difficult to accurately obtain, it has been reported that, among adults, 70 percent of alcohol-dependent users experience at least one relapse within four years after treatment. Similar relapse rates for heroin, nicotine, and marijuana users have also been documented.[6] As with other chronic illnesses, relapses to drug use can occur during or after successful treatment episodes. Recovering individuals may require prolonged treatment and multiple episodes of treatment to achieve long-term abstinence.

Relapses are most likely to occur within the first 12 months of the discontinuance of substance use. Relapses may be triggered by a number of life stressors (e.g., divorce, death of a loved one, loss of job or income, periods of illness or poverty), or to a seemingly ordinary exposure to a person or place associated with previous substance use. It is believed that two primary factors may play a key role in protecting against relapse, the development of adaptive life skills and ongoing drug-free social support, such as that found in 12-step programs. In fact, a meta-analysis study of adults that investigated the relationship between long-term sobriety and AA attendance and involvement found positive outcome effects.[147] Another potentially important protective factor is social support for the individual in recovery. Ongoing therapy and social support assistance for family members is also recommended because substance dependence has a serious impact on family functioning, and because family members may inadvertently maintain behaviors that initially tolerated or supported the substance use behavior.

FUTURE DIRECTIONS IN ADOLESCENT SUBSTANCE ABUSE TREATMENT

The above sections of this chapter suggest that much more research on adolescent substance abuse is needed, including its natural history, epidemiology, etiology, assessment, prevention, and treatment. Because existing treatment strategies have shown modest outcomes at best, a very immediate need exists to develop and test *newer* forms of psychosocial treatment.

A Consideration of Youth Development

One very important, yet relatively untapped, area for treatment research focuses on the developmental changes occurring between early adolescence and young adulthood (from approximately age 16 to 25), when new challenges, pressures, and responsibilities increase as individuals transition into independent, adult roles. Although substance dependence can begin at any age, individuals from 18 to 24 have relatively high substance use rates, and substance use dependence often arises sometime during the ages of 20 to 49. Treatment of substance use disorders among young people must be designed to reflect their unique developmental needs.

Treatment providers should continue to address and emphasize issues that play significant roles in adolescent development, such as cognitive, emotional, physical, social, moral, and career development, as well as family and peer environment factors. Those teens who abuse drugs are relatively unlikely to experience normative developmental trajectories. They may experience truncated development (taking on tasks before they are ready) or childhood dependence (not learning skills of independence).

Accordingly, there is a need to understand some of the developmental challenges spanning this entire transitional period, which can lead to or be affected by drug use. During young adolescence, youth begin to place a greater importance on their peers relative to their parents and primary family members (e.g., brothers and sisters). They tend to experiment with new behaviors in the context of a group of three to eight same-sex peers, as opposed to one-on-one interactions. Dynamic social changes occur between early adolescence (junior high school) and later adolescence (high school). In later adolescence, youth spend more time away from adults, and their lives become less dominated by social interactions with these small groups of same-sexed peer groups. Concomitantly, they become exposed to a wider range of interactions with crowds in unsupervised social gatherings, more dyadic relationships such as dating, and more weak ties (liaisons) than in earlier years.[148–150] Older teens begin to experience new challenges (e.g., jobs, team sports, unsupervised recreational time). Perhaps, as individuals grow closer in age to adulthood, their peers place more and more direct pressure on them to show autonomy or to hurry into adult-like roles.[151]

Emerging adulthood (approximately 16 to 25 years) is characterized by the general goal of developing a stable, sustained identity as an adult within an environmental context that tends to be rapidly changing in its demands on the individual.[152] This is a period in which young people tend to move away from dependence on caretakers toward self-sufficiency, as a transitional period prior to taking on the obligations to others that structure adult life for most people. The age at which this self-care transition actually occurs may vary as a function of life circumstances. Youth in relatively deviant life trajectories tend to reach a period of relative independence at younger ages than others.[2] There may be an expectation of many life possibilities, but with this optimism is a sense of being "in-between" and capable of becoming trapped in an undesired life role. Most emerging adults will move out of the parents' home, generally more than once, and take a job to obtain independence. They are relatively likely to live alone. They tend to go in and out of additional school or vocational training. Main developmental tasks appear to be learning to accept responsibility for oneself, making independent decisions, and becoming financially independent. One considers what type of person one wants to have as a partner, what type of person one views oneself as, and what type of careers one can realistically take on.[152] Not surprisingly, this is the age range in which people are at highest risk for drug abuse.

Young people leaving high school are expected to seek new opportunities.[152, 153] These may include: (1) assuming career avenues and financial independence, (2) learning skills of independent living (e.g., buying or renting a place to live apart from one's parents),[153] (3) growth in self-care skills (e.g., cooking, cleaning, grooming, buying goods, traveling), and (4) social adventures (e.g., love and young adult groups). Social adventures lead eventually to commitment in relationships (e.g., marriage and children). Relatively high levels of family conflict in adolescence may diminish in emerging adulthood, as the individual achieves an emotional distance from parental demands and begins to associate more as a junior peer.[154]

One may argue that youth enter a protracted life phase. Within this phase, there is a trade-off between commitments and new areas of exploration that must be abandoned. For example, getting married would tend to preclude further dating. Beginning a full-time job would tend to preclude taking on another full-time job with a different directional emphasis. Events characteristic of young and middle adulthood, such as taking on the role of a parent, economic provider, and nurturer, leads to new experiences but often in sacrifice for others, and also leads to increasing law abidance, diligence, and conservatism.[155]

Youth who receive parental support, are academically and socially competent, are strongly bonded to school, attend church, and hold normatively popular attitudes are relatively likely to transition smoothly into normatively defined young adult roles.[156–159] Normatively popular attitudes include such sentiments as valuing one's health, affirming the importance of hard work, and expressing respect of family. On the other hand, youth that exhibit unconventional behavior (e.g., cheating, having a child out of wedlock), unconventional attitudes (e.g., tolerance of deviance and preference for sensation seeking), poor emotional control, anger, intrapsychic distress, and interpersonal difficulty are relatively likely to use drugs in emerging adulthood.[154,160] These youth tend to enter adult roles early ("precocious development"), before they are really prepared to take them on. They tend to drop out of high school or attend part-time, get married and quickly divorced, have children while relatively young, and take on relatively undesired full-time employment. Those teens who exhibit precocious development are at particularly high risk for drug use in emerging adulthood.[158]

Successful marriage (often forestalled until later in emerging adulthood) is inversely related to drug use, possibly because social opportunities to use decrease, and relationship commitment and consideration of the other person may reduce one's desire to use. This effect applies to males and females, though more strongly for females. Pregnancy and parenthood, in the context of happy marital relationships, are statuses that are also inversely related to drug use. On the other hand, cohabitation, which is relatively strongly associated with holding nontraditional beliefs, is positively associated with drug use. Job stability in young adulthood is negatively related to drug use, although participation in the military or in hourly jobs may be relatively strongly associated with use of cigarettes and alcohol.[153]

Another major predictor of drug use in emerging adulthood is drug use in adolescence.[156] The stability of cigarette smoking from high school graduation over the next 10 years is very high, is moderately high for alcohol and marijuana use, but decreases dramatically for other illicit substance use.[153,161] Finally, age is a major curvilinear predictor of drug use. Experimental drug use tends to peak during this period of emerging adulthood,[153] and then tends to decline later in young adulthood (around 25 years of age).

Treatment programs focusing on emerging adulthood must not only acknowledge the features of emerging adulthood (e.g., increased exploration of various experiences), but also must link these features to feasible strategies of treatment (e.g., enhancing prosocial skills). Relevant strategies include addressing the tangible needs of emerging adults, such as employment, housing, education, parenting resources, family counseling, transportation, recreation, and dental/medical care. In fact, research has shown that the best predictors of successful substance abuse treatment are gainful employment, adequate family support, and lack of coexisting mental illness.[162] Optimally, new treatment programs will not only focus on the addiction but also consider integrating substance abuse treatment with, for example, vocational services.

A Consideration of Integrated and Matched Treatment Programs

Future treatment research should also be directed at developing interventions tailored to adolescents with co-occurring substance use and mental disorders, because these disorders often coexist in the same individual. However, to date, substance abuse treatment researchers have sought to develop an understanding of the treatment of single psychiatric conditions, and have virtually failed to incorporate treatment of co-occurring problems.

It is likely that there would be a greater yield from treating adolescents diagnosed with a substance use disorder and a co-occurring mental disorder using treatment that follows an integrated protocol addressing both conditions.[163,164] Adolescents may find it difficult to adhere to parallel or sequential treatments in separate substance abuse and mental health systems, thus compromising the effectiveness of treatment.[165]

An integrated treatment approach would allow continuous attention to both problems, a synthesis of treatment principles, and prioritization of treatment goals.[165] Furthermore, studies of integrated treatments would help to bridge the gap between the substance use and mental health treatment literatures, which has the potential to produce better outcomes among adolescents than either treatment alone.

Gender, age, socioeconomic, and cultural background factors also need much more investigation, as these factors may suggest a need to match treatment to young clients with different needs to maximize effects on their behavior.

Regarding comorbid conditions or variations in social-environmental contexts, data on patient-treatment matching would aid in designing the most efficient treatment programs for groups of persons.

Conclusions

Much more work is needed to advance knowledge in the arena of adolescent substance abuse and dependence. Most notably, treatment strategies remain relatively underdeveloped in relation to other areas of medicine, and among older populations. As indicated in this chapter, it appears that no single treatment is likely to be appropriate and effective for all adolescents. Still, to the best of our knowledge, all treatment programs should include some type of continuing care or self-care regimen. One may speculate that treatment programs should include a programming component that encourages adolescents to form attachments with prosocial, non-drug abusing people in their community, and assist them in finding leadership or service opportunities that enable them to contribute to their community. Ideally, the treatment intervention, along with treatment setting and services, should be matched to the particular problems and needs of the individual, and some means of attaching the individual to his or her community after treatment, and helping him or her to maintain sobriety, is essential.

Future directions in treatment research must continue to target the development, implementation, evaluation, and diffusion of evidence-based adolescent substance abuse programming. Most importantly, use of empirical program development methods will assist in constructing programming that is needed.[165] Input from those in treatment (particularly among those participating in the natural support systems within the recovery movement), pilot studies, and consideration of mechanisms of lifestyle change will provide the ingredients for the development of effective treatment programming. Further, the knowledge gained from this research should be utilized to develop guidelines and public health policies that will prevent the development of adolescent substance use disorders.

REFERENCES

1. Brannigan, R., Schackman, B. R., Falco, M., & Millman, R. B. (2004). The quality of highly regarded adolescent substance abuse treatment programs: Results of an in-depth national survey. *Archives of Pediatrics and Adolescent Medicine, 158*, 904–909.
2. Newcomb, M. D., & Bentler, P. M. (1988b). Impact of adolescent drug use and social support on problems of young adults: A longitudinal study. *Journal of Abnormal Psychology, 97*, 64–75.

3. Leccese, M., & Waldron, H. B. (1994). Assessing adolescent substance use: A critique of current measurement instruments. *Journal of Substance Abuse Treatment, 11*, 553–563.
4. Winters, K. C. (1999). Treating adolescents with substance use disorders: An overview of practice issues and treatment outcome. *Substance Abuse, 20*(4), 203–225.
5. American Psychiatric Association (2000). *Diagnostic and statistical manual of mental disorders* (4th ed., text revision).Washington, DC: Author.
6. Sussman, S., & Ames, S. L. (2001). *The social psychology of drug abuse.* Buckingham, UK: Open University Press.
7. Kandel, D. B., Yamaguchi, K., & Chen, K. (1992). Stages of progression in drug involvement from adolescence to adulthood: Further evidence for the gateway theory. *Journal of Studies on Alcohol, 53*, 447–457.
8. Graham J. W., Collins, L. M., Wugalter, S. E., Chung, N. K., & Hansen, W. B. (1991). Modeling transitions in latent stage-sequential processes: A substance use prevention example. *Journal of Consulting and Clinical Psychology, 59*, 48–57.
9. Collins, L. M., Graham, J. W., Rousculp, S. S., & Hansen, W. B. (1997). Heavy caffeine use and the beginning of the substance use onset process: An illustration of latent transition analysis. In K. Bryant, M. Windle, & S. West (Eds.), *The science of prevention: Methodological advances from alcohol and substance abuse research* (pp.79–99). Washington, DC: American Psychological Association.
10. Newcomb, M. D., & Bentler, P. M. (1989). Substance use and abuse among children and teenagers. *The American Psychologist, 44*, 242–248.
11. Tarter, R. E. (2002). Etiology of adolescent substance abuse: A developmental perspective. *American Journal on Addictions, 11*, 171–191.
12. Newcomb, M. D. (1995). Identifying high-risk youth: Prevalence and patterns of adolescent drug abuse. *NIDA Research Monograph, 156*, 7–38.
13. Arria, A. M., Tarter, R. E., & Van Thiel, D. H. (1991). Vulnerability to alcoholic liver disease. *Recent Developments in Alcoholism, 9*, 185–204.
14. Bailey, S. L., & Rachal, J. V. (1993). Dimensions of adolescent problem drinking. *Journal of Studies on Alcohol, 54*, 555–565.
15. Deas, D., Riggs, P., Langenbucher, J., Goldman, M., & Brown. (2000). Adolescent are not adults: Developmental considerations in alcohol users. *Alcoholism: Clinical and Experimental Research, 24*, 232–237.
16. Abrantes, A. M., Brown, S. A., & Tomlinson, K. L. (2004) Psychiatric comorbidity among inpatient substance abusing adolescents. *Journal of Child and Adolescent Substance Abuse, 13*(2), 83–101.
17. Tomlinson, K. L., Brown, S. A., & Abrantes, A. M. (2004) Psychiatric comorbidity and substance use treatment outcomes of adolescents. *Psychology of Addictive Behaviors, 18*, 160–169.
18. Cornelius, J. R., Maisto, S. A., Pollock, N. K., Martin, C. S., Salloum, I. M., Lynch, K. G., & Clark, D. B. (2003). Rapid relapse generally follows treatment for substance use disorders among adolescents. *Addictive Behaviors, 28*, 381–386.

19. O'Leary, T. A., Brown, S. A., Colby, S. M., Cronce, J. M., D'Amico, E. J., Fader, J. S., Geisner, I. M., Larimer, M. E., Maggs, J. L., McCrady, B., Palmer, R. S., Schulenberg, J., & Monti, P. M. (2002). Treating adolescents together or individually? Issues in adolescent substance abuse interventions. *Alcoholism: Clinical and Experimental Research*, *26*, 890–899.

20. Blum, R. W. (1995). Transition to adult health care: Setting the stage. *Journal of Adolescent Health, 17*, 3–5.

21. Martin, C. S., & Winters, K. C. (1998). Diagnosis and assessment of alcohol use disorders among adolescents. *Alcohol Health and Research World, 22*, 95–105.

22. Chung, T., Martin, C. S., & Winters, K. C. (2005). Diagnosis, course, and assessment of alcohol abuse and dependence in adolescents. *Recent Developments in Alcoholism, 17*, 5–27.

23. Langenbucher, J., Martin, C. S., Labouvie, E., Sanjuan, P. M., Bavly, L., & Pollock, N. K. (2000). Toward the *DSM-V*: The withdrawal-gate model versus the *DSM-IV* in the diagnosis of alcohol abuse and dependence. *Journal of Consulting and Clinical Psychology, 68*, 799–809.

24. Substance Abuse and Mental Health Services Administration, Office of Applied Studies. (2002). *Report from the 2001 National Household Study on Drug Abuse. Volume 1: Summary of national findings.* Rockville, MD: Author.

25. Johnston, L. D., O'Malley, P. M., Bachman, J. G., & Schulenberg, J. E. (2004). *Monitoring the Future national survey results on drug use, 1975–2003. Volume I: Secondary school students.* Bethesda, MD: National Institute on Drug Abuse (NIH Publication No. 04–5507).

26. Chen, K., Sheth, A .J., Elliott, D. K., & Yeager, A. (2004). Prevalence and correlates of past-year substance use, abuse, and dependence in a suburban community sample of high-school students. *Addictive Behaviors, 29*, 413–423.

27. Sussman, S., Dent, C. W., & Galaif, E. R. (1997). The correlates of substance abuse and dependence among adolescents at high risk for drug abuse. *Journal of Substance Abuse, 9*, 241–255.

28. Newcomb, M. D., & Bentler, P. M. (1988a). Consequences of adolescent drug use. Newbury Park, CA: Sage.

29. Bennett, M. E., McCrady, B. S., Frankenstein, W., Laitman, L. A., Van Horn, D.H.A., & Keller, D. S. (1993). Identifying young adult substance abusers: The Rutgers Collegiate Substance Abuse Screening Test. *Journal of Studies on Alcohol, 54*, 522–527.

30. National Institute on Alcohol Abuse and Alcoholism. (1998). http://www.niaaa.nih.gov/ResearchInformation/ExtramuralResearch/AdvisoryCouncil/prevention.htm. Retrieved June 20, 2005.

31. Hawkins, J. D., Catalano, R. F., & Miller, J. Y. (1992). Risk and protective factors for alcohol and other drug problems in adolescence and early adulthood: Implications for substance abuse prevention. *Psychological Bulletin, 112*, 64–105.

32. Petraitis, J., Flay, B. R., & Miller, T. Q. (1995). Reviewing theories of adolescent substance use: Organizing pieces in the puzzle. *Psychological Bulletin, 117*, 67–86.

33. Beman, D. S. (1995). Risk factors leading to adolescent substance abuse. *Adolescence*, *30*, 201–208.

34. Sussman, S., Dent, C. W., & Leu, L. (2000). The one-year prospective prediction of substance abuse and dependence among high-risk adolescents. *Journal of Substance Abuse*, *12*, 373–386.

35. Denton, R. E., & Kampfe, C. M. (1994). The relationship between family variables and adolescent substance abuse: A literature review. *Adolescence*, *29*, 475–495.

36. Gabel, S., Stallings, M. C., Young, S. E., Schmitz, S., Crowley, T. J., & Fulker, D. W. (1998). Family variables in substance-misusing male adolescents: The importance of maternal disorder. *American Journal of Drug and Alcohol Abuse*, *24*, 61–84.

37. Hoffmann, J. P., & Cerbone, F.G. (2002). Parental substance use disorder and the risk of adolescent drug abuse: An event history analysis. *Drug and Alcohol Dependence*, *66*, 255–264.

38. Kilpatrick, D. G., Acierno, R., Saunders, B., Resnick, H. S., Best, C. L., & Schnurr, P. P. (2000). Risk factors for adolescent substance abuse and dependence: Data from a national sample. *Journal of Consulting and Clinical Psychology*, *68*, 19–30.

39. Humes, D. L., & Humphrey, L. L. (1994). A multimethod analysis of families with a polydrug-dependent or normal adolescent daughter. *Journal of Abnormal Psychology*, *103*, 676–685.

40. Weinberg, N. Z., Rahdert, E., Colliver, J. D., & Glantz, M. D. (1998). Adolescent substance abuse: A review of the past 10 years. *Journal of the American Academy of Child and Adolescent Psychiatry*, *37*, 252–261.

41. Miles, D. R., Stallings, M. C., Young, S. E., Hewitt, J. K., Crowley, T. J., & Fulker, D. W. (1998). A family history and direct interview study of the familial aggregation of substance abuse: The adolescent substance abuse study. *Drug and Alcohol Dependence*, *49*, 105–114.

42. Brown, S. A., Goldman, M. S., Inn, A., & Anderson, L. (1980). Expectations of reinforcement from alcohol: Their domain and relation to drinking patterns. *Journal of Consulting and Clinical Psychology*, *48*, 419–426.

43. Goldman, M. S., Greenbaum, P. E., & Darkes, J. (1997). A confirmatory test of hierarchical expectancy structure and predictive power discriminant validation of the alcohol expectancy questionnaire. *Psychological Assessment*, *9*, 145–157.

44. Fromme, K., Katz, E. C., & Rivet, K. (1997). Outcome expectancies and risk-taking behavior. *Cognitive Therapy and Research*, *21*, 421–442.

45. Leigh, B. C. (1989). In search of the seven dwarves: Issues of measurement and meaning in alcohol expectancy research. *Psychological Bulletin*, *105*, 361–373.

46. Leigh, B. C., & Stacy, A. W. (1993). Alcohol outcome expectancies: Scale construction and predictive utility in higher order confirmatory factor models. *Psychological Assessment*, *5*, 216–229.

47. Wiers, R. W., Hoogeveen, K. J., Sergeant, J. A. & Gunning, W. B. (1997). High and low dose expectancies and the differential associations with drinking in male and female adolescents and young adults. *Addiction*, *92*, 871–888.

48. Ames, S. L., Franken, I.H.A., & Coronges, K. (in press). Implicit cognition and drugs of abuse. In R. W. Wiers & A. W. Stacy (Eds.), *Handbook on implicit cognition and addiction*. Thousand Oaks, CA: Sage.

49. Stacy, A. W. (1997). Memory activation and expectancy as prospective predictors of alcohol and marijuana use. *Journal of Abnormal Psychology, 106*, 61–73.

50. Wiers, R. W., & Stacy, A. W. (Eds., in press). *Handbook on implicit cognition and addiction*. Thousand Oaks, CA: Sage.

51. Galaif, E. R., Stein, J. A., Newcomb, M. D., & Bernstein, D. P. (2001). Gender differences in the prediction of problem alcohol use in adulthood: Exploring the influence of family factors and childhood maltreatment. *Journal of Studies on Alcohol, 62*, 486–493.

52. Wu, P., Hoven, C. W., Liu, X., Cohen, P., Fuller, C. J., & Shaffer, D. (2004). Substance use, suicidal ideation and attempts in children and adolescents. *Suicide and Life-Threatening Behavior, 34*, 408–420.

53. Jaycox, L. H., Ebener, P., Damesek, L., & Becker, K. (2004). Trauma exposure and retention in adolescent substance abuse treatment. *Journal of Traumatic Stress, 17*, 113–121.

54. Myers, M. G., Stewart, D. G., & Brown, S. A. (1998). Progression from conduct disorder to antisocial personality disorder following treatment for adolescent substance abuse. *American Journal of Psychiatry, 155*, 479–485.

55. Rivers, S. M., Greenbaum, R. L., & Goldberg, E. (2001). Hospital-based adolescent substance abuse treatment: Comorbidity, outcomes, and gender. *The Journal of Nervous and Mental Disease, 189*, 229–237.

56. Sullivan, M. A., & Rudnik-Levin, F. (2001). Attention deficit/hyperactivity disorder and substance abuse: Diagnostic and therapeutic considerations. *Annals of the New York Academy of Sciences, 931*, 251–270.

57. Wise, B. K., Cuffe, S. P., & Fischer, T. (2001). Dual diagnosis and successful participation of adolescents in substance abuse treatment. *Journal of Substance Abuse Treatment, 21*, 161–5.

58. Scheier, L. M., & Botvin, G. J. (1996). Cognitive effects of marijuana. *Journal of the American Medical Association, 275*, 1547.

59. Kaminer, Y., Burleson, J. A., & Jadamec, A. (2002). Gambling behavior in adolescent substance abuse. *Substance Abuse, 23*, 191–198.

60. Smith, D. E., Schwartz, R. H., & Martin, D. M. (1989). Heavy cocaine use by adolescents. *Pediatrics, 83*, 539–542.

61. Myers, M. G., & Brown, S. A. (1994). Smoking and health in substance-abusing adolescents: A two-year follow-up. *Pediatrics, 93*, 561–566.

62. Marshall, M. J., Marshall, S., & Heer, M .J. (1994). Characteristics of abstinent substance abusers who first sought treatment in adolescence. *Journal of Drug Education, 24*, 151–162.

63. Hsieh, S., Hoffmann, N. G., & Hollister, C. D. (1998). The relationship between pre-, during-, post-treatment factors, and adolescent substance abuse behaviors. *Addictive Behaviors, 23*, 477–488.

64. Latimer, W. W., Newcomb, M., Winters, K C., & Stinchfield, R. D. (2000). Adolescent substance abuse treatment outcome: The role of substance abuse problem severity, psychosocial, and treatment factors. *Journal of Consulting and Clinical Psychology, 68,* 684–696.

65. Latimer, W. W., Winters, K. C., Stinchfield, R., & Traver, R. E. (2000). Demographic, individual, and interpersonal predictors of adolescent alcohol and marijuana use following treatment. *Psychology of Addictive Behaviors, 14,* 162–173.

66. Blood, L., & Cornwall, A. (1994). Pretreatment variables that predict completion of an adolescent substance abuse treatment program. *Journal of Nervous and Mental Disease, 182,* 14–19.

67. Brown, S. A. (1999). Treatment of adolescent alcohol problems: Research review and appraisal. *NIAAA Extramural Scientific Advisory Board: Treatment* (chapter 14, pp. 1–26). Bethesda, MD: National Institute on Alcohol Abuse and Alcoholism.

68. Myers, M. G., Brown, S. A., & Mott, M. A. (1993). Coping as a predictor of adolescent substance abuse treatment outcome. *Journal of Substance Abuse, 5,* 15–29.

69. Stinchfield, R. D., Niforopulos, L., & Feder, S. H. (1994). Follow-up contact bias in adolescent substance abuse treatment outcome research. *Journal of Studies on Alcohol, 55*(3), 285–289.

70. Brown, S. A., Vik, P.W., & Creamer, V A. (1989). Characteristics of relapse following adolescent substance abuse treatment. *Addictive Behaviors, 14*(3), 291–300.

71. Schottenfeld, R. S. (1994). Assessment of the patient. In M. Galanter & H. D. Kleber (Eds.), *The American Psychiatric Press textbook of substance abuse treatment* (pp. 109–120). Washington, DC: American Psychiatric Press.

72. Rychtarik, R. G., Koutsky, J. R., & Miller, W. R. (1998). Profiles of the alcohol use inventory: A large sample cluster analysis conducted with split-sample replication rules. *Psychological Assessment, 10,* 107–119.

73. Rychtarik, R. G., Koutsky, J. R., & Miller, W. R. (1999). Profiles of the alcohol use inventory: Correction to Rychtarik, Koutsky, and Miller (1998). *Psychological Assessment, 11,* 396–402.

74. Annis, H. M. (1984). *Situational Confidence Questionnaire short form.* Toronto, Ontario, Canada: Addiction Research Foundation.

75. Newcomb, M. D., & Felix-Ortiz, M. (1992). Multiple protective and risk factors for drug use and abuse: Cross-sectional and prospective findings. *Journal of Personality and Social Psychology, 63,* 280–296.

76. First, M. B., Spitzer, R. L., Gibbon, M. (1996). *Structured Clinical Interview for DSM-IV.* New York: Biometrics Research Department, New York Psychiatric Institute.

77. Ewing, J. A. (1984). Detecting alcoholism: The CAGE questionnaire. *Journal of the American Medical Association, 252,* 1905–1907.

78. Riggs, S. G., & Alario, A. J. (1989). Adolescent substance abuse. In C. E. Dube, M. G. Goldstein, D. C. Lewis, D. C. Myers, & W. R. Zwick (Eds.), *The Project ADEPT curriculum for primary care physician training* (p. 27). Providence, RI: Brown University, Center for Alcohol and Addiction Studies.

79. Knight, J. R., Shrier, L. A., Bravender, T. D., Farrell, M., Vanderbilt, J., & Shaffer, H. J. (1999). A new brief screen for adolescent substance abuse. *Archives of Pediatrics and Adolescent Medicine, 153,* 591–596.

80. Mayer, J., & Filstead, W .J. (1979). The Adolescent Alcohol Involvement Scale: An instrument for measuring adolescents' use and misuse of alcohol. *Journal of Studies on Alcohol, 40,* 291–300.

81. Brown, S. A., Christiansen, B. A., & Goldman, M. S. (1987). The Alcohol Expectancy Questionnaire: An instrument for the assessment of adolescent and adult alcohol expectancies. *Journal of Studies on Alcohol, 48,* 483–491.

82. Fromme, K., Stroot, E. A., & Kaplan, D. (1993).Comprehensive effects of alcohol: Development and psychometric assessment of a new expectancy questionnaire. *Psychological Assessment, 5,* 19–26.

83. Stroot, E. A., & Fromme, K. (1989, November). *Comprehensive effects of alcohol: Development of a new expectancy questionnaire.* Paper presented at the 23rd annual meeting of the Association for Advancement of Behavior Therapy, Washington, DC.

84. D'Amico, E. J. & Fromme, K. (1997). Health risk behaviors of adolescent and young adult siblings. *Health Psychology, 16,* 426–432.

85. DiClemente, C. C., Carbonari, J. P., Montgomery, R. P., & Hughes, S. O. (1994). The Alcohol Abstinence Self-Efficacy scale. *Journal of Studies on Alcohol, 55,* 141–148.

86. Miele, G. M., Carpenter, K. M., Smith Cockerham, M., Trautman, K. D., Blaine, J., & Hasin, D. S. (2000). Substance Dependence Severity Scale (SDSS): Reliability and validity of a clinician-administered interview for *DSM-IV* substance use disorders. *Drug and Alcohol Dependence, 59,* 63–75.

87. Harrell, T. H., Honaker, L. M., & Davis, E. (1991). Cognitive and behavioral dimensions of dysfunction in alcohol and polydrug abusers. *Journal of Substance Abuse, 3,* 415–426.

88. Rahdert, E. (1991). *Adolescent assessment/referral system manual.* Washington, DC: U.S. Department of Health and Human Services (Publication No. [ADM] 91–1735).

89. Klitzner, M., Schwartz, R., Gruenwald, P., & Blasinsky, M. (1987). Screening for risk factors for adolescent alcohol and drug use. *American Journal of Diseases of Children, 141,* 45–49.

90. White, H. R., & Labouvie, E. W. (1989). Toward the assessment of adolescent problem drinking. *Journal of Studies on Alcohol, 50,* 30–37.

91. Annis, H. M. (1982). *Inventory of Drinking Situations.* Toronto, Ontario, Canada: Addiction Research Foundation of Ontario.

92. Annis, H. M., & Graham, J. M. (1991). *Inventory of Drug-Taking Situations (IDTS): User's guide.* Toronto, Ontario, Canada: Addiction Research Foundation of Ontario.

93. Winters, K. C., & Henly, G. A. (1993). *Adolescent Diagnostic Interview Schedule and Manual.* Los Angeles: Western Psychological Services.

94. Winters, K. C., Stinchfield, R. D., & Henly, G. A. (1993). Further validation of new scales measuring adolescent alcohol and other drug abuse. *Journal of Studies on Alcohol, 54,* 534–541.

95. McLellan, A. T., Luborsky, L., Woody, G. E., & O'Brien, C. P. (1980). An improved diagnostic evaluation instrument for substance abuse patients: The Addiction Severity Index. *Journal of Nervous and Mental Disease, 168,* 26–33.

96. Friedman, A. S., & Utada, A. (1989). A method for diagnosing and planning the treatment of adolescent drug abusers (the Adolescent Drug Abuse Diagnosis [ADAD] instrument). *Journal of Drug Education, 19,* 285–312.

97. Meyers, K., McLellan, A. T., Jaeger, J. L., & Pettinati, H. M. (1995). The development of the Comprehensive Addiction Severity Index for Adolescents (CASI-A): An interview for assessing multiple problems of adolescents. *Journal of Substance Abuse Treatment, 12,* 181–193.

98. Nishimura, S. T., Hishinuma, E. S., Miyamoto, R. H., Goebert, D. A., Johnson, R. C., Yuen, N. Y., & Andrade, N. N. (2001). Prediction of DISC substance abuse and dependency for ethnically diverse adolescents. *Journal of Substance Abuse, 13,* 597–607.

99. Rogers, R., Cashel, M. L., Johansen, J., Sewell, K. W., & Gonzalez, C. (1997). Evaluation of adolescent offenders with substance abuse: Validation of the SASSI with conduct-disordered youth. *Criminal Justice and Behavior, 24,* 114–128.

100. Dennis, M. L., Funk, R., Godley, S. H., Godley, M. D., & Waldron, H. (2004). Cross-validation of the alcohol and cannabis use measures in the Global Appraisal of Individual Needs (GAIN) and Timeline Followback (TLFB; Form 90) among adolescents in substance abuse treatment. *Addiction, 99* Suppl 2, 120–128.

101. Petchers, M. K., & Singer, M. I. (1987). Perceived-Benefit-of-Drinking Scale: Approach to screening for adolescent alcohol abuse. *Journal of Pediatrics, 110,* 977–981.

102. Petchers, M. K., Singer, M. I, Angelotta, J. W., & Chow, J. (1988). Revalidation and expansion of an adolescent substance abuse screening measure. *Journal of Development and Behavioral Pediatrics, 9,* 25–29.

103. Moberg, D. P., & Hahn, L. (1991). The Adolescent Drug Involvement Scale. *Journal of Adolescent Chemical Dependency, 2,* 75–88.

104. Metzger, D., Kushner, H., & McLellan, A. T. (1991). *Adolescent Problem Severity Index.* Philadelphia: University of Pennsylvania.

105. Goldberger, B. A., & Jenkins, A. J. (1999). Drug toxicology. In P. J. Ott, R. E. Tarter, & R. T. Ammerman (Eds) *Sourcebook on substance abuse: Etiology, epidemiology, assessment, and treatment* (pp. 184–196). Boston: Allyn and Bacon.

106. ADE, Inc. (1987). *Juvenile Automated Substance Abuse Evaluations (JASAE).* Clarkston, MI: ADE.

107. Sussman, S., Earleywine, M., Wills, T., Cody, C., Biglan, T., Dent, C. W., & Newcomb, M. D. (2004). The motivation, skills, and decision-making model of drug abuse prevention. *Substance Use and Misuse, 39*(10–12), 1971–2016.

108. Skara, S., & Sussman, S. (2003). A review of 25 long-term adolescent tobacco and other drug use prevention program evaluations. *Preventive Medicine, 37,* 451–474.

109. Evans, R. I. (1976). Smoking in children: Developing a social psychological strategy of deterrence. *Preventive Medicine, 5,* 122–127.

110. Botvin, G. J., Baker, E., Dusenbury, L., Botvin, E. M., & Diaz, T. (1995). Long-term follow-up results of a randomized drug abuse prevention trial in a white middle-class population. *Journal of the American Medical Association, 273,* 1106–1112.

111. Sussman, S., Dent, C. W., Burton, D., Stacy, A. W., & Flay, B. R. (1995). *Developing school-based tobacco use prevention and cessation programs.* Thousand Oaks, CA: Sage.

112. Sussman, S., Dent, C. W., & Stacy, A. W. (2002). Project Towards No Drug Abuse: A review of the findings and future directions. *American Journal of Health Behavior, 26,* 354–365.

113. Sussman, S., Sun, P., McCuller, W. J., & Dent, C. W. (2003). Project Towards No Drug Abuse: Two-year outcomes of a trial that compares health educator delivery to self-instruction. *Preventive Medicine, 37,* 155–162.

114. Godley, M. D., & White, W. L. (2005). A brief history and some current dimensions of adolescent treatment in the United States. In M. Galanter (Ed.), *Recent developments in alcoholism. Volume 17: Alcohol problems in adolescents and young adults* (pp. 367–382). New York: Kluwer.

115. Substance Abuse and Mental Health Services Administration Center for Substance Abuse Treatment. (2001). *Quick Guide for Clinicians Based on Tips 31 and Tips 32: Screening and Assessing Adolescents for Substance Use Disorders.* Pub # (SMA) 01–3596. Rockville, MD: U.S. Department of Health and Human Services.

116. Blum, R. W. (1997). Adolescent substance use and abuse. *Archives of Pediatric and Adolescent Medicine, 151,* 805–808.

117. Tims, F. M., Dennis, M. L., Hamilton, N. J., Buchan, B., Diamond, G., Funk, R., & Brantley, L. B. (2002). Characteristics and problems of 600 adolescent cannabis abusers in outpatient treatment. *Addiction, 97* Suppl 1, 46–57.

118. Weiner, M. D., Sussman, S., McCuller, W. J., & Lichtman, K. (1999). Factors in marijuana cessation among high-risk youth. *Journal of Drug Education, 29,* 337–357.

119. Weddle, M., & Kokotailo, P. (2002). Adolescent substance abuse: Confidentiality and consent. *Pediatric Clinics of North America, 49,* 301–315.

120. Jainchill, N., Bhattacharya, G., & Yagelka, J. (1995). Therapeutic communities for adolescents. *NIDA Research Monograph, 156,* 190–217.

121. Liddle, H. A., & Dakof, G. A. (1995). Family-based treatment for adolescent drug use: State of the science. *NIDA Research Monograph, 156,* 218–254.

122. Meichenbaum, D. (1977). *Cognitive behavior modification: An integrative approach.* New York: Plenum.

123. Kaminer, Y. (1995). Pharmacotherapy for adolescents with psychoactive substance use disorders. *NIDA Research Monograph, 156*, 291–324.

124. Sussman, S. (2002). Effects of sixty-six adolescent tobacco use cessation trials and seventeen prospective studies of self-initiated quitting. *Tobacco Induced Diseases, 1*, 35–81.

125. Kaminer, Y., Burleson, J. A., & Goldberger, R. (2002). Cognitive-behavioral coping skills and psychoeducation therapies for adolescent substance abuse. *The Journal of Nervous and Mental Disease, 190*, 737–745.

126. Kaminer, Y., & Burleson, J. (1999). Psychotherapies for adolescent substance abusers: 15-month follow-up. *The American Journal on Addictions, 8*, 114–119.

127. Battjes, R. J., Gordon, M. S., O'Grady, K. E., Kinlock, T. W., Katz, E. C., & Sears, E. A. (2004). Evaluation of a group-based substance abuse treatment program for adolescents. *Journal of Substance Abuse Treatment, 27*, 123–134.

128. Liddle, H. A., Rowe, C. L., Dakof, G. A., Ungaro, R. A., & Henderson, C. E. (2004). Early intervention for adolescent substance abuse: Pretreatment to posttreatment outcomes of a randomized clinical trial comparing multidimensional family therapy and peer group treatment. *Journal of Psychoactive Drugs, 36*, 49–63.

129. Kaminer, Y., & Slesnick, N. (2005). Evidence-based cognitive-behavioral and family therapies for adolescent alcohol and other substance use disorders. In M. Galanter (Ed.), *Recent developments in alcoholism. Volume 17: Alcohol problems in adolescents and young adults* (pp. 383–405). New York: Kluwer.

130. Curry, J. F., Wells, K. C., Lochman, J. E., Craighead, W. E., & Nagy, P. D. (2003). Cognitive-behavioral intervention for depressed, substance-abusing adolescents: Development and pilot testing. *Journal of the American Academy of Child and Adolescent Psychiatry, 42*, 656–665.

131. Dasinger, L. K., Shane, P. A., & Martinovich Z. (2004). Assessing the effectiveness of community-based substance abuse treatment for adolescents. *Journal of Psychoactive Drugs, 36*, 27–33.

132. Funk, R. R., McDermeit, M., Godley, S. H., & Adams, L. (2003). Maltreatment issues by level of adolescent substance abuse treatment: The extent of the problem at intake and relationship to early outcomes. *Child Maltreatment, 8*, 36–45.

133. Rounds-Bryant, J. L., Kristiansen, P. L., & Hubbard, R. L. (1999). Drug abuse treatment outcome study of adolescents: A comparison of client characteristics and pretreatment behaviors in three treatment modalities. *American Journal of Drug and Alcohol Abuse, 25*, 573–591.

134. Dinges, N. G., & Duong-Tran, Q. (1993). Stressful life events and co-occurring depression, substance abuse and suicidality among American Indian and Alaska Native adolescents. *Culture, Medicine, and Psychiatry, 16*, 487–502.

135. Deas, D., & Thomas, S. E. (2001). An overview of controlled studies of adolescent substance abuse treatment. *The American Journal on Addictions, 10*, 178–189

136. Henggeler, S. W., Clingempeel, W. G., Brondino, M. J., & Pickrel, .G. (2002). Four-year follow-up of multisytemic therapy with substance-abusing and

substance-dependent juvenile offenders. *Journal of the American Academy of Child and Adolescent Psychiatry, 41*, 868–874.

137. Bosworth, K. (1996). *Definition of SAP: Teacher Talk.* Available at: ⟨http://education.indiana.edu/cas/tt/v3i3/sapdef.html⟩. Retrieved July 15, 2005.

138. Levy, S., Vaughan, B. L., & Knight, J. R. (2002). Office-based intervention for adolescent substance abuse. *Pediatric Clinics of North America, 49*, 329–343.

139. Kaye, D. L. (2004). Office recognition and management of adolescent substance abuse. *Current Opinion in Pediatrics, 16*, 532–541.

140. Farrow, J. A. (1995). Service delivery strategies for treating high-risk youth: Delinquents, homeless, runaways, and sexual minorities. *NIDA Research Monograph, 156*, 39–48.

141. Alcoholics Anonymous. (2001). *Alcoholics Anonymous 2001 Membership Survey.* New York: Alcoholics Anonymous World Services.

142. Kaminer, Y. (2001). Alcohol and drug abuse: Adolescent substance abuse treatment: Where do we go from here? *Psychiatric Services, 52*, 147–149.

143. Kelly, J. F., Myers, M. G., & Brown, S. A. (2000). A multivariate process model of adolescent 12-step attendance and substance use outcome following inpatient treatment. *Psychology of Addictive Behaviors, 14*, 376–389.

144. Grenard, J. L., Ames, S. L., Pentz, M. A., & Sussman, S. Y. (in press). Motivational interviewing with adolescents and young adults for drug-related problems. *International Journal of Adolescent Medicine and Health* (Special issue on adolescence and alcohol).

145. Miller, W. R., & Rollnick, S. (2002). *Motivational interviewing: Preparing people for change* (2nd ed.). New York: Guilford.

146. Council of Philosophical Studies (1981). *Psychology and the philosophy of mind in the philosophy curriculum.* San Francisco: San Francisco State University.

147. Tonigan, J. S., Toscova, R., & Miller, W. R. (1996). Meta-analysis of the literature on Alcoholics Anonymous: Sample and study characteristics moderate findings. *Journal of Studies on Alcohol, 57*, 65–72.

148. Dunphy, D. C. (1963). The social structure of urban adolescent peer groups. *Sociometry, 26*, 230–246.

149. Gavin, L. A., & Furman, W. (1989). Age differences in adolescents' perceptions of their groups. *Developmental Psychology, 25*, 827–834.

150. Shrum, W., & Cheek, N. H. (1987). Social structure during the school years: Onset of the degrouping process. *American Sociological Review, 52*, 218–223.

151. Jessor, R. (1984). Adolescent development and behavioral health. In J. D. Matarazzo, S. M. Weiss, J. A. Herd, N. E. Miller & S. M. Weiss (Eds.), *Behavioral health: A handbook of health enhancement and disease prevention* (Chap. 4). New York: Wiley.

152. Arnett, J. J. (2000). Emerging adulthood: A theory of development from the late teens through the twenties. *American Psychologist, 55*, 469–480.

153. Bachman, J., Wadsworth, K., O'Malley, P., Johnston, L., & Schulenberg, J. (1997). *Smoking, drinking, and drug use in young adulthood: The impacts of new freedoms and new responsibilities.* Mahway, NJ: Erlbaum.

154. Aseltine, R. H., & Gore, S. L. (2000). The variable effects of stress on alcohol use from adolescence to early adulthood. *Substance Use and Misuse, 35*, 643–668.

155. Stein, J. A., Newcomb, M. D., & Bentler, P. M. (1986). Stability and change in personality: A longitudinal study from early adolescence to young adulthood. *Journal of Research in Personality, 20*, 276–291.

156. Brook, J. S., Whiteman, M., Cohen, P., Shapiro, J., & Balka, E. (1995). Longitudinally predicting late adolescent and young adult drug use: Childhood and adolescent precursors. *Journal of the American Academy of Child Adolescent Psychiatry, 34*, 1230–1238.

157. Guo, J., Hawkins, J. D., Hill, K. G., & Abbott, R. D. (2001). Childhood and adolescent predictors of alcohol abuse and dependence in young adulthood. *Journal of Studies on Alcohol, 62*, 754–762.

158. Krohn, M. D., Lizotte, A. J., & Perez, C. M. (1997). The interrelationship between substance use and precocious transitions to adult statuses. *Journal of Health and Social Behavior, 38*, 87–103.

159. Maggs, J. L., Frome, P. M., Eccles, J. S., & Barber, B. L. (1997). Psychosocial resources, adolescent risk behaviour and young adult adjustment: Is risk taking more dangerous for some than others? *Journal of Adolescence, 20*, 103–119.

160. Brook, J. S., Balka, E. B., Gursen, M. D., Brook, D. W., & Shapiro, J. (1997). Young adults' drug use: A 17-year longitudinal inquiry of antecedents. *Psychological Reports, 80*, 1235–1251.

161. Brook, D. W., Brook, J. S., Zhang, C., Cohen, P., & Whiteman, M. (2002). Drug use and the risk of major depressive disorder, alcohol dependence, and substance use disorders. *Archives of General Psychiatry, 59*, 1039–1044.

162. Rohrbach, L. A., Sussman, S., Dent, C. W., & Sun, P. (2005). Tobacco, alcohol, and other drug use among high-risk young people: A five-year longitudinal study from adolescence to emerging adulthood. *Journal of Drug Issues, 35*(2), 333–356.

163. Center for Substance Abuse Treatment (CSAT). (2000). Integrating substance abuse treatment and vocational services. *Treatment Improvement Protocol (TIP) Series* 38. Washington, DC: U.S. Government Printing Office (DHHS Publication No. (SMA) 00–3470).

164. Greenbaum, P. E., Prange, M. E., Friedman, R. M., & Silver, S. E. (1991). Substance abuse prevalence and comorbidity with other psychiatric disorders among adolescents with severe emotional disturbances. *Journal of the American Academy of Child and Adolescent Psychiatry, 30*, 575–583.

165. Osher, F. C., & Kofoed, L. L. (1989). Treatment of patients with psychiatric and psychoactive substance abuse disorders. *Hospital and Community Psychiatry, 40*, 1025–1030.

166. Sussman, S., Petosa, R., & Leventhal, H. (2001). Needs for the future of program development. In S. Sussman (Ed.), *Handbook of program development for health behavior research and practice.* Thousand Oaks, CA: Sage.

Chapter 8

Workaholism

Ronald J. Burke

This review examines the literature on workaholism in organizations. Workaholism is acknowledged to be a stable individual characteristic, although how it is distinguished from other characteristics is often unclear.[1] The review addresses the following areas: definitions of workaholism, measures of workaholism, the prevalence of workaholism, types of workaholics, validating job behaviors, antecedents of workaholism, work consequences, health consequences, extrawork satisfactions and family functioning, evaluating workaholism components, possible gender differences, reducing workaholism, and future research directions.

Although the popular press has paid considerable attention to workaholism,[2–9] very little research has been undertaken to further our understanding of it. Most writing has been anecdotal and clinical;[2,6,10,11] basic questions of definition have not been addressed and measurement concerns have been avoided.[12]

It should come as no surprise, then, that opinions, observations, and conclusions about workaholism are both varied and conflicting. Some writers view workaholism positively from an organizational perspective.[8,12–14] Machlowitz[8] conducted a qualitative interview study of 100 workaholics and found them to be very satisfied and productive. Others view workaholism negatively.[6,10,11] These writers equate workaholism with other addictions and depict workaholics as unhappy, obsessive, tragic figures who are not performing their jobs well and are creating difficulties for their coworkers.[10,15,16] The former would advocate the encouragement of workaholism; the latter would discourage it.

DEFINITIONS OF WORKAHOLISM

Research on workaholism has been hindered by the absence of acceptable definitions and measures.[12] Mosier defined workaholism in terms of hours worked; workaholics were those who worked at least 50 hours per week.[17] Cherrington sees workaholism as "an irrational commitment to excessive work.[18] Workaholics are unable to take time off or to comfortably divert their interests" (p. 257). Machlowitz defines workaholics as people "who always devote more time and thoughts to their work than the situation demands ... what sets workaholics apart from other workers is their attitude toward work, not the number of hours they work" (p. 11).[8] Killinger defines a workaholic as "a person who gradually becomes emotionally crippled and addicted to control and power in a compulsive drive to gain approval and success" (p. 6).[6] Robinson defines workaholism "as a progressive, potentially fatal disorder, characterized by self-imposed demands, compulsive overworking, inability to regulate work habits and an over-indulgence in work to the exclusion of most other life activities" (p. 81).[19]

Oates, generally acknowledged as the first person to use the word *workaholic*, defined it as "a person whose need for work has become so excessive that it creates noticeable disturbance or interference with his bodily health, personal happiness, and interpersonal relationships, and with his smooth social functioning" (p.4).[10] Porter defines workaholism as "an excessive involvement with work evidenced by neglect in other areas of life and based on internal motives of behavior maintenance rather than requirements of the job or organization" (p. 71).[16]

Scott, Moore, and Miceli used a three-step process to develop what they term a reasonable definition of the construct.[12] They first collected characteristics attributed to workaholics in the practical and clinical literature. They then looked for conceptual similarities among these characteristics. They also differentiated the workaholic concept from similar constructs (e.g., job involvement) to reduce redundancy. They identified three elements in workaholic behavior patterns using this process: discretionary time spent in work activities, thinking about work when not working, and working beyond organizational requirements.

Spence and Robbins were the first researchers to define workaholism.[20] They define the workaholic as a person who "is highly work involved, feels compelled or driven to work because of inner pressures, and is low in enjoyment at work" (p. 62). Most writers view workaholism as a stable individual characteristic.[12,20] In addition, most definitions of workaholism have negative connotations. Finally, most writers use the terms *excessive work, workaholism,* and *work addiction* interchangeably.

Despite these broad and varying definitions, a compelling case could be made for devoting more research attention to workaholism. There have been suggestions that workaholism may be increasing in North America.[2,21] It is not clear whether workaholism actually has positive or negative organizational consequences.[6,8] There is also debate on the association of workaholic behaviors with a variety of personal well-being indicators, such as psychological and physical health and self-esteem. Finally, different types of workaholic behavior patterns likely exist, each having unique antecedents and outcomes. The question of whether workaholism can, or should be, reduced has also been raised.[6,16,22]

MEASURES OF WORKAHOLISM

Some writers have developed measures of workaholism,[2,6,8,20,23,24,25] but with the exception of Robinson and Spence and Robbins, most were not based on a clear definition of workaholism, nor do they provide psychometric information on the measure and its validity.[19,20]

A number of measures of workaholism have been reported in both the popular and academic literatures. Many of these are listings of behaviors in checklist form, are used once, and are never validated. Machlowitz lists 10 characteristics (e.g., "Do you get up early, no matter how late you go to bed?") in a yes/no format.[8] She writes that if a person answers yes to eight or more questions, the person may be a workaholic. Doerfler and Kammer used this measure in a study of male and female attorneys, physicians, and psychologists.[25] Killinger lists 30 items in her workaholic quiz (e.g., "Do you think you are special or different from other people?"), also answered in a yes/no format.[6] She suggests that 20 or more yes answers indicate the respondent is likely a workaholic. There is no information about where these items came from nor any psychometric information about the properties of these two scales.

Two other measures of workaholism have been developed and reported along with information of some of each measure's properties.[19,20] Robinson and his colleagues developed the Work Addiction Risk Test (WART). WART contains 25 items drawn from symptoms (characteristics) reported by writers on workaholism.[26] Respondents rate items on a four-point Likert scale (1 = Never true, 4 = Always true) according to how well each item describes their work habits (e.g., "It's important that I see the concrete results of what I do"). Scores can range from 25 to 100. Robinson states that scores of 25 to 56 indicate that a respondent is not work addicted, scores from 57 to 66, mildly work addicted, and scores from 67 to 100, highly work addicted.[19] Scores above 65 fall greater than one standard deviation above the mean. The items on WART, based on a review of available literature, were grouped into five categories: overdoing, self-worth, control–perfectionism, intimacy, and preoccupation-future reference.

Robinson and his colleagues report a number of short studies providing psychometric information for WART. They indicate a test-retest reliability over a two-week period in a sample of 151 university students of .83, with a coefficient alpha of .85.[27] Robinson and Post reported a split-half reliablities in three data sets:169 college students, 106 graduate students, and 194 members of Workaholics Anonymous.[28] Based on 442 respondents, a Spearman-Brown split-half coefficient of .85 was obtained.

Face validity was determined by having 50 working adults place each of the 25 WART items into one of the five broader categories (e.g., overdoing). On average, the 25 items were correctly allocated to the five umbrella categories by 70 percent of these graduate students.[29]

Robinson tested the criterion-related validity of WART, again in sample of students, by correlating WART scores with measures of Type-A behavior and anxiety.[30] Comparing high, medium, and low WART scorers showed that students scoring higher on WART also scored higher on anxiety and some Type-A components. These findings are not surprising given the conceptual and content overlap between WART and the two criterion measures.

Spence and Robbins report the development of their workaholism measure, providing both reliability and concurrent validity information.[20] Based on their definition of workaholism, developed from a review of the literature, they prepose three workaholism components: work involvement, feeling driven to the work, and work enjoyment. They developed multi-item measures of these components, each having internal consistency reliabilities greater than .67 in a study of 368 social workers holding academic appointments.

PREVALENCE OF WORKAHOLISM

Not surprisingly, given the varied and ambiguous nature of workaholism definitions, estimates of the prevalance of workaholics vary. Machlowitz estimated that 5 percent of the U.S. population were workaholics.[8] Doerfler and Kammer, using Macholwitz's measure, reported that 23 percent of their sample of physicians, lawyers, and psychiatrists/therapists were workaholics.[25] Kanai, Wakabayashi, and Fling, in a large Japanese sample consisting primarily of managers, found that about 21 percent fell into the Spence and Robbins Work Addict profile.[31] Spence and Robbins reported, in a sample of professors of social work, that 8 percent of men and 13 percent of women fell into their Work Addict profile.[20] Elder and Spence (unpublished manuscript), based on a sample of MBA graduates in the United States, observed percentages falling into workaholism profiles similar to those noted in the earlier (1992) Spence and Robbins study.[31]

TYPES OF WORKAHOLICS

Some researchers have proposed the existence of different types of workaholic behavior patterns, each having potentially different antecedents and associations with job performance and work and life outcomes.[12,15,20] Naughton presents a typology of workaholism based on the dimensions of career commitment and obsession-compulsion.[15] Job-involved workaholics (high work commitment, low obsession-compulsion) are hypothesized to perform well in demanding jobs, be highly job satisfied with low interest in nonwork activities Compulsive workaholics (high work commitment, high obsession-compulsion) are hypothesized to be potentially poor performers (staff problems resulting from impatience and ritualized work habits). Nonworkaholics (low work commitment and obsession-compulsion) spend more time on nonwork commitments. Compulsive nonworkaholics (low work commitment, high obsession-compulsion) compulsively spend time in nonwork activities.

Scott, Moore, and Miceli suggest three types of workaholic behavior patterns: compulsive-dependent, perfectionist, and achievement-oriented.[12] They hypothesize that compulsive-dependent workaholism will be positively related to levels of anxiety, stress, and physical and psychological problems, and negatively related to job performance and job and life satisfaction. Perfectionist workaholism will be positively related to levels of stress, physical and psychological problems, hostile interpersonal relationships, low job satisfaction and performance, and voluntary turnover and absenteeism. Finally, achievement-oriented workaholism will be positively related to physical and psychological health, job and life satisfaction, job performance, low voluntary turnover, and prosocial behaviors.

Spence and Robbins, using profile analysis, identified three workaholic types based on their workaholic triad notion.[20] The workaholic triad consists of three concepts: work involvement, feeling driven to work, and work enjoyment. Work Addicts (WAs) score high on work involvement and feeling driven to work and low on work enjoyment. Work Enthusiasts (WEs) score high on work involvement and work enjoyment and low on feeling driven to work. Enthusiastic Addicts (EAs) score high on all three components. Three other studies using the same three scales have produced essentially the same profiles.[31,32,33] These researchers offer a number of hypotheses as to how these three workaholic patterns might differ from each other. Thus, WAs would be more perfectionistic, would experience greater stress, and would report more physical health symptoms. The existence of different types of workaholic patterns might help reconcile the conflicting observations and conclusions cited above.

Oates identified five types of workaholics: dyed-in-the-wool workaholics, converted workaholics, situational workaholics, pseudoworkaholics, and escapists posing as workaholics.[10] Fassel described four types of workaholics: compulsive workers, binge workers, closet workers, and work anorexics.[2] Robinson distinguished four types of workaholics: relentless workaholics, bulimic workaholics, attention deficit workaholics, and savoring workaholics.[19] The three Spence and Robbins workaholism types are the only types that have received research attention.[20]

RESEARCH FINDINGS

The following sections of the chapter will review selected research findings that compare the three types of workaholics proposed by Spence and Robbins on personal demographic and work situation characteristics, job behaviors likely to be associated with workaholism, work outcomes, personal life and family functioning, and indicators of psychological well-being. Other studies not based on the Spence and Robbins workaholism types will also be incorporated in this review as relevant.

Personal Demographic and Work Situational Characteristics

A critical question involved potential differences between the three workaholism types on both personal demographic and work-situation characteristics such as hours and extra hours worked per week. If the workaholism types were found to differ on these (e.g., organizational level, marital status, hours worked per week), these demographic or work-situation differences might account for any differences found on work and health outcomes.

A number of studies have reported essentially no differences between the workaholism types on a variety of personal and work situation characteristics.[20,34–36] The workaholism types work the same number of hours and extra hours per week—significantly more hours and extra hours per week than the nonworkaholism types. The workaholism types were similar in terms of age, gender, marital and parental status, job and organizational tenure, income, and organizational size.

Validating Job Behaviors

There has been considerable speculation regarding the job behaviors likely to be exhibited by workaholics. This list includes job involvement, job stress, nondelegation of job responsibilities to others, levels of job performance, levels of interpersonal conflict, and of lack of trust. Empirical research has examined some of these hypothesized relationships.

Both Spence and Robbins and Burke provide evidence of the concurrent validity of the Spence and Robbins workaholism profiles.[20,34] Both studies included the same measures of validating job behaviors (e.g., job involvement, job stress, time committed to job, perfectionism, nondelegation of tasks).

Comparisons of the workaholism types on a number of behavioral manifestations strongly supported the hypothesized relationships. First, EAs devoted more psychological sense of time to job than did both WEs and WAs. Second, WAs reported greater job stress than did EAs, both reporting greater job stress than did WEs. Third, both EAs and WEs reported greater job involvement than did WAs. Fourth, WAs indicated greater unwillingness to delegate than did both EAs and WEs. Fifth, EAs were more perfectionistic than were WEs.

Spence and Robbins found that WAs reported higher levels of job stress, perfectionism, and unwillingness to delegate job duties to others then did WEs. Kanai, Wakabayashi, and Fling, using the Spence and Robbins measures, reported that EAs and WAs scored higher than WEs on measures of job stress, perfectionism, nondelegation, and time committed to job.[31] Elder and Spence (unpublished manuscript), in a sample of women and men MBA graduates, report that WAs and EAs scored higher than WEs on measures of perfectionism, job stress, and nondelegation.[32] Taken together, these studies consistently showed that WAs exhibited higher levels of these validating job behaviors than did one or both of the two other workaholic profiles (WEs and EAs).

Antecedents of Workaholism

Three potential antecedents of workaholism have received some conceptual and research attention. Two of these, family of origin and personal beliefs and fears, are the result of socialization practices within families and society at large. The third, organizational support for work-personal life balance, represents organizational values and priorities.

Family of Origin

Robinson has written about work addiction as a symptom of a diseased family system.[19,37,38] Work addiction, similar to other addictive behaviors, is intergenerational and passed on to future generations through family processes and dynamics. In this view, work addiction is seen as a learned addictive response to a dysfunctional family of origin system. Pietropinto suggests that children of workaholics learn that parental love is contingent on their (the children's) high performance.[39]

Although not tested directly (i.e., workaholism scores of parents were not examined in relation to workaholism scores of their children), Robinson and his colleagues equate elevated health symptoms of workaholic fathers with elevated health symptoms in their children (e.g., anxiety and depression) as support for such a relationship.[40,41]

Personal Beliefs and Fears

Burke examined the relationship of personal beliefs and fears and workaholism.[42] Beliefs and fears, a reflection of values, thoughts, and interpersonal styles, have been shown to be precursors of Type-A behavior.[43] Three measures of beliefs and fears developed by Lee, Jamieson, and Early were used.[44] One, striving against others, had six items (e.g., "There can only be one winner in any situation"). A second, no moral principles, had six items (e.g., "I think that nice guys finish last"). The third, prove yourself, had nine items (e.g., "I worry a great deal about what others think of me"). A total score was also obtained by combining these three scales.

Burke compared the three Spence and Robbins types on these measures of beliefs and fears. Was there a relationship between the cognitions that managers and professionals hold about their broader environment and levels of workaholism? Analyses provided evidence of such a relationship. First, all three beliefs and fears were significantly correlated with measures of feeling driven to work (positively) and work enjoyment (negatively). Second, comparisons of workaholism types showed significant type effects on all three measures of beliefs and fears as well as on their composite score.

More specifically, WAs scored significantly higher than WEs and EAs on measures of striving against others and no moral principles, as well as on the composite measure . In addition, WAs scored higher on the need to prove self than did WEs. Workaholism thus emerges as work behaviors in response to feelings of insecurity and low self-worth. This is best reflected in managers' feelings of being driven to work. Paradoxically, these beliefs and fears were also found to be associated with lower levels of work enjoyment .

Organizational Values

Burke[45] compared perceptions of organization culture values supporting work-personal life imbalance across the Spence and Robbins profiles. Organizational values encouraging work-family balance and imbalance were measured by scales proposed by Kofodimos.[46] Organizational values encouraging balance was measured by nine items (e.g., "Setting limits on hours spent at work"). Organizational values supporting imbalance was measured by eight items (e.g., "Traveling to and from work destinations on weekends"). A total imbalance score was obtained by combining both scales, reversing the balance scores.

There was considerable support for the hypothesized relationships. WAs reported lower balance values than both WEs and EAs and higher imbalance values than did WEs. In summary, WAs saw their workplaces as less supportive of work-personal life balance.

Work Outcomes

The relationship between workaholism and indicators of job and career satisfaction and success is difficult to specify. It is likely that different types of workaholics will report varying work and career satisfactions.[12]

Burke[47] compared levels of work and career satisfaction and success among the workaholism profiles observed by Spence and Robbins. Four work outcomes, all significantly intercorrelated, were used. Intent to quit was measured by two items (e.g., "Are you currently looking for a different job in a different organization?"). This scale had been used previously by Burke.[48] Work Satisfaction was measured by a seven-item scale developed by Kofodimos.[46] An item was "I feel challenged by my work." Career satisfaction was measured by a five-item scale developed by Greenhaus, Parasuraman, and Wormley.[49] One item was "I am satisfied with the success I have achieved in my career." Future career prospects were measured by a three-item scale developed by Greenhaus, Parasuraman and Wormley.[49] An item was "I expect to advance in my career to senior levels of management."

WAs scored lower than WEs and EAs on job satisfaction, career satisfaction, and future career prospects, and higher than WEs on intent to quit. Interestingly, all three workaholic profiles (WAs, EAs, and WEs) worked the same number of hours per week, had the same job and organizational tenure, and were the same ages.

Psychological Well-Being

There is considerable consensus in the workaholism literature on the association of workaholism with poorer psychological and physical well-being.[50] In fact, some definitions of workaholism incorporate aspects of diminished health as central elements. It is not surprising that this relationship has received research attention.

Burke compared workaholism types identified by Spence and Robbins (1992) on three indicators of psychological and physical well-being.[51] Data were obtained from 530 employed women and men MBAs using questionnaires. Psychosomatic symptoms were measured by nineteen items developed by Quinn and Shepard.[52] Respondents indicated how often they experienced each physical condition (e.g., headaches) in the past year. Lifestyle behaviors were measured by five items developed by Kofodimos.[46] One item was "I participate in a regular exercise program." Emotional well-being was measured by six items developed by Kofodimos.[46] An item was "I actively seek to understand and improve my emotional well-being."

The comparisons of the workaholism types on the three measures of psychological and physical well-being provided considerable support for the hypothesized relationships. Thus, WAs had more psychosomatic symptoms than both WEs and EAs and poorer physical and emotional well-being than did WEs.

Kanai, Wakabayashi, and Fling, using the workaholism triad components developed by Spence and Robbins in a sample of 1,072 Japanese workers from 10 companies, found that both WAs and EAs reported more health complaints than did WEs.[31] There were no differences between these three groups on measures of smoking, alcohol consumption, and serious illness, however. Spence and Robbins, in a sample of men and women social-work professors, noted that WAs indicated more health complaints than did individuals in their other two workaholic profiles.[20] Elder and Spence (unpublished manuscript), in their study of women and men MBA graduates, observed that WAs and EAs indicated more health complaints than did WEs. They also reported that WAs were less satisfied with their jobs and lives than were EWs and WEs.[32]

These studies indicate that WAs generally report greater psychological distress than either of the two other workaholism types.

Extrawork Satisfactions and Family Functioning

A number of writers have hypothesized that workaholism is likely to negatively affect family functioning.[6,16,19] Empirical examinations of this hypothesis are unfortunately few. Robinson and Post (1997) report data from a sample of 107 self-identified workaholics (members of Workaholics Anonymous chapters in North America) who completed WART and a family assessment instrument.[41] Three levels of WART scores representing increasing levels of workaholism were compared. High scores differed from low and medium scores on six of the seven family assessment scales, indicating lower (poorer) family functioning in all cases.

Robinson also reviews the literature on children of workaholics.[53] Robinson and Kelley asked 211 young adults (college students) to think back to their childhoods and rate the workaholism of their parents using WART.[40] Participants also completed measures of depression, anxiety, self-concept, and locus of control. College students who perceived their parents as workaholics scored higher on depression and external locus of control. Children of workaholic fathers scored higher on anxiety than did children of nonworkaholic fathers. Interestingly, mothers' workaholism had no effect on these outcomes. Robinson and Rhoden (1998) attribute the distress of children of workaholic fathers to the presence of a diseased family system, more evidence that work addiction contributes to family dysfunction.[54]

Burke[42] considered the relationship of workaholism types identified by Spence and Robbins and extrawork satisfactions in a sample of 530 employed women and men MBAs.[55] Three aspects of life or extrawork satisfaction were included. Family satisfaction was measured by a seven-item scale developed by Kofodimos.[46] One item was "I have a good relationships with my family members." Friends satisfaction was measured by three items developed by Kofodimos.[46] An item was "My friends and I do enjoyable things together." Community satisfaction was measured by four items also developed by Kofodimos.[46] A sample item was "I contribute and give back to my community."

The comparisons of the workaholism types on the three measures of life or extrawork satisfactions provided moderate support for the hypothesized relationships. WAs reported less satisfaction on all three measures than did WEs and less satisfaction on one measure (family) than did EAs.

Evaluating Workaholism Components

The two workaholism measures used in two or more research studies all contain components or factors.[19,20] Do these individual factors have similar and independent relationships with particular outcomes? Or might they have opposite relationships with some outcomes and no relationship with others?

Burke considered the question of whether the workaholism triad components had different consequences.[55] A research model was developed to guide both variable selection and analysis strategy. There have been suggestions that both personal and work setting factors are antecedents of workaholic behaviors.[11,12] Thus, both individual-difference characteristics and organizational factors were included for study. Five panels of predictor variables were considered. The first consisted of individual demographic characteristics (e.g., age, gender, marital status). The second consisted of three measures of personal beliefs and fears.[44] The third consisted of work situation demographic factors (e.g., years with present employer, size of organization). The fourth included measures of perceived organizational values supporting work-life balance.[46] The fifth included the workaholism triad components (work involvement, feeling driven to work, work enjoyment). The important questions were whether the workaholism triad components would add significant increments in explained variance on particular work and personal well-being measures, and if they did, which of the workaholism triad components accounted for these increments.

Outcome measures included aspects of job behaviors, work satisfaction (e.g., job satisfaction, career satisfaction, future career prospects, intent to quit), psychological well-being (e.g., psychosomatic symptoms, emotional well-being, lifestyle behaviors) and elements of life satisfaction (e.g., family satisfaction, friends satisfaction, community satisfaction).

Although significantly intercorrelated, the three workaholism components had only moderate interrelationships, none of these correlations exceeding .25. The three workaholism components, considered together, almost always accounted for significant increments in explained variance on outcome measures, controlling for a number of personal and work-setting factors. The components had a greater impact on job behaviors and work outcomes likely to be evidenced by workaholic behaviors and less impact on psychological well-being and extrawork satisfactions. It is likely that the latter would be affected by a wider array of work and life experience, workaholic behaviors being only one of them.

An examination of the relationships among specific workaholism components and the various types of outcome variables revealed an interesting, and complex, pattern of findings. First, work enjoyment and feeling driven to work were significantly related to all seven job-behavior measures, while work involvement was significantly related to about half of them. Respondents scoring higher on the workaholism components also scored higher on job behaviors reflecting workaholism, with one exception—difficulty in delegating. In this instance, respondents scoring higher on work involvement and feeling driven to work and lower on work enjoyment reported greater difficulty in delegating.

Second, joy in work was the only workaholism component related to work outcomes. Respondents reporting greater work enjoyment also reported more job satisfaction, more optimistic future career prospects, and more career satisfaction to date.

Third, both work enjoyment and feeling driven to work were related to indicators of psychological well-being but in opposite directions. Respondents reporting greater work enjoyment and lesser feelings of being driven to work indicated more positive psychological well-being.

Finally, workaholism components had a significant effects on only one of the three measures of extrawork satisfactions. Respondents reporting greater work involvement and lesser feelings of being driven to work reported greater community satisfaction.

In sum, although work enjoyment and feeling driven to work had consistent and similar effects on job behaviors reflecting workaholism, these two workaholism components had different effects on work outcomes and psychological well-being. One, work enjoyment, was associated with positive outcomes; the other, feeling driven to work, was associated with negative outcomes. Finally, none of the workaholism components showed consistent relationships with measures of extrawork satisfactions.

Gender Differences

Research has also focused on gender differences in workaholism and workaholism-related variables. Spence and Robbins compared men and women social workers in academic positions on their workaholism triad (work involvement, feeling driven to work, work enjoyment), behavioral correlates (e.g., perfectionism, nondelegation) and health complaints.[20] In this sample, women scored significantly higher than men on feeling driven to work, work enjoyment, job stress, job involvement, and time commitment scales; no differences were found on work involvement, perfectionism, and nondelegation scales. Women also reported more health complaints.

Elder and Spence reported comparisons of men and women MBA graduates on these measures along with a few others.[32] Few differences were found. Men did score significantly higher than women on job involvement. There were also similar, though not identical, relationships among the measures for both genders. The three workaholism triad measures were significantly correlated for men; the feeling driven to work and work enjoyment scales were uncorrelated for women.

Doerfler and Kammer examined the relationships of levels of workaholism with both sex and sex-role orientation (masculine, feminine, androgynous).[25] They collected data from attorneys, physicians, and psychologists. Workaholism was measured by the 10 characteristics proposed by Machlowitz.[8] They reported that 23 percent of their respondents were workaholics, consistent across the two sexes and three professional groups. Interestingly, a majority of single workaholics were female, and female workaholics reported more masculine and androgynous characteristics than feminine characteristics.

Burke compared responses of 277 men and 251 women in his study of workaholism.[57] He first compared the prevalance of Spence and Robbins workaholism types separately in men and women. There were no significant gender differences in these distributions. Women and men fell into each of the three workaholism types to a similar degree.

He then compared responses of these men and women on the three workaholism components and on a number of validating job behaviors. It is important to first examine gender differences on personal and situational characteristics before considering gender differences on the workaholism measures to put the latter into a larger context. Females and males were similar on a minority of the items: organizational level, organizational size, and the proportion having worked part-time at some point in their careers. However, there were considerably more statistically significant female-male differences on these demographic items. Males were older, more likely to be married, to be in longer marriages, more likely to have children, to have more children, had completed their MBA degrees earlier, were less likely to have gaps in their careers, earned higher incomes, and had been in their present jobs and with their present employers longer. It should be noted that many of these demographic characteristics were themselves significantly correlated and the sample sizes of both female and males were large.

Female-male comparisons were undertaken on the three workaholism components as well as on the seven job-behavior validation measures. Significant differences were present on 6 of the 10 measures. Females were less work involved, devoted less time to their jobs, worked fewer hours, and worked fewer extra hours, but reported greater job stress and greater perfectionism than males. Females and males reported similar levels of work enjoyment, feeling driven to work, job involvement, and difficulties in delegating.

ADDRESSING WORKAHOLISM

There is a large speculative literature suggesting ways to reduce levels of workaholism. One part of this work focuses on individual and family therapy;[19,58] a second part emphasizes organizational and managerial interventions.

Individual Counseling

Workaholics Anonymous chapters have sprung up in some North American cities. These groups, patterned after Alcoholics Anonymous self-help groups, endorse the 12-step approach common to the treatment of a variety of addictions. Killinger and Robinson include chapters outlining actions an individual might pursue to reduce levels of workaholism.[6,19]

It has also been suggested that workaholics must examine their feelings as well as their thought patterns.[59] Korn, Pratt, and Lambrou advise individuals to reduce impulses supporting workaholism and reestablish healthy priorities.[13] Other writers have advocated self-help programs for workaholics.[4,5,7,10,60] These include identifying alternatives to work, exploring new hobbies and outside interests, and enjoying doing nothing. Professional help, in the form of both individual and group counseling, may be useful for those interested in developing new patterns of behavior.[15,22].

Burwell and Chen apply rational-emotive behavior therapy (REBT) to an analysis of the causes of workaholism and its treatment.[61] Workaholism has, as one of its possible causes, low self-image and low self-esteem. One of the basic irrational beliefs in REBT is that one must impress others through accomplishments and outperform them. The difficulty in treating workaholism is compounded by the societal acceptance of workaholism and denial of the problem. REBT addresses the irrational beliefs that drive workaholism. REBT tackles irrational beliefs using cognitive reframing, practicing unconditional self-acceptance, and behaving in ways that are opposite to previously held beliefs. The latter might involve, for example, delegating tasks to others, setting boundaries between work and home, attempting to balance work and life, and engaging in more leisure activities.

Family Therapy

Robinson and his colleagues, consistent with their clinical and consulting perspective, focus on treatment, both individual and family. This is not surprising, given the central role they give to both family of origin and current family functioning in the development maintenance and intergenerational transmission of workaholism. The treatment recommendations Robinson offers are similar to those offered to alcoholic families.[19]

In this view, denial is common among workaholics and their family members. Family members are reluctant to complain. Workaholics define their behaviour and symptoms in a favorable light.[6,16] Parental expectations of children, often unrealistic, must be addressed. Family structures need to be identified. How do family members collude with the workaholic parent? Family members need help in expressing their negative feelings (e.g., frustration, hurt, and anger) to the workaholic. Families need to learn to set boundaries around the amount they work together and talk about work. Family members can set goals to improve family dynamics (e.g. communication, roles, expression of feelings). Families can also gain a deeper understanding of the intergenerational transmission of addictions. Family involvement and counseling is another vehicle for assisting workaholics. These initiatives may uncover family dynamics that contribute to the workaholic pattern, make spending time with families more satisfying, and create rewards for workaholics for their family participation.

Workplace Interventions

How can employers help workaholics and workaholics help themselves? Schaef and Fassel offer the following ideas.[11] Employers should pay attention to the performance and work habits of employees and be alert to warning signs of workaholism. They should not reward addictive behavior, but recognize those employees who are productive but also lead balanced lives. They should ensure that employees take vacation time away from work. Finally, job insecurity, work overload, limited career opportunities, and lack of control can make employees feel compelled to work longer hours. If these factors exist, employers should try to minimize their impact on the atmosphere within the organization.

Haas also highlights the role that managers can play in helping their workaholic employees to change.[62] Workaholic employees should be referred to an employee assistance program or a recovery program to start treatment processes. Managers should help prioritize projects for employees as long-term and short-term assignments. Workaholics must be encouraged and helped to delegate their work. At the end of each day, the manager should meet with the employee to discuss what has been accomplished during that day and to plan (down to short intervals) for the following day. The employee should be given specific times to take breaks and to leave work so that positive terms may be acquired through training. It may also be possible to reduce the negative effects of workaholism, particularly well-being and health consequences, through stress management training.[63]

The development of workplace values that promote new, more balanced priorities and healthier lifestyles will support workaholics who want to change their behaviors.

CONCLUSIONS AND IMPLICATIONS

There is general agreement that workaholism is a stable individual difference characteristic. There is also some consensus that workaholism is likely to be a central concept in understanding the relationship of workplace experiences, typically involving work stressors, and a variety of work outcomes (satisfaction, job performance), extrawork satisfactions (family, friends), and health indicators (psychosomatic symptoms, medication use).

Workaholism has been shown to have little relationship to more generic ethics (work, achievement, leisure time) or to other concepts suggested to be similar (Type-A behavior, obsessive thinking, compulsive finishing, delayed gratification). Thus, workaholism likely will have an impact on the satisfaction and well-being of organizational members.[50]

This review has identified some definitions of workaholism that appear adequate for research purposes.[12,19,20] However, progress needs to be made on the measurement front. Two measures of workaholism warrant further attention.[19,20] Both the Spence and Robbins measure and the Robinson measure have been used in 10 or more studies. There is considerable support for the workaholism profiles identified by Spence and Robbins; at least five separate studies using different samples in several countries have confirmed their existence. More work needs to be done with the Robinson measure to verify his five factors in other studies. Although almost all of Robinson's studies have used a total score over the 25 items, it may be that one of the five factors is the most toxic.

More effort must be undertaken on several fronts to validate those measures of workaholism that show promise. First, workaholism must be shown to predict validating job and work behaviors (e.g., perfectionism, nondelegation). Second, workaholism must be shown to predict extrawork satisfactions (e.g., family satisfaction and family functioning). Third, workaholism must be shown to predict psychological well-being (e.g., emotional health). Fourth, self-reports of workaholism must be shown to predict others' reports (spouse, coworkers). Fifth, measures of workaholism must be shown to be stable over time. So far, only Robinson, Post, and Khakee have examined this.[27]

It is also important to understand the relationship of workaholism to concepts having potential overlap (e.g., Type-A behavior, compulsion-obsession). Robinson's measure, in particular, includes elements common to most depictions of Type-A behavior.

More research must be devoted to understanding the antecedents of workaholism. Research to date has considered family of origin,[19] personal beliefs and fears,[42] and workplace organizational norms and values.[45] It would also be worthwhile to more systematically consider the role played by demographic factors (e.g., age, gender, occupation).

Porter explores reasons people feel compelled toward excess work when externally imposed demands are absent.[63] There are several reasons why people work hard, and each reason may have both desirable and undesirable consequences to the individual, the organization, or both. Porter provides a description of the workaholic consistent with the addiction paradigm. She concludes with a plea for a healthier approach to hard work that includes a balance of nonwork interests.

Hours worked, in itself, is not particularly informative in explaining health and satisfaction. Is working hard always problematic? The answer is a definite no! It seems to make a difference why the person is working hard (low self-esteem) and how the person is working hard (perfectionistic, obsessive-compulsive, high levels of stress). The old adage that "hard work never killed anyone" may need to be revised.

The development of norms based on large representative samples would be a significant contribution to the field. With few exceptions, most research on workaholism has involved relatively small samples. It becomes difficult to make comparisons across studies. The two more commonly used measures face these limitations.[19,20] That is, different values are used to create the workaholism types, or high, medium, or low levels of workaholism on the Robinson measure in each study.[20]

Several specific questions require further attention. Do women and men exhibit similar levels of workaholism? Does workaholism have the same antecedents and consequences in women and men? Although workaholics likely exist in all professions and jobs, and in all organizations, are some professions more likely to attract and develop workaholics than others (e.g., stock brokers versus primary school teachers)? And again, although workaholics are likely to exist in all countries, at least in developed and industrialized countries, are some countries more likely to develop workaholics, (e.g., Japan and the United States versus Spain and France)?

It is also important to undertake longitudinal studies of the development and impact of workaholism. Most studies, involving one-time data collection only, cannot address issues of causality in a meaningful way. Does workaholism cause dissatisfaction, or does dissatisfaction cause workaholism?

Since almost all studies to date have employed self-report data to assess levels of workaholism as well as any other variables of interest, it is critical to begin to add more independent and objective measures. These might involve the use of an organization's performance-evaluation data to assess work contributions, coworker data to assess workplace relationships, spouse and children data to assess marital and family functioning, objective medical data to assess physical health and physiological data (e.g., heart rate) to determine levels of daily biological functioning.

It is also useful to make a distinction between statistical significance and practical significance. Some of the statistical findings reported in the manuscripts that were reviewed, while significant, may represent relatively small differences or effects. Nevertheless, if these identify a few individuals who may be at risk and result in positive change, the practical significance of these findings is large.

Although useful information about workaholism and its correlates can be gleaned from studies of college students, it is imperative that efforts to replicate and extend such studies use samples of employed men and women, particularly in occupations where they have the freedom to give free rein to their drive to work.

It is also important to link and integrate two streams of research initiatives that have existed relatively independently. The older stream resides in clinical and counseling psychology and family dynamics; the newer stream has emerged in organizational behavior and work psychology, with a link to health. Useful insights and contributions have been made in both.

ACKNOWLEDGMENTS

Preparation of this manuscript was supported in part by the Schulich School of Business, York University. I am grateful to Janet Spence for permission to use her workaholism measures. Louise Coutu prepared the manuscript.

REFERENCES

1. McMillan, L.H.W., O'Driscoll, M. P., Marsh, N. V., & Brady, E. C. (2001). Understanding workaholism: Data synthesis, theoretical critique, and future design strategies. *International Journal of Stress Management, 8,* 60–92.
2. Fassel, D. (1990). *Working ourselves to death: The high costs of workaholism, the rewards of recovery.* San Francisco: HarperCollins.
3. Garfield, C. A. (1987). *Peak performers: The new heroes of American business.* New York: William Morrow.
4. Kiechel, W. (1989, April 10). The workaholic generation, *Fortune,* 50–62.
5. Kiechel, W. (1989, August 14). Workaholics Anonymous. *Fortune,* 117–118.
6. Killinger, B. (1991). *Workaholics: The respectable addicts.* New York: Simon and Schuster.
7. Klaft, R. P., & Kleiner, B. H. (1988). Understanding workaholics. *Business, 33,* 37–40.
8. Machlowitz, M. (1980). *Workaholics: Living with them, working with them.* Reading, MA: Addison-Wesley.
9. Waddell, J. R. (1993). The grindstone. *Supervision, 26,* 11–13.
10. Oates, W. (1971). *Confessions of a workaholic: The facts about work addiction.* New York: World.
11. Schaef, A. W., & Fassel, D. (1988). *The addictive organization.* San Francisco: Harper and Row.
12. Scott, K. S., Moore, K. S., & Miceli, M. P. (1997). An exploration of the meaning and consequences of workaholism. *Human Relations, 50,* 287–314.
13. Korn, E. R., Pratt, G. J., & Lambrou, P. T. (1987). *Hyper-performance: The A.I.M. strategy for releasing your business potential.* New York: Wiley.
14. Sprankle, J. K., & Ebel, H. (1987). *The workaholic syndrome.* New York: Walker.
15. Naughton, T. J. (1987). A conceptual view of workaholism and implications for career counseling and research. *The Career Development Quarterly, 14,* 180–187.

16. Porter, G. (1996). Organizational impact of workaholism: Suggestions for researching the negative outcomes of excessive work. *Journal of Occupational Health Psychology, 1,* 70–84.

17. Mosier, S. K. (1982). *Workaholics: An analysis of their stress, success and priorities.* Unpublished masters thesis. University of Texas at Austin.

18. Cherrington, D. J. (1980). *The work ethic.* New York: American Management Association.

19. Robinson, B. E. (1998). *Chained to the desk: A guidebook for workaholics, their partners and children and the clinicians who treat them.* New York: New York University Press.

20. Spence, J. T., & Robbins, A. S. (1992). Workaholism: Definition, measurement, and preliminary results. *Journal of Personality Assessment, 58,* 160–178.

21. Schor, J. B. (1991). *The overworked American.* New York: Basic Books.

22. Seybold, K. C., & Salomone, P. R. (1994). Understanding workaholism: A view of causes and counseling approaches. *Journal of Counseling and Development, 73,* 4–9.

23. Engstrom, T. W., & Juroe, D. J. (1979). *The work trap.* Old Tappan, NJ: Fleming H. Revell.

24. Spruel, G. (1987). Work fever. *Training and Development Journal, 41,* 41–45.

25. Doerfler, M. C., & Kammer, P. P. (1986). Workaholism: Sex and sex role stereotyping among female professionals. *Sex Roles, 14,* 551–560.

26. Robinson, B. E. (1996). Concurrent validity of the Work Addiction Risk Test. *Psychological Reports, 79,* 1313–1314.

27. Robinson, B. E., Post, P., & Khakee, J. E. (1992). Test-test reliability of the Work Addiction Risk Test. *Perceptual and Motor Skills, 74,* 9–26

28. Robinson, B. E., & Post, P. (1995). Split-half reliability of the Work Addiction Risk Test: Development of a measure of workaholism. *Psychological Reports, 76,* 1226.

29. Robinson, B. E., & Post, P. (1994). Validity of the Work Addiction Risk Test. *Perceptual and Motor Skills, 78,* 337–338.

30. Robinson, B. E. (1999). The Work Addiction Risk Test: Development of a tentative measure of workaholism. *Perceptual and Motor Skills, 88,* 199–210

31. Kanai, A., Wakabayashi, M., & Fling, S. (1996). Workaholism among employees in Japanese corporations: An examination based on the Japanese version of the workaholism scales. *Japanese Psychological Research, 38,* 192–203.

32. Elder, E. D., & Spence, J. T. (1998). *Workaholism in the business world: Work addiction versus work-enthusiasm in MBAs.* Unpublished manuscript. Department of Psychology, University of Texas at Austin.

33. Robbins, A. S. (1993). *Patterns of workaholism in developmental psychologists.* Unpublished manuscript. Department of Psychology, University of Texas at Austin.

34. Burke, R. J. (1999). Workaholism in organizations: Measurement validation and replication. *International Journal of Stress Management, 6,* 45–55..

35. Burke, R. J., Richardsen, A. M., & Mortinussen, M. (2004). Workaholism among Norwegian senior managers: New research directions. *International Journal of Management, 21*, 415–426.

36. Bonebright, C. A., Clay, D. L., & Ankenmann, R. D. (2000). The relationship of workaholism with work-life conflict, life satisfaction, and purpose in life. *Journal of Counseling Psychology, 47*, 469–477.

37. Robinson, B. E. (2000). Adult children of workaholics: Clinical and empirical research with implications for family therapists. *Journal of Family Psychotherapy, 11*, 15–26.

38. Robinson, B. E. (2001). Workaholism and family functioning: A profile of familial relationships, psychological outcomes and research considerations. *Contemporary Family Therapy, 23*, 123–135.

39. Pietropinto, A. (1986). The workaholic spouse. *Medical Aspects of Human Sexuality, 20*, 89–96.

40. Robinson, B. E., & Kelley, L. (1998). Adult children of workaholics: Self-concept, anxiety, depression, and locus of control. *American Journal of family Therapy, 26*, 35–50.

41. Robinson, B. E., & Post, P. (1997). Risk of work addiction to family functioning. *Psychological Reports, 81*, 91–95

42. Burke, R. J. (1999). Workaholism in organizations: The role of beliefs and fears. *Anxiety, Stress and Coping, 14*, 1–12.

43. Price, V. A. (1982). What is Type A behavior? A cognitive social learning model. *Journal of Occupational Behavior, 3*, 109–130.

44. Lee, C., Jamieson, L. F., & Earley, P. C. (1996). Beliefs and fears and Type A behavior: Implications for academic performance and psychiatric health disorder symptoms. *Journal of Organizational Behavior, 17*, 151–178.

45. Burke, R. J. (1999). Workaholism in organizations: The role of organizational values. *Personnel Review, 30*, 637–645.

46. Kofodimos, J. (1995). *Balancing act.* San Francisco: Jossey-Bass.

47. Burke, R. J. (1999). Are workaholics job satisfied and successful in their careers? *Career Development International, 26*, 637–745.

48. Burke, R. J. (1991). Early work and career experiences of female and male managers: Reasons for optimism? *Canadian Journal of Administrative Sciences, 8*, 224–230.

49. Greenhaus, J. H., Parasuraman, S., & Wormley, W. (1990). Organizational experiences and career success of black and white managers. *Academy of Management Journal, 33*, 64–86.

50. McMillan, L. H. W., O'Driscoll, M. P., & Burke, R. J. (2003). Workaholism in organizations: A review of theory, research and future directions. In C. L. Cooper & I. T. Robertson (Eds.), *International Review of Industrial and Organizational Psychology* (pp. 167–190). New York: John Wiley.

51. Burke, R. J. (1999). Workaholism in organizations: psychological and physical well-being consequences. *Stress Medicine, 16*, 11–16.

52. Quinn, R. P., & Shepard, L. J. (1974). *The 1972–73 Quality of Employment Survey.* Ann Arbor: Institute for Social Research, University of Michigan.

53. Robinson, B. E. (1990). Workaholic kids. *Adolescent Counselor, 2,* 24–47

54. Robinson, B. E., & Rhoden, L. (1998). *Working with children of alcoholics: The practitioner's handbook* (2nd ed). Beverly Hills, CA: Sage.

55. Burke, R. J. (1999). Workaholism and extra-work satisfactions. *International Journal of Organizational Analysis, 7,* 352–364.

56. Burke, R. J. (1999). Its not how hard you work but how you work hard: Evaluating workaholism components. *International Journal of Stress Management, 6,* 235–239.

57. Burke, R. J. (1999). Workaholism in organizations: Gender differences. *Sex Roles, 41,* 333–345.

58. Robinson, B. E. (1992). *Overdoing it: How to slow down and take care of your self.* Deerfield Beach, FL: Health Communications.

59. Minirth, F., Meier, P., Wichern, F., Brewer, B., & Skipper, S. (1981). *The workaholic and his family.* Grand Rapids, MI: Baker Book House.

60. Franzmeier, A. (1988). To your health. *Nations' Business, 76,* 73.

61. Burwell, R., & Chen, C.D.F. (2002). Applying REBT to workaholic clients. *Counseling Psychology Quarterly, 15,* 219–228.

62. Haas, R. (1991). Strategies to cope with a cultural phenomenon—workaholism. *Business and Health, 36,* 4.

63. Porter, G. (2004). Work, work ethic, work excess. *Journal of Organizational Change Management, 17,* 424–439.

63. Robinson, B. E. (1997). Work addiction: Implications for EAP counseling and research. *Employee Assistance Quarterly, 12,* 1–13.

Chapter 9

The Remarkable Normalcy of Dying to Kill in Holy War

Rona M. Fields

Abraham Maslow raised the question of normalcy in the midst of the madness of terror and genocide when he asked, Which was normal: The SS guards who dropped pellets of Zyclon B gas into a chamber full of helpless men, women and children, watched their death agonies, and went home at the end of the day to kiss their wives and play with their children? Or the terrified inmates of the concentration camp, who, realizing their helplessness in the face of certain death, became clinically depressed, suffering delusions, hallucinations, and depersonalization?

I was reminded of this passage in *The Psychology of Being*[1] in 1998, in Santiago, Chile, after recording hours of interviews with torture survivors and reviewing some of the decades-old case affidavits from the Truth and Justice Commission files. Chile had adopted an impunity system whereby testimony and affidavits did not eventuate in trials, convictions, and penalties. The bound documents were filed away with limited access. Instances of torture and disappearance started on the day of the coup, September 11, 1973. Everyone except President Allende, who died in his office, was led out the side door of the presidential palace at gunpoint, bound, and trucked off to the stadium, which became a makeshift concentration camp. Photos of this became iconic of the coup. There was a significant effort made to destroy all such evidence, but many photos appeared in the foreign press. Memory was restructured in Chile, no less than it was by Pol Pot in Cambodia. By reinventing reality, literally putting a different frame on the same picture, predators rationalize their actions.

Ideological framing, calling a military initiative a "war to defend democracy" rather than a "preemptive attack," changes the action from an offensive initiative to a defensive response. Similarly, identifying the enemy as a "terrorist" rather than a "patriot" or "freedom fighter" changes the subject and the object of aggression. General Augusto Pinochet, several years later, explained his actions as having martyred himself. In the same vein, he presented the death of Allende and the disappearances of thousands of his political adversaries as preventive actions to ensure that his opposition did not have martyrs around whom to rally. In fact, dealing with this issue of normalcy 30 years later, Pinochet, charged with crimes against humanity, used the issue of mental competency to thwart efforts to extradite him from England and try him in Spain. In this kind of contest of normalcy the subject claims, or his doctors claim, he cannot meet the norms for acting rationally, thoughtfully, and with adequate memory to contribute to his own defense.[2] Thus, over time, whether an action was planned and executed by a normal person becomes instead an issue of their normalcy to stand trial for the action.

This re-creation of reality is physically evident in the presidential palace itself. On that September day in 1998, a cursory examination revealed a visible difference between stones and bricks that had been recently replaced and the patina of the old masonry of the original structure.

I asked a young military guardsman what had happened to the brickwork and whether there hadn't been a doorway at this spot. He said he hadn't noticed anything, but then, given that he was less than 25 years old, he referred the inquiry to his superior. This man, perhaps five to ten years his senior, also had no idea of what had happened in this spot 25 years before. He explained that be was from the countryside and hadn't ever been in the capitol until he turned 18. And so it went. I snapped photos and then, lest my interest in this history endanger me, walked quickly away.

But the questions remained. The files of affidavits detail torture, murder, and disappearances. Thirty-five thousand were tortured. More than 3,000 were killed and made to "disappear."

The affidavits from the Truth and Justice Commission hearings not only detail the torture, but they also often include the names of the torturers and the places where these obscenities transpired. Several of the identified torturers were easily found. One of them, a former policewoman, had trained German Shepherd dogs to rape women prisoners. I asked her to talk with me about the dogs.

I started by asking how in the world she could train dogs to do what was so completely unnatural to their species. She was quite forthcoming in explaining how the women were spread-eagled by male guards and what she did to train and reinforce the dogs. When asked how she felt now about what she had done and how she dealt with her memories. She said: "That was a long time ago. Now is the time for Christian forgiveness!" Another infamous torturer was a policeman whose specialty was manipulating electrical charges on prisoners strapped to an iron bedspring. His particular "genius" was that he knew how far to go without killing the subject. When this kind of torture was first used, most prisoners died before they could reveal anything. Therefore, experienced police were brought in to replace the military interrogation personnel. This man had later become a suburban wine merchant, and when interviewed he claimed that he didn't know what the electrodes were engaging because he could only see his control panel and was directed by his superiors on the voltage. It was all so "normal"! In fact, it is remarkably reminiscent of the Stanley Milgram experiments in which he tested obedience to authority by asking subjects to deliver a n electric shock to a person in a glass booth, who enacted increasing pain and discomfort with every elevation of the feigned voltage. The subjects obeyed the authoritative director rather than considering the obvious misery of the "victim."[3] Social psychologist Phillip Zimbardo did a variant on this experiment. He divided a group of undergraduate student volunteers into two groups, "guards" and "prisoners." The fake prison contained barred cells, sparsely furnished emulating the local jail. The guards were told that these prisoners were violent and would try to break out and riot. Very soon, the guards became brutal and the prisoners, aggressive. When he saw what was happening, Zimbardo called off the experiment before the scheduled completion date.[4]

FINDING A SYSTEM FOR MEASUREMENT

War, intercommunal violence, terrorism, genocide, and criminal violence engender an abnormal social mind-set. After all, the idea of normalcy is predicated on a static, two-dimensional, bell-shaped curve. But children growing up in conditions of violence and social prejudice are likely to map their many dimensions of emotion and motivation on other parameters that incorporate their own dimensions of motivation, emotion, values, and beliefs. In order to place the individual in relation to a larger population, it is necessary to use measurement instruments that are multifactor tests. Further, these instruments yield norms and profiles they are readily influenced by the test takers' life experiences at the time they are answering the questions. Thus, an individual who is under great stress will more likely produce a Minnesota Multiphasic Personality Inventory (MMPI) profile that is high on the Pd (Psychopathic) index of the MMPI even though the individual is not necessarily psychopathic.

Emotions, motivation, attitudes, and values not generally measured on a scaling device amenable to a bell curve are also not indices of normalcy per se as much as they are measures of an individual's state at the time of testing. In that regard, profiles and scores can be anywhere on the bell curve for a given time and place. These are more dynamic indices than the cognitive measures.

Projective tests can reveal information that is obscured from behavioral observations and even from the awareness of the individual himself or herself. In this respect, projective tests more effectively mirror the multidimensionality of the individual. One of the most useful tools for examining achievement motivation has been Murray's Thematic Apperception Test.[5] The test consists of 20 ambiguous picture cards with instructions to make up a story. Thus the individual projects his or her fantasy, and since the stimuli are ambiguous, the stories themselves are individual and neither right nor wrong. Murray predicated his system of interpretation on the assumption of "need states" and postulated "n-achievement." Working with patients who had been in combat during WWII and with mental patients, Magda Arnold began elaborating on the n-achievement thesis when she became convinced that need states did not describe motivation and that achievement is only one of several basic motivational objectives. She developed and standardized a system of scoring this qualitative instrument in a multidimensional and dynamic manner.[6] This became one of the standard instruments in my studies of trauma survivors, children growing up under conditions of violence, and members of paramilitary (aka, terrorist) groups.[7] Motivational Index scores on Story Sequence Analysis of the Thematic Apperception Test (SSA TAT) have been validated with an interscorer reliability coefficient of .86. The curve deviates to the left on the populations described in these studies, as do other measurements of cognitive and moral development. But statistically, it is to be expected that a subset of a population will tend to deviate toward the low end. In order to fix the norms for these children, the social scientist would have to shift the scaling of T scores, or, as is often done, weight the scores accordingly. But the obvious fact these data provide is that the conditions of these subjects' daily lives mandate against their development of moral judgment, as might their age peers in a secure society.[8]

This is not to suggest that children growing up in violence are essentially abnormal and that their behavior will be abnormal and therefore antisocial. Studies of children and members of paramilitary organizations indicate that on measures of intelligence and personality, they are distributed as normally as any large population (except in some particulars, where there is a pattern that is still within the range of normal distribution). I found these children of violence to be healthy, intelligent, charming, and attractive. Certainly they are not the psychopaths described in the media and by so-called experts on terrorism. Nor are they withdrawn isolates suffering from chronic post-traumatic stress syndrome.

Similarly, studies of adult members of paramilitary organizations found them to be of normal or above average intelligence, very concerned with issues of right and wrong, and see themselves as vulnerable members of a threatened group, unprotected by and isolated from the institutions of the larger society—in short, alienated, socially marginalized, and politically ineffectual.

Research using standardized psychological tests shows remarkable similarities among holy warriors who kill themselves in the act of killing others and those who operate within organizations called "terrorist" in many different cultures, countries, and historical periods. Furthermore, all criteria applied in the laboratory and on-site show that torturers are within the normal standard deviations from the mean on the bell-shaped curve. After all, under other social circumstances they might devise and execute freshman pledge tasks for high school or college fraternities. People were generally shocked to learn that the young American soldiers at Abu Ghraib committed horrific acts against prisoners and took pictures of themselves doing it. No one even claimed temporary insanity.

Formerly, when I presented these facts about members of groups labeled "terrorist," I was often branded a terrorist sympathizer, or even, in the United Kingdom, a terrorist. Studies of the neuropsychological damage done through the forced application of extreme stress, beatings, sensory deprivation, and sensory overstimulation on detainees alleged to be members of the Irish Republican Army (IRA) provoked Sir William Deeds, Member of Parliament and publisher-editor of the *Daily Telegraph*, to a heated charge on Thames-TV in late October 1973. In reference to *Society on the Run*,[9] which reported measurable brain damage in two-thirds of the men tested, Deeds declaimed, "Those Irish republicans and your other friends in Long Kesh are all low IQ types anyway!"

The book was subsequently removed from the market and 10,000 copies were shredded. Its author, Rona M. Fields, was on the terrorist list for many years afterward; was denied admission to the United Kingdom and denied access there. Thirty-two years later, British police and intelligence reported in stunned press statements to an equally stunned public that the suicide bombers presumed responsible for the July 7 and July 21, 2005, transit attacks in London are normal young British subjects of the kind that might live next door in any city or town.

This marks a turning point in understanding extraordinary behaviors by ordinary people. But perhaps it is actually a revisited turning point. Hannah Arendt, in writing about Adolph Eichmann on trial in Jerusalem, subtitled her book, "On the Banality of Evil."[10] And indeed, the very normalcy of a logistician filling cattle cars with prisoners and estimating the costs and amounts of Zyclon B needed to murder them is a study in the normalization of the abnormal.

As clinical psychologists generally hold the view that normalcy is measurable and that which is abnormal will be evidenced through our toolbox of well-standardized tests. But we are measuring individuals and not societies. In company with the SSA TAT, the Tapp Kohlberg questions of legal socialization,[11] predicated on Jean Piaget's stages of moral development,[12] and Spielberger's State Trait Personality Index (STPI)[13] proved themselves, over time and many different cultures and languages, the measuring instruments that would provide insights into the mind of the terrorists and the motivation for suicide-homicide.

PREDICTING A TERROR VOCATION

Certain environmental circumstances are likely to limit choices generally: conditions of fear, violence, chaos, and positioning as marginal within the larger society. As Piaget describes it, conditions that limit a child's experience of a variety of roles—particularly representations of political efficacy—may lead them to the barricades rather than the bar of justice. A child who is able to identify either as a victim of aggression or as an aggressor becomes truncated at what Piaget and Tapp and Kohlberg describe as Level II on the developmental scale of moral judgment-retributive justice or vendetta. Aligned with this system of assigning stages of moral justice are some personality traits or states that combine with or emanate out of this truncation. Individuals are angry when they feel violated, and they may engage in angry behaviors without any remorse or guilt feelings, although they do feel guilt about other behaviors. Furthermore, they do not experience anxiety about their anger and angry behaviors, although they do admit to anxiety about other things. One other characteristic is curiosity. The individual who joins a paramilitary or terrorist group has a higher level of risk taking because he or she is curious. These personality and moral development factors on diagnostic tests present a distinctive profile. They are also characteristics of what Eric Hoffer designated "true believer."[14] Such individuals are well within the norms for other personality traits and follow a bell-shaped curve of distribution in intelligence.

Arnold's SSA TAT is another useful measure for predicting the prospect for a terror vocation, and it also has some value, in predicting the likelihood of suicide/homicide. Using 10 standard TAT cards, stories are elicited that tell what is happening, what did happen, what will happen, and how it will end. These stories, regardless how sparse, can indicate the choice behaviors of the individual as well as their decision-making process. The themes of the stories are extracted and listed in order. These "imports" form a story themselves—the story sequence alluded to in the test's title. The imports are then scored on a template ranging between −2 and +2. Added up, the 10 stories provide a motivation index score. These are frequently elaborations on the responses to the Tapp Kohlberg questions of legal socialization used to determine the level of moral judgment/political socialization. SSA includes the categories right and wrong, achievement, response to adversity, and human relationships. In addition, the profile was formulated on the Spielberger STPI.

Children evaluated for predicting a terror vocation were also administered a Violence Distance Scale interview. This was composed of questions assessing exposure to acts generally considered threatening. During the first several years of the study, the precise proximity and kind of violence experienced had no correlation with the individual's scores on this and other tests.[15]

In one study of Palestinian suicide bombers during the second Intifada it was found that each of them had experienced personally or within the primary or extended family violence or fatal trauma at the hands of the Israeli Defense Forces (IDF). However, the suicide bombers who acted during the period of the Oslo accords were raised in poverty but had not had proximal experience of deadly violence.[16]

Finally, studies of Palestinian children living in a variety of environments during 1982–1983 found that children living in Beit Safafa, a Palestinian village incorporated into Jerusalem, who had not experienced proximal violence, had, by January 1983, so thoroughly identified with the victims of the Sabra-Shatila massacre through watching television that they reported personally experiencing bombing and shootings and that they wanted vengeance or vindication. In the Palestinian camps on the West Bank children were talking about taking vengeance with stones.

It was four years later that the first Intifada started with the Children of the Stones. The predictive formula that evolved out of these researches was presented in a paper at a conference on Children and War in Stockholm Sweden in 1990. The formula summarized these findings as $T = SPV(LSIII)(MI.SSA)$.[17] Social political violence as quantified by the average level of legal socialization, multiplied by the quantity derivative from the average motivation index score as measured by story sequence analysis, yields the likelihood for a terrorist vocation.

Martyrdom homicide did not originate with Palestinian suicide bombers, nor, for that matter, with Muslims. Eighteenth-century nationalists, anarchists, and nihilists, in their respective quests for attention to their cause, conducted terror operations including targeted assassination, suicide-homicide actions, and public self-immolations. Though they were often dubbed "fanatics" and were usually imprisoned or deported, they were not considered mentally ill. Instead, they were much like the profile derived from using the Spielberger STPI on members of terrorist organizations. From all published reports, they were angry people, and although they felt guilt about other things, were not guilty about expressing their anger; were not anxious (therefore unlikely to have met the diagnostic conditions for neurosis), and were curious—risk takers.

SUICIDE

There is a body of research and theory on suicide and the issue of whether a suicide is ever committed in a state of mental normality. The question might better be phrased, What are the motivational dynamics of the individual who chooses to take his or her own life? In so-called sanctioned suicide, or choosing to end one's life when faced with terminal illness, the sanctions specify that the individual must be of sound mind. Does the same distinction apply for suicide-homicide? Undoubtedly there are instances in which the subject would be diagnosed as pathological. However, the post-mortem psychological studies of the nine suicide-homicide bombers who acted during the period of the Oslo accords, as well as journalistic accounts of the Palestinian suicide bombers who followed, produce a standard bell curve. If the study is extended to Al-Qaeda operatives, there are few if any indices of diagnosable pathologies, although in some instances there were apparent symptoms of depression or attention deficit hyperactivity disorder (ADHD). In others, there is a history of head trauma that might have had behavioral consequences. These latter cases cannot be adequately diagnosed. But even though the majority of members of paramilitary or terrorist organizations test at the level of Retributive Justice, which is Level II on the Tapp-Kohlberg or Piagetian model, and average a −1 motivation index score, they are not pathological nor retarded. The motivation index score is calculated on a basis of likelihood for successful achievement or conclusion in strategies for achievement, human relationships, right and wrong, and dealing with adversity. These are predictable outcomes for people growing up in war, violence, disadvantaged social circumstances, and restricted opportunities to engage in politically effective roles.

The first suicide-homicide by a Palestinian in Israel was on Friday, April 16, 1993, near Mechola in the Jordan Valley. The perpetrator, a member of Hamas, placed a car loaded with explosives in between two buses next to a restaurant and then detonated the explosives with himself inside the car. There is a methodological problem in studying this specific Palestinian suicide bomber to gain insight into a more generalized population of suicide-homicide perpetrators. While much more is known about a particular case allowing more complete analysis, the motivation, social influences, demographics and behavioral dynamics vary widely from person to person. But in studying the Palestinian suicide-homicide and terrorist population, several theoretical models have emerged that may be quite productive in wider application.

One such is the model based on Durkheim's classic work on suicide, particularly his formulation of altruistic and fatalistic suicide.[18] These two categories of suicide can best be applied to traditional societies going through political, social, and economic transitions. Working in the period (1897) of the emergence of nationalist, anarchist, and nihilist terrorism, Durkheim recognized that these emanated from traditional societies undergoing transitions, in contrast to postindustrialized societies in which suicide was categorized as egoistic and anomic. People who commit altruistic suicide, according to Durkheim, have become deeply integrated into a social group and suicide becomes a "duty" for members of that group. Examples of this include the Peoples' Temple mass suicide in Guyana and David Koresh and his Branch Davidians in Waco, Texas. There is a socialization trajectory that may be compared with the socialization for membership in a gang or a paramilitary organization. The major difference is that the suicide objective obviates much of the training and the need to avoid capture, and subsequent integration into the community. The successful mission is termination. This, of course, engenders fatalism because the suicide act satisfies the group. This sacrifice has helped the collective achieve its goals. The pattern of suicide terrorism indicates that members of religious organizations carry out most of these acts of suicide terrorism. Religiously motivated suicide terrorists are of course not necessarily Islamic militants. However, profiles of perpetrators in the Middle East indicate that most of them were educated in religious schools and were known to have been diligent practitioners of Islam in their everyday life. Their suicidal acts stem from a strong religious conviction in the glorious destiny that awaits the perpetrator in the afterlife having fulfilled his mission on earth.[19] This corresponds to the altruistic typology espoused by Hazbolah, Hamas, and Islamic Jihad. According to Ganor,[20] the typical Hamas *shahid* is a religious, young, unmarried, unemployed male. This same profile fits the Liberation Tigers of Tamil Edem (LITR) in Sri Lanka.[21] Women, who have carried out the majority of suicide attacks in behalf of the Kurdish Workers Party (PKK) in Turkey, also match the same socioeconomic profile. They ranged in age from 17 to 27, and generally came from poor families and lacked professional skills.[22] Despite propaganda that represents the Chechen women suicide terrorists as the Black Widows, most of them are single and have the same socioeconomic profile.

The phenomenon of suicide terrorism can be seen as a manifestation of the altruistic type or the fatalistic type, or, most often, a combination of the two. According to Young,

> These two types should be treated as twin sisters nursed in the same type of socio-cultural system. Their differences can be sought only from the subjective meaning of the suicidal action if a person commits suicide to fulfill his duty, his psychological state may either be one of serene conviction [altruism] or it may be of extreme fear and despair [fatalism].[23]

Several theorists have characterized fatalistic suicide emanate from continuous political and economic oppression. As noted by Stack,

> Fatalistic suicide ... results from excessive regulation, such as that of persons with futures blocked, aspirations choked by oppressive discipline and persons living under physical or moral despotism ... Fatalistic suicides involve an escape from a normative situation from which there is no appeal.[24]

The specific vector needn't be a foreign oppressor. Stack contends that rates of fatalistic suicide are related to the degree of political totalitarianism

Durkheim's subcategory acute altruistic suicide refers specifically to the suicide of martyrs who perceive a lofty and glorious place for themselves beyond life on earth. According to Young, the person who commits acute altruistic suicide must be certain he has no life of his own and believes in a beautiful conception of the afterlife and a serene conviction. This person is carried to his or her death in a burst of faith and enthusiasm.[25]

The other subcategory Durkheim introduced is fatalistic suicide. Acts of fatalistic suicide are characteristic of situations of hopelessness that result from continuous political and economic oppression. Stack noted that

> In such a totalitarian environment marked by relatively low freedom and respect for human dignity, already suicidal persons have an additional reason for viewing life as meaningless and are more apt to commit suicide.[26]

Researchers on terrorism at Haifa University theorize that the Durkheim models of altruistic and fatalistic suicide are appropriate categories to use in the study of terrorism, and they particularly related this model to suicide terrorism. They note that none of the previous researchers have linked it to terrorism at all.[27]

SOCIAL NORMS IN RELATION
TO THE LARGER SOCIETY

Violence, marginalization, and repression have been linked together with a "failed polity" as the recruiting ground for prospective terrorists. These conditions are also the foundation for collective violence and revolution. The demographics are not identical for terrorists and the smaller percentage that become suicide bombers. There are socioeconomic differences between the two groups, but this varies by location.

European political history, too, has seen cases in which a marginalized minority seeks to reclaim its *legendary* history (witness Northern Ireland and the Bosnian and Kosovar aspirations).

The intellectual achievement and tolerant attitudes of the Moors—the Caliphate that instituted the Golden Age of Spain—sustained the scientific and mathematical enlightenment of ancient Greece during the millennium of the European Dark Ages. Later, by contrast, he refugees from economic and political degradation in contemporary Muslim countries arrived in Europe as uneducated laborers who, along with their children and grandchildren, occupied slum ghettoes that were uniformly Muslim, albeit of varied national origins. In some instances there was a colonial connection between their places of origin and of refuge, and that connection fomented bitter nationalist struggles. France became home to North African Muslims from its former colonies; England had already opened its doors to former colonials now emanating from the South Asian subcontinent as well as the Caribbean and the Middle East. Large numbers of Turkish *Gastarbeiters* were in Germany and the Scandinavian countries. In each of these countries, a different pattern was applied for resettling immigrant populations. These respective patterns reflected the political expectations of the host government for the group's incorporation.

Germany's model was segregation, reflecting the expectation that there would be no assimilation: the immigrants would not become naturalized Germans. In France the emphasis was on assimilating and homogenizing immigrants with the indigenous French. However, that scheme failed to take into account that Muslim immigrants were not only a formerly colonized population, but also the winners in the anticolonial war, who were quite resistant to French iconography. For example, France has national martyrs who represent the union of the populace in wars for French dignity and sovereignty. But there is no martyr icon for the French Algerian War, which cost more French lives than did World War I. In Holland there was an idealistic view in which all the ingathered former colonial subjects and the persecuted immigrants from Africa and Asia would integrateinto the Dutch population under conditions of liberal democracy. A large number, however, didn't come to Amsterdam for liberation from their rigid religious orthodoxies.

No less important is the attraction for second-generation immigrants of a positive identity—an identity conferred by the very circumstance of their difference from the indigenous population that has subordinated them, restricting them to inferior jobs and housing. Many European minorities revive their old cultures and languages in the course of asserting their uniqueness preserving their identity. This is particularly the case in nationalist struggles such as Northern Ireland, Kosovar Albanians, Bosnian Muslims, and Chechen nationalists. But the current second and third generations of Muslims in Europe time-warped back 600 years to propose as most attractive the reestablishment of the Caliphate. Not coincidentally, this is the rallying cry for Osama bin Laden.

Their legend of the Caliphate and aspirations for a revival are antagonistic toward modernism and toleration. Their alienation has been fomented or mobilized by imams of Salafi Islam, the least tolerant and most radical opponents of modernism. This philosophy, in turn, breaks into several subgroups, one of which is Salafi Jihadists. Among these are the *takfiri*, who can remove all signs of Islam from body and behavior in service of jihad. Thus, the 9/11 bombers were able to drink in bars, shave their faces, and eat non-halal food to blend into the majority population when it suited their jihadi purposes. The same ethic is invoked to allow women to become suicide bombers. It is in fact an ideology rather than a theology.

For jihadis Iraq is the most immediate training ground because it pits "infidel occupier" against a "captive" Muslim population in a Muslim land. Jihadis recall the Crusaders of 600 years ago, including Richard the Lion Hearted, who invaded primarily Muslim territories in southern and eastern Europe en route to Jerusalem. Reiterated and memorialized, this piece of history permits a parallel rationalization for contemporary vendetta.

One of the persistent questions about the recent spate of suicide bombers is their level of education and assimilation into European culture. The assumption is that suicide-homicide or martyrdom killings are the last-resort behavior of young, uneducated, and economically disadvantaged men who lack the resources to deal with a technological, sophisticated modern society.

It is true that many of the Shia suicide bombers in Lebanon in the 1980s were drawn from these social ranks. It is also the case for the first nine homicide-suicide bombers from Gaza who acted during the period of the Oslo accords. But that demographic has changed during the second Intifada and among the ranks of recruits to Al-Qaeda and related organizations. Many of the suicide bombers have completed undergraduate and graduate work. Their education in technology does not intrude or challenge bedrock belief systems, as an education in the humanities and social sciences might do.

To understand this change one must look both to developmental psychology and geography.

The early followers of Muhammad were subjected to persecution much as the early Christians and Jews. Every clan that contained Muslims subjected them to torture and death to force them to deny the supremacy of Allah. This martyrology, particularly noted in the death of Husayn, grandson of Muhammad who was martyred by the dominant Sunni religious establishment. He is the penultimate martyr of Shia Islam and an icon for acts of martyrdom, notably suicide-homicide. Death on the path to declaring the supremacy of Allah is, for many Muslims, martyrdom. Education in Islam includes this knowledge, these icons, and these ideals.

In the late 20th century, the economic lure of western Europe, with its recent history of colonial occupation of land masses with large Muslim populations in Africa, Asia, and southern and eastern Europe, brought guest workers and illegal immigrants eager to partake of prosperity and freedom. But what they find, besides low-paying jobs, is an atmosphere of discrimination. Particularly painful to North African Muslim immigrants in France is the political denial of their suffering in the Algerian War, which their parents and grandparents fled as refugees. Immigration of Palestinians and Lebanese contributed fuel to the rhetorical flames about Jewish (Zionist) occupation of Muslim lands.

Studies of immigrant populations indicate that while the best adjustment to their new environment is reported by immigrants living in close proximity to their expatriate group, the children of immigrants in the United States and in Europe have tended to have a significantly higher incidence of delinquency and adult criminal behavior than their parents' generation and indigenous age peers.[28]

My own studies indicate that alienation from the institutions of the host society and recognition that their family is external to the access trajectory for success in those institutions provides the breeding ground for violent behavior. Limited opportunities to participate in the machinery of power—legislative bodies, courts, administration, elected and appointed officialdom—restrict development of political efficacy. Political inefficacy truncates the development of moral judgment. No less important to second-generation immigrants is a positive identity—an identity conferred by the very circumstance of their difference from the indigenous population that has subordinated them, restricting them to inferior jobs and housing.

TRAUMA, TORTURE, AND POST-TRAUMATIC STRESS

It is significant that the overwhelming majority of Muslims in Europe are not seduced by appeals by jihadis, and that those who are, regardless of their level of education and social status origins, are (according to their own final martyrdom statements) motivated to vendetta for either primary (victimization) or secondary trauma-identification with victims. Some theorists on the motivation for suicide-homicide have focused on the experience of the perpetrator as a torture survivor or a close family member of a victim of the opponent's predations.

Particularly dramatic examples are the Black Widows of Chechnya who embarked on suicide-homicide actions in Russia. They are women who allegedly lost their husbands and brothers to the predations of the Russian army in Chechnya. The several Palestinian women who attempted or succeeded in suicide-homicide missions are also reported to have lost close relatives either in Israeli Defense Forces (IDF) assassinations or in fighting the IDF. Generally women suicide-homicide perpetrators are likely to have suffered primary rather than secondary trauma as the instigation of their choice for suicide-homicide.

But this was the case for neither the 9/11 nor the 7/7 suicide bombers. Also notable are the social class and educational background of the 9/11 suicide bombers, 15 of whom came from Saudi Arabia, where they had education and more-or-less middle-class family backgrounds. If they experienced primary trauma, it was when they volunteered to go to Afghanistan. But they were exposed to secondary trauma through the recruiting materials used by Al-Qaeda that feature scenes of Palestinians attacked and killed by the IDF. Now, of course, the photos and videos of the infamous Abu Ghraib prisoner abuse have become recruiting posters, videos, and repetitive media features in the Arab world. Basel Saleh studied the demographics and traumatic experiences of 219 male and female political activists in Islamic Jihad, Islamic Resistance Movement, and Al Aqsa, between 2000 and 2003, and found that there was a significant history of trauma inflicted by the IDF. But of the 214 "martyrs" in his demographic analysis, the majority were in their 20s, and all were affiliated with one of the three organizations before their mission. Their occupations ranged from unemployed laborer to teachers in Islamic universities. Individuals assassinated by the IDF are also identified by their organizations as martyrs. One of the confounding issues in identifying an Islamic martyr psychology is that in Islam, unlike Christianity or Judaism, the amorphous "death on the path to Allah" doesn't distinguish between heroes and martyrs, fighters and the pious. Those who were middle class were more often killed by assassination, while most of the younger casualties were less educated and worked at occupational levels. On the other hand, my own study of nine Palestinian suicide bombers who killed themselves between 1990 and 1999 during the period of the Oslo accords indicated that their trauma was primarily secondary—through identification with travesties of the occupation and religious commitment to martyrdom.[29]

Normally, this stage of moral-legal development occurs between ages 13 and 19. In a peaceful egalitarian society, late adolescence is the beginning of the stage of universal justice—that is, right and wrong are considered universally applicable regardless of individuals' relationships with each other or affinity or identity group. But the earlier stage of retributive justice is not merely a desire for vengeance consequent to experiencing violent trauma. It is also predicated on the affinity group relationships and identity groups' social valuation. It is particularly likely if the victim of violent trauma is an adolescent or young adult male in a patriarchal culture. Gang warfare easily becomes intercommunal violence. Less often recognized is the impact of secondary trauma that is generated through identification with a victim by reason of affiliation, race, ethnicity, or communion.

The Martyrdom Ethos Is Generated through These Two Levels of Trauma

In an earlier study of primary and secondary traumatization, I found that Palestinian children who had not personally witnessed the massacres at Sabra and Shatila in 1982 identified so completely with the event and the victimization that they reported experiencing bombings and killings and had nightmares about their parents being massacred and themselves confronted by armed soldiers. They evidenced symptoms of post-traumatic stress, as did the children who were in those places at the time of the massacre. This secondary traumatization during childhood and adolescence fuels vendetta and truncates the development of moral judgment in the stage of retributive justice. This is the dynamic that in adult members of terrorist groups is manifested as righteous indignation.

If we examine Muslims in Europe who have engaged in suicide-homicide through this paradigm we find all of the elements of the cycle: fear into hatred into violence. The fear is fear of victimization—physical, political, and discrimination experienced as an immigrant. Hatred is too often reciprocal and enacted as violence, as exemplified in race riots and the cycle of retaliatory violence following the murder of Theo Van Gogh, for example.

Historically, social class and level of formal education are more likely to yield a positive correlation with positions of leadership in a revolutionary group. Neither these indices nor the indices of psychological normality and intelligence are the conclusive determinants of emotionally driven moral choices. Instead, these alternatives are mediated by experience. Behavior is chosen (motivated) from the iconic brain images in the circuits of affective memory.[30]

DETERMINING DEVIANT BEHAVIOR

Young people who commit suicide and/or homicide are choosing a center-stage role for themselves. Whether the ultimate objective is fatalistic or altruistic, the individual believes that the future depends on him or her and the incipient act. All who join a terrorist organization make a commitment of their lives and fortunes to the shared project. This is much the same as the volunteer to military service. The latter expects training, discipline, and esprit de corps. Unlike the perpetrator of suicide-homicide, the military volunteer envisions the future with *himself or herself in it.* The soldier's commitment is to the institutions of the prevailing society, of which the military or security institution is a vital conservator.

Nevertheless, there are similarities in the training program. Foot soldiers are trained to take orders and fulfill their mission. However, a soldier fights for his comrades in arms and counts as a victory the mission in which his group fought bravely and survived. Military training also deplores civilian casualties. In fact, post-traumatic stress disorder or combat stress disorder is often triggered by killing innocent women and children. Diametrically opposite, the terrorist trainee lives entirely in an "us/them" framework. A "good" death is killing "them." A "bad" death is one inflicted on us by them and demands vengeance. When terrorists identify themselves and prospective membership with commonalities in religious or national origins and seek iconic status through attacking "the oppressors" and "the impure," they are able to rationalize the death of coreligionists by the latter's collaboration. National armies rationalize deaths of civilians as "collateral damage."

In the earlier days of suicide-homicide through the Hezbollah in Lebanon, martyrs were promoted like rock stars are in the West. They made death films, photos on posters, and cassette tapes that would get played on broadcast media. Similarly, in the Palestinian cases, suicide-homicides achieved instant fame and their families received payment of death benefits and celebrated the holy death. Since martyrdom is accorded as well to those who are killed on the path to Allah, many killed by the IDF were celebrated as martyrs. It was commonplace in the apartments of Palestinians in Sabra and Shatila in Beirut to see these posters commemorating and celebrating a close relative who was killed at the Munich airport after participating in the massacre at the Olympic Games. There is no question that such representations had inspirational impact on the young. To ensure the direction of the impact, a younger brother of the deceased would often take his name. In a society in which millions live in anonymity and anomie, this fragile glimmer of eternal recognition exerts a powerful appeal.

There is another essential difference between an army and a terrorist organization. The former recruits and trains persons who have reached the age of consent. The latter may well commence training in childhood, or junior organizations, but will accept as recruits for martyrdom missions volunteers of whatever age, preferably steeped in their ideology but not necessarily tested for the depth of their knowledge. Such recruits are for a single mission and need few qualifications apart from ideological commitment. They do not receive lengthy training in terrorism or undertake a series of missions of varying tasks.

More experienced members of terrorist organizations with skills like bomb making and finance become too valuable to become martyrs by suicide missions. In fact, the trajectory of a suicide bomber within an organization is relatively brief. The usual scenario is that a prospective suicide bomber joins a terror organization in order to fulfill that objective.

Psychologists and psychiatrists providing services to people living in communities with high incidence of recruits, such as Gaza, emphasize the demographics of poverty and hopelessness as motivating factors and traumatic experiences as the triggering factor.[31] As of this writing there are two primary sources for diagnostic determination, and neither is clinically acceptable. First, there are postmortem interviews based on psychological tests administered to close family members and friends of the deceased. These are presumably predicated on norms for the population. The other method is through clinical interviews with suicide bombers who have been intercepted by the Israelis and jailed.[32]

Finally, journalists recently began doing interviews of suicide-bombers-in-training volunteered by their organization press offices or handlers.[33]

All of the data when subjected to story sequence analysis motivation index indicate that these men and women are not motivated by pathology but have rationalized their chosen pathway to notoriety and eternity in total disregard for their victims. Or perhaps by prejudging their intended victims as evil and a danger to their identity group, they rationalize their target population. The rationalization thesis seems to be that dying for the cause is holy and good. The death of others caused in pursuit of "our cause" is trivial and justified by the overriding importance of the cause. But how is this different from the gang members who in the course of their gang wars kill innocent people who happen to be in the way?

As individuals, those who turn to deadly force as the only alternative are not necessarily diagnosable as social deviants, criminals, intellectually marginal, or even as fanatics. They are often more concerned than their peers with right and wrong and with justice.

THE FORENSIC IMPLICATIONS OF FLUID BOUNDARIES OF ABNORMALITY

In presenting a mental health defense and/or a mental health mitigating circumstance, it is a struggle to try to somehow "fix" what are very fluid boundaries of diagnoses of abnormality. This comes to the fore when dealing with culprits such as Timothy McViegh, Jim Jones, David Koresh, and John Muhamed. Each of them was responsible for multiple deaths and either died with his victims or gave himself over to capital sentencing to be put to death for his crimes. Minimal psychological evaluations and postmortem psychological assessments revealed no recognizable pathologies. Certainly there was nothing that might have led to a finding of not guilty by reason of insanity. For lack of anything more substantive, they are consigned to the diagnosis, "sociopath or character disorder." But had these men been studied before their mass killing event, would they have been found outside the norms on intelligence, personality, and other tests? Would they have profiled on the MMPI as significantly high Pd scores? The fact is that many of the responses and conditions of early life that place a respondent into that category are commonplace in poverty, domestic violence, poor family interactions, alcohol and other substance abuse, and membership in a victimized minority group. The Hare Psychopathy Checklist-Revised (PCL-R) is an example of a test frequently used in forensic settings to determine the likelihood that a felon has potential for rehabilitation or is simply a sociopath. Scoring is adversely affected by all of these named sociodemographic circumstances.[34] As for intelligence tests, it is easy to understand that members of minority groups—either by dint of language or ethnicity—would not respond satisfactorily to the culturally biased vocabulary questions on a standard individual intelligence test, and that if they are not familiar with solving matrix puzzles and/or conceptualizing a three-dimensional object as a two-dimensional drawing, would have a terrible time on the nonverbal tests of intelligence. And so it goes.

All of this brings us to questions raised by many generations of students of psychology: Isn't killing an abnormal act? Isn't suicide an indication of a disturbed personality? And finally, would anyone in his or her right mind choose no resuscitation and no extraordinary measures in a life or death medical crisis? The answer to the last question may be extended to the other two questions. The implementation and legitimacy of a Living Will presumes that a human being can choose to die. When, then, is killing an abnormal act?

We know that damage to the frontal and temporal lobes, particularly on right side, can result in impaired judgment and impulsivity. Mature moral judgment is a function of the frontal lobe and is presumed to be undeveloped until that part of the brain reaches adulthood. Neuroscientists have demonstrated that damage to the frontal and temporal lobes is one of the three characteristics of multiple killers.[35] In federal law and most state laws in the United States and in Europe, an individual with a subnormal IQ and/or an individual incapable of reasoned judgment cannot be assigned a death penalty. But on the other hand, an elderly person can be ruled incompetent to handle his or her own funds or make personal choices if the individual is diagnosed with dementia. That diagnosis is made apart from psychological tests, on the basis of behavioral observations. We would like to believe that a diagnosis is a scientific statement and not a subjective estimation. And perhaps in the case of an elderly person suffering dementia it is. But for the disaffected youths recruited into terrorist organizations, there is a normalcy that is abnormal. Very much like the American immigrant youths who become gang members, the disaffected young Muslims of Europe, also second-generation, drift into radicalism under the blind eyes of parents who are often perplexed on parenting these children born in freedom and relative affluence. These parents are likely to be working very hard at whatever jobs or enterprises they can command convinced that making money will provide everything that is needed for their children's success. Clearly, the model of their own, traditional upbringing is not appropriate for this urban modern environment.

The Leeds bombers are typical of these young men. According to the report about them in *Time* magazine, they drifted into "groups whose zeal and camaraderie offer a sense of purpose."[36]

Often it is a youth outreach center or a radical Islamist Inam. When their talent and enthusiasm for jihad are recognized, they are offered travel to Pakistan and Afghanistan for training. Sometimes they have been offered missions in Palestine and die blowing up themselves and others in a Tel Aviv nightclub. Usually parents and neighbors haven't tracked a particular pattern, but in retrospect they recall the youth having gotten into racial fights at school or showing proclivities for religious orthodoxies. Ironically, it may be parents who, trying to settle a rebellious son, mistakenly blame his problems on "modernism." They send him back to Pakistan to a madrassa to learn Arabic and the Qur'an and discipline.

THE TERRORIZING EFFECTS OF NORMAL TERRORISTS

The sheer irrationality of a terrorist attack is what traumatizes the subject population. When the terrorists come across to their target population as normal, they become individuals with whom their victims can sympathize or even empathize (as is theorized in the Stockholm Syndrome).[37] Anne Speckhard in her paper, "Soldiers for God: A Study of the Suicide Terrorists in the Moscow Hostage Taking Siege," notes the following example:

Given the general Russian attitude toward Chechans, it is interesting that the Stockholm effects were so pronounced . . . Indeed, the Chechans were willing to die and take the hostages with them if necessary, but were also individually kind and relational with their hostages so much so that afterwards their hostages felt grief and pity for them.[38]

She also notes in writing about women suicide bombers generally that:

> In terms of producing the desired effect of terror, female bombers are likely more potent in this regard since they defy all traditional stereotypes of women as nurturing, sympathetic and kind.[39]

This raises the question of societal norms themselves. At the same time we recognize that there are relative norms for behavior in various social roles. We recognize this with remarks such as "Well, mothers are like that!" or "What else could you expect of a teen-ager?"

Thus, when an evangelical preacher of any sect exhorts his or her followers to murderous hatred against an out-group in their midst, some may tend to accept this is normal behavior and fail to recognize the zealotry and fanaticism that are intrinsic to an act of terrorism. In a society in which there is a historic and political link with the psychology of xenophobia, such fanaticism is incorporated within the bounds of the social norms. At the time of this writing, the United Kingdom is considering enacting laws to criminalize "incitement to hatred" when it is perpetrated by a nonnative radical Muslim imam. Hate speech and publication have been banned in Germany since the establishment of the Federal Republic of Germany following World War II. Similar measures are under consideration in The Netherlands and France. Ironically, no such consideration was applied in the case of the Reverent Ian Paisley, who is presently a member of the European Parliament despite his acts of hate speech. Similarly, a century ago, in the pre–Civil War United states, no such legal measure impeded fanatical antiabolitionists such as Wendell Phillips and other Garrisonian abolitionists who inspired the terrorist tactics of John Brown and of Nat Turner. Clearly, it is a matter of the societal norms and political hegemony for enmity. Adolf Hitler, against the backdrop of a liberal democratic Weimar Republic, was able to incite xenophobic hatred of such proportions as to set off a war of conquest and the Holocaust. He and his political philosophy established an us/them psychology. It incorporated a good death/bad death ideology without room for moderation.

While we would like to believe that this dynamic can only be established when there is preexisting climate of fear and intolerance, the pre–Civil War abolitionists, with their zealotry for democracy, and Ian Paisley's fierce anti-Catholic and anti-Ecumenical rantings against the World Council of Churches, actually helped to create a climate of fear not much different from the Reichstag fire of 1933 that established Hitler and the Nazi Party as the Third Reich.

When terrorism achieves its intentions, the target society is vulnerable to the politics of fear. Societal norms on acceptable behavior—or what is normal—change.

There is further evidence of this normalization in the data on suicide bombers demographics from the beginning of the Palestinian bombings to the present phenomenon in Iraq. The marginality of the early suicide-homicide bombers, both demographically and psychologically, contrasts with the many volunteers from throughout the Muslim world who are volunteering for these missions in Iraq. In even stronger contrast is their move to relative anonymity—no more video- or audiotaped messages of farewell. No more photo posters with background icons of the Dome of the Rock or Al Aqsa. In short, the normalization of the abnormal is being completed.

NOTES

1. A. Maslow, *Toward a Psychology of Being* (New York: Van Norstrand Reinhold, 1968).

2. A. Dorfman, *Exorcising Terror* (New York: Seven Stories Press, 2002).

3. S. Milgram, *Obedience to Authority: An Experimental View* (New York: Harper and Row, 1974).

4. P. Zimbardo, "Obedience to Authority," *American Psychologist* 27 (1974): 566–567.

5. H. Murray, Thematic Apperception Test, *Manual for the Thematic Apperception Test* (Cambridge, MA: Harvard University Press, 1943).

6. M. Arnold, *Story Sequence Analysis of the Thematic Apperception Test* (New York: Columbia University Press, 1963).

7. R. M. Fields, *Society on the Run* (Hammondsworth, UK: Penguin, 1973); R. M. Fields, *Society Under Siege* (Philadelphia: Temple University Press, 1976).

8. J. Piaget, *The Moral Judgment of the Child* (New York: Harcourt, Brace and World, 1932).

9. Fields, *Society on the Run.*

10. H. Arendt, *A Report on the Banality of Evil* (New York: Viking, 1963).

11. J. Tapp and L. Kohlberg, "Developing Senses of Law and Legal Justice," *Journal of Social Issues* 27 (1971): 65–91.

12. J. Piaget, *The Language and Thought of the Child* (New York: Meridian Books, World Publishing, 1963).

13. C. Spielberger, *State-Trait Personality Indices* (Tampa, FL: Psychology Assessment Services, 1985).

14. E. Hoffer, *The True Believer* (New York: Harper and Row, 1951).

15. R. M. Fields, *Society Under Siege* (Philadelphia: Temple University Press, 1976).

16. R. M. Fields, S. Elbedour, and F. A. Hein, "The Palestinian Suicide Bomber," in *The Psychology of Terrorism, Vol. 2*, ed. C. E. Stout (Westport, CT: Greenwood/Praeger, 2002) pp. 193–224.

17. G. Reuven, "Impact of the Intifada on Israeli Youth," the 2nd International Conference on Wartime Medical Services, Stockholm, Sweden, June 25–29, 1990.

18. E. Durkheim, *Suicide* (New York: Free Press, 1951).

19. Fields, Elbedour, and Hein, *The Palestinian Suicide Bomber*; and Hein, "The Palestinian Suicide Bomber."

20. B. Ganor, "Suicide Terrorism: An Overview" (paper presented at Countering Suicide Terrorism: An International Conference, International Policy Institute for Counter-Terrorism, Herzlia, Israel, March 10, 2000).

21. R. Gumaratna, "Suicide Terrorism in Sri Lanka and Israel" (paper presented at Countering Suicide Terrorism: An International Conference, International Policy Institute for Counter-Terrorism, Herzlia, Israel, March 10, 2000).

22. D. Ergil, "Suicide Terrorism in Turkey: The Workers' Party of Kurdistan" (paper presented at Countering Suicide Terrorism: An International Conference, International Policy Institute for Counter-Terrorism, Herzlia, Israel, March 10, 2000).

23. Young Lung-Chang, "Altruistic Suicide: A Subjective Approach," *Sociological Bulletin* 21 (1972): 103–121.

24. Stack, S., *Durkheim and His Study of Suicide* (London: Hutchinson, 1982), p. 162.

25. Young, "Altruistic Suicide," p. 105.

26. Stack, *Durkheim*.

27. G. Ben-Dor, A. Pedahzur, Arie Perliiger, L. Weinberg, and Daphna Canetti-Nisim, "Latest Research and Information about Terrorism and Terrorists," (Haifa, Israel: National Security Studies Center at the University of Haifa, April 22, 2006). Available at http://www.terrorismexperts.org/.

28. E. E. Huyck and R. M. Fields, "Impact of Re-Settlement on Refugee Children," *International Migration Review* 15 (1981): 246–251.

29. Fields, Elbedour, and Hein, "The Palestinian Suicide Bomber."

30. M. Arnold, *Memory and the Brain* (London: Lawrence Erlbaum, 1984).

31. R. L. Punamaki, "Can Ideological Commitment Protect Children's Psychosocial Well-Being in Situations of Violence?" *Child Development* 67 (1996): 55–69.

32. J. Post, E. Sprinzak, and L. Denny, "The Terrorists in Their Own Words: Interviews with 35 Incarcerated Middle Eastern Terrorists," *Terrorism and Political Violence* 15 (2003): 171–184.

33. A. Ghosh, "Inside the Mind of an Iraqi Suicide Bomber," *Time*, July 4, 2005, pp. 25–29.

34. R. Hare, "PLC-L Normalization Standards," *Manual for the Hare PLC* (San Antonio, Tex.: Harcourt Assessment, 1998).

35. J. H. Pincus, *Base Instincts: What Makes Killers Kill?* (New York: W. W. Norton, 2001).

36. Ghosh, "Inside the Mind."

37. F. Ochberg, "The Victim of Terrorism: Psychiatric Considerations" (paper presented at International Seminar on Dimensions of Victimization in the Context of Terrorists Acts conference in Evian, France, June 3–5, 1977).

38. A. Speckard, "Soldiers for God: A Study of the Suicide Terrorists in the Moscow Hostage Taking Siege" (paper presented at Centra Conference, Arlington, Va., 2004).

39. Speckard, "Soldiers for God," pp. 8–9.

Chapter 10

Culture in Psychopathology—Psychopathology in Culture: Taking a New Look at an Old Problem

Juris G. Draguns

THREE ILLUSTRATIONS

Tim is a 24-year-old graduate student in biochemistry at a prominent midwestern research university. Characteristically ambitious, energetic, and productive, he has not been himself lately. His professors and peers have noticed a kind of indifference, bordering on apathy, in the laboratory, in seminars, and in casual social give-and-take. His friends are at a loss to account for this change, except that, as some of them recall, it started rather rapidly, after a couple of academic and social setbacks. The paper he had worked on for three months, his first solo publication, was peremptorily rejected by a refereed journal. And he could not hold his own in arguments and debates with an exceptionally brilliant and articulate new graduate student. His girlfriend's support and encouragement were now increasingly mixed with criticism and sarcasm, or so Tim thought. At one time, he suddenly burst into tears between classes. A short hospitalization and prescription for antidepressants followed, and cognitive-behavioral treatment was initiated. Diagnostic interviews revealed a guilt- and doubt-ridden young man who was blaming himself for promise unrealized and potential wasted.

Shiro is a 26-year-old junior executive in a major corporation in Japan. Married a year ago, he is the father of a baby girl. His ascent from a lower-middle-class family was a model Japanese success story. Groomed for admission into a prestigious university from his preschool days, he studied hard through grade and high school, eschewing idle pastimes. He passed the entrance examination to the university of his choice with flying colors. Upon gradu-ation, luck smiled on him again. He was selected as an executive trainee by a prominent Japanese company with the prospect of lifetime employ-ment and steady promotions, and his superior took a liking to him. He was singled out for praise, but also assigned responsibilities. Sooner than many of his peers he was included in the obligatory late suppers with entertain-ment for company's suppliers and customers. Returning home on the last train, he had to be ready to start early the next day. He married an attractive and charming young woman of a more prominent social background than himself. There was little time for courtship or romance or the development of an intimate relationship. He barely saw his new daughter, although he constantly thought about her. One day, he overslept. Once he got up, the whole world looked dark to him. Catching the commuter train was out of the question. Deeply depressed, he was treated with a combination of anti-depressants, Japanese residential Morita therapy, and cognitive-behavioral interventions. He spoke little, but complied conscientiously with all treat-ments. Occasionally, he was heard to mutter: "I've let them all down. I've failed them miserably." "They" included his wife, but more prominently his parents, who had sacrificed so much for the sake of his education and career, his mentors and tutors at different stages of his life, his supervisor, who had pinned such high hopes on him, and even the company president, whom he had met once for a handshake.

Barnaby is a son of a family of moderately successful shopkeepers in Lagos, Nigeria. Devout Evangelical Christians, his parents instilled in him a sense of duty and an ethic of self-improvement. Graduated from a secondary school with fairly good grades, he quickly got married and became father of three children. Working at a succession of clerical jobs, he attended night school to improve his English and to qualify for a coveted entry-level position in the civil service. At age 25, he seemed on the verge of attaining his goal when, while studying for an important test, he lost his ability to understand what he was reading. Language was not an issue, but words remained unconnected in his mind, sen-tences did not add up, and paragraphs had no meaning. At the same time, head-aches and a sense of general physical distress overwhelmed him. Examined at a modern medical center, he was found to be free of neurological disorder, and no standard psychiatric diagnosis appeared to fit him. Informally, Barnaby and others called his condition "brain fag" and attributed it to his having worked too hard. Antianxiety and antidepressant medications brought some relief.

Barnaby and his parents were utterly unresponsive to the suggestion by one of his physicians that he seek psychiatric consultation. Traditional African healing methods were briefly considered, but Barnaby's family rejected then as "unchristian." Instead, reliance was placed on prayer, which brought about some symptomatic improvement.

SIMILAR CHALLENGES, DIFFERENT RESPONSES

Three ambitious, hardworking, upwardly mobile young men who found themselves entangled in the pursuit of their goals! The challenges that they faced were more similar than different, but the distress and dysfunction that they experienced bore the earmarks of their respective milieus. American individualistic culture rewarded Tim for his successes and held him responsible for any hint of imperfection or failure. He internalized these values, measured his progress by the most demanding standards, and felt self-loathing when he found himself short of his objectives. His blame was concentrated on himself, and the discrepancy between what he was and what he should have been was experienced most painfully. Shiro, too, saw his dreams disintegrate before his eyes. Yet his sense of inadequacy was not focused upon himself, but upon his parents and mentors whom his failure, he thought, had so grievously disappointed. His sense of obligation was directed at specific people, and it was their sorrowful, reproachful glances that he dreaded to imagine, yet was unable to banish. Barnaby's distress was more globally and organismically experienced. Apparently, it was not pinned to either himself or his significant others. Yet it was felt most painfully, perhaps because of the helplessness in being unable to correct, control, or make sense of his predicament. In contrast to his counterparts in the United States and Japan, Barnaby faced another problem. Three systems of conceptualization and care were available to him, and yet none of them quite fit him. That was true of modern secular scientific resources, traditional African approaches, and Christian religious practices.

THE PROBLEM

In what ways and to what extent do people differ across cultures in responding to stresses and challenges of living, especially when they cannot cope with them adequately on the basis of their experience and resources? This chapter will seek to provide answers to these questions on the basis of clinical observations and research findings that have been accumulating ever more rapidly in the course of the last few decades. To this end, the two pivotal terms in this chapter must be defined.

KEY DEFINITIONS

What is culture? An elegant classical definition by Melville Herskovits equates it with the environment that human beings have created.[1] Emphasis in this pithy statement is placed upon artifacts, from hand tools to computers and from huts to skyscrapers. However, it is implicitly recognized that the environment to which this definition refers is both external and internal. In particular, the aspects of culture that are crucial in the context of this chapter are to be found within rather than outside human beings. Tseng[2] focuses upon "the unique behavior patterns and lifestyle shared by a group of people which distinguish it from others" as the defining features of culture. Moreover, in Tseng's formulation, culture encompasses "views, beliefs, values and attitudes," as well as "rituals, customs, etiquette, taboos, [and] laws" (p. 5). As Ember and Ember[3] assert, culture is learned, shared, and transmitted.

These statements primarily pertain to geographically distinct and separate cultures in locations where all people speak the same language and abide by the same customs. In pluralistic cultures, of which the United States is perhaps the most prominent exemplar, people of a variety of cultures inhabit the same area, interact, and are mutually influenced. They share to varying degrees some core values and beliefs while retaining certain of their original or ancestral cultural characteristics. Investigation of cultural impact upon psychopathology in pluralistic cultures faces the challenge of disentangling the various threads of cultural influence.

Psychopathology as a concept encompasses the totality of mental disorders or mental illnesses. The fundamental criteria of mental disorder, as embodied in the current *Diagnostic and Statistical Manual of Mental Disorders* (fourth edition, text revision), or *DSM–IV–TR*,[4] are distress and disability, that is, personal suffering and impairment in dealing effectively with the challenges of daily life. The authors of *DSM-IV* and other experts[5] are adamant in sharply differentiating mental disorder from social deviance and from conflict between an individual and his or her society.

HOW MUCH DOES CULTURE INFLUENCE PSYCHOPATHOLOGY?

There is a virtual consensus that the expressions of psychopathology are not identical around the world. Disagreement, however, does arise when the extent and importance of these differences are considered. Are they fundamental or trivial, striking or minor?

Ruth Benedict, an eminent cultural anthropologist, maintained that psychological disturbance is a social category defined independently within each culture.[6] One culture may exalt as its mystics and poets persons who would be considered crazy in another culture. Conversely, people admired and emulated as heroes within their culture might be regarded as seriously disturbed outside of it. On the other side of the ledger, Eric Berne has minimized the importance of cultural differences in psychopathology.[7] On the basis of his observations of institutionalized psychiatric patients in French Polynesia, he concluded that" clinically, cultural differences can be treated as mere dialects or accents of a common language; the Italian schizophrenic speaks schizophrenic with an Italian accent, and the Siamese manic speaks manic with a Siamese accent" (p. 108).

RESEARCH FINDINGS

Global Uniformities in Psychopathology

A series of large-scale multinational studies by the World Health Organization (WHO) greatly advanced the state of knowledge on the symptoms of schizophrenia throughout the world. In the initial study, in which schizophrenic patients at clinical research centers in Colombia, Czechoslovakia, Denmark, England, India, Nigeria, Russia, Taiwan, and the United States participated, seven virtually invariant symptoms were identified at all of the nine sites: lack of insight, flat affect, delusional mood, ideas of reference, perplexity, auditory hallucinations, and feeling of external control.[8] Follow-up observations two years later demonstrated that positive symptoms, such as delusions, were likely to disappear, while negative symptoms, such as flat affect, tended to persist.[9] Additional findings, gathered at 12 centers in 10 countries, bolstered the case for commonalities across cultures in prevalence[10] and in the number of stressful events.[11] Coordinators of this research concluded that schizophrenia occurred in all countries in which it was investigated and that rates of incidence were similar in all of the populations studied.[11] Moreover, there was no support obtained for the oft-voiced expectation, going back to Ruth Benedict,[6] that schizophrenic symptoms would be labeled and construed differently depending on the culture.

WHO teams have also investigated hospitalized depressed patients in Canada, Iran, Japan, and Switzerland.[12] They succeeded in identifying a set of six symptoms that were widely prevalent at all locations: sadness, absence of joy, lowered pleasure, reduced concentration, lack of energy, and a sense of inadequacy. In a more recent, comprehensive epidemiological investigation of rates of depression in 10 major cities around the world, Weissman and coworkers[13] reported that insomnia and lack of appetite were among the most prevalent symptoms at all of the research sites. These findings are consistent with the conclusions by several reviewers[14–17] who regard such vegetative symptoms as sleep disturbance, poor appetite, and lack of energy to be the pancultural substrate of depressive experience.

Sequential research of a comparable scope has not yet been extended beyond schizophrenia and depression, so that our knowledge of universalistic features of other disorders remains fragmentary. In any case, no worldwide constancies have emerged in the 14-nation Collaborative Study of Psychological Problems in General Health Care,[18] nor, in light of Tseng's recent comprehensive review,[17] in several bicultural, multicultural, and multiethnic studies of anxiety disorders.

Cultural Differences in Psychopathology

Reports of cultural differences in psychopathology are much more numerous than demonstrations of uniformity, and they extend over a much wider range of psychiatric conditions. In the WHO projects, prognosis for schizophrenia was unexpectedly found to be better in developing countries, such as Nigeria, than in developed ones, exemplified by Denmark.[11] Another paradoxical result was the negative correlation between educational level and favorable prognosis for schizophrenia in developing countries, the exact obverse of the relationship between these two variables observed time and again in the United States and other economically advanced nations. Moreover, although the worldwide trend toward similar, convergent prevalence rates of schizophrenia is solidly established,[11] Murphy was able to identify a limited number of social settings characterized by unusually high or low rates of schizophrenia.[19] He then hypothesized that high rates of schizophrenia were in part caused by the patterns of confusing and contradictory messages from the community to the person—an intriguing, but as yet untested, possibility. Expressed emotion, however, has proved to be a fruitful area of investigation, and Indian schizophrenics were found to receive about half as many emotionally toned, disparaging communications from their families by comparison with their British counterparts.[20] According to Al-Issa,[21] hallucinations, a prominent symptom in schizophrenia, vary in their cultural meaning and are embedded in a cultural context. Thus, the choice of sensory modality, visual or auditory, is in part influenced by culture.

Two axes of cultural difference have been identified for depression. Somatic distress and vegetative symptomatology appear to loom larger in verbal reports and self-presentation of depressed individuals in Asia and Africa as compared to their counterparts in Europe and North America. Conversely, guilt has been found to be more prominently featured and more articulately expressed by European and North American depressives.[17] Moreover, self-accusations and self-blame by Japanese patients were focused on specific individuals whom they had allegedly let down or disappointed, while depressed individuals in

Germany castigated themselves for their presumed violations of abstract and absolute principles.[22] Abe[23] noted convergence between the personality traits of depressives in Japan and in Spain who, in both countries, tended to be hardworking, scrupulous, and orderly, in keeping with the characteristics of *homo melancholicus*, originally described in Germany.[24] Cross-cultural comparisons of depression are complicated, and were for a long time stymied by the difficulty of arriving at an intercultural consensus on the basic and intrinsic manifestations of depression. Marsella[15] and other reviewers have commented on the absence of terms equivalent to *depression* in many languages, even though descriptors for some of the components or facets of depressive experience may exist. Cultural complications in defining depression are further illustrated by the findings of the US-UK Diagnostic Project,[25] in the course of which apparent disparities in prevalence of schizophrenia and depression between London and New York were investigated. Upon application of standardized diagnostic criteria, differences between patients in the two cities virtually disappeared. What remained was the difference between diagnosticians, who can be regarded as their culture's agents, with a special proclivity for identifying schizophrenia in the United States and depression in Great Britain.

Less research-based information is available on anxiety disorders, personality disturbances, and various forms of dissociative experience. This paucity of findings is paradoxical because anecdotal observations and theoretical considerations argue for the importance of cultural factors in all of these syndromes. This very feature, however, increases difficulties in making symptoms of these conditions comparable. Besides, many of the varieties of personality disorders have only recently been incorporated into international diagnostic practices, and do not have the rich tradition and history of identification, observation, and treatment characteristic of schizophrenia and depression. Beyond specific diagnostic categories, emphasis on bodily distress appears to be a hallmark of psychopathology in many cultures. In China, Ots[26] succeeded in "cracking the code" of cultural communication of emotional states through specific somatic complaints. Associations between liver and anxiety, heart and anger, and spleen and melancholy were established in China. This implicit code was understood by doctors, and perhaps more dimly and preverbally, by the patients. Bodily symptoms of mental distress are both prominent and common in East Asia, India, Africa, and Latin America, and Kirmayer[27] cautioned Western clinicians lest they dismiss such reports as defensive and trivial. In fact, recognition of various bodily sensations that accompany stressful life experiences may bespeak perceptiveness and sensitivity.

Eating disorders, especially anorexia nervosa and bulimia, have acquired prominence and visibility in recent decades. Internationally, two trends are worth noting. Anorexia nervosa, in particular, appears to be a syndrome of affluent societies.[28] Rarely seen in periods of widespread food shortages and little noted outside of Europe and North America, anorexia nervosa has experienced a spread to the affluent and partially Westernized segments of the population in China, Japan, and India.[17] Culturally variable aspects of eating disorders include idealized body image, emphasis upon slimness, and attitudes toward body exposure. These variables are affected by the global spread of Euroamerican standards, but are also mediated by traditional cultural attitudes. Anorexic teenage girls in Hong Kong, for example, are less openly preoccupied with gaining weight, but tend to complain of intolerable fullness in the stomach and distaste for food.[29]

Alcohol abuse is one of the most culturally variable mental disorders, both internationally and interethnically.[17] Chinese, Italians, and Jews have low rates of problem drinking, both in their countries of origin and in the United States as well as in other countries to which they or their ancestors have migrated. Common characteristic of these and other low alcohol-consumption groups is the manner in which alcohol consumption is regulated and socialized. Often, drinking of a small amount of alcohol is introduced at a festive occasion within the family context, and remains under parental supervision or control. Alcohol then serves as an adjunct to special events and social rituals and is more of a treat or food, rather than a means of bringing about mood change or surcease from frustration. In cultures and ethnic groups in which alcohol consumption is associated with self-assertion, rebellion, or release of normally suppressed emotions, the risk of alcohol abuse tends to be higher.[30] International comparisons of alcohol abuse rates and of amounts of alcohol consumption leave several questions unanswered. Among them is the contrast in the rates of alcohol-related problems between adjacent and culturally related countries, such as France and Italy and Korea and China.

Suicide has been investigated in relation to culture for over 100 years. Durkheim's pioneering comparisons of suicide rates across the states of Europe highlighted the role of social cohesion in preventing and of alienation in promoting suicide.[31] Durkheim's seminal ideas have received a great deal of support in the ensuing century.[32] The psychoanalytically based formulation, that suicide is the result of aggression turned against the self, has fared less well as a general explanatory principle, even though the dramatic increase of suicide in some regions torn by strife and racked by violence, such as Sri Lanka, is consistent with this explanation.[32] By this time, suicide rates are widely regarded as an indicator of unresolved social problems, tensions, and frustrations. Tseng and McDermott[33] have pointed out that national rates of completed suicide tend to vary less than rates of attempted suicide, which they consider the more sensitive social indicator.

In age distribution of suicides, four culturally distinctive patterns have been distinguished: continuous increase of suicide with age, characteristic of Czechoslovakia; increase in suicide rate up to a peak between the ages of 50 and 60 followed by a decrease, as found in Finland; a bimodal curve with peaks in young adulthood and old age, exemplified by Japan; and a unimodal distribution with a peak around the age of 20, observed in Micronesia.[17] These spikes point to periods of vulnerability in their respective cultures that may be kept in mind in developing prevention and early intervention programs.

Culture-Bound Disorders

Culture-bound disorders refer to recurrent patterns of behavior that are recognized as disturbed in the cultural settings in which they occur, are distinct in their manifestations from the disorders included in the international, historically Western-based, diagnostic categories, and are typically encountered in circumscribed geographic areas or culture regions. Within their cultures, culture-bound disorders are explicitly named and labeled. Their etiology tends to be explained in culturally meaningful terms. Typically, but not always, culture-bound disorders are dramatic, acute, and reversible. A glossary of 25 such syndromes is included in *DSM–IV*.[4]

Amok refers to episodes of hypermotility and dissociation that culminate in homicidal outbursts.[34] People are attacked at random, without any detectable motive. Amok runners are heedless of danger to themselves, and not uncommonly precipitate their own death. Young men of precarious social status and fragile self-esteem are especially susceptible to these eruptions; among women, amok is an exceptional occurrence. Typically, the amok episode is preceded by a slight or injury to one's pride, real or imagined. Community response aims to restrain the amok runner and to prevent harm to him or others. Frenzy is quick to subside, and a period of exhaustion, sleep, and stupor follows, from which the person emerges bewildered and depressed, with partial or total amnesia for the amok experience. Amok in its prototypical form occurs throughout Southeast Asia.

Homicidal rampages that bear various degrees of resemblance to amok have been reported in other regions. *Koro* principally afflicts young men in Southern China, Singapore, Malaysia, and Thailand.[33] Its cardinal symptom is the person's conviction that his penis is receding into his abdomen, frequently accompanied by fears of his impending death. Persistent worry, agitation, anxiety, and panic are experienced. Persons suffering from koro seek help from local healers and take traditional herbal medicine. Epidemic outbreaks of koro have occurred in the course of which hysteric symptoms overshadow direct expressions of anxiety.

Most of the koro victims quickly return to their baseline of functioning, and only a few cases become chronic.

In Japan, excessive shyness and fear of people assume the culturally distinctive form of *taijin-kyofushu* (TK), translated as *anthropophobia*.[34] Symptoms of TK include causing other people discomfort by body odor, blushing, or staring. In this respect TK differs from social phobia in *DSM–IV*, in which the overriding features are fear of rejection by others and avoidance of social interaction; TK engenders morbid self-consciousness, intermingled with embarrassment and shame. Consequently, spontaneity is inhibited and social interaction is severely disrupted, but not systematically avoided. TK primarily occurs in adolescents and young adults, with a three to one ratio of men to women. Patients with TK are treated with a gamut of interventions, from psychotropic drugs through behavioral therapy to verbal psychotherapy of several orientations. A distinctive Japanese approach, Morita therapy, involves highly structured time-limited residential treatment designed to distract patients from preoccupation with themselves or others. Conditions similar to TK have been described in Korea and China, for example.[35]

In Mexico, Puerto Rico, and throughout Central America and Caribbean countries, personal losses and catastrophic events precipitate an intense emotional reaction that is somewhat anticlimactically termed *attaque de nervios* (ADN) or an attack of nerves.[33] In its early stages, heat sensations are reported to rise from the chest to the head. The cardinal feature of ADN is loss of control over motoric, affective, and verbal expressions. Shouting, crying, and trembling are common, often accompanied by aggression in word or deed. Fighting in an apparently dissociative state may occur. ADN is often precipitated by death or separation from a loved one or by the threat or the experience of desertion. Middle-aged or older women with less than complete high school education who are not employed and are separated are at risk for ADN. Episodes of AND tend to be brief and self-corrective.

Bouffée délirante aigüe (BDA) is a diagnostic term in the official French diagnostic system. It refers to brief and reversible psychotic episodes marked by dramatic confusional symptoms. BDA is prevalent in West Africa and has also been encountered in Haiti and Cuba.[36] What sets BDA apart from the better-known psychotic syndromes is its good prognosis. Most experiences of BDA are transitory, and return to the person's premorbid functioning is the expected outcome, although recurrence is sometimes experienced. The onset of BDA is frequently triggered by dread, often related to the culturally shared beliefs in malevolent magic. BDA responds well to both traditional herbal remedies and modern psychotropic drugs.

Descriptive information on culture-bound disorders has been accumulating for over a century. Research effort has now shifted to the search for empirically based generalizations about the nature and variety of culture-bound disorders as well as their antecedents, concomitants, and consequences. The relativistic view accords central importance to culture in shaping these syndromes, and emphasizes the inherent difficulty and perhaps even futility of fitting these disorders into a worldwide classificatory grid. The proponents of the opposite, universalistic, conception consider all mental disorders to be fundamentally identical throughout the world and concede to culture only the external trappings of symptom expression.

INTERIM REFLECTIONS

The Current State of Evidence

In light of the findings reviewed, both worldwide uniformity and cultural variability of psychopathology have been demonstrated. A limited number of culturally constant symptoms have been identified in schizophrenia and depression. Incidence and prevalence rates for schizophrenia exhibit little variation around the globe. Definitive information on the rates of depressive disorders has been somewhat more difficult to obtain, as the criteria of depression vary greatly in space and perhaps in time. The old notion that depression is a hallmark of advanced or of Western civilization has been dispelled, although it would be incautious to maintain that the rates of depression are constant throughout the world. Epidemiological research by Weissman et al.[13] in 10 metropolitan centers in several countries has demonstrated that there is less cultural variation in the rates of bipolar mood disorder than of unipolar depression. However, some of the differences in the rates of depression appear to be counterintuitive and may turn out to be spurious. It is somewhat baffling to find that markedly less depression is reported in Beirut, Lebanon, racked by civil strife and violence at the time of the survey, than in a Paris that was free of major upheavals during the same period.

Evidence in favor of cultural malleability of psychopathological manifestations is a lot ampler. Questions remain about the extent and nature of this variation and its surface versus fundamental quality. What cultural characteristics do they reflect and at what angle of refraction? If the relationship between culture and psychopathology is stable and solid, it should be possible eventually to infer the prevailing patterns of disturbance from the characteristics of the culture. Conversely, knowledge of disturbance within a culture should make it possible to generate realistic inferences about its fundamental and prominent features.

Research Approaches and Directions

If culture affects psychopathology, as the evidence reviewed in this chapter appears to indicate, what dimensions or characteristics of culture are responsible for this influence? In a project of an unprecedented scope, Hofstede[37] identified five basic cultural factors, derived from multivariate research on values at the workplaces of 53 countries or regions. Hofstede's variables have been found relevant and applicable across several areas of psychology. Draguns and Tanaka-Matsumi[14] sought to extend them to the cross-cultural study of psychopathology. To this end, predictions pertaining to Hofstede's five fundamental axes of cultural variation were formulated. So far, a team of researchers from eight countries[39] was able to confirm predictions pertaining to individualism-collectivism by establishing that social anxiety was more frequent and intense in collectivistic countries of East Asia than in individualistically oriented countries in Western Europe, North America, and Australia. Hypotheses formulated in reference to the other four Hofstede dimensions, power distance, uncertainty avoidance, masculinity-femininity, and short versus long time orientation, await being put to a test.

How then is culture reflected in psychopathology? The answer to this question is to be sought through qualitative studies of subjective experience and in part, through the observation of culture-bound disorders. Kimur,[22] a phenomenological psychotherapist in Japan, contributed findings on the characteristic experience of interpersonality, so different from the self-contained and autonomous self, as revealed by his patients. Glimpses into personal experience that psychotherapy provides constitute invaluable raw data about internalized culture, especially as it is expressed in conjunction with distress and disability.

In 1904, Kraepelin, one of the founding fathers of modern psychiatry, published an account of his observations of mental disorders in Indonesia and Algeria that contains some prescient comments: "We may also hope that the psychiatric characteristics of a people can further the understanding of its entire psychic character. In this sense, comparative psychiatry may be destined to one day become an important auxiliary science of comparative ethnopsychology" (p. 231).[40]

UNFINISHED TASKS

Symptom as the Traditional Object of Investigation

To what extent has Kraepelin's vision been realized, and what, if any, questions remain unanswered? A lot of information has been amassed with the psychiatric symptom as the basic unit of comparison, usually investigated at two or more sites across national frontiers, geographic distance, and high cultural contrast.

This research strategy is exemplified by the WHO surveys of schizophrenia and depression[8–12] designed to provide a bird's-eye view of psychopathology around the globe. Moreover, the priority of the WHO research teams has been to identify the common core of the major psychopathological syndromes. Cross-cultural differences were noted and described, but were not the focus of these worldwide projects. In the process, the interpersonal and social context was overlooked, and this imbalance remains to be corrected.

The fact that the symptom is not the only source of cultural variation in psychopathology was recognized rather early, and three carriers of cultural influence were recognized: patients, diagnosticians, and community agents.[42] The last category encompassed all the persons in direct contact with the person presenting signs of distress or disability, in his or her household and beyond its walls in the community at large. Collectively, all of these observers, including the patient, participate in recognizing psychological disturbance, imposing a label on it, and initiating culture's corrective, punitive, compassionate, or curative response to it. To investigate and assess these processes, a more elaborate model has been developed.[43] It goes beyond observing and recording a patient's symptoms, inquires into their meaning from the person's as well as his or her family's and community's points of view, explores the patient's social identifications and identity, and specifies the family's and community's responses to the behaviors and experiences presented by the family. Thus, psychopathology is viewed not as a circumscribed occurrence, but as a social transaction that unfolds in time and involves several participants. The transactional point of view carries with it two implications. First, physicians, psychiatrists, psychologists, social workers, and other designated agents of the community can be studied as contributors to cultural differences in perception and identification of psychopathology, on the basis of a given culture's sensitivities and thresholds of tolerance. This was done in the case of the US-UK Diagnostic Project,[25] which provided important correctives in the understanding of the nature of differences in modes of experience and perception of the psychopathology in the community. Second and more fundamentally, recognition of transactions as fundamental in psychopathology has stimulated the development of research approaches for studying the manifestations of psychopathology in family, community, and institutional contexts by means of a variety of quantitative, qualitative, and mixed methodologies, as exemplified by Kleinman' work.[44,45] More generally, conceptualization and research on psychopathology and culture is moving toward the recognition of the inescapable complexities in this area of investigation. Within this framework, the impact of the external, cultural, and the internal, somatic, framework is incorporated and the gap between them is bridged. To convert these guidelines into systematic observations, shifting among and pooling a wide range of research strategies is advocated, from worldwide surveys to thoroughly documented, in-depth case studies.

Rapid Sociopolitical Transformations

Consistent with the contextual point of view, it is expected that the cultural influence is not imprinted upon psychopathological manifestations once and for all, but that it changes with time, and especially so when social transformations are abrupt, dramatic, and far-reaching. The last two decades of the 20th century were particularly rich in such cataclysmic revolutionary events, from the unexpected collapse of the Soviet Union and its satellites to the dismantling of apartheid in South Africa. It is unfortunate that any impact of these developments on psychopathology has largely gone undocumented. An exception is the observations by Russian psychiatrists, Korolenko and Dmitriyeva,[46] in Siberia, who reported that hypochondriacal and neurasthenic symptoms, prominent during the Soviet era, had markedly declined, and an upsurge of free-floating anxiety and of adjustment disorders had occurred, presumably in response to the sense of social and economic insecurity and consequent feelings of helplessness. On the other hand, in the wake of the Maoist Cultural Revolution, neurasthenic symptoms of diffuse bodily malaise, together with chronic fatigue, passivity, and lack of energy, were exacerbated in frequency in China.[47] Such manifestations were often encountered in individuals traumatized and alienated in the course of these upheavals. Skultans,[48] writing about the period of Soviet domination in Latvia, suggested that neurasthenic manifestations represented a form of inarticulate political protest and rejection of the externally imposed social reality.

Psychopathology and Culture: Direction and Nature of Links

The accumulated store of findings demonstrates that culture and psychopathology are interrelated, but what is the nature of the links before them? It has been suggested that psychopathological symptoms represent an exaggeration of modal cultural characteristics and are the caricature of their respective culture.[42] This hypothesis has received support in a study of both ambulatory patients suffering from anxiety disorders and their normal, psychiatrically undisturbed counterparts at six sites around the Pacific rim: mainland China, Taiwan, Japan, South Korea, Bali, and Thailand.[49] In the same investigation it was demonstrated that there was a greater similarity between the two Chinese sites, in Shanghai and Taipei, respectively, than between the other four samples, from as many countries. In another comparative research project that included both normal and depressive samples from Egypt and Germany,[50] significantly greater reliance on external locus of control was uncovered in both Egyptian samples compared to Germans, without, however, an accentuation of these differences between the two depressive groups. Unexpectedly, however, Radford[51] reported that culture obliterated differences between Japanese and Australian depressive samples, while such differences remained pronounced between the normal control groups. Marsella[52] predicted that severity of psychopathology would produce convergence in symptomatology across cultures. In line with this expectation, schizophrenics in Nicaragua and Sweden were more similar in their defense mechanisms than borderline patients, who, in turn, were less different in the two countries than adequately functioning individuals with no psychiatric diagnosis.[53] Thus, the results are moot and the road is open to further explorations and to more refined and differentiated predictions.

On a semi-intuitive basis it would appear that there is the greatest degree of cross-cultural uniformity in rates in schizophrenia and in bipolar disorder. However, these results tend to coexist with substantial and meaningful cultural differences in modes of expression. Depression and anxiety appear to provide more room for cultural variation in both incidence and symptomatology, but specific conclusions about the manner and scope of such variation are premature. Specific symptoms, especially in mildly depressed or anxious people, are more likely to bear the stamp of their place and time, and fluctuations in alcohol or substance abuse, suicide, eating disorders, and interpersonal disturbance may come closer to being the psychopathological barometers of their culture or, in Di Nicola's phrase, "cultural chameleons" (p. 245).[28]

Psychopathology and Self: A Key Relationship

The self has emerged as a key construct in tying together personal experience and culture. In sociocentric cultures, the self acts as a bridge between a person and other human beings; in cultures where autonomy and individuality are emphasized, the self is surrounded by a boundary that separates that person from others.[54] Actual investigations of the link between culturally characteristic modes of psychopathology and self-experience have barely been initiated, even though measures of both variables are available. If such connections are established, they will shed light on the manner in which internalized culture is expressed through disturbed behavior and personal distress.

CONCLUDING COMMENTS

Psychopathology and culture is no longer a blank slate but neither is it a completed canvas. In light of the information presented in this chapter, cultural components of psychopathology are far from being trivial. Yet, a great many syndromes are recognizable in different regions of the world, although they are not identical. Vegetative and affective symptoms of depression, general and specific expressions of anxiety, and components of cognitive distortion and disorganization associated with schizophrenia, all recur in disparate locations. Regardless of milieu or site, psychopathological experience and expression can be placed on four axes of appraisal:[55] (1) from high to low in affect or mood; (2) consensual and reality bound to idiosyncratic and unrealistic in the perceptual-cognitive domain; (3) from tense to relaxed in organismic experience; and (4) reliable or appropriate in social behavior, as opposed to unreliable or inappropriate. Subjective experience and social judgment determine the boundary between the normal and abnormal in any single case. Often, there are disagreements within the culture, for example between the person directly affected and his or her observers and associates. More frequently, the line between normal and abnormal is drawn differently across cultures. And yet, no culture stands idly by in the presence of extremes of mood, misperception, anxiety, or unacceptable behavior. In the psychological transaction that ensues, culture is expressed and reflected, and yet the unity of humankind is affirmed.

REFERENCES

1. Herskovits, M. (1949). *Man and his works*. New York: Knopf.
2. Tseng, W.-S. (2003). *Clinician's guide to cultural psychiatry*. San Diego: Academic Press.
3. Ember, C. R. & Ember, M. (1996). *Cultural anthropology* (8th ed.) Saddle River, NJ: Prentice Hall.
4. American Psychiatric Association (1994). *Diagnostic and statistical manual of mental disorders* (4th ed., text rev.). Washington, DC: Author.
5. Draguns, J. G. (2002). Universal and cultural aspects of counseling and psychopathology. In P. B. Pedersen, J. G. Draguns, W. J. Lonner, & J. E. Trimble (Eds.), *Counseling across cultures* (5th ed., (pp. 29–50). Thousand Oaks, CA: Sage.
6. Benedict, R. (1934). Culture and the abnormal. *Journal of General Psychology, 10*, 59–82.
7. Berne, E. (1956). Comparative psychiatry and tropical psychiatry. *American Journal of Psychiatry, 113*, 193–200.
8. World Health Organization (1973). *Report of the International Pilot Study of Schizophrenia*. Geneva: Author.
9. World Health Organization (1980). *Schizophrenia: An international follow-up study*. Geneva: Author
10. Jablensky, A., Sartorius, N., Ernberg, G., Anker, M., Korten, A., Cooper, J. E., Day, R., & Bertelsen, A. (1992). *Schizophrenia: Manifestations, incidence, and course in different cultures: A World Health Organization ten country study*. Geneva: Author.

11. Day, R., Nielsen, J. A., Korten, A., Ernberg, G., Dube, K. C., Gebhart, J., Jablensky, A., Leon, C., Marsella, A. J., Olatawura, M., Sartorius, N., Takahashi, R., Wig, N., & Wynne, L. (1987). Stressful life events preceding the acute onset of schizophrenia: A cross-national study from the World Health Organization. *Culture, Medicine, and Psychiatry, 11*, 123–205.

12. World Health Organization (1983). *Depressive disorders in different cultures: Report of the WHO collaborative study of standardized assessment of depressive patients.* Geneva: Author.

13. Weissman, M. M., Bland, R. C., Canino, G. J., Faravelli, C., Greenwald, S., Hwu, H. G., Joyce, P. R., Karam, E. G., Lee, E. G., Lellouch, J., Lepine, J. R., Newman, S. C. Rubio-Stipec, M., Wells, J. E., Wickmaratne, P. J., Wittchen, H. U., & Yeh, E. K. (1996). Cross-national epidemiology of major depressive and bipolar disorder. *Journal of the American Medical Association, 276*, 293–299.

14. Draguns, J. G., & Tanaka-Matsumi, J. (2001). Assessment of psychopathology across and within cultures: Issues and findings. *Behaviour Research and Therapy, 41*, 755–776.

15. Marsella, A. J. (1980). Depressive experience and disorder across cultures. In H. C. Triandis & J. G. Draguns (Eds.), *Handbook of cross-cultural psychology. Volume 6:, Psychopathology* (pp. 237–289). Boston: Allyn and Bacon.

16. Pfeiffer, W. (1994). *Transkulturelle Psychiatrie: Ergebnisse und Probleme* (Transcultural psychiatry) (2nd ed.). Stuttgart, Germany: Thieme.

17. Tseng, W.-T. (2001). *Handbook of cultural psychiatry.* San Diego: Academic Press.

18. Ustun, T. B. & Sartorius, N. (Eds.) (1995). *Mental health in general health care: An international study.* Chichester, UK: Wiley.

19. Murphy, H.B.M. (1982). Culture and schizophrenia. In I. Al-Issa (Ed.), *Culture and psychopathology* (pp. 221–250). Baltimore, MD: University Park Press.

20. Wig, N. N., Menon, D. K., Bedi, H., Ghosh, A., Kuipers, L., Leff, J., Karten. A., Day, R., Sartorius, N., Einberg, G., & Jablensky, A. (1987). Expressed emotion and schizophrenia in Northern India: I. Cross-cultural transfer of ratings of relatives' emotions. *British Journal of Psychiatry, 151*, 156–160.

21. Al-Issa, I. (1995). The illusion of reality or the reality of illusion: Hallucinations and culture. *British Journal of Psychiatry, 166*, 369–373.

22. Kimura, B. (1995). *Zwischen Mensch und Mensch* (Between one human being and another). Darmstadt, Germany: Akademische Verlagsanstalt.

23. Abe, Y. (2001). Algunos razgos de pacientes depresivos en Japon (Some characteristics of depressive patients in Japan). Paper presented at Andorra 2001 Transcultural Psychiatry Section Symposium, Andorra la Vella.

24. Tellenbach, H. (1976). *Melancholie* (Melancholia). Heidelberg, Germany: Springer.

25. Cooper, J. E., Kendell, R. E., Gurland, B. J., Sharpe, L., Copeland, J.R.M., & Simon, R. (1972). *Psychiatric diagnosis in New York and London.* Oxford: Oxford University Press.

26. Ots, T. (1990). The angry liver, the anxious heart, and the melancholy spleen: The phenomenology of perception in Chinese culture. *Culture, Medicine, and Psychiatry, 14*, 21–58.

27. Kirmayer, L. J. (1984). Culture, affect, and somatization. Parts 1 and 2. *Transcultural Psychiatric Research Review, 21*, 159–188 & 237–262.

28. Di Nicola, V. F. (1990). Anorexia multiforme: Self starvation in historical and cultural context. Part 2. Anorexia nervosa as a culture-reactive syndrome. *Transcultural Psychiatric Research Review, 27*, 245–286.

29. Lee, S. & Hsu, L. K. G. (1995). Eating disorders in Hong Kong. In Y T. Lin, W. S. Tseng, & E. K. Yeh (Eds.). *Chinese societies and mental health* (pp. 197–208). Hong Kong: Oxford University Press.

30. Helzer, J., Canino, G., & Chen, C. N. (1998). *Cross-national studies of alcoholism.* New York: Oxford University Press.

31. Durkheim, E. (1951). *Suicide* (J. A. Spaulding & G. Simpson, trans.). Glencoe, IL: Free Press (originally published in 1897).

32. Desjarlais, R., Eisenberg, L., Good, B., & Kleinman, A. (1995). *World mental health. Problems and priorities in low-income countries.* New York: Oxford Universities Press.

33. Tseng, W. S. & McDermott, J. F. Jr. (1981). *Culture, mind, and therapy: An introduction to cultural psychiatry.* New York: Brunner/Mazel.

34. Jilek, W. G. & Jilek-Aal, L. (2001). Culture-specific mental disorders. In E. Henn, N. Sartorius, H. Helmchen, & H. Lauter (Eds.), *Contemporary Psychiatry. Volume 2. Psychiatry in special situations* (pp. 219–245). Berlin: Springer-Verlag.

35. Tanaka-Matsumi, J. (1979). Taijin Kyofusho. Diagnostic and cultural issues in Japanese psychiatry. *Culture, Medicine, and Psychiatry, 3*, 231–245.

36. Zhang, A. Y., Yu, L. C., Draguns, J. G., Zhang, J., & Tang, D. (2000). Sociocultural context of anthropophobia: A sample of Chinese youth. *Social Psychiatry and Psychiatric Epidemiology, 35*, 418–426.

37. Collomb, H. (1965). Bouffées délirantes en psychiatrie africaine. *Psychopathologie Africaine, 1*, 167–239.

38. Hofstede, G. (2001). *Culture's consequences: Comparing values, behaviors, institutions, and organizations across nations* (2nd ed.). Thousand Oaks, CA: Sage.

39. Heinrichs, N., et al. (in press). Cultural differences in perceived social norms and social anxiety. *Behaviour Research and Therapy.*

40. Kraepelin, E. (1904). Vergleichende Psychiatrie (Comparative psychiatry). *Zentralblatt fur Nervenheilkunde und Psychiatrie 27*, 433–437.

41. Jilek, W. G. (1995). Emil Kraepelin and comparative sociocultural psychiatry. *European Archives of Psychiatry and Clinical Neuroscience, 245*, 231–238.

42. Draguns, J. G. (1973). Comparison of psychopathology: Issues, findings, directions. *Journal of Cross-Cultural Psychology, 4*, 9–47.

43. Kleinman, A. (1992). How is culture important for *DSM-IV?* In J. E. Mezzich, Kleinman, H. Fabrega, B. Good, G. Johnson-Powell, K. M. Lin, S. Manson, & D. Parron (Eds.), *Cultural proposals for DSM-IV* (pp. 7–28). Pittsburgh: University of Pittsburgh.

44. Kleinman, A. (1986). *Social origins of distress and disease.* New Haven: Yale University Press.
45. Kleinman, A. (1988). *Rethinking psychiatry: From cultural category to personal experience.* New York: Free Press.
46. Korolenko, C., & Dmitriyeva, N. (1999). *Sotsiodinamicheskaya psikhiatriya* (Sociodynamic psychiatry). Novosibirsk, Russia: Novosibirsk Pedagogical University Press.
47. Kleinman, A., & Kleinman, J. (1985). Somatization: The interconnections in Chinese society among culture, depressive experiences, and the meaning of pain. In A. Kleinman & B. Good (Eds.), *Culture and depression* (pp. 429–490). Berkeley: University of California Press.
48. Skultans, V. (1995). Neurasthenia and political resistance in Latvia. *Anthropology Today, 11,* 14–17.
49. Tseng, W. S., Asai, M., Kieqiu, L., Wibulswasd, P., Suryani, L. K., Wen, L. K., Brennan, J., & Heiby, E. (1990). Multicultural study of psychiatric disorders in Asia: Symptom manifestations. *International Journal of Social Psychiatry, 36,* 252–264.
50. Rader, K. K., Krampen, G., & Sultan, A. S. (1990). Kontolluberzeugungen Depressiver im transkulturellem Vergleich (Beliefs about control of depressives in a cross-cultural comparison). *Fortschritte der Nerologie und Psychiatriy, 58,* 207–214.
51. Radford, M.H.B. (1989). *Culture, depression, and decision-making behaviour: A study with Japanese and Australian clinical and nonclinical populations.* Unpublished doctoral dissertation, Flinders University of South Australia.
52. Marsella, A. J. (1988). Cross-cultural research on severe mental disorders: Issues and findings. *Acta Psychiatrica Scandinavica* Suppl. 344, 7–22.
53. Sundbom, E., Jacobson, L., Kullgren, G., & Penayo, U. (1998). Personality and defense: A cross-cultural study of psychiatric patients and healthy individuals in Nicaragua and Sweden. *Psychological Reports, 83,* 1331–1347.
54. Chang, S. C. (1988). The nature of the self: A transcultural view. Part I: Theoretical aspects. *Transcultural Psychiatric Research Review, 25,* 169–204.
55. Draguns, J. G. (1980). Psychological disorders of clinical severity. In H. C. Triandis & J. G. Draguns (Eds.), *Handbook of cross-cultural psychology. Volume 6: Psychopathology* (pp. 99–174). Boston: Allyn and Bacon.

Chapter 11

How the Effects of Traumatic Experiences Are Passed "Unto the Following Generations"

Judith Issroff

The future belongs to those who give the next generation reason to hope.
Pierre Teilhard de Chardin[1]

Those who come in contact with traumatized people cannot avoid experiencing some of the overwhelming, "indigestible" feelings roused during the traumatic events. I call these inevitable onward transmission effects "affect contagion phenomena" because the emotions are spread directly, as in transmission of contagious infections, a domino-like effect.[2] Traumatized individuals affect those around them and also the communities and societies within which they live.[3–5] Onward transmission occurs not only directly but also indirectly, often with scaled up, exaggerated effects occurring remotely in time, place, and person that are understandable in terms of chaos theory.[2] In various ways these reverberations of traumatic experiences are passed on to subsequent generations when insufficiently ameliorated, contained, and worked through. All societies have developed strategies that serve as "cultural containers"[2,6–8] to deal with traumatic events: religious rituals, theatrical and other cultural and national happenings, and therapy situations are examples of cultural containers—communally sanctioned events where intense emotions may safely be expressed and played out in socially acceptable fashion. Individuals grieve, fantasize, and privately work through traumatizing experiences that have disrupted their inner and outer personal sense of continuity-of-being and disrupted their life-course function in physical, social, psychic, cognitive, and spiritual ways in their personal private inner worlds, in their sleeping dreams, play, and creative compositions. Because they communicate powerfully, here diverse case stories are presented to illustrate the social and transgenerational problems encountered in traumatized individuals and the reverberations in their wake.[10,11]

No society can survive as a democracy when the numbers of those who are damaged and dependent exceeds the "containing" or "carrying" capacity of those who are healthy and mature.[12] Governments very rarely allocate adequate resources for the treatment and management of traumatized individuals. Children cannot be other than what their parents make them, and, as will be shown, the damage of traumatized parents is often unwittingly and unintentionally passed on their children.[13-45] Governments seldom budget to support parenting adequately. But dealing with trauma and quality of parenting are critical issues for any society, not only for humanitarian, moral, and medical reasons, but also in sociopolitical and economic long-term social cost-benefit effect terms. Just as it is dangerous for us to ignore the possible scenarios of global disaster,[46] unless basic reliable knowledge about how to foster healthy human beings capable of behaving in nondestructive ways with their environments and fellow human beings is given the respect it merits, society will pay a heavy price. It is within life-worlds, situations, occasions, and circumstances that calamity, when it occurs, takes intelligible shape that determines both the response to it and the effects that it has. Global warming and policies for mutually assured destruction (MAD) using nuclear weapons exist and require urgent attention. However material they may be, and however unpredictable or unintended, collapse and catastrophe are also social events, like coups and recessions, riots, religious movements, and our incapacity effectively to face human-generated problems locally and globally is clear. Geertz[46] advocates a monographic literature about particular disasters. This chapter presents such detailed case scenarios. The implications we can draw should help us to think about how we might try to build tolerant, healthy individuals and societies. In personal and planetary terms we are doomed if we cannot deal better with ourselves. Although natural disasters dramatically compel our attention, our own violence, our violations of our role in planetary ecology, our propensity to neglect and abuse each other, bring about our major preventable disasters and traumas. In this respect we should not avoid thinking about our own identity formation, difference, diversity, the role of dissidents and outsiders versus social pressures toward conformity,[47-49] and "groupthink"[50,51] tendencies. We need to cultivate our ability to perceive and tolerate paradox, to manage conflict, value and support traditional cultural containers and relief valves for safe expression of trauma-induced feelings. We also need professionals trained to cope with the overwhelming, indigestible affects unavoidably raised by trauma[2] in order to mitigate the spread of such affect contagion phenomena.

Awareness of transgenerational transmission of traumatization has been with us since biblical times. We have long been told that the sins of the fathers are visited upon their sons unto the fifth generation (Exodus 20:5). Now evidence from many sources shows that the damage done to survivors of trauma is visited on their children and their children's children.[13–45,52] Further, a price is paid by the offspring of both victims and witnesses, and perpetrators.[19,32,33] The ongoing reverberations of trauma affect not only individuals, but also the life course of families, peoples, and nations.[53–58]

I suspect that it is the nonimmediate damage to the offspring of victims of traumatization and their relative strength that can often enable them to become vehicles for working through what their parents or grandparents had been unequipped to process. The mission or "transgenerational mandate" to remember and work through the trauma that parents could not deal with, along with the relative health to allow traumatically generated abscesses of memory to surface and drain, often falls on offspring. However, this happens only if environmental impingement is sufficiently in abeyance, and if the disruptive, foreign body–like introjects[37,62] of their parents' disturbances do not erupt within them too disastrously. It is no wonder that clinicians who work in relatively stable, affluent, democratic societies see so many second- and third-generation offspring of trauma victims.[2,3,63–87] In many societies family and tribal vendettas are legendary and ongoing.[88–102] We have to remember that while some think violent behaviour is largely learned, holding that humans are "polymorphously educable," "can learn virtually anything," and "among other things ... can learn to be virtually wholly unaggressive,"[103] others view humankind as killer apes,[104] proliferating cancerously on Gaia, our planet.[105] Whichever view we hold,[106,107] no one can deny that violence is a monster that devours its own children. It does not solve anything; it only prolongs itself. It is the bedfellow of intolerance, ignorance, insecurity, threat, and fear. To the extent that recovery is possible, sufficient time without further traumatic life disruptions is necessary for pain and healing after destruction and loss. It is the healthy, secure, and sufficiently mature members in a group that contain the disturbed and damaged, that is, the traumatized, the rigid, the dogmatic, the intolerant and immature in their midst.[12] No society can remain open to diversity and contain its injured and malfunctioning individuals without eventually itself suffering severe and perhaps irreversible damage (e.g., Colin Turnbull's report of the Ik[108]).

Understanding what facilitates healthy development is integral to comprehending how traumatized people malfunction as parents and transmit beliefs, values, and coping styles.[5,109–125] Adaptive survival mechanisms, understandable in originally life-fracturing experiences, may be inappropriate for current circumstances. *Loss and depression interfere with infant nurture,*[126-131] *child rearing and social integration.* Ongoing reverberations of trauma are especially severe in cases of childhood abuse, neglect, and exploitation.[52-54,123-129,132-136] Exigencies of situations in which survivors find themselves often necessitate involvement in life-rebuilding tasks. Working through of events is deferred. When behavior that ensured someone's survival becomes habitual it may be maladaptive, and preclude working through recrudescence of traumatic memories or grieving.

Still, traumatized parents do not necessarily pass on their trauma or act pathogenetically with their children.[79,132-134] Not every once-tortured father decides to "toughen" his daughter by extinguishing cigarette stubs on her bare flesh. Nor does transgenerational transmission of traumatization always lead to breakdown and illness: many survivors' descendents are in helping professions, or work as social and environmental activists. Their "compulsive caretaking" behavior shows their sensitivity to suffering. They work through personal legacies of parental trauma in valuable personal and social ways.

Dr. Jack Kevorkian assisted patients who wished to end their lives. He had lived through the genocide in which half the Armenian people died in all manner of brutal ways. At one point, he himself was starved. His struggle was devoted to allowing people to end their suffering in a humane fashion. Surely his ancestors' exposure to pain enhanced his personal sensitivity and gave him courage to confront such issues as quality of life and dignity of dying when pain is unendurable.

RECURRENT CYCLES OF TRAUMATIZATION

Traumatically generated attitudes, behavior, memory, and unassimilable feelings directly and indirectly retraumatize both survivors and those in contact with them, a contribution to the reverberating aftereffects of trauma. Not surprisingly, conflicts of previously deeply traumatized populations recrudesce into violent intolerant conflagrations, as, for example, in ex-Yugoslavia, Gujarat, India–Pakistan, and the Middle East.

Depending on the way one chooses to look at history, either wars periodically interrupt peace, or war is the more natural state, one intermittently in abeyance because of needs to recuperate, along with mankind's natural tendencies to bonding and cooperative interaction, without which we would not be here today.

Forgiveness? Vengeance? Coexistence? Different views are held about "an eye for an eye" or forgiveness,[135-137] whether or not violent behavior is innate or largely learned. Although relevant to understanding living with inter- and transgenerational trauma, here neither these large topics nor detailed attention to mechanisms of onward transmission can be addressed.

Variations, malfunction, and/or deviations of the modes of healthy transgenerational development follow trauma. Healthy development in any particular social context is a huge topic.[109–125] Adequate personal and social development toward age-appropriate behavior reflecting health and maturity is an achievement not to be taken for granted. Multiple developmental factors and strands interact in complex ways. Knowledge about the process has increased exponentially.[128] Historically, child rearing consisted of almost ubiquitous neglect, abuse, and torture—reflected in high infant mortality rates until recently—and this is key to understanding cultural history, war, human violence, and cruelty.[53,54,55] An end to this terrible record of transgenerational transmission of trauma is possible in relatively humane, prosperous societies and has recently been expressed in various declarations of human, women's, and children's rights.

Does the impact of traumatic events impair a survivor's ability to enjoy life, to live creatively in a healthy state? Does that affect survivors' ability to enjoy and interact creatively with their offspring? What happens when appropriate emotional attunement,[130, 131] mirroring, and ability to sustain illusion, imagination, play, life-zest, and joy[109–112] are damaged? What happens when the environmental ambience necessary for positive nurture[113–119] is absent, deficient, or insufficient?

The preceding questions indicate some subtle but important components of parenting that are basic to children's health and resilience[114,120–122] in adversity. They are underemphasized in the literature.[63–93] describing the mechanisms by which the adverse after-impact of trauma wields its nefarious effects on subsequent generations and societies.

WORKING DEFINITION OF TRAUMA

Trauma is a disruption of continuity-of-being at any level—physical, intrasubjective, psychic, spiritual, or sociocultural. Accordingly, healing necessitates restoration of the sense of continuity-of-being by reconnecting to the pretraumatized state, memories, or condition.

Disruption arises from within, and/or outside the child when the social and physical realm impinges or when parenting is untimely, insensitive, remote, rejecting-dismissive, coercive or enmeshing, intrusive-disruptive, abusive, and/or inconsistent-teasing.

For nontraumatizing development, instinctual need has to be met within the child's capacity to tolerate need-frustration. Need-frustration can occur during absence of a specific significant other person, sometimes a transitional object endowed with specific subjective meaning to a particular individual child.[138]

An implication of this particular definition of trauma is that one of the prime tasks of parenting is to protect the child from any (avoidable) disruption of the child's sense of continuous-ongoing-being,[139] wherever the potential disruption arises.

Parents provide the social cohesion and contextual infrastructure of mind that enables human development in a particular culture. Socioeconomic, spiritual, and/or emotional states can lead to withdrawal from an infant: any pressing attention-diverting preoccupations adversely affect a parent's ability to be sufficiently attuned to an infant to respond to its needs in sensitive and timely fashion. Any peculiarities of the parent's mind-set and life-philosophy will affect the child's outlook. *Transgenerational damage occurs when traumatized parents malfunction and cannot meet their children's demands and needs to provide an appropriate facilitating environment for the maturational processes.*

Death anxieties or death instinct? Part of the legacy of generations of trauma? Like 99.9 percent of all species of life that have existed, humankind struggles toward survival or self-elimination in the face of natural or human-engineered disaster. Conditions that allowed the transgenerational working-through of traumatization have probably enabled the spread of improved childrearing, along with relative success of democratization, and technologies that have qualitatively improved living conditions in the developed world. Four-fifths of the collective world budget is spent on defense (armaments), while a mere fifth of what is spent on that amount could eliminate most of humankind's most obvious, pressing problems.[140]

Why is there such universal governmental disinterest in dealing with soluble problems that cause untold miseries, traumatize billions of people and their offspring? Why invest in and promote arms industries that will certainly add to the cumulative traumatization of mankind on earth and endanger planetary life itself? Is it death instinct? Or persistent fears and anxieties that are the legacy of generations of traumatization?

History, Psychohistory, and Childhood Abuse

Lloyd DeMause [53-55] documented the ubiquitously traumatizing history of childhood. His scholarly account of parents' historical neglect, exploitation, and brutal abuse of children is numbingly difficult to read, comprehend, and digest. Even today, abuse remains the fate of all too many children, even if they are not victims of long-standing generations of war or zealous madness such as Nazi Germany or China's Cultural Revolution, Pol Pot's Cambodia, Rwanda, or other societies in psychotic states or disintegration such as the Ik.[108]

We have to remember how relatively recent in the developed world are the reduction in infant mortality, the increase in longevity, affluence, liberation of women, recognition of and legislation aimed at women's and children's rights, the abolition of slavery, and interest in developing reliable public knowledge about both what enables humans to develop in the direction of health, resilience,[121,122] and fosters salutogenic attitudes,[113,114] and about what happens, how, and why, to the development and function of offspring of traumatized, damaged, and suboptimally functioning parents.

A number of possible transgenerational transmission mechanisms have been described. Among these is trauma transmission from parents to children when early nurture is inadequate.

Grieving, bereft mothers who have suffered massive traumatizing losses, including their own sustaining environments, are often psychically concussed, preoccupied, depressed, and empathically numbed.[68,141] This occurs in abused women, refugees, immigrants, those living in conditions of strife, war, famine, those traumatized during the process of giving birth or ill. Their vulnerable, temperamentally difficult infants may adversely interact, aggravating dyadic relational problems.

Integration of several fields of scholarship enables us to comprehend how the very structure-functioning of the developing infant's brain becomes altered in conditions of maternal insufficiency or incapacity.[128] Subsequent ability to develop and interact as a compassionate, empathic, intuitive, "creatively alive" human being, capable of joy and "peak" experiences, is adversely affected. Sufficiently sensitive affective attunement.[111,112,117,119,125,130,131] within a secure, loving, not overly ambivalent nor enmeshed-coercive, nonimpinging, nonteasing attachment bonding situation is essential to overall healthy development.

This is not to overlook or underestimate the impact of later influences: The basis for vulnerability to later stresses becomes entrenched when the mother is unable to meet her infant's needs and then gradually fails over time to nurture in ways that are within the coping ability of her dependent, developing infant and child—that is, in nontraumatizing ways. The process of nurture becomes cumulatively traumatizing when it is insensitive and inadequate, as often occurs in grieving mothers.

Attitude and Resilience to Traumatic Events

A basic fault in her infant's development cannot be avoided by a distressed, traumatized mother or caregiver during the critical first two months of life's course. The infant's resilience will be adversely affected by these conditions.

Vulnerability is laid down in early infancy. Without overlooking the significance of any of the numerous other mechanisms identified that operate later in life's course and the life-trauma dialect, the environmentally derived, enhanced vulnerability to later traumatization overrides resilience potential or compounds genetic susceptibility. Probably the commonest major mechanisms for transgenerational transmission of vulnerability to later trauma are perinatal problems that impair earliest interactions between infants and mothers.[109,111,112,118,125,130,131]

Trauma affects people in their totality: spiritual and physical dimensions of transgenerational transmission cannot be overlooked. Various factors coexist, interact, summate: teasing them out is no simple matter, as they influence each other over the life span.[79,80]

Space limitations preclude consideration and illustration of many modes of transmission, including physical mechanisms, the way family dynamics are affected by post-traumatic stress reactions and disorders, and so-called image-contagion phenomena.[45] All are important, as are the additional complex problems burdening survivors of human savagery. Nor can psychosocial implications be addressed adequately. Here I concentrate on one mode of transgenerational transmission of trauma commonly encountered: *transgenerational maternal depression; abuse, neglect, disorganized attachment patterns, and organized perverse abuse.*

We cannot properly relate to abstractions that dehumanize and distance us from the plight of the traumatized. I therefore present individual cases and then discuss politicosocial situations in the African context. Permission was given to discuss cases.

Mark

For eight months I daily treated a homicidal-suicidal 14- to 15-year-old adolescent. He was confused and experienced himself as without an identity when not switching persona, often without knowing he had done so. Like Mark, both parents suffered from dissociative disorders and disorders of attachment behavior.

Both Mark's mother's mother and his father's mother had lost their respective mothers during their pregnancies. Both his grandmothers had suffered severe postnatal depression. Both the boy's parents had been traumatized when they witnessed their mothers repeatedly humiliated and terrorized by unsupportive, brutal spouses—in father's case, also alcoholic. The unsurprising result was that both the boy's parents show bizarre, emotionally flat and/or inappropriate, unempathic, anxious-insecure, dismissive, sometimes rejecting, and extremely disorganized attachment behaviors. Mark was often punished by solitary confinement for endless hours in an unstimulating room. Both parents have neglected, emotionally abused, humiliated, and also abused Mark physically at times.

This potential terrorist's heroes were Timothy McVeigh, Charles Manson, and the Columbine School killers, until the advent of the "superheroes" whose destructive attacks on World Trade Center and Pentagon greatly excited him.

Mark has made several cold, vicious, calculated, unprovoked murderous attacks on unsuspecting persons in states of apparent calm while obsessed with fantasies about how to kill his own family members. His nightmares are gruesome and unrelenting. His only regret at being sent to a secure unit is that he may not be able to experience the power and control of actual murder to which he aspires.

Kimberley

Kimberley suffered transgenerational familial organized ritualized abuse. She and Mark were both hospitalized in a unit where I worked closely with several other complexly traumatized adolescents. Some further cases had also suffered perverse abuse and torture in organized, ritualized, terrifying groups. Like Mark, Kimberley was dangerous, unempathic, suicidal, and capable of vicious, destructive or even murderous behavior toward herself and others. Her incestuously abusive grandfather—who was possibly also her father—had told her she could never be rid of the blood tie to him. So, she not only cut through her own nerves and tendons, and later tried to dissect down through sensation-dead areas to find the biggest vein to slit to bleed herself dry, but also sliced other adolescents' wrists "to help them end their misery," provided Mark with a cigarette lighter to encourage him to burn down the hospital, and pushed a girl (who was hesitating to jump) over a railway bridge balustrade. Later she slit her own throat.

Like Kimberley, several aunts, uncles, and cousins, her mother had been abused by her father, the girl's grandfather. He raped Kimberley regularly from infancy, and was ringleader of the group who sadistically terrorized the girl and several other members of the family for years. Her mother, too, suffered from dissociative identity disorder (DID), compounded by alcoholism and other substance abuse. As in Mark's case (where sexual abuse was not an issue), this girl suffered from post-traumatic multiple personalities, the basis set in infancy by her abused mother's defective affect-attunement ability, postnatal depression, and lifelong rejection of her child.

Both youngsters are currently in secure units: their prognosis is extremely poor. Like their parents, they are affectively cold, out of touch to the point of being emotionally blind and deaf, unable to relate ordinarily or cross-identify with others. They suffer from feelings of unreality, of themselves and/or their surroundings, known as depersonalization and derealization, consequent psychosomatization, and they engage in self-cutting in attempts to experience themselves as embodied through pain and bleeding. Both are highly intelligent, but their thinking is distorted. Both hallucinate and suffer horrific nightmares.

They act out dangerously and impulsively, but also plan and execute cool murderous attacks on others and/or themselves. They are certainly capable of murderous social terrorism but have not been exposed to ideologies that might appeal to their psychopathological makeups and provide group support for directed terrorism. They are ambivalent, confused, and anxious in their attachment to their abusers. They both switch personalities and are aware of multiple selves. They suffer from psychiatrically accepted descriptive criteria for dissociative identity disorder (by *DSM-IV* criteria, dissociative disorder not otherwise specified [DDNOS]), and *International Classificatory Diagnostic manual (ICD-10)* multiple personality disorder and comorbid disorganized anxious insecure ambivalent attachment patterns. While their personalities can be described as mood disordered, borderline, psychotic, or neurotic, they are psychopathic-sociopathic in their behavior.

I was able to compare these two dangerous youngsters with other cumulatively, complexly or ritually group-abused/traumatized youngsters who had become perpetrators, witnesses, and victims of perverse atrocities. However, in contrast with the first two cases, these youngster came from warm, caring backgrounds where ordinary, good enough relationships and secure, loving attachment bonds existed. They and their parents could interact and respond appropriately. The youngsters who had experienced good enough mothering and fathering were securely attached even though their parents had been unable to protect them from abuse perpetrated from outside the family. One feels fellow feeling with them, not as if they came from another planet, as with the first two cases and their respective parents. They are treatable—a completely different prognosis.

The early life experiences suffered by Mark and Kimberley sharply contrast with development that occurs within secure attachments. In the afflicted youngsters and their parents, their traumatized, malattuned depressed mothers and grandmothers, and, respectively, their abusive, disorganizing spouses provided a setting for the development of severe dissociative phenomena and lack of fellow human empathy, comorbid with disorganized insecure and/or dismissive-rejecting attachment patterns.

The case vignettes support the thrust of important work on early brain development, and its dependence on good mothering, mirroring, and appropriate affective attunement[130, 131] facilitated by secure attachment[115–119] if right-brain development necessary to positive social interaction is to occur.[128] Such development is essential for ordinary life-appreciative social bonding and fellow feeling for others.

Following predictable life-event traumas such as bereavement, mourning occurs throughout life, affecting life course.[68,141] Many survivor parents are intermittently overwhelmed by grief that takes on pathological or complicated mourning proportions.[73] Survivor parents who are preoccupied with unresolved grief have difficulty interacting with and setting limits to their children's activities; indeed coping with their robust activity.

Maternal depression and interfering images[45] can haunt bereft mothers who have lost previous infants or witnessed atrocities. Such images interfere with maternal responsiveness during early critical-sensitive periods of maternal-infant interaction and nursing, as clearly evident in the case of Betty.

Betty

Betty, born 10 months after the death of an infant brother, was a depressed 14-year-old with suicidal ideation. She presented with various manifestations of confused body image, personal and sexual identity, and was miserably, inextricably involved in relationships with unsuitable immature male friends. During the five years of her psychoanalysis, we speculated that her bereaved, depressed mother had related to her "replacement" infant daughter[35] with a confusing set of interfering memories of her dead son.

At Betty's request, when analysis ceased, her still very depressed mother was seen. Betty's mother opened her interview by describing how she had never been able to relate to handling her infant daughter. After her baby son's death, she had been and was still haunted by memories of him. Sometimes she had been surprised to notice that she was handling a girl baby.

Later Betty's youngest son presented with transsexual identity.

Inappropriate parental expectations of those who relate to their infants through idolization or idealization or with interfering images of significant others preclude ordinary development: it cannot take place under distorted mirroring, maladaptive expectations, and/or bombardments of projections from disturbed, traumatized parents.

Nora

Nora, a gaunt, divorced Israeli woman in her early 30s, underwent analysis in London more than 30 years ago. She felt she had but two alternatives: suicide, or serving as an escort to visiting Japanese men, despite her skills, talents, and training. She could relate to no one and felt misunderstood.

Nora was born a twin to peasant parents in middle Europe. Her father had escaped being killed by the Nazis, together with his first wife, children, and the rest of his family. He then found refuge with his second wife's family and became engaged to Nora's mother's sister. Then Nazis arrived again. His fiancée was killed. Nora's father and mother escaped in heavy snow, the sole survivors of the village. Beset with survival guilt, they clung together. Nora's mother became pregnant with twins, so they married. Nora's twin died in infancy. Like Betty's mother, Nora's mother lost an infant whom she alternately confused with her dead sister. Transmission (projection) of her mother's negative affects and bizarre objects caused devastating damage to Nora. She bore the confused projections of her mother's survival guilt, and all her mother's ambivalent feelings about being alive instead of her sister. Constant adverse comparisons with the idealized infant twin sister emotionally battered her. Nora wrote a poem: "My mother never had a charm to give me: my mother only had her pain to give me, to live with me, to be my guardian, my company, my memory."

Nora was insecure, confused, untrusting, demanding, arrogant, off-putting, a panic-spreading person. She was lonely, friendless, a misfit, stumbling about in Great Britain, as her parents had in Europe, surprised to find themselves where they were, lives derailed and unfocused, without a safety net. Nora abhorred her parents' lack of education and poverty, felt little in common with them, pitied and hated them. She related to them dutifully, as they had to her. She suffered from, and, in turn, manifested their confusions, anxieties about eating and health, and their constant persecutory verbosity, often screaming in "a voice trenchant with weaponry." Like others who have lost the sense of their own reality, on the basis of "because I go on talking, I know that I exist," incessantly she talked at, rather than with, her interlocutors. In lieu of suicide, Nora had aborted nine fetuses in five pregnancies in Jerusalem. Why should she bring children into this world to suffer like her parents and herself? What her parents had experienced at the hands of the Nazis, they thereafter unwittingly caused her to experience. She evoked similar feelings in me in the treatment countertransference, and when I reported these difficulties at a survivor syndrome workshop, remote in time, place, and person, similar affects and defense mechanisms were irrationally displayed toward me by colleagues. So I came to identify one of the modes of transgenerational transmission of massive traumatization as affect-contagion phenomena.[2]

Death anxiety is frequently roused in traumatizing situations. In the following case, abreactive narration (which sometimes amounts to reexperiencing with a quality akin to reliving the original traumatizing situation) almost caused actual death; the horrific account roused great anxiety in both those present and those who heard of the incident later, including a secretary who was so distressed she could not transcribe the tape recording.

Job

An elderly gentleman in Tel Aviv, a twin experimented on by Josef Mengele, with great difficulty broke years of silence and told me and his wife a particularly sickening, bizarre, and gruesome image- and affect-contagion-generating traumatic episode. He suffered a heart attack during the telling. Fortunately, he survived, felt better for having told what he had witnessed, and later organized a reunion of the remaining survivor twins. He remembered Mengele collecting skeletons of dwarfs for a medical school. Mengele threw the dwarfs live into glass vats of acid, and as a further experiment stood 10-year-old children to watch to witness the impact on them. Like many survivors, such as the very few *Sonderkommando* survivors, Job had spared himself and his family this recollection: *silence does not always mean shame, or guilt.* The silence of one of Hitler's personal bodyguards and its impact on his analyzed daughter stems from a very different set of experiences, but however a family secret is generated, whatever its content, silence and fantasies about that silence can have equally destructive effects on family relationships and the next generation. Silence caused by similar and different situations afflicts many survivors of African civil war atrocities, their families, and communities.

Cases from contemporary Africa illustrate direct trauma impact after generations of traumatization in impoverished and illness-stricken populations during civil war and political repression. In these debilitated populations, death, population movement, and detribalization wreak havoc: protective parenting is handicapped.

Cultural factors aggravate and/or alleviate stress. One cannot overlook the specific local context of living with trauma and its ramifications when trying to understand the complexity of its ongoing reverberations, inter- and transgenerational transmission. In Mozambique, after decades of civil war, countless survivors—child victim, witnesses, participants, and perpetrators—illustrate the importance of African cultural beliefs in omnipresent ancestral spirits and of local rituals and cultural memes when living with trauma. Shangaan-speaking tribes believe omnipresent ancestral spirits require daily appeasement rituals to avoid illness, strife, and other disasters.

Zinha

Zinha, age 12, survived three years in a military camp as a brutal commandant's sexual slave. Her fingers and ears were chopped off when, sent to prepare soup, inadvertently she picked leaves from an unmarked plot that belonged to someone else. When this happened, Zinha's mother abandoned her, believing that the incident had occurred because Zinha had been promised to the spirit of a long-deceased uncle who had been offended.

After the civil war had ended and purification ceremonies been performed that allowed the "contaminated" girl to return to her village, Zinha was ceremonially married off to the spirit of this dead uncle and sent to live alone in a hut in the bush.

Boi

The same belief system drastically further traumatized "Boi." At the age of 10 he was abducted by soldiers, abused, and saw his village burned and his kinfolk mutilated and slaughtered. He escaped, and again fled when he found a hut in the forest full of the fresh corpses of his classmates. He found a job with a vicious farmer, escaped after the war, and was ceremonially purified, and taken in by a local Christian bishop and his family, despite dire warnings that because they did not know whose ancestral spirit inhabited and controlled this boy stranger, Boi's presence was bound to cause grief to the villagers.

As was inevitable, when further misfortune struck, the bishop, too, accepted the customary traditional belief and verdict of the traditional diviner (*njango sora*) that his Christian belief-led adoption of Boi had offended local ancestral spirits and brought further afflictions on the already stricken villagers. In front of Boi and eight other former child soldiers who belonged to the small group with whom he was working, including his own sole surviving biological son, he committed suicide by deliberately stepping on a marked landmine. Boi fled to the further trauma of becoming a Maputo street child.

Because of the power of belief in ancestral spirits, already complexly traumatized children witnessed the horrifying death of their mentor. For similar reasons, at least 80 children in remote areas of South Africa's Northern Province annually witness their mothers burned as witches, designated as such by traditional diviners who name them responsible for their villages being struck by lightning.

Mozambican ex-Renamo and Frelimo boy soldiers who destroyed each other's homes, villages, and families are unlikely to become rehabilitated as ordinary citizens of a recovered society. They were recruited by forced participation in gruesome terrorization, often themselves vehicles of the destruction of their own parents, homes, villages, and friends. In their belief system, they also destroyed the chance for their victims' and ancestors' souls to find rest. Their cultures and country are ravaged, their previous values and self-esteem shattered. In their own eyes they are shamed, lack self-respect, are guilty in their very survival.

Traditional healers have always played a central part in tribal life and still occupy important positions. Cultural rituals can "decontaminate" and enable reintegration into village life by appeasing the particular ancestral spirits who inhabit each tribe member from birth. These spirits are identified by diviners who purport to know who the ancestral spirits were in whichever animal-masked man ritually raped a particular mother at the onset of her first menstruation. The animal whose mask the man wears is then supposed to protect the girl by passing on its particular characteristic of cunning or strength. The ejaculated "salt" (semen) of the ritual rapist passes on the particular ancestral spirit to the girl. Children born to her will be of this ancestral spirit. Enormous social power is thus invested in the *njanga soras*. What happens after civil war, when so many traditional diviners have disappeared or lost track of which spirits are present concretely in whomever returns?

After the purification-reintegration ceremony the traumatized parties are forbidden to speak (or even think) of what happened—contrary to widespread therapeutic techniques for dealing with trauma. These traditional cultural methods have positive as well as negative implications for inter- and transgenerational trauma impact transmission.

The cautionary message for Western-trained trauma therapists is clear: they cannot function adequately without knowledge of specific local beliefs and mores and cooperation with traditional community healers.

A further terrible blow of fate, or restless ancestral spirits, compounded the tragic and terrible situation for war orphans in Mozambique. Floods struck. People were trapped in trees. Many parents pushed their children into helicopters and later drowned. Large camps of displaced, orphaned children formed. They know not from whence they came, nor whether or not their war-traumatized parents had survived. Who would dare adopt them? Societies do disintegrate.

Political complications exacerbate difficulties and adversely affect the entire situation in an extremely poor, infrastructureless, and natural disaster-prone country like Mozambique. Finally triumphant in intertribal strife, power-wielding politicians and industrialists, themselves former coerced child soldiers, were leaders of the lawless warring faction, uneducated except in pillage, murder, rape, and violent atrocity. It would be surprising were corruption and the usually brutal, callous methods that brought these 'leaders' to such positions not widespread in the aftermath of hostilities.

What can we learn from the South African situation, where politically generated trauma of the apartheid era[137] did not allow nonwhite mothers to keep their infants and children with them when they went to work as servants in white homes, resulting in a situation of widespread nonprovision of stable affectional bonding and nurture?

Affectional bonding is basic to prosocial behavior and caring identifications The seeds of the destruction of the South African apartheid system were sown in its futile attempt at implementation when laws conceived and maintained by the racist regime separated infants and small children from their working mothers and fathers. Apartheid ideology inevitably produced generations of detribalized urban psychopaths, the violent, compassionless sociopathic elements that run rampant in the new South Africa, handicapping and threatening its future peaceful development. The merit of the revolution, led by children who rationally refused to learn in Afrikaans, was spoiled by the behavior of transgenerationally and directly violated, deeply traumatized elements among them.[142]

Rendered vulnerable to traumatization by early deprivation of sensitive mothering, youth in South African townships[142] were multiply traumatized. Most children witnessed violent deaths, including "necklacing," in which a victim with a gasoline-filled tire around his or her neck was ignited without trial. The deprived, largely uneducated youth were oppressed, detribalized, and brutalized. Their futures were uncertain, as was their ability to rear the next generation in a direction against violence. They were set on continuation of a traumatization-prone pattern that continues in the violent crime-plagued newly democratic South Africa.

AFFECT-CONTAGION PHENOMENA

Reporting in a large group situation of the impact of Nora on me, I discovered a mode of onward trauma transmission, affect-[2] (and image-) contagion phenomena.[45] How are the effects of affect-contagion phenomena generated? How do they spread? How may their effects be contained and ameliorated in the inner world of the psyche, and in the social world? What are the sociopolitical implications?

A simple linear application of the concept of the umbrella term *affect-contagion phenomena* is not intended by comparing their impact to shock waves or contagion. We think of spread in terms of homeostasis, linearity and predictable causality, and also nonlinear dynamics, dynamic systems theory, chaos and complexity theory, networking, process, and interconnectedness.

Affect-contagion phenomena behave like chaotic strange attractors, the foundation for hidden order in natural systems.[143] Ongoing traumatizing effects exist, like Mandelbrot fractal factors in the general chaotic systems that comprise society, have scaling (recurring, magnifying) and summative effects, spread in uncertain ways, dissipate, and stimulate self-organization in different levels of systems the trauma has effected. An irreducible degree of randomness, uncertainty, and unpredictability is a fundamental feature of nature. Trauma effects are modified by innumerable factors, including resilience or hardiness possessed by any individual, family, or group, and the buffering, ameliorative, and container effects of various social and cultural structures and practices.

The ongoing impact initiated by a traumatic event is liable to bifurcate and keep branching, leading to scaling fractal effects in the patterns of turbulence, particularly at crisis points where fluctuations occur at boundaries and interfaces. The processes caused by the initial trauma lead to periods of spontaneous reorganization or punctuated equilibria in the lives of affected individuals, families, groups, and societies.

Affect-contagion phenomena are both self-organizing and dissipative in their effects. They are autopoietic, in that the people they affect couple with their diverse environments and with others in a manner that makes them continually self-generating. Affect-contagion phenomena affect others and this changes their effects, both on the initial victim and per se.

Trauma initially causes disequilibrium, which leads to spontaneous new structure-function organization in afflicted individuals. Trauma causes losses of trust, empathy, sense of being grounded and connection to personal history, body, identity, meaning, faith, boundaries, power, autonomy, capacity for vitality and personal agency, safety, and initiative. Trauma makes people susceptible to death imagery and illness.

But there are positive, helpful structures and influences in society that counteract affect-contagion phenomena. Their influence is disseminated in similar ways. Both personal and shared social containers and buffers that enable safe expression and a measure of working through of trauma are considered in more detail below.

In what is known as *transitional space*, where individual and group subjectivity finds and makes use of what objectively exists,[139] there are everywhere cultural resources for expression and safe containment of trauma in imaginative ways: failure of containment is traumatizing. Ways of containment have to be found and promoted in therapy to mitigate, moderate, and buffer uncontained or unassimilated affect-contagion phenomena from inadequate digestion of the overwhelming feelings (memories, images) of trauma. "The management of the individual's emotional economy becomes his primary concern, in terms of which all else is rationalized" (p. 135).[8]

To different individual extents, people make use of cultural expression in transitional cultural arenas as externalized equivalents of the inner dream space, including interactions that take place in therapies, play, cultural containers,[5–8] art, music, dance, theater, social life, religious rituals, and sports. Examples might include activities like the social use of cockfights in Indonesia,[9] or ritualized communal containers like the fast of the ninth day of the month of *Av* (*Tisha B'Av*), when Jews still mourn the destruction of the Second Temple in Jerusalem that occurred at the hands of the Romans in 70 c.e. Similarly, the rich traditions of African dance, song, fireside dramatic storytelling (*indaba*), purification rituals, strong sense of community with its in-built supportive structures, all play positive roles in reducing the impact of accretions of individual and communal pain consequent on the manifold impacts of trauma and injustice that Africa's populations have suffered, and continue to endure.

The significance of symbolization cannot be underestimated.[143] Symbolism per se has a container function in language, and in both the inner container (or play or symbolism) of the dream space and in outer social and cultural containers, such as games and rituals.

The inner sleeping-dream space, dream experience, and dream symbolism comprise a personal individual container for working through traumatic events rather than promoting onward transmission. The various kinds of group therapies and expressive therapies devised by Western society exemplify particular forms of cultural containers, as do the ritual purification ceremonies run by Shangaan tribal diviners.

I chose the first and last letters of the Hebrew alphabet, ʔ-*aleph* and ʔ-*tav*, to describe the function of external intersubjective and social phenomena. I term the way these cultural containers function positively to hold society in a more-or-less stable equilibrium as ʔ-*aleph*-functioning to differentiate them from disruptive ʔ-*tav*-functioning affect-contagion phenomena. This terminology was suggested by Wilfred Bion's designation of the functioning of good enough intrapsychic introjected "containers" with the Greek letter *alpha* and Gianna William's use of *omega*-functioning to describe that of disruptive, "foreign body" introjects.[62]

It would be surprising if the ways in which disruptive ʔ-*tav*-functioning aftereffects of traumatization, affect- and image-contagion phenomena spread are not similar to those of positive, healing, ʔ-*aleph*-functioning, buffering, stabilizing effects of good enough parenting and effective therapies. The input of buffering, moderating, and ameliorating factors effects change in similar ways to those by which affect-contagion phenomena spread, and include therapeutic situations. These contribute to a salutogenic attitude to life and resilience, not entirely innate givens. Salutogenic survivors are not broken but overcome adversity, stress, and trauma, to bounce back and even transcend their life-shattering experiences.[113,114]

Affect-contagion phenomena are unavoidable. Their role in transgenerational impact of massive traumatization cannot be underestimated. Spreading traumatization occurs because personal and social containers deal inadequately with overwhelming ego defense-breaching affects. Reenactments inevitably take place within transference-countertransference situations, in the family and elsewhere.

Assuredly there are social implications of inter- and transgenerational transmission of trauma aftershock. Do universal patterns and laws such as those of the Mandelbrot relate across all manner of states of organization of humans? They do seem to when one considers the after impact of trauma and its spread.

Using catastrophe theory, when there are too many deeply traumatized people, is there a critical catalytic turning point at which an individual will break, or a family collapse, or society degenerate at an alarming rate, almost irrecoverably? Is this what we have seen, for example, in Nazi Germany, Stalin's Soviet Union, Pol Pot's Cambodia, the Chinese Cultural Revolution, in Lebanon, in Mozambique, among the Ik mountain people,[108] in Rwanda, in ex-Yugoslavia, in the Palestinian territories, and elsewhere in generations of displaced refugees? Are we seeing the aftereffects and trans- and intergenerational transmission and propagation of terrorization and traumatization in places where people had lived together in apparent harmonious coexistence, tolerating their diversity at times for several generations? Or is there rather a constant balance and shift between stabilizing and destabilizing factors, a kind of periodicity? Can the so-called butterfly effect of weather forecasting apply also to humans and their interactions? In other words, does some seemingly insignificant and unrecorded/unrecordable event in the life of an individual result in large societal changes? Theoretically, yes.

Trauma management is crucial in sociopolitical and personal life if we are to build healthy individuals and societies over and beyond basic needs and infrastructure. Democratic societies cannot survive when the numerical mass of those who are damaged and dependent exceeds the "containing" or "carrying" capacity of those who are relatively mature, healthy individuals.[12] Trauma etches indelible changes in the brain.[128,144,145]

Is tolerant coexistence achievable in the face of humankind's ubiquitous destructiveness, and continuous or intermittent but recurrent and cumulative damage? Prevention, amelioration, and minimalization of the effects of traumatization are possible. In order safely to contain the natural grief, rage, pain, and desire for revenge so that eventually tolerant, nonviolent coexistence may become possible, society needs not to forget, but rather to promote conditions to facilitate overall healthy development, treatment, and support communal ritual containers.

Politicians, industrialists, educators need to understand, value, and support parenting, cultural containers, and professionals trained to cope with inevitable affect-contagion phenomena in the short- and long-term aftermath of trauma to mitigate their inter- and transgenerational spread.

REFERENCES

1. Teilhard de Chardin, P. (1964). *The phenomenon of man*. London: Collins.
2. Issroff, J. (1979). *Affect contagion phenomena: Ongoing effects subsequent to massive traumatisation: A study of a large group discussion of the Holocaust in a "Survivor Syndrome" workshop and further implications*. Paper presented at First Conference of Children of Survivors of the Holocaust, November 4–5, 1979, New York City; published in German (1993) as Phänomene der Affekt-Kontamination—Fortdauernde Auswirkungen massiver Traumatisierung: Untersuung einer Grossgruppendiskussion

über den Holocaust in einem Workshop zum "Survivor-Syndrom." *Gruppenpsychother. Gruppendynamik, 33,* 83–112.

3. Figley, C. (1985). *Trauma and its wake.* New York: Brunner/Mazel.
4. Van der Kolk, B. A., McFarlane, A. C., & Weisaeth, L. (Eds.). (1996). *Traumatic stress: The effects of overwhelming experience on mind, body, and society.* New York and London: Guilford.
5. Pearlman, L. A., & Saakvitne, K. W. (1995). *Trauma and the therapist: Countertransference and vicarious traumatization in psychotherapy with incest survivors.* New York and London: W. W. Norton.
6. Mead, M. (1941). Community drama—Bali and American. *American Scholar, 11,* 78.
7. Mead, M. (1948). The concept of culture and the psychosomatic approach. In D. Harding (Ed.), *Personal character and cultural milieu: A collection of readings* (p. 530). New York: Syracuse University Press.
8. Geertz, C. (1993). *The interpretation of cultures.* London: Harper Collins/Fontana.
9. Geertz, C. (1995). *After the fact: Two countries, four decades, one anthropologist.* The Jerusalem-Harvard Lectures. Cambridge, MA, and London: Harvard University Press.
10. Ehrensaft, M. K., Cohen, P., Brown, J., Smailes, E., Chen, H., & Johnson, J. G. (2003). Intergenerational transmission of partner violence: A 20-year prospective study. *Journal of Consulting and Clinical Psychology, 71,* 741–753.
11. Epstein, H. (1979). *Children of the Holocaust.* New York: J. B. Putnam.
12. Winnicott, D. W. (1951). Some thoughts on the meaning of the word "democracy." *Human Relations,* 3,175–186.
13. Kellermann, N.P.F. (2000). *Children of Holocaust survivors: A bibliography (as of 31 December 1999).* Jerusalem: AMCHA—The National Israeli Center for Psychosocial Support of Survivors of the Holocaust and the Second Generation.
14. Kellermann, N.P.F. (2000). *Transmission of Holocaust trauma.* Jerusalem: AMCHA—The National Israeli Center for Psychosocial Support of Survivors of the Holocaust and the Second Generation.
15. Bergmann, M., & Jucovy, M. E. (1982). Prelude: The second generation. In M. Bergmann & M. Jucovy (Eds.), *Generations of the Holocaust* (pp. 18–32). New York: Basic Books.
16. Danieli, Y. (Ed). (1998). *International handbook of multigenerational legacies of trauma.* New York: Plenum Press.
17. Davidson, S. (1980). The clinical effects of massive psychic trauma in families of Holocaust survivors. *Journal of Marital Family Therapy, 6,* 11–21.
18. Zaidi, L. Y., Knutson, J. F., & Mehm, J. B. (1989). Transgenerational patterns of abusive parenting: Analogue and clinical tests. *Aggressive Behavior, 15,* 137–152.
19. Mitscherlich, A., & Mitscherlich, M. (1975). *The inability to mourn* (B. R. Blaczek, Trans.). New York: Random House/Grove. (Original work published 1967).
20. De Wind, E. (1949). The confrontation with death: Symposium on psychic traumatization through social catastrophe. *International Journal of Psychoanalysis, 49,* 302–305.

21. Davidson, S. (1987). Trauma in the life-cycle of the individual and the collective consciousness in relation to war and persecution. In H. Dasberg, S. Davidson, G. L. Durlacher, B. C. Filet, & E. de Wind (Eds.), *Society and trauma of war.* Assen/Maastricht, Nederlands: Van Gorcum.

22. Barocas, H. A., & Barocas, C. D. (1979) Wounds of the fathers: The next generation of Holocaust victims. *International Review of Psychoanalysis,* 6, 331–340.

23. Borocas, H., & Borocas, C. (1973). Manifestations of concentration camp affects on the second generation. *American Journal of Psychiatry,* 130, 830–841.

24. Danielli, Y. (1980). Families of survivors of the Nazi Holocaust: Some long and short term effects. In N. Milgram (Ed.), *Psychological stress and adjustment in time of war and peace.* Washington, DC: Hemisphere.

25. Eitinger, L., Krell, R., & Rieck, M. (1973).*The psychological and medical effects of concentration camps and related persecutions on survivors of the holocaust, a research bibliography.* Vancouver, Canada: University of British Columbia Press.

26. Greenblatt, S. (1978). The influence of survival guilt on chronic family crisis. *Journal of Psychology and Judaism,* 2, 19–28.

27. Kestenberg, J. S., & Kestenberg, M. (1982). The experience of survivor parents. In M. S. Bergman, & M. E. Jucovy (Eds.), *Generations of the Holocaust* (pp. 46–61). New York: Basic Books.

28. Kogan, I. (1995). *The cry of mute children: A psychoanalytic perspective of the second generation of the Holocaust.* London and New York: Free Association Press.

29. Laub, D., & Auerhahn, N. C. (1984). Reverberations of genocide: Its expression in the conscious and unconscious of post-Holocaust generations. In S. Luel & P. Marcus (Eds.), *Psychoanalytic reflections on the Holocaust: Selected essays* (pp. 287–303). New York and Tel Aviv, Israel: University of Denver and Ktav.

30. Laub, D., & Auerhahn, N. C. (1993). Knowing and not knowing massive psychic trauma: Forms of traumatic memory. *International Journal of Psychoanalysis,* 74, 287–302.

31. Moscovitz, S. (1982, July). Today's parents: yesterday's children in turmoil. Symposium on Child Survivors as Parents. International Conference on Child Psychiatry and Allied Professionals, Dublin, Ireland.

32. Moscovitz, S. (1983). *Love despite hate: Child survivors of the Holocaust and their adult lives.* New York: Schocken Books.

33. Müller-Hohagen, J. (1993). Nazi perpetrators as victims—consequences on their descendants. Paper presented at the Hamburg Conference on Children in War and Persecution, Hamburg, Germany, September 26–29, 1993.

34. Newman, L. (1973). Emotional disturbance in children of Holocaust survivors. *Social Casework: The Journal of Contemporary Social Work,* 63, 43–50.

35. Poznanski, E. O. (1972). The "replacement child": A saga of unresolved parental grief. *Behavioral Pediatrics,* 81, 1190–1193.

36. Prince, R. M. (1985). Second generation effects of historical trauma. *Psychoanalytic Review, 72,* 9–29.

37. Rakoff, V., Sigal, J., & Epstein, N. B. (1966). Children and families of concentration camp survivors. *Canada's Mental Health, 14,* 24–26.

38. Rogers, R. R. (1979). Intergenerational exchange: Transference of attitudes down the generations. In J. Howells (Ed.), *Modern perspectives in the psychiatry of infancy* (pp. 339–349). New York: Brunner/Mazel.

39. Rogers, R. R. (1990). Intergenerational transmission of historical enmity. In V. Volkan, J. Montville, & D. A. Julius (Eds.), *The psychodynamics of international relationships: Vol. 1 Concepts and theories* (pp. 86–91). Lexington, MA: Lexington Books/Heath.

40. Rosenthal, P. A., & Rosenthal S. (1980). Holocaust effect in the third generation: Child of child of survivors. *American Journal of Psychotherapy, 34,* 572–580.

41. Schwartz, S., Dohrenwend, B. P., & Levav, I. (1994). Nongenetic familial transmission of psychiatric disorders? Evidence from children of Holocaust survivors. *Journal of Health and Social Behavior, 35,* 395–402.

42. Sigal, J., & Weinfeld, M. (1989). *Trauma and rebirth: Intergenerational effects of the Holocaust.* New York: Praeger.

43. Sigel, I. E. (Ed.). (1985). *Parental belief systems: The psychological consequences for children.* Hillsdale, NJ: Erlbaum.

44. Sorcher, N., & Cohen, L. J. (1997). Trauma in children of Holocaust survivors: Transgenerational effects. *American Journal of Orthopsychiatry, 67,* 493–500.

45. Stelzer, J., & Issroff, J. (1983). La mere et l'image de la mort [The mother and the image of death: A specific way of traumatization of a collective traumatization from one generation to the other]. *Dialogue recherches Clinique Sociologiques sur le couple et la famille, 79,* 53–61.

46. Geertz, C. (2005, March 24). Very bad news [Review of the book *Collapse: How societies choose to fail or succeed*]. *New York Review of Books,* 4–6.

47. Asch, S. E. (1956). Studies of independence and submission to group pressure: I. A minority of one against a unanimous majority. *Psychological Monographs, 70,* 512–522.

48. Kelman, H., & Hamilton, V. L. (1989). *Crimes of obedience: Toward a social psychology of authority and responsibility.* New Haven, CT, and London: Yale University Press.

49. Milgram, S. (1980). *Obedience to authority: An experimental view.* New York: Harper and Row.

50. Janis, L. I. (1972). *Victims of groupthink.* Boston: Houghton Mifflin.

51. Janis, L. I., & Mann, L. (1977). *Decision making: A psychological analysis of conflict, choice, and commitment.* New York and London: Free Press and Collier Macmillan.

52. Danieli, Y., Brom, D., & Sills, J. (Eds.). (2005). *The trauma of terrorism: Sharing knowledge and shared care: An international handbook.* Binghamton, NY: Haworth.

53. DeMause, L. (Ed.). (1975). *The history of childhood*. New York: Harper Torchbooks.
54. DeMause, L. (2001). The evolution of childrearing. *The Journal of Psychohistory*, 28, 362–451.
55. DeMause, L. (2002). *Psychohistory: Childrearing and the emotional life of nations*. New York: Harper Torchbooks.
56. Atlas, J. (2001). The central paradigm: Childrearing as the fulcrum of psychohistorical explanation. *The Journal of Psychohistory*, 29, 9–38.
57. Volkan, V. D. (2003). Traumatized societies. In S. Varvin & V. D. Volkan (Eds.), *Violence or dialogue? Psychoanalytic insights on terror and terrorism* (pp. 217–236). London: International Psychoanalysis Library.
58. Volkan, V. D., Ast, G., & Greer, W. (2002). *The Third Reich in the unconscious: Transgenerational transmission and its consequences*. New York: Brunner/Routledge.
59. Allport, G. W., Bruner, J. S., & Jandorf, E. M. (1959). Personality under social catastrophe: Ninety life histories of the Nazi revolution. In C. Kluckhohn, H. M. Murray, & D. M. Schneider (Eds.), *Personality in Nature, Society and Culture* (pp. 347–366). New York: Knopf. (Reprinted from *Character and Personality*, 10, 1–22).
60. Becker, D. (2000). Dealing with the consequences of organized violence in trauma work. In D. Bloomfield, M. Fischer, & B. Schmelzle (Eds.), *The Berghof Handbook for Conflict Transformation*. Berghof, Germany: The Berghof Research Center for Constructive Conflict Management.
61. Boothby, N. (1993). Mobilizing communities to the psychosocial needs of children in war and refugee situations. In R. J. Apfel & B. Simon (Eds.), *Minefields in their hearts: The mental health of children in war and communal violence*. New Haven, CT, and London: Yale University Press.
62. Williams, G. (1997). Reversal of the container/contained relationship, On introjective Processes, and *Omega* function in "The No-Entry System of Defences." In G. Williams (Ed.), *Internal landscapes and foreign bodies: Eating disorders and other pathologies*. London: Duckworth, Tavistock Clinic Series.
63. Boszormyenyi-Nagy, I.. & Spark, G. M. (1973). *Invisible loyalties*. New York: Harper and Row.
64. Des Pres, T. (1976) *The survivor*. New York: Pocket Books.
65. Eitinger, L. (1964). *Concentration camp survivors in Norway and Israel*. Oslo, Norway: Universitets Forlaget.
66. Fields, R. (1980). Victims of terrorization: The effects of prolonged stress. *Evaluation and Change* [Special issue on victimization], 137, 76–83.
67. Figley, C. (1978). *Stress disorders among Vietnam veterans*. New York: Brunner/Mazel.
68. Figley, C. (Ed.). (1999). *Traumatology of grieving: Conceptual, theoretical, and treatment foundations*. Philadelphia and London: Brunner/Mazel.

69. Freud, A., & Burlingham, D. (1943). *War and children*. New York: International Universities Press.

70. Fried, M. (1982). Endemic stress: The psychology of resignation and the politics of scarcity. *American Journal of Orthopsychiatry, 52*, 4–9.

71. Grubrich-Simitis, I. G. (1981). Extreme traumatization as cumulative trauma. *Psychoanalytic Study of the Child, 36*, 415–450.

72. Herman, J. L. (1992). *Trauma and recovery: The aftermath of violence from domestic abuse to political terror*. New York: Basic Books.

73. Issroff, J. (1983). Pathological mourning in families and certain cases of suicide: On "not being good enough" and "not being wanted enough." In E. Chigier (Ed.), *Counselling and therapy in grief and bereavement* (pp. 197–212). Tel Aviv, Israel: Freund.

74. Jucovy, M .E. (1992). Psychoanalytic contributions to Holocaust studies. *International Journal of Psychoanalysis, 73*, 267–283.

75. Kestenberg, J. S. (1972). How children remember and parents forget. *International Journal of Psychoanalytic Psychotherapy, 1–2*, 103–123.

76. Kestenberg, J. S, & Brenner, I. (1996). *The last witness: The child survivor of the Holocaust*. Washington, DC: American Psychiatric Press.

77. Kielson, H. (1979). *Sequential traumatization of children*. Stuttgart, Germany: Ferdinand

78. Rabonowitz, D. (1976). *New lives: Survivors of the Holocaust living in America*. New York: Knopf.

79. Valent, P. (1998). *From survival to fulfillment: A framework for the life-trauma dialectic*. Philadelphia and London: Brunner/Mazel.

80. Valent, P. (1999). *Trauma and fulfillment therapy: A wholistic framework*. Philadelphia and London: Brunner/Mazel.

81. Vardi, D. (1990). *Memorial candles: Children of the Holocaust*. London: Routledge.

82. Vogel, M. L. (1994). Gender as a factor in the transgenerational transmission of trauma. *Women and Therapy, 15*, 35–47.

83. Volkan, V. D. (1981). *Linking objects and linking phenomena: A study of the forms, symptoms, metapsychology, and therapy of complicated mourning*. New York: International Universities Press.

84. Walker, M. (1992). A web of secrets: Generations of abuse. In *Surviving Secrets* (pp. 6–33). Buckingham, UK, and Philadelphia: Open Universities Press.

85. Wanderman, E. (1976). Children and families of Holocaust survivors: A psychological overview. In Y. Steinitz & D. M. Szonyi. (Eds.), *Living after the Holocaust: Reflections by the post-war generation in America*. New York: Bloch.

86. Weisaeth, L. (1993). Disasters: Psychological and psychiatric aspects. In L. Goldberger & S. Breznitz (Eds.), *Handbook of stress: Theoretical and clinical aspects* (pp. 591–616). New York: Free Press/Macmillan.

87. Volkan, V. D. (1991). On 'chosen trauma.' *Mind and Human Interaction, 3*, 13.

88. Volkan, V. D. (1988). *The need to have enemies and allies: From clinical practice to international relationships.* Northvale, NJ: Jason Aronson.

89. Volkan, V. D. (1993). Immigrants and refugees: A psychodynamic perspective. *Mind and Human Interaction, 7*(3), 110–127.

90. Volkan, V. D. (1997). *Bloodlines: From ethnic pride to ethnic terrorism.* New York: Farrar, Strauss, and Giroux.

91. Volkan, V. D. (2002). Large-group identity: Border psychology and related processes. *Mind and Human Interaction, 13,* 49–76.

92. Volkan, V. D. (2003). Traumatized societies. In S. Varvin & V. D. Volkan (Eds.), *Violence or dialogue? Psychoanalytic insights on terror and terrorism* (pp. 217–236). London: International Psychoanalysis Library.

93. Rogers, R. R. (1979). Intergenerational exchange: Transference of attitudes down the generations. In J. Howells (Ed.), *Modern perspectives in the psychiatry of infancy* (pp. 339–349). New York: Brunner/Mazel.

94. Rogers, R. R. (1990). Common security: A psychological concept. In V. Volkan, J. Montville, & D. A. Julius (Eds.), *The psychodynamics of international relationships: Concepts and theories.* Lexington, MA: Lexington Books/Heath.

95. Rogers, R. R. (1990). Intergenerational transmission of historical enmity. In V. Volkan, J. Montville, & D. A. Julius (Eds.), *The psychodynamics of international relationships: Concepts and theories* (Vol. 1, pp. 86–91). Lanham, MD: Lexington Books.

96. Lifton, R. J. (1968). *Death in life: Survivors of Hiroshima.* New York: Random House.

97. Lifton, R. J. (1970). *History and human survival: Essays on the young and old, survivors and the dead, peace and war, and on contemporary psychohistory.* New York: Random House.

98. Lifton, R. J., & Olsen, E. (Eds.). (1974). *Explorations in psychohistory: The Wallfleet Papers.* New York: Simon and Schuster.

99. Lifton, R. J. (1979). *The broken connection: On death and the continuity of life.* New York: Simon and Schuster.

100. Lifton, R. J. (1988). Understanding the traumatized self: Imagery, symbolization, and transformation. In J. P. Wilson, Z. Harel, & B. Zahana (Eds.), *Human adaptation to extreme stress* (pp. 7–31). London: Plenum.

101. Lifton, R. J. (1993). *The protean self: Human resilience in an age of fragmentation.* New York: Basic Books.

102. Lifton, R. J., & Olsen, E. (1974). *Living and dying.* London: Wildwood House.

103. Montagu, A. (1970). *Learning non-aggression.* New York and Oxford: Oxford University Press.

104. Thompson Jr., A. J. (2003). Killer ppes on the planet. In S. Varvin and D. V. Vamik (Eds.), *Violence or dialogue: Psychoanalytic insights on terror and terrorism* (p. 73). London: International Psychoanalytical Association.

105. Reader, J. (1990). *Man on earth.* Harmondsworth, UK: Penguin.

106. Arendt, H. (1978).We refugees. In *Jew as pariah* (p. 55). New York: Grove. [Reprinted from *The Menorah Journal*, Jan. 1943, p. 69.]

107. Arendt, H. (1963). *Eichmann in Jerusalem: A report on the banality Of evil.* Harmondsworth, UK: Penguin.

108. Turnbull, C. (1987). *The mountain people.* New York: Touchstone.

109. Winnicott, D.W. (1965). Providing for the child in health and in crisis. In *The maturational processes and the facilitating environment* (pp. 64–72). London: Hogarth Press/ Institute of Psychoanalysis.

110. Winnicott, D. W. (1986). Living creatively. In *Home is where we start from: Essays by a psychoanalyst* (pp. 39–54). Harmondsworth, UK: Penguin.

111. Winnicott, D. W. (1988). *Human nature* (esp. pp. 55–64). London: Free Association Books.

112. Winnicott, D. W. (1988). *Babies and their mothers.* London: Free Association Books.

113. Antonovsky, A. (1986). Life span developmental psychology: Intergenerational relations and transmitting the sense of coherence. In N. Datan, A. L. Green, & H. W. Haynes (Eds.), *Life-span developmental psychology: Intergenerational relations.* Hillside, NJ: Erlbaum.

114. Antonovsky, A. (1987). *Unravelling the mystery of health: How people manage stress and stay well.* Jossey-Bass Joint Social and Behavioural Science Series and Health Series. San Francisco and London: Jossey-Bass.

115. Bowlby, J. (1979). *The making and breaking of affectional bonds.* London: Tavistock.

116. Bowlby, J. (1981). *A secure base: Clinical applications of attachment theory.* London: Routledge.

117. Brazelton, T. B., & Cramer, B. G. (1991). *The earliest relationship: Parents, infants and the drama of early attachment* London: Karnac.

118. Bretherton, I. (1990.) Communication patterns, internal working models, and the intergenerational transmission of attachment telationships. *Infant and Mental Health* Journal, *11,* 237–252.

119. Emde, R. N., & Samerhoff, A. J.(1989). Understanding early relationship disturbances. In R. N. Emde and A. J. Samerhoff (Eds.), *Relationship disturbances in early childhood: A developmental approach* (pp. 1–12). New York: Basic Books.

120. Haggerty, R., Sherrod, L. R., Garmezy, N., & Rutter, M. (1994). *Stress, risk, and resilience in children and adolescents: Process, mechanisms, and interventions.* Cambridge, New York, and Melbourne, Australia: Cambridge University Press.

121. Kobasa, S. C., Maddi, S. R., & Kahn, S. (1982). Hardiness and health. *Journal of Personality and Social Psychology, 42,* 168–177.

122. Masten, A. S., Best, K. M., & Garmezy, N. (1990). Resilience and development: Contributions from the study of children who overcome adversity. *Development and Psychopathology, 2,* 425–426.

123. Benedict, R. (1938). Continuities and discontinuities in cultural conditioning. *Psychiatry, 1,*167–177.

124. Murray, L., & Cooper, P .J. (1997). Effects of postnatal depression on infant development, *Archives of Disease in Childhood, 77*, 99–101.

125. Raphael-Leff, J. (2000). *"Spilt milk": perinatal loss and breakdown*. London: Institute of Psychoanalysis.

126. Schwartz, S., Dohrenwend, B. P., & Levav, I. (1994). Nongenetic familial transmission of psychiatric disorders? Evidence from children of Holocaust survivors. *Journal of Health and Social Behavior, 35*, 395–402.

127. Sigel, I. E. (Ed.). (1985.) *Parental belief systems: The psychological consequences for children*. Hillsdale, NJ: Erlbaum.

128. Schore, A. N. (2003). *Affect dysregulation and disorders of the self*. New York and London: W. W. Norton.

129. Seligmann, M.E.P. (1975). *Helplessness: On depression, development and death*. San Francisco: W. H. Freeman.

130. Stern, D. N. (1986). *The interpersonal world of the human infant*. New York: Basic Books.

131. Stern, D. (1998). *The maternal constellation*. New York: Basic Books.

132. Rubenstein, R. L. (1992). *After Auschwitz and the age of triage*. Baltimore: Johns Hopkins University Press.

133. Berenbaum, M. (1979). *The vision of the void*. Middletown, CT: Wesleyan University Press.

134. Bettlheim, B. (1979). *Surviving and other essays*. New York and London: Thames and Hudson/A. Knopf.

135. Wiesenthal, S. (1970). *"The Sunflower" by Simon Wiesenthal with a symposium*. London: W. H. Allen.

136. Weisenthal, S. (1998). *The Sunflower: On the possibilities and limits of forgiveness* (Rev. ed.) New York: Shocken.

137. Krog, A. (1998). *Country of my skull: Guilt, sorrow, and the limits of forgiveness in the new South Africa*. New York: Three Rivers Press.

138. Winnicott, D. W. (1984).Transitional objects and transitional phenomena. In *Through paediatrics to psychoanalysis: Collected papers* (pp. 229–242). (Reprinted from *Through paediatrics to psychoanalysis*, London: Tavistock, 1958; paper originally published 1951).

139. Winnicott, D. W. (1971). *Playing and reality*. London: Tavistock

140. Economists Allied for Arms Reduction. (1993). New York: Arias Foundation for Peace and Human Progress.

141. Parkes, C. M. (1972). *Bereavement: Studies of grief in adult life* New York: International Universities Press.

142. Straker, G. (with Moosa, F., Becker, R., & Nkwale, M.). (1993). *Faces in the revolution: The psychological effects of violence on township youth in South Africa*. Cape Town, South Africa: David Philip.

143. Deri, S. K. (1984). *Symbolization and creativity*. New York: International Universities Press.

144. Van der Kolk, B. A. (1987). The psychobiology of the trauma response: Hyperarousal, constriction, and addiction to traumatic re-exposure. In B. A. Van der Kolk (Ed.), *Psychological trauma* (pp. 63–87). Washington, DC: American Psychiatric Press.
145. Van der Kolk, B. A. (1986). *Post traumatic stress disorder: Psychological and behavioral sequelae.* Washington, DC: American Psychiatric Press.

Chapter 12

Conclusion: How Might We Prevent Abnormal Behavior from Occurring and Developing?

Thomas G. Plante

This book series has tried to bring the contemporary world of abnormal psychology and behavior to you in an informative, updated, and understandable manner. Hopefully, you have learned much about how abnormal behavior impacts all those around us including those we care most about. The book has tried to articulate what is currently known about a wide variety of abnormal psychology topics so that you will be much better informed about these issues that are often discussed in the news and elsewhere.

After reading and reflecting on these important topics, one might wonder what can be done to minimize, eliminate, or prevent these kinds of problems from occurring. There is clearly no simple answer to this question. There are a variety of reasons why abnormal behavior emerges and develops. Some are due to biological or physiological factors such as genetics, hormonal and biochemical influences, and the exposure to both legal and illegal substances. Others are due to internal psychological conflicts associated with personality, mood, and stress mechanisms. Still others are due to the interactions of many social and interpersonal relationships with loved ones, work or school associates, neighbors, and community members. There are many different roads that lead to abnormal and problematic behavior. However, this does not mean that we can't do much more to improve the odds that abnormal behavior won't develop within ourselves and others. We clearly can make a better world for ourselves and for society if we can follow some key principles of prevention.

After reading this book series and carefully evaluating the advice of many leading experts, several important principles of prevention emerge as being especially important in preventing abnormal behavior from either developing or getting worse. While we cannot do justice to each prevention strategy articulated, we can at least introduce these seven principles to the reader. This list is not meant to be exhaustive or exclusive. It merely provides some very brief reflections and observations as well as prevention and coping principles.

AVOID ABUSE AND NEGLECT OF CHILDREN

As clearly articulated in several chapters of the series, the abuse and neglect of children occurs at alarming and disturbing rates. Abused and neglected children are much more likely to develop certain troubles with depression, anxiety, violence, substance abuse, interpersonal difficulties, and a host of other problem behaviors. Once developed, these problems impact others around them and can be passed on from generation to generation. Somehow, efforts must be increased to minimize child abuse and neglect. Public policy experts, child protection professionals, family attorneys, politicians, mental health professionals, and others must work closely to help children stay safe and to ensure that those entrusted with the welfare of children (e.g., parents, teachers, coaches, child care providers) are capable of providing the competent and effective care that children need, which is free from any abuse or neglect. While we can't totally eliminate child abuse and neglect, we can certainly try to minimize it by pooling our collective resources and expertise making a firm commitment to the safety and well-being of all children. Like a lot of things, it will take a selfless commitment of time, money, and other resources to make significant progress in this area. It will involve working with many different community, civic, religious, educational, law enforcement, mental health, political, and other agencies. Perhaps as former President Nixon argued for a "War on Cancer" or former President Johnson's "War on Poverty," we may need a "War on Child Abuse and Neglect."

MINIMIZE POVERTY

Those who are poor are less likely to have access to professional mental and physical health care services and are much more likely to be impacted by the stress that is associated with poverty (e.g., unemployment, poor housing, and exposure to community violence). As poverty levels increase and the gap between the rich and poor widens, it is likely that the psychological and behavioral problems associated with poverty will increase. Therefore, efforts to reduce poverty will likely minimize the development of or the worsening of a variety of abnormal psychology problems. Again, politicians, business leaders, mental health professionals, family advocates, and others must somehow work together in order to minimize poverty both here and abroad. Perhaps former President Johnson's "War on Poverty" needs to be waged once again.

MINIMIZE EXPOSURE TO VIOLENCE

Sadly, we live in an often highly violent world. Violence is not only perpetrated during wars and in street crime but also in the seclusion and privacy of one's own home. Domestic violence, child abuse, date rape, and other kinds of violence are all too common. Furthermore, research has clearly indicated that exposure to violence through entertainment sources (e.g., movies, video games) also increases the risk of both violence and other mental health–related problems among vulnerable viewers. The entertainment industry, politicians, mental health professionals, family advocates, and others must somehow work together in order to minimize violence exposure in entertainment, in the media in general, and in both public communities and private homes.

DEVELOP AND NURTURE EFFECTIVE AND AFFORDABLE TREATMENTS (INCLUDING PHARMACEUTICALS)

The development of quality and effective intervention strategies including pharmaceutical agents has the potential ability to greatly reduce the impact of abnormal behavior, assuming these options are available to all those in need. For example, medications such as Prozac and other selective serotonin reuptake inhibitors have revolutionized the treatment of depressive disorders during the past decade and a half. These medications, while not perfect or right for everyone with depression, have greatly improved the odds of effectively dealing with a number of psychiatric troubles including obsessive-compulsive disorder, depression, bulimia, and so forth. Recent quality research using empirically supported psychological interventions has also demonstrated remarkable results for a wide variety of abnormal behavior problems. Quality behavioral and psychological interventions for panic disorder, depression, eating disorders, post-traumatic stress disorder, and many other problems are available. Research and development on affordable medications and psychosocial interventions to help those who suffer from abnormal behavior offer hope to not only those afflicted with these conditions but also to those loved ones who suffer too.

However, medications in particular can often too easily be seen as a magic pill to solve all problems. Medications can also be extremely expensive in the United States in particular. A careful and thoughtful effort to make appropriate medications available to those who can truly benefit from them will likely help to minimize the severity of abnormal behavior for not only identified patients but also for all those who are connected to them via family, work, school, or other relationships. The best available research and practice is needed to ensure that interventions that can help people with abnormal behavior are readily available and used.

ALTER CULTURAL EXPECTATIONS ABOUT BEHAVIOR

In previous decades, children rode in cars without seat belts and rode their bikes without bike helmets. Parents physically hit their children at will and in public. People were allowed to smoke wherever they wanted to do so. Women who sought to work outside of the home were considered odd or too bold. Cultural expectations about how we live our lives that have impacted social customs and expectations can be applied to abnormal behavior risk factors as well. For example, violence exposure, maintaining zero tolerance for child abuse, alcohol and other substance abuse, poverty, and so forth may help to create a society where abnormal behavior cannot flourish. Public policy can be used to help decrease the odds that abnormal behavior risks are tolerated. Cultural expectations and policy decisions can be used to ensure that those who experience particular problems seek appropriate resources. There is too often a social taboo to request help from mental health professionals about abnormal psychology related problems. This resistance and avoidance tragically often allows potential problems to become more severe and serious.

AVOID EXPOSURE TO ABNORMAL PSYCHOLOGY RISK FACTORS

While Americans demand individual freedoms, exposure to particular risks increases the chance of abnormal behavior of developing. For example, legalized gambling in some form (e.g., Indian gaming, lotteries, Internet gambling) is now allowed in just about all states and is certainly not confined to Las Vegas and Atlantic City. Bars and liquor stores are open and available around the clock in just about every city. Pornography and online gambling are available on the Internet and thus just about everyone who has a computer or can get to one can be exposed to these influences. These trends increase the odds that those who are vulnerable to developing certain abnormal problems (e.g., alcoholism, pornography, gambling) will do so. As I have heard many times, "An alcoholic probably shouldn't work as a bartender." Controlling the environment so that temptations are not available very easily would go a long way in minimizing the development of many abnormal behavior problems. Furthermore, vulnerable children and those with predilections to particular behavioral problems can all too easily access materials that can contribute to further abnormal psychology problems. Therefore, being thoughtful about the environmental influences that increase the odds of developing problems later in life should make all of us more sensitive to these influences.

MAXIMIZE ETHICS—ESPECIALLY SOCIAL RESPONSIBILITY AND CONCERN FOR OTHERS

At the end of the day, somehow we all must find a way to live together, sharing the planet and its resources. If we have any hope of living in a world that is humane and just and where abnormal behavior and problems are managed better and minimized, we'll need to maximize our social responsibility and concern for others. The ethical treatment of all persons and our efforts to make the world a better place for all will hopefully prevent or at least minimize many of the troubles associated with abnormal behavior. A global effort to support ethical interactions among all may help us better live with social responsibility and concern for others.

While abnormal behavior is likely to be with us forever, there is much that we can do as a society to minimize the possibility that abnormal behavior will develop in at-risk individuals and groups as well as to help those who experience these troubles. Mental health professionals working with others including public policy leaders, industries such as the pharmaceutical companies, and experts in many other fields can help a great deal. Can our culture and society make the commitment to do this? Let us hope so.

Index

About the Editor and the Contributors

EDITOR

Thomas G. Plante, *PhD*, *ABPP*, is professor and chair of psychology at Santa Clara University and adjunct clinical associate professor of psychiatry and behavioral sciences at Stanford University School of Medicine. He has authored, coauthored, edited, or co-edited six books, including *Sin against the Innocents: Sexual Abuse by Priests and the Role of the Catholic Church* (2004), *Bless Me Father for I Have Sinned: Perspectives on Sexual Abuse Committed by Roman Catholic Priests* (1999), *Faith and Health: Psychological Perspectives* (2001), *Do the Right Thing: Living Ethically in an Unethical World* (2004), and *Contemporary Clinical Psychology* (1999, 2005), as well as over 100 professional journal articles and book chapters. He is a fellow of the American Psychological Association, the American Academy of Clinical Psychology, and the Society of Behavioral Medicine. He maintains a private practice in Menlo Park, California.

CONTRIBUTORS

Susan L. Ames, *PhD*, is a research associate with the Transdisciplinary Drug Abuse Prevention Research Center (TPRC) at the Institute for Prevention Research (IPR), Department of Preventive Medicine, Keck School of Medicine, University of Southern California. Her research emphasis is on the mediation of implicit processes and competing social, personality, and cultural constructs in the etiology and prevention of risk behaviors (e.g., drug use and HIV-risk behavior) among at-risk youth and adults. Her research focuses on new prevention and harm-reduction strategies for addictive behaviors and prediction models of substance use and risky sexual behavior.

Michael Axelman is an assistant professor in counseling psychology at Santa Clara University, where he teaches graduate-level courses in child and family areas. He is the clinical director of the South Bay/San Jose, California, chapter of the Children's Psychotherapy Project. Michael Axelman has taught in urban public schools and published on school violence, childhood aggression, and the making of safe schools. He is a licensed psychologist who maintains a child, adolescent, and family psychotherapy practice in Palo Alto, California.

Sara Bonnell is a graduate student in the counseling psychology program at Santa Clara University. Her current research interests focus on the psychology of disenfranchised urban communities.

Ronald J. Burke, PhD, is professor of organizational behavior, Schulich School of Business, York University, in Toronto, Ontario, Canada. He has edited or co-edited 15 books and published over 500 journal articles. The founding editor of the *Canadian Journal of Administrative Sciences,* he has been a member of the editorial boards of more than 15 journals. Burke is also a consultant to organizations on human resource management issues.

Christina M. Dalpiaz founded CHANCE (Changing How Adults Nurture Children's Egos, 1996), a nonprofit organization dedicated to making family violence socially unacceptable through advocacy and education. Ms. Dalpiaz has written two parenting books, *Here's Your CHANCE* (1995) and *Breaking Free, Starting Over* (2004). She has also assisted in the production of two training videos entitled *Through the Eyes of a Child* (1997) and *Family Violence: Debunking the Myths* (2000). Additionally, Ms. Dalpiaz contributed to a documentary for television entitled, *The Truth about Teen Violence* (1999). Ms. Dalpiaz's background includes working as a security research analyst for an international research firm and as an intelligence officer for the U.S. Navy Reserves. She is currently a graduate student in psychology at Walden University.

Juris G. Draguns, PhD, is professor emeritus of psychology at the Pennsylvania State University. He has held visiting appointments and has lectured, in six languages, in Germany, Sweden, Australia, Taiwan, Latvia, and Mexico, as well as at the East-West Center in Honolulu, Hawaii. His principal area of research interest is cross-cultural psychology, with a focus on the interplay of culture and psychopathology. In 2001, Draguns received the Award for Distinguished Contributions to the International Advancement of Psychology.

Rona M. Fields, PhD, is senior research fellow in cognitive science in the Cyber Security Policy and Research Institute, School of Engineering and Applied Sciences, George Washington University. She is a fellow of the American Psychological Association and a diplomate in forensic evaluation. Her publications include books on terrorism, social change, gender studies and, most recently, *Martyrdom: The Psychology Theology and Politics of Self Sacrifice* (2004). She served on the Amnesty International Medical Commission in the Campaign to Abolish Torture in 1973–1976, developed the protocol for the psychological examination of torture victims while a fellow at the Peace Research Institute of Oslo, Norway, in 1975. She continues to be actively engaged in forensic psychology and consults with police and sheriff's departments as well as with United Nations Peace Keeping operations. She has worked as a print and broadcast journalist in Europe, Africa, and the Middle East. Most recently she is using her expertise on terrorism to develop high-tech programs to predict, analyze, and prevent terror actions.

Judith Issroff, M.B., B.Ch. (Witwatersrand), D.P.M. M.R.C.Psych; M.Inst. Psychoanal., is a consultant child, adolescent, and family psychiatrist and psychoanalyst in the United Kingdom and Israel and has been a consultant in the adolescent unit of the Tavistock Clinic and School for Family Psychiatry and Community Mental Health in London. She has edited a book on Winnicott and Bowlby and has published numerous book chapters and journal articles. She has also written for *The Jerusalem Times* and has been a UNICEF consultant in post–civil war Mozambique and elsewhere.

Stanley Krippner, Ph.D., is professor of psychology at Saybrook Graduate School and Research Center, San Francisco, and President of the International Division of the Institute for Medicine and Advanced Behavioral Technology, Ciudad Juarez, Mexico. He has authored, co-authored, edited, or co-edited several books including *The Psychological Effects of War Trauma on Civilians: An International Perspective* (Greenwood, 2002), and *The Varieties of Anomalous Experience: Examining the Scientific Evidence* (American Psychological Association, 2000). He was the 2002 Recipient of the American Psychological Association's Award for Distinguished Contributions to the International Advancement of Psychology, and the 2003 Recipient of the Ashley Montagu Peace Award.

Maria D. Llorente, MD, is an associate professor of medicine in the Department of Psychiatry at the University of Miami School of Medicine and is currently chief of psychiatry at the Miami VA Medical Center. Dr. Llorente has participated in several large clinical demonstration projects that have investigated suicidal ideations and comorbid psychiatric pathology in older adults, and serves on the board of the American Psychiatric Foundation, where a primary focus is funding programs that aim at preventing youth suicides. She has authored and coauthored publications in the areas of suicide, homicide-suicide, and associated psychopathology. Current research interests include increasing access to mental health services and improving early identification and treatment of psychiatric disorders.

Julie. E. Malphurs, PhD, is an assistant professor of research at the University of Miami School of Medicine and research investigator at the Miami VA Medical Center. Dr. Malphurs has coauthored more than 20 research publications in the areas of pediatric and geriatric mental health. Her current research investigates interventions for older adults with co-occurring medical and psychiatric illnesses, specifically depressive disorders.

Cheryl L. Meyer, PhD, J.D., is a professor at Wright State University School of Professional Psychology and conducts research that incorporates legal, educational, psychological, and sociological perspectives. She has published *The Wandering Uterus* (1997) and *Mothers Who Kill Their Children: Understanding the Acts of Moms from Susan Smith to the "Prom Mom"* (2001).

Daphne Nahmiash, PhD, is director of professional services in a health and social service center in Montreal, Canada. She is a recently retired assistant professor from the School of Social Service, Laval University, Quebec. She has coauthored two books: *When Seniors are Abused* (1995) and *Home Care: A Love Affair* (1993). She has also coauthored and authored several book chapters and articles on abuse and neglect of older adults.

Michelle Oberman J.D., M.P.H., is a professor of law at Santa Clara University and conducts research on legal and ethical issues relating to sexuality, pregnancy, and motherhood. She has been widely published on the regulation and intervention in the treatment of pregnant women, statutory rape, and modern American infanticide. In 2001 she coauthored *Mothers Who Kill Their Children: Understanding the Acts of Moms from Susan Smith to the "Prom Mom."*

Daryl S. Paulson, PhD, is president and CEO of BioScience Laboratories, Inc. Dr. Paulson is the author of numerous articles and seven books, including *Handbook of Regression Analysis* (in press), *Applied Statistical Designs for the Researcher* (2003), *Handbook of Topical Antimicrobial Testing and Evaluation* (1999), *In the Jaws of Demons: Modern Warfare* (in press), *Competitive Business, Caring Business: An Integral Perspective for the 21st Century* (2002), and *Walking the Point: Male Initiation and the Vietnam Experience* (1994). In addition he is the editor of *Handbook of Topical Antimicrobials: Industrial Applications in Consumer Products and Pharmaceuticals* (2002).

Silvana Skara, PhD, M.P.H., is a research associate at the Institute for Health Promotion and Disease Prevention Research within the University of Southern California, Keck School of Medicine, Department of Preventive Medicine. She is currently involved in research on school- and community-based tobacco, alcohol, and other drug abuse prevention and cessation interventions, focusing on the needs assessment, design, implementation, evaluation, and dissemination of programs.

Steve Sussman, PhD, FAAHB, is a professor of preventive medicine and psychology at the University of Southern California. He studies the utility of empirical program development methods in tobacco and drug abuse prevention and cessation research, and has over 200 publications in this arena. His projects include Towards No Tobacco Use, Towards No Drug Abuse, and EX, which are considered model programs at numerous agencies (e.g., Centers for Disease Control and Prevention, National Institute on Drug Abuse [NIDA], Center for Substance Abuse Prevention [CSAP], Health Canada, U.S. Department of Education).

About the Series Advisers

Patrick H. DeLeon, *PhD., ABPP, MPH, JD,* is a former president of the American Psychological Association and has served on Capitol Hill for over three decades working on health and educational policy issues. A fellow of the APA, he has been active within the APA governance, having been elected president of three practice divisions. A former editor of *Professional Psychology: Research and Practice,* he has been on the editorial board of the *American Psychologist* since 1981. He has received several APA Presidential citations as well as the APA Distinguished Professional and Public Interest Contributions awards. He has also been recognized by the leadership of professional nursing, social work, and optometry. He is a Distinguished Alumnus of the Purdue University School of Liberal Arts. He has authored in excess of 175 publications.

Nadine J. Kaslow, *PhD, ABPP,* is professor and chief psychologist at Emory University School of Medicine in the Department of Psychiatry and Behavioral Sciences. She is president of the American Board of Clinical Psychology, -former president of the Divisions of Clinical Psychology and of Family Psychology of the American Psychological Association, past chair of the Association of Psychology Postdoctoral and Internship Centers, and associate editor of the *Journal of Family Psychology.* Her research interests and numerous publications focus on the assessment and treatment of suicidal behavior in abused and nonabused women, family violence (intimate partner violence, child abuse), child and adolescent depression, and training issues in psychology. She is currently principal investigator on grants funded by the Centers for Disease Control and Prevention on the treatment of abused suicidal African American women, the treatment of suicidal

African American women. She is a licensed psychologist who maintains a psychotherapy practice in Atlanta, Georgia, for adolescents with eating disorders, adults, couples, and families.

Lori Goldfarb Plante, *PhD,* is a clinical lecturer at Stanford University School of Medicine. She conducts a private practice in clinical psychology in Menlo Park, California, where she specializes in the assessment and treatment of adolescents and young adults. She is the author of a book addressing chronic illness and disability within the family as well as the author of numerous professional articles on eating disorders, sexuality, and sexual abuse in adolescents and young adults.